A BIBLIOGRAPHY OF
EDITH, OSBERT AND SACHEVERELL SITWELL

RICHARD FIFOOT

SECOND EDITION, REVISED

RUPERT HART-DAVIS LONDON

Granada Publishing Limited

First published 1963 by
Rupert Hart-Davis Ltd
3 Upper James Street
London W1R 4BP

Second (revised) edition 1971

ISBN 0 246 64022 7

Printed in Great Britain by Richard Clay (The Chaucer Press), Ltd.,
Bungay, Suffolk

THE SOHO BIBLIOGRAPHIES

XI

EDITH, OSBERT AND SACHEVERELL SITWELL

TO MY WIFE

CONTENTS

ILLUSTRATIONS

PREFACE TO THE SECOND EDITION

This bibliography lists the first publications of the writings of each author in turn. Of their own books, and of those to which they contributed (this is not always a simple distinction), the first English and American editions are given in chronological sequence. Later editions are included only when they contain textual revisions or variations, and no attempt is made to list unrevised reprints even when they have been reset. Anthologies which include the Sitwells' works are included only when their publication preceded that of the relevant works in a book wholly by one of the Sitwells. Similarly, items reprinted in periodicals without alteration from previously published books of the Sitwells are not included.

In the book sections (i.e. the A and B sequences) the source of each item previously published in a periodical or elsewhere is given. Subsequent publication is not, for reasons of space, noted in the periodical sections (the C sequences); but the full publication history of each item can be traced by the use of the index. I have paid particular attention to revisions of the texts between one form of publication and another.

Following the periodical sections are lists of books announced but not published, of translations, of musical settings and of gramophone recordings. I have not included the Sitwells' letters to the press; nor have I mentioned or described dust wrappers—an omission I have regretted since reading Sir Sacheverell Sitwell's "A Note for Bibliophiles" (see sC 179) which explains how personal are the wrappers of some of his books.

The colours of cloth bindings were simply described in the original edition of this bibliography, without the use of a standard code of colours. Similarly the texture or graining of the cloth was not usually mentioned, and certainly no code in this respect either was used. Though I am impressed with the ideal desirability of such specification as advocated in recent articles by Mr. G. Thomas Tanselle, I have not been able to provide it in this edition. The chief reason is the lack of time (and it *is* time-consuming to match colours against a comprehensive code) for the purpose in the three months I could spend on the revision; in addition, a good many of the books involved are no longer available to me. I have corrected some errors of the original edition in this respect, and I do not believe that there is much likelihood of confusion between variant bindings in the items in this bibliography, save possibly in one instance.

The extent of revision is considerable, quite apart from the addition of items published after the first edition came out. The information on more than 160 items has been corrected or expanded, twenty-seven items have been deleted, and there are no less than fifty-four items which should have been included in the original edition but were not. I have tried to see copies of everything listed, but without complete success; perhaps the most elusive piece is an exhibition catalogue described by Thomas Balston in his posthumous review of the original edition in *The Library* (see oB 5*A*). Additional items inserted into their places in the original sequences are denoted by an italic letter *A* (*B*, *C*, etc) following the number of the preceding item; though this makes the notation slightly cumbersome it avoids disturbing the numbering of items in the first edition. Page sizes are given in millimetres, as in my draft for the first edition; instead of in inches and fractions of inches, as in the published first edition. And, while I have bibliographically collated copies of all books I have seen, I have deleted the very few collations actually printed in the first edition.

I had hoped to include in this edition details of the Sitwells' radio and television broadcasts. But, though I have some information on these, it is so clearly incomplete that it would be misleading to publish it. I had also contemplated a list of manuscript materials, at least those in institutional libraries; but it is obviously premature to attempt this. It may, however, be worth mentioning the great quantity in the University of Texas, the letters in the British Museum and in Yale University Library, and the manuscripts sold at Christie's on 17 July 1968.

There are three earlier bibliographical works on the Sitwells:

1. *Sitwelliana 1915–1927*, by Thomas Balston, with portraits by Albert Rutherston. (London, Duckworth, 1928; ordinary copies, and seventy numbered copies with signed duplicates of the portraits.)
2. In: *Ten Contemporaries*, by John Gawsworth. (See EB18.)
3. "Edith Sitwell: a critical bibliography 1915–1950," by Lois D. Rosenberg. (*Bulletin of Bibliography*, v. 21, nos. 2–3, pp. 40–43, 57–60, September–December 1953 and January–April 1954; this is a list of critical writings by and about Edith Sitwell.)

I owe a debt to all three.

This bibliography was begun in 1950–51 in partial fulfilment of the requirements for the Diploma in Librarianship at the School of Librarianship and Archives, University College, London. Its resumption was due to the encouragement of Sir Osbert Sitwell and Sir Rupert Hart-Davis.

Edinburgh, March, 1970

ACKNOWLEDGEMENTS

My debt to Dame Edith Sitwell, Sir Osbert Sitwell and Sir Sacheverell Sitwell will be obvious; but I wish to record my sincere gratitude for their courtesy, kindness and patience, which have been a constant encouragement. Errors and omissions in this bibliography, however, are strictly my own.

It is impossible to name all who have given me help over the years, but I cannot fail to thank the authorities of the British Museum Library, the Library of Congress, the New York Public Library and the National Library of Scotland; Mr. W. H. Smettem and Scarborough Public Library; Miss Anne Munro-Kerr and the Foreign Department of the Society of Authors; Mr. Paul Scott, Miss Jean LeRoy and Messrs. Pearn, Pollinger and Higham; Mr. Anthony Newnham; Mr. Alan S. Bell; Mr. Michael Strachan; many of the staff of Messrs. B. H. Blackwell Ltd.; Mr. B. S. Page, Librarian Emeritus, and the University of Leeds for granting me leave to visit the United States; and the University of Edinburgh for granting me three months' leave for this revised edition.

The following persons, publishers and journals have given me information which has been invaluable: Adams and Dart, Publishers; George Allen & Unwin Ltd.; Appleton-Century-Crofts Inc.; The Architectural Press Ltd.; *Argosy*; *The Army Quarterly*; E. J. Arnold & Son Ltd.; Ascher (London) Ltd.; Atheneum Publishers; Mr. Edward Weeks and The Atlantic Monthly Press; A. S. Barnes and Co. Inc.; B. T. Batsford Ltd.; Mr. C. W. Beaumont; Ernest Benn Ltd.; Billing and Sons Ltd.; The Birmingham Repertory Theatre; A. & C. Black Ltd.; Mr. B. N. Brickell, The Blackmore Press; Sir Basil Blackwell and Basil Blackwell &

Mott Ltd.; Geoffrey Bles Ltd.; The Bobbs-Merrill Company Inc.; John Lane, The Bodley Head; William Brendon and Son Ltd.; British Broadcasting Corporation and B.B.C. Publications; The British Council; The British Film Institute; Mr. B. W. Rawlins and The British Fuchsia Society; The British Institute of Recorded Sound; B.P.C. Publishing Ltd.; Mr. Karl Brown and St. Martin's Press Inc.; Mr. Richard Buckle; The Burleigh Press; *The Burlington Magazine*; Business Press Bureau Ltd.; Butler and Tanner Ltd.; Caedmon Publishers; Cambridge University Press; the late Roy Campbell; Jonathan Cape Ltd.; Mr. John Carter; Cassell and Co. Ltd.; The Caxton Press; *Charm*; Chatto and Windus Ltd.; J. & W. Chester Ltd.; Major H. S. Forbes, The Church Lads Brigade; Miss J. A. Wrench, The City Literary Institute; Richard Clay (The Chaucer Press), Ltd.; W. H. & L. Collingridge Ltd.; Collins, Publishers; Columbia Records (New York); The Condé Nast Publications Ltd.; Constable & Co. Ltd.; *Cornhill Magazine*; Country Life Ltd.; *The Countryman*; Coward-McCann Inc.; The Curtain Press Ltd.; The Curwen Press Ltd.; *Daily Express*; *Daily Graphic*; *Daily Mail*; Mr. W. G. Fraser and *Daily Mirror*; *Daily Telegraph & Morning Post*; Mr. Oliver Davies; Peter Davies Ltd.; Decca Record Co. Ltd.; Mr. Alan Denson; J. M. Dent & Sons Ltd.; The Devin-Adair Co.; Doubleday, Doran & Co. Inc.; Miss P. M. Downie; The Dropmore Press Ltd.; Gerald Duckworth & Co. Ltd.; E. P. Dutton & Co. Inc.; Editions Poetry (London) Ltd.; The English Association; *Evening Standard*; Everybody's Publications Ltd.; Eyre and Spottiswoode (Publishers) Ltd.; Faber and Faber Ltd.; Mr. Charles Birnstingl and The Favil Press Ltd.; *The Feathered Warrior*; Fore Publications Ltd.; Funk and Wagnalls Ltd.; *Geographical Magazine*; Glyndebourne Festival Opera; The Golden Head Press Ltd.; Victor Gollancz Ltd.; *Good Housekeeping*; Mr. Stephen Goode, editor of *Studies in the 20th Century*; Mr. John Hale and Robert Hale Ltd.; Hamish

Hamilton Ltd.; Harcourt, Brace and World Inc.; Harper & Bros., and Harper and Row, Publishers, Inc.; *Harper's Bazaar* (London and New York); George G. Harrap & Co. Ltd.; Lamont Library, Harvard College; Hazell, Watson and Viney Ltd.; William Heinemann Ltd.; the late Leonard Woolf and The Hogarth Press Ltd.; Holt, Rinehart and Winston Inc.; Houghton Mifflin Co.; *Housewife*; Hutchinson & Co. (Publishers) Ltd.; Intercultural Publications Inc.; *John o' London's Weekly*; Michael Joseph Ltd.; Alfred A. Knopf Inc.; Mr. John Lehmann; Mr. Oliver F. Brown and the Leicester Galleries; Mr. Jack Lindsay; *Lilliput*; J. B. Lippincott Co.; Mr. Barry Goalby, The Liszt Society; Percy Lund, Humphries & Co. Ltd.; Macdonald and Evans Ltd.; McDowell, Obolensky Inc.; McGraw-Hill Publishing Co. Ltd.; Robert MacLehose and Co. Ltd.; Mr. Thomas Mark, Mr. R. C. Rowland Clark and Messrs. Macmillan and Co. Ltd.; The Macmillan Co., New York; Cie. des Messageries Maritimes; Hon. Robert Gathorne-Hardy, The Mill House Press; *Montreal Daily Star*; National Gallery of Art, Washington; National Portrait Gallery; Neill and Co. Ltd.; New Directions; *New York Herald-Tribune*; New York University Press; Newman Neame Ltd.; George Newnes Ltd. and C. Arthur Pearson Ltd.; *News Chronicle*; W. W. Norton & Co. Inc.; *The Observer*; *L'Œil*; Oxford University Press; Pan Books Ltd.; Max Parrish & Co. Ltd.; Penguin Books Ltd.; Philips Records Ltd.; Phoenix House Ltd.; Mr. Bern Porter; *Picture Post*; G. P. Putnam's Sons; *The Queen*; *Radio Times*; George Rainbird Ltd.; Mr. Robert K. Haas and Random House Inc.; *The Reader's Digest* (London and New York); *Réalités*; Rinehart & Co. Inc.; Mr. Warren Roberts; Mrs. Hazel Elliot, Royal Academy of Arts; Royal Festival Hall; Royal Philharmonic Orchestra; Routledge and Kegan Paul Ltd.; Capt. J. B. E. Radcliffe, of Rudding Park; the late Bertrand Russell, O.M.; St. Martin's Press Inc.; Arthur Sanderson & Sons Ltd.; Mr. Meredith Whittaker and the *Scarborough Mercury*;

Schott and Co. Ltd.; Sheffield City Libraries; Mr Lindars and the Sheffield Philharmonic Society; Sidgwick & Jackson Ltd.; Stein and Day, Publishers; the late Theo. A. Stephens; The Studio Ltd.; *Sunday Graphic*; *Sunday Times*; the late Alan Swallow; *The Tablet*; The Tate Gallery; *The Tatler & Bystander*; Tavistock Publications Ltd.; Mons. F.–J. Temple; Thames and Hudson Ltd.; The Rev. J. W. Thorpe, Rector of Witley; *Time*; The Times Bookshop; Arthur Tooth & Sons Ltd.; *Town and Country Magazine*; Mr. Michael Foot and *Tribune*; The Hon. Patricia Tryon and The Tryon Gallery; University Books Inc.; J. W. Scott, and Ian Angus, University College Library, London; The Viking Press Inc.; Vista Books, Longacre Press Ltd.; *Vogue*; Mr. A. K. Snowman and Messrs. C. & H. Wartski (Llandudno) Ltd.; George Weidenfeld and Nicolson Ltd.; Western Printing Services Ltd.; Westminster Press Ltd.; The Whitefriars Press Ltd.; Williams and Norgate Ltd.; Mr. André L. Simon and the Wine and Food Society; Allan Wingate (Publishers) Ltd.; *Woman's Journal*; *World Digest*; The World Publishing Company; A. A. Wyn Inc.; *The Yorkshire Post*; Yorkshire Television Ltd.; and A. Zwemmer Ltd.

I wish also to record my sincere gratitude to Sir Rupert Hart-Davis for encouragement and help, and for patience, and to the late John Hayward, who purged the original edition of many errors both gross and subtle.

DAME EDITH SITWELL

BOOKS WRITTEN BY EDITH SITWELL
(EA1–EA54)

EA1   THE MOTHER   1915

First edition

THE MOTHER | AND OTHER POEMS | BY | EDITH SIT-
WELL | OXFORD: PRINTED FOR THE AUTHOR | BY B. H.
BLACKWELL, BROAD STREET | 1915

184 × 148 mm.

20 pp.: [i] half-title; [ii] London Agents . . .; [iii] title; [iv] Note;
[v] dedication; [vi] blank; vii Contents; [viii] blank; 9–19 text; [20]
blank.

Dark grey paper wrappers, sewn. Untrimmed edges. Printed in black
on upper cover only.

500 copies printed by Rogers and Broome, Oxford. Published 14
October 1915 at 6*d.*

CONTENTS

Drowned Suns [from *Daily Mirror*, 13 March 1913]—The Web of
Eros—Serenade [from *Daily Mirror*, 22 November 1913]—The
Drunkard—The Mother

EA2   TWENTIETH CENTURY   1916
            HARLEQUINADE

First edition

Twentieth Century | Harlequinade | AND OTHER POEMS |
BY | EDITH AND OSBERT SITWELL | 𝔒𝔵𝔣𝔬𝔯𝔡 | B. H.
BLACKWELL, BROAD STREET | 1916.

187 × 147 mm.

28 pp: [1] title; [2] blank; [3] contents; [4] blank; [5] Edith Sitwell . . .
dedication; [6] acknowledgements; 7–19 text [Edith Sitwell]; [20]

blank; [21] Osbert Sitwell; [22] acknowledgements; 23–27 text [Osbert Sitwell]; [28] Some opinions on The Mother.

Pink paper wrappers, sewn. Untrimmed edges. Printed in black on upper cover only.

500 copies printed by Rogers and Broome, Oxford. Published 7 June 1916 at 1s.

CONTENTS (BY EDITH SITWELL)

The Spider—Clown's Houses—Pedagogues—Trams—Water Music [from *Daily Mirror*, 14 December 1915]—Lullaby [from *Daily Mirror*, 26 March 1915]—Antic Dance

EA3   CLOWNS' HOUSES   1918

First edition

[*Decorative initial, extending four lines down*]
CLOWNS' HOUSES [*ornament*] BY EDITH | SITWELL, AUTHOR OF "THE | MOTHER AND OTHER POEMS" | AND EDITOR OF "WHEELS."

191 × 136 mm.

40 pp.: [1] title; [2] blank; [3] dedication; [4] acknowledgement; [5] contents; [6] blank; 7–36 text; [37] "This fifth of the Initiate Series of Poetry by Proved Hands, was printed in Oxford at the Vincent Works, and finished in August [*sic*], MCMXVIII. Published by B. H. Blackwell, Broad Street, Oxford, and sold in America by Longmans, Green & Co., New York"; [38–40] advertisements.

Russet patterned paper wrappers. Untrimmed edges. White paper labels, printed in black, pasted to upper cover and spine.

750 copies printed. Published 9 June 1918 at 3s.

CONTENTS

Fireworks—Minstrels—Déjeuner sur l'Herbe—What the Dean said to Silenus—Strawberry Paths—Weathercocks [revised from *New Paths 1917–18*]—Two Drunkard Songs—Myself on the Merry-go-Round—Black Coffee—The Old Nurse's Song—Rocking-Horses—On the Guitar—Variations on an Old Nursery-Rhyme—Mariner-Men—Palanquins—The Dancers—Acrobats—Plutocracy at Play—The Madness of Saul [contains parts, revised, from "A Scene from Saul" in *Wheels 2*]

First edition

THE | WOODEN PEGASUS | BY | EDITH SITWELL | Author
of "Clowns' Houses"; Editor of "Wheels" | OXFORD |
BASIL BLACKWELL | 1920

205 × 130 mm.

120 pp.: [1] half-title; [2] "By the same author . . ."; [3] title; [4] blank;
[5] dedication; [6] blank; [7] Acknowledgement; [8] blank; 9–12
contents; 13–119, [120] text, and imprint: "Printed by Hazell, Watson
& Viney, Ld., London and Aylesbury."

Black cloth spine, pink paper boards. Untrimmed edges. Lettered in
white on spine only.

750 copies printed. Published 26 June 1920 at 6s.

CONTENTS

Singerie [from *Wheels 3*]— The Avenue [from *Wheels 3*]—Mandoline
[revised from *Art and Letters* v. 2 no. 4]—Comedy for Marionettes—Falsetto Song [from *Wheels 3*]—Eventail [from *A Miscellany
of Poetry, 1919*]

Fifteen Bucolic Poems. 1. What the Goosegirl said about the Dean
[from *Wheels 4*]—2. Noah—3. The Girl with the Lint-white Locks
[from *Wheels 4*]—4. The Lady with the Sewing-Machine [revised
from *Art and Letters*, v. 2 no. 1]—5. By Candlelight [from *Wheels
4*]—6. Serenade [from *The Mother*]—7. Clowns' Houses [from
Twentieth Century Harlequinade]—8. The Satyr in the Periwig [from
Wheels 2]—9. The Muslin Gown [revised from *Wheels 2*]—10.
Miss Nettybun and the Satyr's Child [from *Wheels 4*]—11. Queen
Venus and the Choir-Boy [revised from *Wheels 4*]—12. The Ape
sees the Fat Woman [from *Saturday Westminster Gazette*, 25
October 1919]—13. The Ape watches Aunt Sally [revised from
Coterie, no. 3]—14. Springing Jack [revised from *Coterie*, no. 3]—
15. "Tournez, Tournez, Bons Chevaux de Bois" [from *Wheels 4*]

Seven Nursery Songs. 1. Old Lady Fly-Away—2. Great Snoring and
Norwich—3. Fat William and the Trains—4. A Penny Fare to
Babylon—5. The Butcher's Shop—6. The King of China's
Daughter [revised from *Wheels 1*]—7. Old King Ptolemy

Pedagogues and Flower-Shows. 1. "Tall cranes with wooden
bodices"—2. What the Professor said to the Editor of "Wheels"
[both from *Art and Letters*, v. 3 no. 2]

Switchback—Trams [revised from *Twentieth Century Harlequinade*]—
Bank Holiday, I & II [both revised from *Oxford & Cambridge
Miscellany*]—Small Talk, I & II [both from *Art and Letters*, v. 3
no. 2]—Dansons la Gigue [from *Oxford & Cambridge Miscellany*]—
Messalina at Margate [from *Wheels 2*]—Pedagogues [revised from
Twentieth Century Harlequinade]—Song from 'The Queen of
Palmyra' [*sic*] [from *Wheels 3*]—The Choir-Boy rides on the
Switchback [from *Art and Letters*, v. 3 no. 2]—Apricot Jam [revised
from *Wheels 3*]—Stopping Place [revised, with additions, from
Wheels 3]—Portrait of a Barmaid [from *Cambridge Magazine*,
April 1919]—Materialism; or, Pastor . . . takes the restaurant car
for Heaven [revised from *Wheels 4*]—Thaïs in Heaven [revised
from *Wheels 4*]

Four Nocturnes. 1. Processions [from *Wheels 1*]—2. Gaiety [revised
from *Wheels 1*]—3. Vacuum [from *Wheels 3*]—4. 'Et l'on Entend
à Peine leurs Paroles' [from *Wheels 3*]

Treats. 1. Funerals—2. The County Calls [revised from *Wheels 2*]—
3. Solo for Ear-Trumpet [from *Saturday Westminster Gazette*, 5
April 1919]

Antic Hay [revised from *Wheels 1*]—Lullaby [from *Twentieth Century
Harlequinade*]—Water Music [from *Twentieth Century Harle-
quinade*]—The Web of Eros [revised from *The Mother*]—Drowned
Suns [from *The Mother*]—The Drunkard [from *The Mother*]—
The Mother [revised from *The Mother*]

EA5 CHILDREN'S TALES FROM THE 1920
RUSSIAN BALLET

a. *First edition (ordinary copies)*

CHILDREN'S TALES | (*FROM THE RUSSIAN BALLET*) |
RETOLD BY | EDITH SITWELL | & | *ILLUSTRATED BY
I. DE B. LOCKYER* | LONDON | LEONARD PARSONS |
PORTUGAL STREET

252 × 190 mm.

80 pp.: [1] half-title; [2–3] blank; [4] frontispiece; [5] title; [6] "First
published, October, 1920, Leonard Parsons, Ltd."; 7–23 introduction;
[24] blank; [25–28], 29–77, [78] text; [79] "Printed in Great Britain by
Richard Clay and Sons, Limited, Brunswick Street, Stamford Street,
S.E.1, and Bungay, Suffolk"; [80] blank.

Eight colour plates pasted on to separate pages.

Grey buckram spine, natural rough cloth boards. Top edge trimmed. Gilt stamped on spine and device blind-stamped on lower cover.

Published in November 1920 at 12s. 6d. (The printers no longer have records of this or the following issues.)

b. *First edition (special copies)*

[I have been unable to find a copy of this issue. The following description is taken from Thomas Balston, *Sitwelliana* (1928), p. 1: "Edition de luxe (12 numbered copies signed by the author) ... (The Bibliographical Note says '75 numbered copies', but not more than twelve were ever signed and issued.) *First edition*. Leonard Parsons, October 1920."

It seems that the Bibliographical Note appeared on page [2], and that the issue was bound in parchment, with top edge gilt.]

c. *second issue*

THE RUSSIAN BALLET | GIFT BOOK | BY | EDITH SIT-WELL | *ILLUSTRATED BY I. DE B. LOCKYER* | LONDON | LEONARD PARSONS | DEVONSHIRE STREET

249 × 187 mm.

80 pp.: as first edition, except for cancels: [1] half-title; [2] blank; [5] title; [6] "Leonard Parsons, Ltd."

Illustrations as in first edition.

Buff buckram spine, grey paper boards. Trimmed edges. Gilt lettered on spine, device blind-stamped on lower cover.

Published in December 1921 at 6s. (Thus the *English Catalogue*, but the book has no date and Balston—*Sitwelliana*, p. 2—says 1922.)

d. *third issue*

CHILDREN'S TALES | (*FROM THE RUSSIAN BALLET*) | RETOLD BY | EDITH SITWELL | & | *ILLUSTRATED BY I. DE B. LOCKYER* | DUCKWORTH | 3 Henrietta Street, London

[This is a re-issue of the original sheets of EA5a, with a cancel title—the verso of which reads: First published ... 1920. Re-issued by Gerald Duckworth & Co. Ltd., 1928.

It was bound in orange cloth boards, with black lettering on the spine and 445 copies were published in 1928 at 12s. 6d.

The contents and text of all issues are identical.]

EA6   FAÇADE   1922

Note: I have here grouped in chronological order three programmes and one book, in which the majority of the poems forming *Façade* first appeared; most were later republished in other volumes and individual poems can be found by use of the Index. See also EA45, EB13, EB31 and EB32.

a. *First edition*

[*Cover:*] "Façade" | Miss Edith Sitwell | on her | Senger-phone | with | accompaniments, | overture & interlude | by | W. T. Walton

Not folded: 15 single leaves. 259 × 205 mm.

15 ll., typed (not duplicated) on the recto only. Contains text only, with note on the last leaf: "Note. All these poems, and some additional ones, will appear in a book called '*Façade*' which Miss Sitwell is publishing privately in a limited edition with a special frontispiece in colour by Gino Severini—at the Faril [*sic*, for Favil] Press, Kensington."

Grey paper covers, stapled. Title on upper cover. Lower cover blank, but with the following stamped inside: "Ainslie, Typist, Translator, 25, Regent Street, S.W. Open all night and Sundays."

Published 24 January 1922 on the occasion of the first private performance of *Façade* at 2 Carlyle Square, Chelsea, London. I do not know how many copies were produced.

CONTENTS

(1. Overture)—2. Dame Souris Trotte—3. The Octogenarian—4. Aubade [from *Saturday Westminster Gazette*, 2 October 1920]—5. The Wind's Bastinado—6. Said King Pompey—(7. Interlude)—8. Jumbo's Lullaby—9. Small Talk, I & II [from *The Wooden Pegasus*]—10. Rose Castles—11. Introduction, and Hornpipe—12. Long Steel Grass [from *Saturday Westminster Gazette*, 3 September 1921]—

13. When Sir Beelzebub—14. Switchback [from *Wheels 3*]—15. Bank Holiday, I & II [from *The Wooden Pegasus*]—16. Springing Jack [from *The Wooden Pegasus*]—17. En Famille [from *The Chapbook*, July 1920]—18. Mariner-Men: presto [from *Clowns' Houses*]

b. *Second edition*

FACADE | *by* | *Edith Sitwell* | *With a Frontispiece by* | *G. Severini*. | THE FAVIL PRESS | KENSINGTON | 1922

184 × 126 mm.

32 pp.: [1] half-title; [2] blank; [3] title; [4] blank; [5] contents; [6] blank; [7–8], 9–27 text; [28] blank; [29] "This edition, which is privately printed for the Author is limited to 150 Copies. This copy is No. "[in ink, with author's signature]; [30–31] advertisements; [32] "Printed by Philip Sainsbury & Charles Birnstingl at The Favil Press, Peel Street, Kensington, London. February mcmxxij." [Device]. "Compositor: Zina Drummond. Pressmen: Crosby Oakes, Kathleen Nutting."

Frontispiece by Gino Severini tipped in.

Red paper boards, printed with brick pattern. Top edge trimmed. White paper label, printed in black, pasted to upper cover.

150 copies privately printed in February 1922. (Five extra un-numbered copies printed for printer's file and copyright purposes.)

CONTENTS

Winter: Early Spring [from *Wheels 6*]—The Doll [from *Form*, October 1921]—Hérodiade [from *Saturday Westminster Gazette*, 20 August 1921]—En Famille [from EA6a]—The Punch and Judy Show

Façade: Long Steel Grass ("Trio for Two Cats and a Trombone") [from EA6a]—Madam Mouse Trots [as "Dame Souris Trotte" in EA6a]—Through Gilded Trellises—Said King Pompey [from EA6a]—The Octogenarian [from EA6a]—Sailors Come [title erased in author's autograph and "Hornpipe" substituted; from EA6a]—The Wind's Bastinado [from EA6a]—Jumbo Asleep [as "Jumbo's Lullaby" in EA6a]—When Sir Beelzebub [from EA6a]

c. *Third edition*

[*Cover:*] THE NEW CHENIL GALLERIES | BY THE TOWN
HALL, CHELSEA | [*line of type ornaments*] | *FAÇADE* |
[*ornament*] | *Poems by Edith Sitwell* | *Music by W. T.*
Walton | [*line of type ornaments*] | Tuesday April 27th at
8.45 p.m. | *Programme one shilling*

211 × 137 mm.

12 pp. (including wrappers): [1] title; [2] blank; [3] list of performers,
and acknowledgements; [4] order of performance; [5–9] text of poems;
[10] list of books "on sale this evening"; [11] blank; [12] The New
Chenil Galleries . . . The Favil Press, 152 Church Street, Kensington.

Yellow paper wrappers, printed in black as above. Stapled. Trimmed
edges.

Published at the concert on 27 April 1926 at 1s. Printing number not
known.

CONTENTS

Daphne [from *Spectator*, 12 May 1923]—Through Gilded Trellises
[from EA6a]—Trio for Two Cats and a Trombone [as "Long Steel
Grass" in EA6a]—Waltz [as "Valse Maigre, 1843" in *Vogue*, late
December 1924]—Four in the Morning [from *Troy Park*]—Sir
Beelzebub [as "When Sir Beelzebub" in EA6a]

Note: The second—and first public—performance of *Façade* was
held in the Aeolian Hall on 12 June 1923 at 3.15 p.m.; in the programme, however, the texts of poems were not printed "owing to
copyright." Thus the second programme to print any of the poems is
this of April 1926.

d. *Fourth edition*

[*Cover:*] THE NEW CHENIL GALLERIES | BY THE TOWN
HALL, CHELSEA | [*line of type ornaments*] | *FAÇADE* | [*type
ornament*] | *Poems by Edith Sitwell* | *Music by W. T.*
Walton | [*line of type ornaments*] | Tuesday June 29th 1926
at 8.45 p.m. | *Programme one shilling*

221 × 142 mm.

12 pp. (including wrappers): [1] title; [2] blank; [3] list of performers;
[4] order of programme; [5–9] text of poems; [10] sources, acknow-

ledgements and list of books; [11] blank; [12] "The New Chenil Galleries . . . The Favil Press, 152 Church Street, Kensington, W.8."

Stiff yellow paper wrappers, printed in black as above. Stapled. Trimmed edges.

Published at the concert 29 June 1926 at 1s. Printing numbers not known.

CONTENTS

Aubade [from EA6a]—Polka—Waltz [from EA6c]—Tarantella

EA7   BUCOLIC COMEDIES   1923

First edition

BUCOLIC | COMEDIES | BY | EDITH SITWELL | [*device*] | DUCKWORTH & CO. | 3 HENRIETTA STREET, COVENT GARDEN, LONDON

185 × 120 mm.

96 pp.: [1] half-title; [2] "Uniform with this volume . . ."; [3] title; [4]: dedication and "First published in 1923. All rights reserved. Printed in Great Britain by Butler & Tanner, Frome and London"; 5–6 contents, & acknowledgements, and errata slip on p. 6; 7–8 quotations from unpublished prose of Edith Sitwell; 9–94 text; 95–96 reviews of other books.

Decorated grey-blue paper boards. Trimmed edges. Printed in brown on plain panels on spine & upper & lower covers.

Published on 24 April 1923 at 3s. 6d. (Publishers' and printers' records of numbers printed do not survive.)

CONTENTS

Nineteen Bucolic Poems. 1. Early Spring [from *Wheels 6*]—2. Spring [from *English Review*, March 1923]—3. Aubade [from *Façade*, January 1922]—4. Fox Trot—5. Cacophony for Clarinet [from *The Chapbook*, May 1923]—6. Rose—7. Gardener Janus catches a Naiad—8. The Five Musicians [from *Wheels 5*]—9. The Higher Sensualism [revised from *Wheels 5*]—10. King Cophetua and the Beggar Maid [revised from *Wheels 5*]—11. Clown Argheb's Song

[from *Wheels 5*]—12. Poor Martha [from *Spectator*, 22 April 1922]
—13. Fleecing Time [from *Wheels 5*]—14. Country Dance—15.
Evening [revised from *Wheels 5*]—16. On the Vanity of Human
Aspirations [from *Wheels 6*]—17. Green Geese [from *Wheels 6*]—
18. Kitchen Song—19. Spinning Song

Why—The Toilette of Myrrhine [from *Wheels 5*]—En Famille [from
Façade, January 1922]

Façade. 1. Père Amelot—2. The Wind's Bastinado [from *Façade*,
January 1922]—3. Lullaby for Jumbo [as "Jumbo's Lullaby" in
Façade, January 1922]—4. Trio for Two Cats and a Trombone
[from *Façade*, January 1922]—5. Dame Souris Trotte [from *Façade*,
January 1922]—6. Dark Song—7. Fête Galante—8. The Owl—
9. Alone—10. Fading Slow and Furred is the Snow—11. Said King
Pompey [from *Façade*, January 1922]—12. The Sky was of Cinna-
mon—13. Ass-Face—14. The Octogenarian [from *Façade*,
January 1922]—15. Said the Noctambulo—16. Herodiade's Flea—
17. Water Party—18. Hornpipe [from *Façade*, January 1922]—
19. Sir Beelzebub [revised from "When Sir Beelzebub" in *Façade*,
January 1922]

Two Promenades Sentimentales. 1. Rain [from *Spectator*, 18 November 1922]—2. The Professor Speaks.

Winter [from *English Review*, March 1923]—Herodiade [from *Façade*,
February 1922]—The Doll [from *Façade*, February 1922]

Spleen. 1. Platitudes—2. Fantoches—3. By the Lake [from *The
Chapbook*, May 1923]—4. Lady Immoraline—5. Fantasia for
Mouth-Organ [revised from *Wheels 6*]

EA8   THE SLEEPING BEAUTY   1924

a. *First edition*

THE | SLEEPING BEAUTY | BY | EDITH SITWELL | [*de-
vice*] | DUCKWORTH & CO. | 3 HENRIETTA STREET,
LONDON, W.C.

187 × 117 mm.

96 pp.: [1] half-title; [2] "By the same author . . ." [3] title; [4] "First
published in 1924. All Rights Reserved. Made and Printed in Great
Britain by Hazell, Watson & Viney, Ld., London and Aylesbury";
[5] dedication; [6] acknowledgements; 7–96 text.

Black cloth boards. Trimmed edges. Lettered in orange on spine and upper cover.

Published in March 1924 at 5s. (Publisher's records of numbers printed do not survive. According to the printers 1000 copies were printed and 400 initially bound.)

CONTENTS

The following previous publications are included:

The Gardener, from "The Princess in the Sleeping Wood," from *The Nation and Athenaeum*, 27 October 1923 [pp. 9–10]

Aubade, from *Spectator*, 22 December 1923 [revised on pp. 18–19]

La Rousse, from *Oxford Outlook*, November 1923 [revised on pp. 44–45]

Daphne, from *Spectator*, 12 May 1923 [revised as "The Soldan's Song," pp. 70–71]

Song from "The Sleeping Beauty," from *The Nation and Athenaeum*, 1 March 1924 [on pp. 77–78]

b. *First edition, American copies*

THE | SLEEPING BEAUTY | BY | EDITH SITWELL | [*device*] | NEW YORK | ALFRED A. KNOPF | 1924 | (*Printed in England*)

Note: 500 copies were imported in sheets, with a cancel title, and the issue was published 1 August 1924 at $1.75. Black cloth spine, decorated paper boards, with top edge red and a pink and blue paper label pasted on the spine. The contents as in the first edition.

EA9 TROY PARK 1925

a. *First edition*

TROY PARK | BY | EDITH SITWELL | [*device*] | DUCKWORTH | 3 HENRIETTA STREET, LONDON, W.C.

184 × 121 mm.

104 pp.: [1] half-title; [2] "By the same Author..." [3] title; [4] "Acknowledgements ... First published in 1925. All rights reserved"; [5] dedication; [6] quotations; 7–8 contents; 9–103 text; [104] Notes, and

imprint: "Printed in Great Britain by Butler & Tanner Ltd., Frome and London."

Black cloth boards. Trimmed edges. Lettered in orange on spine and upper cover.

Published on 12 March 1925, at 5s. (Publisher's and printers' records of numbers printed do not survive.)

CONTENTS

The Child who saw Midas—Colonel Fantock [revised from *Spectator*, 21 May 1924]—Yesterday [from *The Nation and Athenaeum*, 10 May 1924]—The Bird as Confidante—An Old Woman Laments in Spring-Time—The Little Ghost who Died for Love—Two Night Pieces 1. The Shadow's Saracenic Hordes; 2. The Cold Hours Pass—The Mirror—Three Poor Witches [from *Spectator*, 27 December 1924]—The Bear

Country Cousin: three variations. 1. Perrine—2. Song, In summer when the rose-bushes [as "The Country Cousin", in *Vogue*, late August 1924]—3. Song, The clouds are bunchèd roses

When the Sailor . . . —Kitchen Song [a different poem from "Kitchen Song" in *Bucolic Comedies*]—The Drum—The Man with the Green Patch [from *The Criterion*, January 1925]—Clowns' Luck—The Punch and Judy Show [revised from *Façade*, February 1922]—Four in the Morning [from *Vogue*, late December 1924]—'I Do Like to be Beside the Seaside'—Black Mrs. Behemoth—When Cold December—Bells of Grey Crystal—The Picture Book—The Two Dogs [as "Chanson Gris" in *Vogue*, late April 1924]—Pandora's Box—Mademoiselle Richarde [from *Spectator*, 31 May 1924]—The Pleasure Gardens [from *The Nation and Athenaeum*, 22 November 1924]

b. *First edition, American copies*

TROY PARK | BY | EDITH SITWELL | [*device*] | NEW YORK | ALFRED A. KNOPF | MCMXXV

Note: 350 copies were imported in sheets, with a cancel title. Published in Spring 1925 at $1.75, with black cloth spine, floral patterned paper boards, top edge red, and with a pink and blue paper label pasted on the spine. The contents as in the first edition.

First edition

POOR YOUNG PEOPLE | BY | EDITH, OSBERT, AND
SACHEVERELL | SITWELL | WITH DRAWINGS | BY |
ALBERT RUTHERSTON | [*coloured decoration*] | LONDON |
THE FLEURON | 1925

243 × 185 mm.

72 pp.: [i] blank; [ii] "This edition is limited to 375 copies of which
350 are for sale. This is No." [in ink]; [iii] half-title; [iv] drawing;
[v] title; [vi] "Printed and made in England at The Curwen Press,
Plaistow"; [vii–viii] contents; [ix–x], 1–60 text; [61–62] blank.

Drawings by Albert Rutherston on text pages throughout.

Red cloth boards. Top edge trimmed. Gilt lettered on spine.

375 copies printed (350 for sale). Published October 1925 at 42s.

CONTENTS (BY EDITH SITWELL)

Fashionable Intelligence, 1843—Don Egidion—Far Away—Poor
Young People—The Little Nursemaid—Hired Mourners—Widow
Styles—The Letter

EA11   POETRY AND CRITICISM   1925

a. *First edition*

POETRY & CRITICISM | BY | EDITH SITWELL | [*device*] |
Published by | Leonard & Virginia Woolf at The Hogarth
Press | 52 Tavistock Square, London, W.C.1 | 1925

218 × 140 mm.

32 pp.: [1] half-title; [2] The Hogarth Essays . . .; [3] title; [4] "Printed
in Great Britain by Neill & Co., Ltd., Edinburgh."; 5–27, [28] text;
[29–32] back end-papers.

Stiff pale blue paper wrappers with a design by Vanessa Bell printed
in black on upper cover. Trimmed edges.

Published 29 October 1925 at 2s. 6d., as no. XI of "The Hogarth
Essays." (Publishers' and printers' records of numbers printed do not
survive.)

b. *First edition, American issue*

Poetry and Criticism | *By* | *Edith Sitwell* | *[device]* | *New York* | *Henry Holt and Company*

Note: This issue, printed in the United States, was published 1 April 1926. 1500 copies were printed, but only 1000 bound. Blue cloth spine, dark blue paper boards, top edge blue, with a blue paper label pasted on the spine. Contents as in the first edition.

EA12 AUGUSTAN BOOKS OF 1926
MODERN POETRY

First edition

[Cover; within a decorated and ruled border]

THE AUGUSTAN BOOKS OF | *MODERN POETRY* | *[rule]* | EDITH | SITWELL | *[rule]* | *LONDON: ERNEST BENN LTD.* | *8, BOUVERIE STREET, E.C.4*

221 × 139 mm.

32 pp.: [i] title; [ii] The Augustan Books of Poetry; iii note; iv contents; 5–29 text; [30] Bibliography; [31] blank; [32] advertisement, and: Printed in Great Britain by Billing and Sons, Ltd., Guildford and Esher.

No separate covers. Stapled. Trimmed edges.

Published 27 May 1926 at 6*d*. Copies issued "in the early 1930's" had maroon linen wrappers pasted over front and back pages, with a window cut in the upper cover to show the author's name. The series was later transferred to Messrs. Eyre & Spottiswoode, but neither they nor Messrs. Benn nor the printers have records of numbers printed.

CONTENTS

The Little Ghost who Died for Love—Colonel Fantock—Mademoiselle Richarde—Country Cousin ("Perrine") [all from *Troy Park*]

Gardener Janus catches a Naiad—Fleecing Time—Aubade—Herodiade—Winter [all from *Bucolic Comedies*]

The Country Fair—Through Gilded Trellises [both from *The Sleeping Beauty*]

First edition

ELEGY *on* DEAD FASHION | By EDITH SITWELL | ILLUS-
TRATED BY | THOMAS LOWINSKY | [*decoration*] | DUCK-
WORTH | 3 HENRIETTA STREET, LONDON | 1926

243 × 160 mm.

32 pp.: [i] half-title; [ii] "Of this edition there have been printed by
The Westminster Press 225 copies, of which 200 only are for sale.
No." [in ink, with author's holograph signature]. "All rights
reserved"; [iii] blank; [iv] drawing; [v] title; [vi] blank; 1–21, [22]
text; [23–26] back end-papers.

Seven drawings by Thomas Lowinsky.

Smooth yellow cloth boards. Top edge trimmed. Lettered in black
on upper cover, with black ruled border.

225 copies printed (200 for sale). Published 5 November 1926 at
12s. 6d.

CONTENTS

"Elegy on Dead Fashion," being a greatly revised and extended version of "Fashionable Intelligence, 1843" in *Poor Young People*

EA14   POEM FOR A   1926
            CHRISTMAS CARD

a. *First edition, special copies*
[*No title.*] [*decoration*] CHRISTMAS | GREETINGS

Single sheet, quarto. 238 × 159 mm.

8 pp.: [1] decoration; [2–3] blank; [4] text, with author's holograph
signature; [5] full page design; [6–7] blank; [8] "This card is designed
by Albert Rutherston and published by The Fleuron Limited, 101
Great Russell Street, London, W.C. This is No. [in ink] of 210
specially printed and signed copies on Japanese vellum of which 200
are for sale and 10 for presentation."

Decorations by Albert Rutherston, printed in colours.

Unbound. Untrimmed edges.

210 copies printed (200 for sale). Published in December 1926.

"Poem for a Christmas Card"

b. *First edition, ordinary copies*

Note: These are as the special copies, except that: 1. they are printed on ordinary paper; 2. on p. [4] the author's name is printed, instead of being in her holograph; 3. on p. [5] there is no artist's signature; 4. on p. [8] there is no certificate of limitation. These copies were also published in December 1926, but I do not know how many were printed, nor whether they were published before or at the same time as the special copies. The Curwen Press no longer have detailed records.

EA15   RUSTIC ELEGIES   1927

a. *First edition*

RUSTIC ELEGIES | BY | EDITH SITWELL | Author of | "Bucolic Comedies," "The Sleeping | Beauty," "Troy Park," etc. | DUCKWORTH | 3 HENRIETTA STREET, W.C. | 1927

181 × 116 mm.

96 pp.: [1] half-title; [2] blank; [3] title; [4] "All rights reserved"; 5 Contents; [6] blank; 7–94 text; [95] notes; [96] "Printed in Great Britain by Butler & Tanner Ltd., Frome and London."

Frontispiece (photograph of the author by Cecil Beaton) tipped in.

Black cloth boards. Trimmed edges. Lettered in orange on spine and upper cover.

1500 copies printed. Published 10 March 1927 at 5s.

CONTENTS

Elegy on Dead Fashion [from the book of that title]—The Hambone and the Heart [includes 64 lines from "The Mother" in *The Mother*]—Prelude to a Fairy Tale [includes "Valse Maigre, 1843," from *Façade*, April 1926, now under title "Second Sylph"; and revision of "Widow Styles" from *Poor Young People*]

b. *First edition, American issue*

[*Sepia swelled rule*] | [*black:*] *Rustic Elegies* | *By* | *Edith Sitwell* | *Author of "Bucolic Comedies," "Troy Park,"* | *"The Sleeping Beauty," etc.* | *With Frontispiece by William F. Matthews* | *Alfred A · Knopf · New York* | *1927* | [*sepia swelled rule*]

Note: This issue, printed in America by The Marchbanks Press, consists of 72 pages, with a frontispiece drawing by William F. Matthews, bound in green cloth boards, with trimmed edges, gilt lettered and blind-stamped. 950 copies were printed, and the issue was published in 1927 at $2.50. The publishers do not know the date of publication, but the Library of Congress copy is dated 22 August 1927. The contents are as in first edition.

EA16   POPULAR SONG   1928

a. *First edition, special copies*

[*Within an ornamental border*]

POPULAR SONG | BY EDITH SITWELL | DRAWINGS BY EDWARD BAWDEN | LONDON: FABER AND GWYER LTD. | MCMXXVIII

215 × 137 mm.

16 pp.: [1] "This large-paper edition, printed on English hand-made paper, is limited to five hundred copies. This is number..." [in ink, with author's autograph signature]; [2] blank; [3] title design by Edward Bawden; [4] blank; [5] title; [6] Printed in England; [7] decoration; [8] blank; [9–11] text, with p. [10] blank; [12] blank; [13] "The Ariel Poems ..."; [14] "This is no. 15 of The Ariel Poems. Published by Faber and Gwyer Limited at 24 Russell Square, London, W.C.1. Printed at The Curwen Press, Plaistow"; [15–16] blank.

Decorations by Edward Bawden.

Salmon paper boards. Top edge trimmed. Gilt lettered on upper cover.

"About" 500 copies printed (according to the publishers; the Curwen Press no longer have detailed records). Published "about September" 1928 at 7s. 6d., as no. 15 of "The Ariel Poems."

35

b. *First edition, ordinary copies*

[*Cover*]

POPULAR | SONG | *Edith Sitwell* | DESIGNS BY | EDWARD
BAWDEN

184 × 120 mm.

8 pp.: [1]–[2] blank; [3] decoration; [4]–[5] text; [6] List of the Ariel
Poems; [7]–[8] blank.

Stitched in yellow laid paper wrappers, with the title design by
Edward Bawden printed in black on the upper cover (as p. [3] of
special copies).

"Possibly 2300 copies" (according to the publishers) were printed, and
the issue was published in September 1928 at 1s.

Note: Gawsworth said that they "slightly precede in point of time"
the special copies, but the publishers are unable to confirm this. The
contents are as in the special copies.

EA17   FIVE POEMS   1928

First edition

FIVE POEMS | BY | EDITH SITWELL | DUCKWORTH | 3
HENRIETTA STREET, LONDON | 1928

271 × 195 mm.

32 pp.: [i–ii] blank; [iii] half-title; [iv] "This Edition printed on Van
Gelder handmade paper at the Cambridge University Press, consists
of 275 copies only, all signed by the author, of which 250 copies only
are for sale. No. . . ." [in ink, with author's autograph signature]; [v]
title; [vi] Printed in Great Britain; [vii] contents; [viii] blank; [1–2],
3–20, [21] text; [22] "Printed by Walter Lewis MA at the Cambridge
University Press"; [23–24] blank.

Dark blue buckram boards. Untrimmed edges. Gilt lettered on
spine and upper cover.

275 copies printed (250 for sale). Published 26 October 1928 at 15s.

CONTENTS

Four Songs. 1. The Peach Tree [from *Saturday Review of Literature*,
    21 April 1928]—2. The Strawberry—3. The Greengage Tree—
     4. Daphne [a different poem from "Daphne" in *Façade*, April 1926]

Metamorphosis

a. *First edition*

GOLD COAST CUSTOMS | BY | EDITH SITWELL | DUCK-
WORTH | 3 HENRIETTA STREET | LONDON W.C.

183 × 120 mm.

64 pp.: [1] half-title; [2] "By Edith Sitwell"; [3] title; [4] "All Rights
reserved. First published 1929 . . . Printed in Great Britain"; [5] dedication; [6] blank; 7–63 text; [64] "Printed at the Burleigh Press,
Lewin's Mead, Bristol."

Frontispiece (portrait of the author by Pavel Tchelitchew) tipped in.

Black cloth boards. Trimmed edges. Lettered in orange on spine and
upper cover.

2000 copies printed. Published 24 January 1929 at 5s.

CONTENTS

Gold Coast Customs [includes lines from "The Dog" in *The Nation
and Athenaeum*, 22 October 1927]

Six Songs. 1. Between the Amber Portals of the Sea [as "The Peach
Tree" in *Five Poems*]—2. The Strawberry [from *Five Poems*]—
3. The Greengage Tree [from *Five Poems*]—4. The Nectarine Tree
—5. The Cherry Tree [from *Time & Tide*, 11 January 1929]—
6. Daphne [from *Five Poems*]

The Serenade at Morning—The Cat [as "Cendrillon and the Cat" in
Vogue, late July 1925]—The Bat [from *Time & Tide*, 4 January
1929]—Metamorphosis [from *Five Poems*, but omitting two lines]

b. *First edition, American copies*

GOLD COAST CUSTOMS | BY | EDITH SITWELL | [*device*] |
BOSTON AND NEW YORK | HOUGHTON MIFFLIN COM-
PANY | 1929

Note: 500/520 copies were imported in sheets, and the issue was
published 6 September 1929 at $2.00. There is a cancel title, and the
binding is a black cloth spine with gilt patterned paper boards, top
edge black, with a white paper label pasted on the spine. The contents
are as in the first edition.

a. *First edition, special copies*

ALEXANDER POPE | BY | EDITH SITWELL | LONDON | FABER & FABER LIMITED | 24 RUSSELL SQUARE

224 × 146 mm.

336 pp.: [i] "This signed edition, printed on English hand-made paper, is limited to two hundred and twenty copies. Of these, two hundred numbered copies are for sale. This copy is number" [in ink, with author's autograph signature]; [ii] blank; [iii] half-title; [iv] blank; [v] title; [vi] "First published in MCMXXX by Faber & Faber Limited, 24 Russell Square London W.C.1. Printed in Great Britain at The Chiswick Press, London . . ."; [vii] dedication; [viii] blank; [ix] note; [x] blank; xi Contents; [xii] blank; xiii Illustrations; [xiv] blank; [xv–xvi], 1–316 text, appendices & index; [317] "London: Charles Whittingham and Grigg (Printers), Ltd. Chiswick Press, Tooks Court, Chancery Lane"; [318–320] blank.

Eight plates tipped in, each with tissue guard.

Yellow buckram boards. Top edge gilt, others untrimmed. Gilt lettered on spine.

220 copies printed (200 for sale). Published 7 March 1930 at 52s. 6d.

b. *First edition, ordinary copies*

[*Title as in special copies*]

225 × 143 mm.

336 pp.: As in special copies, with the omission of the certificate on the first page.

Eight plates tipped in, and the wrapper design (by Rex Whistler) printed in sepia on green tipped in before the half-title.

Yellow cloth boards. Top edge gilt, others untrimmed. Gilt lettered on spine.

4000 copies printed. Published 14 March 1930 at 15s. (Some of these copies were later used for a cheap edition, March 1935.)

CONTENTS

As in special copies

c. *First edition, American issue*

[*Within a border*]

ALEXANDER | POPE | [*rule*] | *By EDITH SITWELL* |
[*decoration in green*] | *NEW YORK* | COSMOPOLITAN BOOK
CORPORATION | MCMXXX

Note: This issue, printed in America by J. J. Little & Ives Co., was
published 12 April 1930 at $4.00. The publishers no longer have the
printing numbers. Of 384 pages, the volume was bound in black cloth
spine, with green cloth boards, trimmed edges, and lettered in black
and green. The contents are as in the English issues.

EA20   COLLECTED POEMS   1930

a. *First edition, special copies*

THE COLLECTED POEMS | OF | EDITH SITWELL | LON-
DON | GERALD DUCKWORTH AND COMPANY LTD |
HOUGHTON MIFFLIN COMPANY | BOSTON | 1930

233 × 158 mm.

288 pp.: [i] half-title; [ii] blank; [iii] title; [iv] "Of this edition of The
Collected Poems of Edith Sitwell, on handmade paper, numbered, and
signed by the Author, and with a frontispiece designed by Pavel
Tchelitchew, 320 copies have been printed, of which 200 only are for
sale in England and 100 in the U.S.A. No." [in ink, with author's
autograph signature]. "Printed at The Chapel River Press ... All
Rights Reserved"; [v] Preface, with errata slip; [vi] blank; vii–x Contents; [1], 2–278 text, notes and indexes.

Frontispiece (portrait of the author by Pavel Tchelitchew) tipped in,
with tissue guard.

Buff buckram boards. Untrimmed edges. Gilt lettered on spine.

320 copies printed. Published in London 5 June 1930 at 60s., and in
Boston 10 September 1930 at $15.00.

b. *First edition, ordinary copies*

THE COLLECTED POEMS | OF | EDITH SITWELL | DUCK-
WORTH | 3 Henrietta Street, W.C.2 | 1930

196 × 123 mm.

288 pp.: as in special copies, but omitting certificate and imprint on p. [iv].

No frontispiece.

Two bindings: [1] Crushed dark blue morocco boards. Top edge gilt, others trimmed. Gilt lettered on spine. Head and tail bands, blue silk marker, pale blue marbled end-papers.

[2] Black cloth boards, plain endpapers. Trimmed edges. Gilt lettered on spine.

2500 copies printed (250 in binding [1], the rest in binding [2]). Published 5 June 1930 at 16s. and 8s. 6d.

CONTENTS [all copies]

The Sleeping Beauty [from *The Sleeping Beauty*]—The Drum [from *Troy Park*]—The Man with the Green Patch [from *Troy Park*]—Metamorphosis [from *Five Poems*]

Eight Songs. 1. Daphne [from *Five Poems*]—2. The Sylph's Song [as "The Sylph" in *Rustic Elegies*]—3. The Peach Tree [from *Gold Coast Customs*]—4. The Strawberry [from *Five Poems*]—5. The Greengage Tree [from *Five Poems*]—6. The Nectarine Tree [from *Gold Coast Customs*]—7. The Cherry Tree [from *Gold Coast Customs*]—8. The Serenade at Morning [from *Gold Coast Customs*]

Four Elegies. 1. The Hambone and the Heart [from *Rustic Elegies*, but with several new verses]—2. The Little Ghost who Died for Love [from *Troy Park*]—3. The Lament of Edward Blastock—4. The Ghost whose Lips were Warm [two "new poems"—preface]

Prelude to a Fairy Tale [as in *Rustic Elegies*, but omitting "The Sylph," and pp. 81–85 and the last 52 lines of that version]

The Madness of Saul [revised from *Clowns' Houses*]

Troy Park. 1. The Warmth of Spring, from "The Child who Saw Midas" [from *Troy Park*]—2. Colonel Fantock [from *Troy Park*]—3. Mademoiselle Richarde [from *Troy Park*]—4. The Pleasure Gardens [from *Troy Park*]—5. The Cat [from *Gold Coast Customs*]—6. Pandora's Box [revised from *Troy Park*]

Façade. 1. Père Amelot [from *Bucolic Comedies*]—2. The Bat [from *Gold Coast Customs*]—3. Clowns' Houses [from *The Wooden Pegasus*]—4. The Wind's Bastinado [from *Façade*, January 1922]—5. Lullaby for Jumbo [as "Jumbo's Lullaby" in *Façade*, January 1922]—6. Trio for Two Cats and a Trombone [as "Long Steel Grass" in *Façade*, January 1922]—7. Madam Mouse Trots [as "Dame Souris

Trotte" in *Façade*, January 1922]—8. Four in the Morning [from *Troy Park*]—9. "I Do Like to be Beside the Seaside" [as first of that title in *Troy Park*]—10. Ass-Face [from *Bucolic Comedies*]—11. The Octogenarian [from *Façade*, January 1922]—12. Said the Noctambulo [from *Bucolic Comedies*]—13. Came the Great Popinjay [as "Herodiade's Flea" in *Bucolic Comedies*]—14. Black Mrs. Behemoth [from *Troy Park*]—15. Said King Pompey [from *Façade*, January 1922]—16. The Avenue [from *The Wooden Pegasus*]—17. Dark Song [from *Bucolic Comedies*]—18. Mariner Men [from *Clowns' Houses*]—19. Fête Galante [from *Bucolic Comedies*]—20. The Satyr in the Periwig [revised from *The Wooden Pegasus*]—21. The Owl [from *Bucolic Comedies*]—22. Alone [from *Bucolic Comedies*]—23. Fading Slow [from *Bucolic Comedies*]—24. An Old Woman Laments in Spring-Time [from *Troy Park*]—25. Water Party [from *Bucolic Comedies*]—26. Hornpipe [from *Façade*, January 1922]—27. When Sir Beelzebub [from *Façade*, January 1922]

Thirty-Eight Bucolic Comedies. 1. Early Spring [from *Façade*, February 1922]—2. Spring [from *Bucolic Comedies*]—3. Aubade [from *Façade*, February 1922]—4. Fox Trot [revised from *Bucolic Comedies*]—5. Cacophony for Clarinet [from *Bucolic Comedies*]—6. Rose [revised from *Bucolic Comedies*]—7. Gardener Janus catches a Naiad [from *Bucolic Comedies*]—8. Popular Song [from *Popular Song*]—9. The Five Musicians [from *Bucolic Comedies*]—10. Springing Jack [revised from *The Wooden Pegasus*]—11. The Higher Sensualism [from *The Wooden Pegasus*]—12. King Cophetua and the Beggar Maid [from *Bucolic Comedies*]—13. Clown Argheb's Song [from *Bucolic Comedies*]—14. Pavane [as pt. IV of "The Child who Saw Midas" in *Troy Park*]—15. Poor Martha [from *Bucolic Comedies*]—16. Three Poor Witches [from *Troy Park*]—17. Country Cousin [from *Troy Park*]—18. When the Sailor [from *Bucolic Comedies*]—19. Fleecing Time [from *Bucolic Comedies*]—20. Country Dance [from *Bucolic Comedies*]—21. Evening [from *Bucolic Comedies*]—22. On the Vanity of Human Aspirations [from *Bucolic Comedies*]—23. Green Geese [from *Bucolic Comedies*]—24. Two Kitchen Songs [from *Bucolic Comedies* and *Troy Park*]—25. Spinning Song [from *Bucolic Comedies*]—26. The Bear [from *Troy Park*]—27. Why [from *Bucolic Comedies*]—28. The Toilette of Myrrhine [from *Bucolic Comedies*]—29. En Famille [from *Façade*, January 1922]—30. Two Promenades Sentimentales [from *Bucolic Comedies*]—31. Winter [from *Bucolic Comedies*]—32. Herodiade [from *Façade*, February 1922]—33. The

Doll [from *Façade*, February 1922]—34. Platitudes [from *Bucolic Comedies*]—35. Two Night Pieces [from *Troy Park*]—36. Fantoches [from *Bucolic Comedies*]—37. By the Lake [from *Bucolic Comedies*]—38. Lady Immoraline [revised from *Bucolic Comedies*]

Elegy on Dead Fashion [from *Elegy on Dead Fashion*]

Gold Coast Customs [from *Gold Coast Customs*, but with "new and changed ending"—i.e., the last 26 lines are new]

EA21   IN SPRING   1931

a. *First edition, special copies*
[*Within a coloured decoration*]

IN SPRING | by | EDITH SITWELL | [*ornament*] | WOOD ENGRAVINGS | by EDWARD CARRICK | [*below decoration:*] PRIVATELY PRINTED IN LONDON ANNO DOMINI MCMXXXI

233 × 149 mm.

20 pp.: [i–iv] front end-papers; [1] half-title; [2] "The edition is limited to 290 numbered copies, printed on Charles I. handmade paper, all signed by the author. Of these, 250 copies (Nos. 41–290) are for sale. There is also a special edition of 15 copies, lettered A–O: of which 10 (Nos. F–O) are for sale. Copy No. . . ." [in ink, with author's autograph signature]; [3] title; [4] blank; [5] dedication; [6] blank; [7–9] text—the last four lines being written in author's holograph; [10] blank; [11] "Here ends 'In Spring' a poem by Edith Sitwell with 3 wood engraved decorations by Edward Carrick, set up during May MCMXXXI & printed privately for Terence Fytton Armstrong, 60 Frith St. Soho, W.1"; [12] "Charles Mitchell Ltd., Printers"; [13–16] back end-papers.

Three wood engravings by Edward Carrick on text pages.

Green paper boards. Untrimmed edges. Yellow paper label, printed in black, pasted on upper cover.

15 copies printed (10 for sale). Published 23 May 1931 at 21*s*.

b. *First edition, ordinary copies*

As special copies, except title-page is not coloured, and last four lines of text are printed, not in author's holograph.

290 copies printed (250 for sale). Published 23 May 1931 at 6*s*.

a. *First edition, special copies*

JANE BARSTON | 1719–1746 | By | EDITH SITWELL | [star] | *Drawings* | *by* | *R. A. Davies* | LONDON | FABER & FABER LTD | 1931

216 × 140 mm.

12 pp.: [1] "This large paper edition, printed on English hand-made paper, is limited to two hundred and fifty copies. This is Number" [in ink, with author's autograph signature]; [2] blank; [3] title design by R. A. Davies; [4] blank; [5] title; [6] "Printed in England at The Curwen Press"; [7] decoration; [8] blank; [9–11] text; [12] "This is No. 36 of The Ariel Poems, Published in London by Faber & Faber Limited, at 24 Russell Square, W.C.1."

Drawings by R. A. Davies.

Lemon paper boards. Top edge trimmed. Gilt lettered on upper cover.

"Possibly 274" copies (according to the publishers) printed. Published in October 1931 at 7s. 6d., as no. 36 of "The Ariel Poems."

b. *First edition, ordinary copies*

[Cover]

JANE BARSTON | 1719–1746 | BY EDITH SITWELL | [decoration] | *Drawings by R. A. Davies*

186 × 121 mm.

8 pp.: [1]–[2] blank; [3] decoration; [4]–[6] text; [7]–[8] blank.

Stitched in yellow laid paper wrappers with the title and a design by R. A. Davies on the upper cover (as p. [3] of special copies).

"Possibly 2018" copies (according to the publishers) were printed, and the issue was published in October 1931 at 1s.

Note: Gawsworth said these copies "slightly preceded in point of time the special" copies, but the publishers are unable to confirm this. The printers no longer have relevant records. The contents are as in special copies.

a. *First edition, special copies*

EPITHALAMIUM | BY | EDITH SITWELL | Christmas 1931

216 × 152 mm.

8 pp.: [1] half-title; [2] "Of 100 copies of *Epithalamium* numbered, signed by the Author and specially bound, this is No...." [in ink, with author's autograph signature]; [3] title; [4] blank; [5] text; [6] blank; [7] "Set in Caslon Old Face by The Westminster Press, London, printed by them on English hand-made paper and published by Gerald Duckworth & Co. Ltd."; [8] blank.

Pink cloth boards. Untrimmed edges. Marbled end-papers. Gilt lettered on upper cover.

100 copies printed. Published in November 1931 at 5s.

CONTENTS

"Epithalamium"

b. *First edition, ordinary copies*

Note: As the special copies, except: 1. Page [2] blank; 2. No covers; sewn; 3. Issued in a white envelope, lettered in black on front.

900 copies printed. Published in December 1931 at 1s. The contents are as in the special copies.

a. *First edition*

[*Within a treble rule and star border*]

BATH | BY | EDITH | SITWELL | [*star*] | LONDON | FABER & FABER | 24 RUSSELL SQUARE

219 × 141 mm.

288 pp.: [1] half-title; [2] blank; [3] title; [4] "First published in MCMXXXII by Faber and Faber Limited, 24 Russell Square, London W.C.I. Printed in Great Britain by R. MacLehose and Company Limited, The University Press, Glasgow ..."; [5] dedication; [6] blank; 7 Note; [8] blank; 9 Contents; [10] blank; 11–[12] illustrations; 13–288 text.

Wrapper design (by Rex Whistler) printed in red, and sixteen plates, tipped in.

Rough rose-pink cloth boards. Top edge gilt, others untrimmed. Gilt stamped on spine.

Published in May 1932 at 15*s*. (The publishers no longer know how many copies were printed; the printers say there were 1500 copies.)

b. *First edition, American copies*

[*Within a rectangular border*]

BATH | BY | EDITH | SITWELL | [*star*] | [*device*] | 1932 | HARRISON SMITH | NEW YORK

Note: "Probably 1000 copies" (according to the publishers; the printers have no records) were imported, with a cancel title, and the issue was published in November 1932 at $3.50. Rough pale pink cloth boards, top edge yellow, gilt lettered on spine. The contents are as in the first edition.

EA25   THE ENGLISH ECCENTRICS   1933

a. *First edition*

[*Within a red ornamental border*]

THE | ENGLISH | ECCENTRICS | [*red*] BY | [*black*] EDITH | SITWELL | [*red ornament*] | [*black*] LONDON | FABER & FABER | 24 RUSSELL SQUARE

215 × 141 mm.

336 pp.: [1–2] blank; [3] half-title; [4] "Also by Edith Sitwell . . ."; [5] title; [6] "First published in May 1933 by Faber and Faber Limited, 24 Russell Square, London W.C.I. Printed in Great Britain by R. MacLehose and Company Limited, The University Press, Glasgow . . ."; [7] dedication; [8] blank; [9] quotation; [10] blank; 11 Note; [12] blank; 13 Contents; [14] blank; 15 Illustrations; [16] blank; 17–332 text and index; [333–336] blank.

Wrapper design (by Pavel Tchelitchew) printed in black on green paper, and 16 plates, tipped in.

Green cloth boards. Top edge gilt, others untrimmed. Gilt stamped on spine.

2748 copies printed. Published in May 1933 at 15*s*.

b. *First edition, American copies*

[*Within a red ornamental border*]

THE | ENGLISH | ECCENTRICS | [*red*] BY | [*black*] EDITH | SITWELL | [*red decoration*] | [*black*] Boston and New York | HOUGHTON MIFFLIN COMPANY | 1933

Note: 750/780 copies were imported, with a cancel title, and the issue was published 13 September 1933 at $4.00. Smooth green cloth boards, top edge gilt, gilt stamped on spine. The contents are as in the first edition.

c. *Second edition*

[A revised and enlarged edition was published in 1957 by Vanguard Press, New York.]

d. *Second edition, English copies*

[*Within an ornamental border*]

ENGLISH | ECCENTRICS | BY | EDITH | SITWELL | [*decoration*] | LONDON | DENNIS DOBSON

Note: These copies, printed in America, were bound in grey-green cloth boards, top edge red, stamped in red on the spine.

1100 copies were printed. Publication was in September 1958 at 25*s*.

EA26   FIVE VARIATIONS ON   1933
A THEME

First edition

FIVE VARIATIONS ON A | THEME | *by* | EDITH SITWELL | DUCKWORTH | 3 Henrietta Street, W.C.2 | 1933

195 × 127 mm.

48 pp. [i]–[iv] front end-papers: [v] half-title; [vi] "Poems by Edith Sitwell . . ."; [vii] title; [viii] note, "All rights reserved"; [ix] contents; [x] blank; [1], 2–38 text, and imprint: "Printed at The Chapel River Press, Andover, Hants."

Mottled grey paper boards. Trimmed edges. Lettered in red on spine and upper cover.

1000 copies printed. Published November 1933 at 3*s*. 6*d*.

46

Romance—Two Songs, 1. "Come, my Arabia"; 2. "My desert has a noble sun for heart"—Metamorphosis [from *Five Poems*]—Elegy on Dead Fashion [from *Elegy on Dead Fashion*]

EA27 ASPECTS OF 1934
MODERN POETRY

First edition

ASPECTS OF | MODERN POETRY | BY | EDITH SITWELL | DUCKWORTH | 3 Henrietta Street, London, W.C.2

215 × 138 mm.

264 pp.: [1] half-title; [2] advertisement; [3] title; [4] "First Published 1934. (All rights reserved). Printed in Great Britain at The Chapel River Press, Andover, Hants"; [5] dedication; [6] blank; [7] contents; [8] note; 9–264 text. (Errata slips on pp. 39 and 233.)

Brick-red cloth boards. Trimmed edges. Gilt lettered on spine.

2000 copies printed. Published 15 November 1934 at 8s. 6d.

CONTENTS

Part of ch. 1, "Pastors and Masters," is taken from articles by the author in *Morning Post*, 15 January 1934 and 6 March 1934.

EA28 VICTORIA OF ENGLAND 1936

a. *First edition*

VICTORIA | OF ENGLAND | [*short double rule*] | BY EDITH SITWELL | [*drawing by Barnett Freedman*] | FABER AND FABER LIMITED | 24 Russell Square | London

222 × 144 mm.

392 pp.: [1] half-title; [2] "By the same author . . ."; [3] title; [4] "First published in February MCMXXXVI by Faber and Faber Limited . . . Printed in Great Britain at the University Press, Cambridge . . ."; [5] dedication; [6] blank; 7–9 Note; [10] blank; 11–12 contents; 13–14 illustrations; [15–16], 17–390 text, bibliography and index; [392] blank. Sixteen plates tipped in.

Cerise cloth boards. Top edge gilt, others trimmed. Gilt stamped on spine, with blue and gilt silhouette.

8400 copies printed. Published 13 February 1936 at 15s.

b. *First edition, American issue*

[*Red*] Victoria | [*black*] OF ENGLAND | *Edith Sitwell* | WITH ILLUSTRATIONS | [*rule*] | HOUGHTON MIFFLIN COMPANY · BOSTON | 𝕿𝖍𝖊 𝕽𝖎𝖛𝖊𝖗𝖘𝖎𝖉𝖊 𝕻𝖗𝖊𝖘𝖘 𝕮𝖆𝖒𝖇𝖗𝖎𝖉𝖌𝖊 | 1936

Note: This issue, printed in the U.S.A., was published 3 August 1936 at $3.50. Bound in royal blue rough cloth boards, gilt lettered on red panels on the spine. 3500 copies printed. The contents are as in first edition.

EA29   SELECTED POEMS   1936

a. *First edition*

SELECTED POEMS | With an Essay on her own Poetry | *by* | EDITH SITWELL | DUCKWORTH | 3 Henrietta Street, W.C.2 | 1936

197 × 129 mm.

288 pp.: [1] half-title; [2] blank; [3] title; [4] "All Rights Reserved. Made and Printed in Great Britain by the Kemp Hall Press, Ltd. in the City of Oxford"; [5], 6–7 contents; [8] blank; 9–54 Some notes on my own poetry; 55–285 text of poems, and notes; [286–288] blank.

Smooth green cloth boards. Trimmed edges. Gilt lettered on spine.

Published in June 1936 at 8s. 6d. (The publishers have no record of the number printed; the printers' archives do not appear to survive.)

CONTENTS

Some Notes on my Own Poetry [revised and enlarged from *London Mercury*, March 1935]

[All poems are from *Collected Poems*, 1930, unless otherwise stated]

The Sleeping Beauty

Three Variations on a Theme. 1. Romance [revised and shortened from *Five Variations on a Theme*]—2. Metamorphosis—3. Elegy on Dead Fashion

Five Songs. 1. Daphne—2. The Sylph's Song—3. The Peach Tree— 4. The Strawberry—5. The Greengage Tree

Four Elegies. 1. The Heart and the Hambone [as "The Hambone

and the Heart"]—2. The Little Ghost who Died for Love—3. The Lament of Edward Blastock—4. The Ghost whose Lips were Warm

Colonel Fantock

Façade. 1. Père Amelot—2. Clowns' Houses—3. Lullaby for Jumbo 4. Trio for Two Cats and a Trombone—5. Madam Mouse Trots— 6. Four in the Morning—7. I Do Like to be Beside the Seaside— 8. Said the Noctambulo—9. Came the Great Popinjay—10. Two Variations on an Old Nursery Rhyme [as "The King of China's Daughter" from *The Wooden Pegasus*, and another poem of the same title]—11. Black Mrs. Behemoth—12. The Avenue—13. Mariner Men—14. The Satyr in the Periwig—15. The Owl—16. Two Waltzes: Water Party, Sylph's Song ('Daisy and Lily') [from "Prelude to a Fairy Tale"]—17. Hornpipe—18. When Sir Beelzebub

Bucolic Comedies. 1. Early Spring—2. Spring—3. Cacophony for Clarinet—4. The Fox (not in *Collected Poems*, 1930)—5. Rose— 6. Popular Song—7. The Five Musicians—8. Springing Jack— 9. The Higher Sensualism—10. Polka [from EA6d]—11. King Cophetua and the Beggar Maid—12. Serenade [from *The Mother*]—13. Poor Martha—14. Country Cousin, and Two Songs—15. Three Poor Witches—16. Pavane—17. When the Sailor—18. Fleecing Time—19. Evening—20. On the Vanity of Human Aspirations—21. Green Geese—22. Two Kitchen Songs— 23. Spinning Song—24. The Bear—25. Why—26. En Famille

Two Promenades Sentimentales. 1. Rain—2. The Professor Speaks

Winter

Herodiade

Night Piece [as the first of "Two Night Pieces"]

By the Lake

Prelude [from *London Mercury*, June 1935]

Marine. 1. Fireworks [from *Clowns' Houses*]—2. Minstrels [from *Clowns' Houses*]—3. Pedagogues [from *The Wooden Pegasus*]— 4. Switchback [from *The Wooden Pegasus*]—5. Myself on the Merry-go-Round [from *Clowns' Houses*]

Metropolitan. 1. Stopping Place [revised and shortened from *The Wooden Pegasus*]—2. Miss Nettybun and the Satyr's Child [from *The Wooden Pegasus*]—3. Portrait of a Barmaid [from *The Wooden Pegasus*]—4. The Spider [from *The Wooden Pegasus*]—5. The Drunkard [from *The Mother*]

Gold Coast Customs

b. *First edition, American copies*

SELECTED POEMS | With an Essay on her own Poetry |
by | EDITH SITWELL | Boston | HOUGHTON MIFFLIN
COMPANY | 1937

Note: 350/365 copies were imported, with a cancel title, and the issue
published 27 April 1937 at $3.00. Smooth grey cloth boards, lettered
in black on blue panels on the spine and upper cover. The contents
are as in the first edition.

EA30   I LIVE UNDER A BLACK SUN   1937

a. *First edition*

I LIVE UNDER A BLACK SUN | *A NOVEL* | by | EDITH
SITWELL | LONDON | VICTOR GOLLANCZ LTD | 1937

197 × 129 mm.

400 pp.: [1] half-title; [2] blank; [3] title; [4] "Note ... Printed in
Great Britain by The Camelot Press Ltd., London and Southampton";
[5] dedication; [6] blank; [7] quotations; [8] blank; [9] Foreword;
[10] blank; [11–13], 14–400 text.

Smooth black cloth boards. Trimmed edges. Lettered in buff on
spine.

4350 copies printed. Published 27 September 1937 at 8s. 6d. (Later
copies of this printing are found cased in blue cloth, lettered in black.)

b. *First edition, American issue*

[*Within a decorated border*]

I | LIVE UNDER | A BLACK | SUN | *A NOVEL* | By | EDITH
SITWELL | Doubleday, Doran & Co., Inc. | GARDEN
CITY, NEW YORK | *1938*

Note: This issue, printed in America, was bound in green cloth boards,
blind-stamped on upper cover and gilt lettered on spine. 3500 copies
printed. Published 25 February 1938 at $2.50. Contents as in the first
edition.

First edition

TRIO | *Dissertations on* | SOME ASPECTS OF NATIONAL
GENIUS | BY | OSBERT, EDITH AND SACHEVERELL |
SITWELL | *Delivered as the Northcliffe Lectures* | *at the*
University of London in 1937 | LONDON | MACMILLAN &
CO | 1938

195 × 129 mm.

256 pp.: [i] half-title; [ii] blank; [iii] title; [iv] "Copyright. Printed in
Great Britain by R. & R. Clark, Limited, Edinburgh"; [v] dedication;
[vi] blank; vii Contents; viii Illustrations; [1–2], 3–247, [248] text.

Two plates sewn in and six tipped in.

Pink cloth boards. Trimmed edges. Gilt lettered on spine.

2000 copies printed. Published 28 October 1938 at 7s. 6d. (Copies are
found with wove and laid end-papers.)

CONTENTS (BY EDITH SITWELL)

"Three Eras of Modern Poetry, first and second lectures."

(These Lord Northcliffe Lectures in Literature were delivered by the
author in the Great Hall, University College, London at 5.30 p.m. on
25 and 28 October 1937, under the title "On Modern Poetry," in the
general series "Some Phases of National Genius." A leaflet describing
the series, with synopses, was issued in advance by University
College. See also oA28 and sA36.)

EA32 POEMS NEW AND OLD 1940

First edition

POEMS | NEW AND OLD | by | EDITH SITWELL | Faber
and Faber | 24 Russell Square | London

186 × 121 mm.

80 pp.: [1] half-title; [2] blank; [3] title; [4] "First published in
October MCMXL by Faber and Faber Limited, 24 Russell Square,
London, W.C.1. Printed in Great Britain by Western Printing

Services Ltd., Bristol. All rights reserved"; 5 Selected bibliography; 6 Acknowledgements; 7–8 Contents; 9–80 text.

Brown paper boards. Trimmed edges. Lettered in black on spine and upper cover—giving title as "Poems Old and New".

2500 copies printed. Published 31 October 1940 at 2s. 6d., in "The Sesame Books."

CONTENTS

[All poems are from *Collected Poems*, 1930, unless otherwise stated]

Two Poems of the Time. 1. Lullaby [from *Times Literary Supplement*, 16 March 1940]—2. Serenade: Any Man to Any Woman [from *Life and Letters To-day*, April 1940]

From "Gold Coast Customs"—3, 4

From "Bucolic Comedies". 5. Early Spring—6. Aubade—7. On the Vanity of Human Aspirations—8. Green Geese—9. Two Kitchen Songs—10. Spinning Song—11. King Cophetua and the Beggar Maid—12. The Bear—13. Popular Song—14. By the Lake—15. The Drum

From "Façade". 16. Dark Song—17. Trio for Two Cats and a Trombone—18. Four in the Morning—19. I Do Like to be Beside the Seaside—20. The Octogenarian—21. The Wind's Bastinado

Songs from "The Sleeping Beauty". 22. The Governante's Song—23. Reynard-haired Malinn—24. The Soldan's Song—25. Song of the Man from a Far Country—26. Through Gilded Trellises—27. The Mauve Summer Rain

Two Elegies. 28. The Little Ghost who Died for Love—29. The Heart and the Hambone

From "Five Variations on a Theme". 30. Extract from "Metamorphosis"—31. Romance [as the version in *Five Variations on a Theme*]

EA33   STREET SONGS   1942

First edition

STREET SONGS | BY | EDITH SITWELL | LONDON | MACMILLAN & CO. LTD | 1942

212 × 135 mm.

44 pp.: [i] half-title; [ii] blank; [iii] title; [iv] "Copyright. Printed in Great Britain by R. & R. Clark, Limited, Edinburgh"; [v] dedication;

vi Acknowledgments; vii Contents; [viii] blank; 1–33, [34] text; [35] printer's imprint; [36] blank.

Green cloth boards. Trimmed edges. Gilt lettered on spine.

1500 copies printed. Published 20 January 1942 at 3s. 6d.

CONTENTS

Still Falls the Rain [from *Times Literary Supplement*, 6 September 1941]—Lullaby [from *Poems New and Old*]—Serenade: Any Man to Any Woman [from *Poems New and Old*]—Street Song [from *Life and Letters To-day*, January 1941]—Poor Young Simpleton: 1. An Old Song Re-Sung—2. ". . . Damné par l'arc-en-ciel" [both from *Life and Letters To-day*, September 1941]—Song: Once my Heart was a Summer Rose [from *Life and Letters To-day*, September 1941]— Tattered Serenade: Beggar to Shadow, 1. "These are the Nations of the Dead" [from *Life and Letters To-day*, January 1941]; 2. "In the summer, when no one is cold"—Tears—The Flowering Forest— How Many Heavens . . .—Spring ("Deep in the shade . . .")—You, the Young Rainbow—Song: We are the Darkness in the Heat of the Day [revised from *Life and Letters To-day*, November 1940]—The Youth with the Red-Gold Hair [from *Life and Letters To-day*, January 1941]—The Night before Great Babylon—Song: When I was but a child, that Lion—Most Lovely Shade [contains 12 lines, revised, from "Romance," in *Five Variations on a Theme*]—The Weeping Rose [contains lines and phrases from "Romance"]—The Swans—An Old Woman

EA34   ENGLISH WOMEN   1942

First edition

ENGLISH WOMEN | [*swelled rule*] | EDITH SITWELL | [*small swelled rule*] | *WITH* | *8 PLATES IN COLOUR* | *AND* | *27 ILLUSTRATIONS IN* | *BLACK & WHITE* | [*device*] | WILLIAM COLLINS OF LONDON | MCMXXXXII

222 × 158 mm.

48 pp.: [1] half-title; [2] "General editor . . ."; [3] title; [4] "Produced by Adprint Limited London. Printed in Great Britain by William Brown and Co. Ltd. London"; [5–6] List of illustrations; 7–47, [48] text.

Four leaves of plates sewn in, and black and white illustrations in the text.

Pale blue paper boards. Trimmed edges. Printed in white on spine and upper and lower covers.

17,000 copies printed. Published 22 June 1942 at 4s. 6d., in "Britain in Pictures" series.

EA35   A POET'S NOTEBOOK   1943

First edition

A POET'S NOTEBOOK | EDITH SITWELL | LONDON | MACMILLAN & CO. LTD | 1943

216 × 140 mm.

168 pp.: [i] half-title; [ii] "By the Same Author . . ."; [iii] title; [iv] "Copyright. Printed in Great Britain by R. & R. Clark, Limited, Edinburgh"; v–vi Foreword; vii–viii Acknowledgments; ix–xi Contents; [xii] blank; 1–153 text, and printer's imprint repeated; [154–156] blank.

Green cloth boards. Trimmed edges. Gilt lettered on spine.

3000 copies printed. Published 30 April 1943 at 10s. 6d. (*Note:* The American book "A Poet's Notebook" (1950) is so different in content that it is included separately—see EA46, below.)

CONTENTS

Foreword—1. On the Poet's Nature—2. Notes on the Nature of Poetry—3. Notes on Technical Matters—4. On a Necessity of Poetry—5. On Morality in Poetry—6. On Simplicity—7. On the Senses—8. On Over-civilisation—9. The Need for the Refreshing of the Language—10. On the Poet's Labour—11. On Imagery in Poetry—12. On the Poet, the Natural World, and Inspiration— 13. On the Power of Words—14. On the Deaths of Two Poets— 15. Of Ben Jonson—16. Applicable to the Augustans—17. Some notes on Alexander Pope [includes material from *Alexander Pope*]— 18. A note on Byron—19. Applicable to Blake—20. Applicable to Baudelaire—21. Applicable to Verlaine—22. A note on the earliest English poetry—23. Notes on Chaucer [partly from *Edith Sitwell's Anthology*]—24. Notes on certain poems by Dunbar, Skelton, Gower . . .—25. Notes on Herrick [partly from *The Pleasures of Poetry*, 1st series]—26. Notes on Smart . . . [partly from *Aspects of Modern Poetry*]—27. Notes on Wordsworth [partly from *The Pleasures of Poetry*, 2nd series]—28. Notes on Shakespeare

Epilogue, Two Poems by Edith Sitwell. 1. A Mother to her Dead Child [from *Times Literary Supplement*, 24 October 1942]—2. Green Song [from *Life and Letters To-day*, December 1942]

EA36   GREEN SONG   1944

a. *First edition*

GREEN SONG | & | OTHER POEMS | BY | EDITH SITWELL | LONDON | MACMILLAN & CO. LTD | 1944

214 × 138 mm.

48 pp.: [i] half-title; [ii] "Books by Edith Sitwell"; [iii] title; [iv] "Copyright. Printed in Great Britain by R. & R. Clark, Limited, Edinburgh"; [v] dedication: vi Acknowledgments; vii Contents; [viii] blank; 1–35 text; [36] imprint repeated; [37–40] back end-papers. Green cloth boards. Trimmed edges. Gilt lettered on spine.

5000 copies printed. Published 15 August 1944 at 5s.

CONTENTS

Heart and Mind [from *Times Literary Supplement*, 19 June 1943]— Green Song [from *A Poet's Notebook*]—Anne Boleyn's Song [from *Times Literary Supplement*, 24 April 1943]—A Young Girl—Harvest —Song: O Dionysus of the Tree—One Day in Spring [has some lines from "The Ghost whose Lips were Warm," first published in *Collected Poems*, 1930]—Invocation [from *New Writing and Daylight*, Winter 1943/44]—"O Bitter Love, O Death . . ." [from *Times Literary Supplement*, 15 January 1944]—"Lo, this is she that was the world's desire" [has lines, revised, from "Metamorphosis" in *Five Variations on a Theme*]—Song: The Queen Bee sighed—Girl and Butterfly [from *Penguin New Writing* 20, 1944]—"Green Flows the River of Lethe-O"—O Yet Forgive—A Mother to her Dead Child [from *A Poet's Notebook*]—Holiday [from *Times Literary Supplement*, 8 April 1944]

b. *First edition, American issue*

[For title, see Plate I]

Note: This issue, printed in America, consisted of 48 pages. A frontispiece, a portrait of the author by Pavel Tchelitchew, was tipped in. Bound in yellow paper boards, lettered in green on the spine.

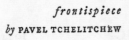

frontispiece
by PAVEL TCHELITCHEW

*G*reen song and
other poems *by*

EDITH SITWELL

view *editions*

distributed by

the vanguard

press · new york

I.   Title page of American issue of *Green Song* [EA36b] (reduced)

1500 copies printed. Published in December 1946 at $3.00. Contents as in the first edition.

EA37   THE WEEPING BABE   1945

First edition

[*See Plate II*]

Two half sheets, folio. 254 × 178 mm.

8 pp.: 1 title, and text; 2–8 text, and imprint: "Printed in England by Augener Ltd., Acton Lane, London, W.4."

Not bound.

Published 2 November 1945 at 8*d*. (The publishers state that any later printings have been made from the same plates and are thus not distinguishable.)

CONTENTS

"The Weeping Babe"

EA38   THE SONG OF THE COLD   1945

First edition

THE SONG | OF THE COLD | BY | EDITH SITWELL | LONDON | MACMILLAN & CO. LTD | 1945

215 × 133 mm.

128 pp.: [i] half-title; [ii] "Books by Edith Sitwell . . ."; [iii] title; [iv] "Copyright. Printed in Great Britain by R. & R. Clark, Limited, Edinburgh"; v Prefatory note; vi Acknowledgments; vii–viii Contents; 1–115, [116] text; [117–120] back end-papers.

Navy-blue cloth boards. Trimmed edges. Gilt lettered on spine.

5000 copies printed. Published 27 November 1945 at 7*s*. 6*d*. (*Note:* The American book, "The Song of the Cold" (1948), is so different in content that it has been listed separately—see EA42.)

CONTENTS

Part I. Invocation [from *Green Song*]—An Old Woman: 1. 'I, an old woman in the light of the sun' [as "An Old Woman" in *Street Songs*]—2. Harvest [from *Green Song*]

Eurydice [from *Horizon*, August 1945]—Song for Two Voices [as "Song: O Dionysus of the Tree" in *Green Song*]

57

II. First page of *The Weeping Babe* [EA37] (reduced)

Part II. Still Falls the Rain [from *Street Songs*]—Lullaby [from *Street Songs*]—Serenade: Any Man to Any Woman [from *Street Songs*]—Street Song [from *Street Songs*]—O Yet Forgive [from *Green Song*]—Poor Young Simpleton [from *Street Songs*]—Song: Once my Heart was a Summer Rose [from *Street Songs*]—Green Flows the River of Lethe-O [from *Green Song*]—A Mother to her Dead Child [from *A Poet's Notebook*]—Tattered Serenade: Beggar to Shadow [from *Street Songs*]—A Song of the Cold [from *Penguin New Writing* 23, 1945]—Tears [from *Street Songs*]—Gold Coast Customs [as in *Collected Poems*, 1930]

Part III. Heart and Mind [from *Green Song*]—Green Song [from *A Poet's Notebook*]—Anne Boleyn's Song [from *Green Song*]—A Young Girl [from *Green Song*]—The Flowering Forest [from *Street Songs*]—How Many Heavens . . . [from *Street Songs*]—Holiday [from *Green Song*]—Song: We are the Darkness in the Heat of the Day [from *Street Songs*]—The Youth with the Red-Gold Hair [from *Street Songs*]—Girl and Butterfly [from *Green Song*]—Song: The Queen Bee sighed [from *Green Song*]—You, the Young Rainbow [from *Street Songs*]—The Soldan's Song [from *The Sleeping Beauty*]—The Song of the Man from the Far Countree [from *The Sleeping Beauty*]—Through Gilded Trellises [from *The Sleeping Beauty*]—The Governante's Song [from *The Sleeping Beauty*]—The Poet Laments the Coming of Old Age [from *Orion* [*I*], 1945]—'O Bitter Love, O Death' [from *Green Song*]—Three Variations on a Theme: 1. Most Lovely Shade [from *Street Songs*], 2. Romance [revised and shortened from *Five Variations on a Theme*], 3. 'Lo, this is she that was the world's desire' [from *Green Song*]—The Swans [from *Street Songs*]—Two Songs: 1. The Greengage Tree, 2. Daphne [both from *Five Poems*]—From 'Façade': 1. Dark Song [from *Bucolic Comedies*], 2. Early Spring [from *Façade*, February 1922], 3. By the Lake [from *Bucolic Comedies*]

Part IV. One Day in Spring [from *Green Song*]—Metamorphosis [revised from *Five Poems*]—From 'The Canticle of the Rose': 1. A Song at Morning [from *Horizon*, December 1944]—The Two Loves [from *New Writing and Daylight*, 1945]

EA39   FANFARE FOR ELIZABETH   1946

a. *First edition*

[*Within a rectangular border*]

[*Row of type ornaments*] | FANFARE FOR | ELIZABETH |
by Edith Sitwell | [*ornament*] | NEW YORK | THE MAC-
MILLAN COMPANY | 1946 | [*row of type ornaments*]

212 × 135 mm.

240 pp.: [i] half-title; [ii] books by Edith Sitwell; [iii] title; [iv] "Copyright, 1946, by Edith Sitwell . . . First printing. Printed in the United
States of America by the Vail-Ballou Press, Inc., Binghampton, N.Y.";
[v] dedication; [vi] blank; [vii] List of illustrations; [viii] blank; [ix]
acknowledgements; [x] blank; [xi–xii], 1–227 text; [228] blank.

Four plates tipped in.

Smooth blue cloth boards. Trimmed edges. Blind-stamped on upper
cover and gilt lettered on spine.

9899 copies printed. Published 15 July 1946 at $2.50.

CONTENTS

The following chapters were previously published in *Life and Letters
To-day*, July–October 1945, and in *Harper's Bazaar*, July 1945:
chapters 5; 13; 17 (second half); 18; and the last chapter

b. *First edition, English issue*

FANFARE | FOR ELIZABETH | BY | EDITH SITWELL |
LONDON | MACMILLAN & CO. LTD | 1946

213 × 135 mm.

212 pp.: [i] half-title; [ii] "Books by Edith Sitwell . . ."; [iii] title; [iv]
"Copyright. Printed in Great Britain by R. & R. Clark, Limited,
Edinburgh"; [v] dedication; vi Acknowledgements; vii List of
illustrations; [viii] blank; 1–202 text; [203–204] blank.

Four plates tipped in.

Smooth green cloth boards. Trimmed edges. Gilt stamped on spine.

20,000 copies printed. Published 6 September 1946 at 12s. 6d.

CONTENTS

As in the first edition

First edition

THE SHADOW | OF CAIN | *by* EDITH SITWELL | JOHN
LEHMANN | LONDON | 1947

212 × 135 mm.

24 pp. (including free end-papers): [1–4] blank; [5] title; [6] "Printed
at The Caxton Press, Christchurch, New Zealand, MCMXLVI";
[7] dedication; [8] blank; 9–18 text; [19] blank; [20–21] notes; [22–24]
blank.

Green paper boards. Trimmed edges. Lettered in black on upper
cover.

3000 copies printed. Published in June 1947 at 3*s.* 6*d.*

CONTENTS

"The Shadow of Cain"

First edition

A Notebook on | WILLIAM | SHAKESPEARE | BY | EDITH
SITWELL | HON. D. LITT. (Leeds), HON. D. LITT. (Dur-
ham) | LONDON | MACMILLAN & CO. LTD | 1948

213 × 135 mm.

248 pp.: [1] half-title; [ii] blank; [iii] title; [iv] "Copyright. Printed in
Great Britain"; [v] dedication; [vi] blank; vii Foreword; [viii] blank;
ix–x Acknowledgements; xi–xii Contents; 1–233 text, and imprint:
"Printed by R. & R. Clark, Ltd., Edinburgh"; [234–236] blank.

Green cloth boards. Trimmed edges. Gilt lettered on spine.

5000 copies printed. Published 15 October 1948 at 15*s.*

CONTENTS

1. The Hymn to Life [revised from "Notes on Shakespeare" in *A
Poet's Notebook*]—2. Of the Clowns and Fools [from *Life and Letters*,
May 1948, and *View*, January 1946]—3. Note on Comedy and

Tragedy—4. Some general notes on the Tragedies [partly from "Notes on Shakespeare" in *A Poet's Notebook*]—5. "Macbeth" [from *View*, 1943 and *A Poet's Notebook*]—6. "King Lear" [revised from *New Writing and Daylight*, 1945]—7. Some Notes on "Hamlet" [partly from *Tribune*, 24 September 1948]—8. "Othello" [partly from *New Writing and Daylight*, 1946]—9. "Timon of Athens"—10. A Note on "Measure for Measure" [from *The Nineteenth Century*, September 1946]—11. The Flowering Darkness: "Romeo and Juliet" [partly from *A Poet's Notebook*]—12. "Antony and Cleopatra" [partly from *A Poet's Notebook*]—13. "Julius Caesar"—14. "Titus Andronicus"—15. Two Notes on "Troilus and Cressida"—16. "Troilus and Cressida," "The Henriad," Shakespeare and Marlow—17. Note on the Historical Tragedies—18. Some general notes on the tragedies relating to the English Kings—19. Some general notes on the Comedies—20. "Twelfth Night"—21. "As You Like It"—22. Note on "All's Well that Ends Well"—23. Some Notes on the Texture of "A Midsummer Night's Dream" [partly from *A Poet's Notebook*]—24. Two Notes on the "Merchant of Venice"—25. Two early comedies—26. The later plays—27. Some notes on "The Winter's Tale"—28. "Pericles"—29. "The Tempest"—30. Notes on the texture of the verse in "Cymbeline" [partly from *A Poet's Notebook*]—31. A Note on Sonnet XIX [from *A Poet's Notebook*]—32. Some General Comments

EA42   THE SONG OF THE COLD   1948

First edition

The Song of the Cold | EDITH SITWELL | [*decoration*] | THE VANGUARD PRESS, INC. | NEW YORK

236 × 155 mm.

120 pp.: [i–ii] blank; [1] half-title; [2] blank; [3] title; [4] "Copyright 1948, by Edith Sitwell ... Manufactured in the United States of America by H. Wolff Book Manufacturing Co., New York, N.Y."; [5–6] contents; [7] Acknowledgements; [8] blank; [9–10], 11–113 text and notes; [114–118] blank.

Smooth black cloth boards. Trimmed edges. Printed in blue on spine and upper cover.

2650 copies printed. Published in November 1948 at $2.75.

Note: This book is included separately from "The Song of the Cold" (London, 1945—see above) as its content is very different.

[Poems not otherwise ascribed were published in *The Song of the Cold* (London, 1945, EA38)]

Three Poems of the Atomic Age. 1. Dirge for the New Sunrise [from *Orion IV*, 1947]—2. The Shadow of Cain [from *The Shadow of Cain*]—3. The Canticle of the Rose [from *Wake* no. 7, 1948]

A Song at Morning—The Two Loves—A Hymn to Venus [from *Poetry London* no. 11, 1947]—Dido's Song [from *Botteghe Oscure*, II, 1948]—Mary Stuart to James Bothwell, casket letter no. 2 [from *Penguin New Writing* 27, 1946]—Two Variations on a Theme—Metamorphosis—Street Acrobat [not from *The Song of the Cold*, 1945]—Said King Pompey [from *Façade*, January 1922]

Twelve Early Poems. 1. Early Spring—2. Dark Song—3. By the Lake—4. The Greengage Tree—5. Daphne [from *Five Poems*]—6. The Soldan's Song—7. Song of the Man from the Far Country—8. The Governante's Song—9. Through Gilded Trellises—10. Waltz [from *The Sleeping Beauty*]—11. The Wind's Bastinado [from *Façade*, January 1922]—12. The Drum [from *Troy Park*]

The Poet Laments the Coming of Old Age—Spring Morning [revised from *Orion IV*, 1947]—The Song of the Cold—The Coat of Fire [from *Horizon*, April 1948]—Gold Coast Customs [as in *Collected Poems*, 1930]—Song: Now that Fate is Dead and Gone [from *Orpheus I*, 1948]—Eurydice—A Sleepy Tune [from *View*, January 1946]—The Bee-Keeper [from *Penguin New Writing* 32, 1947]

EA43   THE CANTICLE OF   1949
THE ROSE

a. *First edition*

THE CANTICLE | OF THE ROSE | SELECTED POEMS | 1920–1947 | BY | EDITH SITWELL | HON. D. LITT. (Leeds), HON. D. LITT. (Durham) | LONDON | MACMILLAN & CO. LTD | 1949

215 × 136 mm.

288 pp.: [i] half-title; [ii] "Books by Edith Sitwell . . ."; [iii] title; [iv] "Copyright. Printed in Great Britain"; v Prefatory note; vi Acknowledgments; vii–x Contents; [1–2], 3–273, [274] text, and imprint:

"Printed by R. & R. Clark, Ltd., Edinburgh"; [275–278] back end-papers.

Smooth blue cloth boards. Trimmed edges. Gilt lettered on spine.

3000 copies printed. Published 20 September 1949 at 15s.

CONTENTS

Part II. Still Falls the Rain—Lullaby—Serenade: Any Man to Any Woman—Street Song—O Yet Forgive—Poor Young Simpleton —Song: Once my Heart . . .—Green Flows the River of Lethe-O —A Mother to her Dead Child—Tattered Serenade: Beggar to Shadow—A Song of the Cold—Tears

Part III. Heart and Mind—Green Song—Anne Boleyn's Song—A Young Girl—How Many Heavens . . .—The Flowering Forest— Holiday—Song: We are the Darkness in the Heat of the Day— The Youth with the Red-Gold Hair—Girl and Butterfly—Song: The Queen Bee sighed—The Poet Laments the Coming of Old Age—'O Bitter Love, O Death'—Most Lovely Shade—'Lo, this is she that was the world's desire'—The Swans

Part IV. One Day in Spring—Metamorphosis—A Song at Morning [as 'From "The Canticle of the Rose"']—The Two Loves.

POEMS 1945–47 [all, except one, as in *The Song of the Cold*, New York 1948]

The Canticle of the Rose:
    The Bee-Oracles. 1. The Bee-Keeper—2. A Sleepy Tune
    Mary Stuart to James Bothwell, casket letter no. 2
    The Song of Dido [as "Dido's Song"]
    Hymn to Venus
    Spring Morning
    A Simpleton [revised from *Horizon*, July 1947]
    Song: Now that Fate is Dead and Gone
    The Coat of Fire

Three Poems of the Atomic Bomb. 1. Dirge for the New Sunrise— 2. The Shadow of Cain—3. The Canticle of the Rose

b. *First edition, American issue*

The Canticle of | the Rose | POEMS: 1917–1949 | [*rose*] | Edith Sitwell | THE VANGUARD PRESS, INC. | New York

235 × 154 mm.

328 pp.: [i] half-title; [ii] Books by Edith Sitwell; [iii] title; [iv] "Copyright, 1949, by Edith Sitwell . . . Manufactured in the United States of America by H. Wolff, New York, N.Y. Designed by Marshall Lee"; [v] Prefatory note; [vi] Acknowledgments; [vii–x] Contents; xi– xxxviii Some notes on my own poetry; [1], 2–290 text.

Black cloth boards. Trimmed edges. Blind-stamped on front and gilt lettered on spine, with pink decoration.

3700 copies printed. Published in December 1949 at $3.75.

CONTENTS

"Some Notes on my Own Poetry" [partly from *Selected Poems*, 1936, and partly from *Orpheus II*, 1949]. Thence as in the first edition

EA44 POOR MEN'S MUSIC 1950

a. *First edition*

[*Within a rectangular border*]

POOR MEN'S MUSIC | *Edith Sitwell* | *Hon. D. Litt. (Leeds)* | *Hon. D. Litt. (Durham)* | [*short rule*] | Key Poet | I | [*device*] | *LONDON* | *FORE PUBLICATIONS LIMITED* | *1950*

159 × 103 mm.

24 pp.: [1] half-title; [2] blank; [3] title; [4] "Copyright by Fore Publications . . . Printed and made in Great Britain by the Blackmore Press, Gillingham, Dorset . . ."; [5] Contents; [6] blank; 7–24 text.

Pink and white paper wrappers. Stapled. Trimmed edges. Printed in black, white and pink on upper and lower covers.

Published on 20 September 1950, as no. 1 of ten volumes of "Key Poets." 1. In an unnumbered edition of 100 copies, all ten volumes sold boxed at 21s., all being signed by their authors on page [2]; 2. In an ordinary edition of about 1650 copies, separately, at 1s., otherwise identical.

CONTENTS

The Stone-Breakers: a prison song [as "Chain-gang: penal settlement" in *Sunday Times*, 4 July 1948]—Street Acrobat [revised from *Arena* 1, (1949), and *The Song of the Cold* (1948)]—A Song of the Dust [from *Penguin New Writing* 40, 1950]—The Madwoman in the Park—Out of School [from *Atlantic Monthly*, June 1949, and *Horizon*, August 1949]

b. *First edition, American copies*

[*Within a rectangular border*]

POOR MEN'S MUSIC | *Edith Sitwell* | Hon. *D. Litt.* (*Leeds*) |
Hon. *D. Litt.* (*Durham*) | [*short rule*] | Key Poet | I | [*device*] | *DENVER* | *ALAN SWALLOW* | *1950*

Note: This was the description given to me by the late Alan Swallow.
I have not seen such a copy, but the American distribution was
confused. The following derives from information from Mr. Jack
Lindsay (the original publisher), the printers, The Swallow Press
Inc. of Chicago and Mrs. Swallow. Swallow imported 250 sets of
the "Key Poets" with his imprint, for sale at $2.50 the signed set,
$0.30 separately, unsigned. These were received in late 1950. In
January 1951 this volume was withdrawn from sale, after U.S. copyright and agency difficulties, but later made available again with the
London imprint. "No more than a dozen copies" were sold with
the Denver imprint; total American distribution, to 1954, was "no
more than 150 copies", including 40 review copies. I do not know
how many of these were signed.

Some of the copies imported were re-issued in 1960 as part of a volume
called *Anthology III*, edited by Alan Swallow. This included nine of
the "Key Poets," all with Denver imprints except for *Poor Men's
Music* which has the London imprint.

EA45   FAÇADE AND OTHER POEMS   1950

First edition

FAÇADE | AND OTHER POEMS | 1920–1935 | BY | EDITH
SITWELL | HON. D. LITT (LEEDS), HON. D. LITT. (DUR-
HAM) | *With an Introductory Essay by* | JACK LINDSAY |
[*device*] | GERALD DUCKWORTH & CO. LTD. | 3 Henrietta
Street, London, W.C.2

182 × 122 mm.

212 pp.: [1] half-title; [2] blank; [3] title; [4] "*Collected Poems* first
published 1930. This Selection first published 1950. All rights reserved. Printed in Great Britain by The Riverside Press, Edinburgh";
5–6 Contents; 7–24 Introductory essay; 25–212 text and indexes.

Pink cloth boards. Trimmed edges. Gilt lettered on spine.

2700 copies printed. Published late October 1950 at 8s. 6d.

First edition

[*Within a rectangular border*]

[*Swelled rule*] | [*rule*] | A Poet's Notebook | by | EDITH
SITWELL | [*decoration*] | *An Atlantic Monthly Press Book* |
Little, Brown and Company · Boston | 1950 | [*rule*] |
[*swelled rule*]

212 × 143 mm.

296 pp.: [i] half-title; [ii] blank; [iii] title; [iv] "Copyright 1943, 1948,
1950 by Edith Sitwell. All rights reserved . . . First edition. Published
October 1950. Atlantic—Little, Brown Books are published by Little,
Brown and Company in association with the Atlantic Monthly Press.
Printed in the United States of America"; v–x Acknowledgments;
xi–xvi Preface; xvii–xviii Contents; [1–2], 3–276 text; [277–278] blank.
Rough tan cloth boards. Trimmed edges. Stamped in blue and gilt on
spine and upper cover.

2000 copies printed. Published 26 October 1950 at $4.00.

CONTENTS

Contains most of *A Poet's Notebook* (1943) and *A Notebook on
William Shakespeare* (1948):

A Notebook on William Shakespeare: omits from the 1948 edition ten
pages of "Some Notes on 'Hamlet,'" two pages of "Othello," and
the whole of chapters XI, XIV–XVI, XVIII, XX and XXI

A Poet's Notebook: omits from the 1943 edition chapters XIV, XVIII,
XXII, XXVIII, and Epilogue: Two Poems; and the following
chapters are revised: I–IV, IX, XIII, XXIII, XXVII

EA47   SELECTED POEMS   1952

First edition

SELECTED POEMS | [*short swelled rule*] | EDITH SITWELL |
PENGUIN BOOKS | HARMONDSWORTH · MIDDLESEX

180 × 111 mm.

176 pp.: [i] half-title; [ii] blank; [iii] title; [iv] "This selection from Dr
Edith Sitwell's Poems first published in Penguin Books, 1952. Made

and printed in Great Britain for Penguin Books Ltd by Unwin Brothers Ltd Woking and London"; [v] Acknowledgements; [vi] blank; vii–viii Contents; ix–xxxix "Some notes on my own poetry"; [xl] blank; 1–134 text, notes and index; [135–136] blank.

Sandy-yellow stiff paper wrappers. Trimmed edges. Printed in green and black on spine and upper and lower covers.

20,000 copies printed. Published 21 March 1952 at 2s. 6d., as no. D16 in "The Penguin Poets".

CONTENTS

[As in *The Canticle of the Rose*, New York, 1949, unless otherwise attributed]

Some notes on my own poetry

Three Poems of the Atomic Age. 1. Dirge for the New Sunrise—2. The Shadow of Cain—3. The Canticle of the Rose

The Coat of Fire—Song: Now that Fate is Dead and Gone—Invocation—An Old Woman—Eurydice—Still Falls the Rain—Lullaby—Street Song—Poor Young Simpleton—A Mother to her Dead Child—The Song of the Cold—Heart and Mind—Green Song—Anne Boleyn's Song—How Many Heavens . . .—Holiday—Song: We are the Darkness in the Heat of the Day—The Youth with the Red-Gold Hair—Girl and Butterfly—Song: The Queen Bee sighed—Most Lovely Shade—'Lo, this is she that was the world's delight' [*sic*]—The Two Loves—The Bee Oracles. 1. The Bee-Keeper—2. A Sleepy Tune—A Bird's Song [not from *The Canticle of the Rose*]—Medusa's Love Song [from *Penguin New Writing* 38, 1949]—A Hymn to Venus—Spring Morning—Earlier Poems: The Drum—Early Spring—Aubade—Popular Song—Waltz—Fox Trot—The Wind's Bastinado—Black Mrs. Behemoth—Gold Coast Customs

EA48   GARDENERS AND   1953
              ASTRONOMERS

a. *First edition*

GARDENERS | AND | ASTRONOMERS | BY | EDITH SITWELL | Hon D Litt (Leeds) Hon D Litt (Durham) | Hon D Litt (Oxford) | LONDON | MACMILLAN & CO. LTD | 1953

216 × 138 mm.

56 pp.: [i] half-title; [ii] blank; [iii] title; [iv] "This book is copyright . . . Printed in Great Britain"; v Acknowledgments; [vi] blank; vii Contents; [viii] blank; 1–45, [46] text, notes, and imprint: "Printed by R. & R. Clark, Ltd., Edinburgh"; [47–48] blank.

Cerise cloth boards. Trimmed edges. Gilt lettered on spine.

4000 copies printed. Published 20 November 1953 at 8s. 6d.

CONTENTS

Bagatelle [from *The Listener*, 9 October 1952]—Gardeners and Astronomers [from *Times Literary Supplement*, 24 August 1951]

The Road to Thebes: three poems on a theme. 1. Beside the yellow foam [from *Atlantic Monthly*, July 1953]—2. Interlude—3. The Night Wind [both from *New World Writing* 3, May 1953]

Three Songs. 1. You said, "This is the time of the wild spring"—2. The Song of the Beggar Maid to King Cophetua—3. A Bird's Song [from *Selected Poems*, 1952]

Butterfly-Weather—The Blinded Song-Bird near the Battle-Field—The Stone-Breakers: a prison song [from *Poor Men's Music*]—Out of School [from *Poor Men's Music*]—The Wind of Early Spring—Sailor, What of the Isles [from *The Listener*, 9 April 1953, and *Atlantic Monthly*, June 1953]—A Love Song [revised from "Medusa's Love Song" in *Selected Poems*, 1952]—The April Rain [from *Times Literary Supplement*, 17 April 1953, and *Atlantic Monthly*, April 1953]—Two Songs: 1. Prometheus's Song [from *The Listener*, 19 June 1952, and *Atlantic Monthly*, February 1953]—2. The Queen of Scotland's Reply [from *Atlantic Monthly*, February 1953, and *New Statesman*, 20 June 1953]

A Song of the Dust [revised from *Poor Men's Music*]

b. *First edition, American issue*

Gardeners | & | Astronomers | NEW POEMS BY | Edith Sitwell | THE VANGUARD PRESS, INC. | NEW YORK

234 × 154 mm.

64 pp.: [1] half-title; [2] decoration; [3] title; [4] "Copyright, 1953, by Edith Sitwell . . . Designed by Marshall Lee. Manufactured in the United States of America by H. Wolff, New York. Library of Congress Catalogue Card Number: 53–10804"; [5] Other books by Edith Sitwell; [6] blank; [7] Contents; [8] blank; [9] decoration; [10] blank; [11–12], 13–60 text; [61] notes; [62–64] blank.

Black-and-white drawings on text pages.

Green cloth and black paper boards. Trimmed edges. Stamped blind and in silver and ivory on upper cover, and in silver on spine.

2500 copies printed. Published November 1953 at $2.75.

CONTENTS

As in the first edition, but omitting "A Bird's Song," "The Stone-Breakers," "Out of School" and "A Love Song"

EA49   COLLECTED POEMS   1954

a. *First edition*

The | Collected | Poems | of | Edith Sitwell | [*five stars arranged as the Dipper*] | THE VANGUARD PRESS | NEW YORK

235 × 153 mm.

496 pp.: [a] half-title; [b] blank; [i] title; [ii] "Copyright 1949, 1953, and 1954 by Edith Sitwell. . . . Library of Congress Catalogue Card Number: 54–11518. Designed by Marshall Lee. Manufactured in the United States of America by H. Wolff, New York"; [iii] Prefatory note; [iv] Acknowledgments; [v] dedication; [vi] blank; [vii–xiii] Contents; [xiv] blank; xv–l "Some notes on my own poetry"; [1–2], 3–442 text and indexes; [443–444] blank.

Black cloth boards. Trimmed edges. Gilt lettered on upper cover, and gilt and lilac stamped on spine.

5000 copies printed. Published December 1954 at $6.50.

CONTENTS

Some Notes on My Own Poetry [revised from *Selected Poems*, 1952]

EARLY POEMS—[from *Collected Poems*, 1930, unless otherwise stated]

Serenade—Mandoline [from *The Wooden Pegasus*]—Singerie [from *The Wooden Pegasus*]—The Avenue—The King of China's Daughter [from *The Wooden Pegasus*]

Bucolic Comedies. 1. Early Spring—2. Spring—3. Aubade—4. Three Poor Witches—5. Two Kitchen Songs—6. King Cophetua and the Beggar Maid—7. Gardener Janus Catches a Naiad—8. Green Geese—9. The Higher Sensualism—10. Springing Jack—11. Pavane—12. When the Sailor—13. Evening—14. Winter—

15. Spinning Song—16. Two Songs [as I and II of "Country Cousin"]—17. The Bear—18. On the Vanity of Human Aspirations—19. The Man with the Green Patch [revised]

The Sleeping Beauty

Façade. 1. The Drum—2. Clowns' Houses—3. Père Amelot—4. Ass-Face—5. Said King Pompey [revised]—6. The Bat—7. Lullaby for Jumbo—8. Trio for Two Cats and a Trombone—9. Madam Mouse Trots—10. Four in the Morning [revised]—11. Black Mrs. Behemoth—12. Came the Great Popinjay—13. The Wind's Bastinado—14. En Famille—15. Country Dance—16. Mariner Man [as "Mariner-Men"]—17. The Octogenarian—18. Bells of Grey Crystal [from *Troy Park*]—19. When Cold December [as in *Façade & other Poems*, 1950]—20. Fox Trot—21. Polka [as "Neptune—Polka"]—22. Mazurka [as "Pluto—Mazurka"]—23. Jodelling Song [revised]—24. Waltz [as "Sylph's Song"]—25. Popular Song—26. By the Lake—27. Dark Song—28. Water Party—29. The Satyr in the Periwig—30. I Do Like to be Beside the Seaside—31. Hornpipe—32. Scotch Rhapsody [as in *Façade & other Poems*, 1950]—33. Something Lies beyond the Scene [as in *Façade & other Poems*, 1950]—34. Sir Beelzebub

Marine. 1. Why?—2. Fireworks [as in *Clowns' Houses*]—3. Switchback [from *The Wooden Pegasus*]—4. Minstrels [from *Clowns' Houses*]—5. Pedagogues [from *The Wooden Pegasus*]—6. Portrait of a Barmaid [from *The Wooden Pegasus*]—7. Myself in the Merry-Go-Round [from *Clowns' Houses*]

The Drunkard [from *The Mother*]—Colonel Fantock

Three Rustic Elegies. 1. The Little Ghost who Died for Love—2. The Hambone and the Heart [revised, and as in *The Canticle of the Rose*]—3. The Ghost whose Lips were Warm

Fragment: The Madness of Saul—Elegy on Dead Fashion [revised and abbreviated]—Metamorphosis: first version, 1929—Metamorphosis: second version, 1946 [from *The Song of the Cold*]—Romance [from *The Song of the Cold*]

Five Songs. 1. Daphne—2. The Peach Tree—3. The Strawberry—4. The Greengage Tree—5. The Nectarine Tree

Gold Coast Customs

LATER POEMS, 1940–45. [Unless otherwise stated, all from *The Song of the Cold*, 1945]

Part I. 1. Invocation—2. An Old Woman—3. Eurydice—4. Song for Two Voices

Song: Where is All the Bright Company gone? [revised from *Encounter*, October 1953]

Of the Wise and Foolish [not previously published]

A Song of the Dust

b. *First edition, English issue*

Edith Sitwell | [*short swelled rule*] | COLLECTED | POEMS | LONDON | MACMILLAN & CO LTD | 1957

213 × 138 mm.

496 pp.: [i] half-title; [ii] "Other books by Edith Sitwell"; [iii] title; [iv] "This book is copyright ... Printed in Great Britain"; [v] dedication; [vi] blank; vii Prefatory note; viii Acknowledgments; ix–xiv Contents; xv–xlvi "Some notes on my own poetry"; [1–2], 3–444, [445] text, indexes, and imprint: "Printed by R. & R. Clark, Ltd., Edinburgh"; [446–450] blank.

Blue cloth boards. Trimmed edges. Gilt stamped on spine, with a red panel.

3000 copies printed. Published 25 July 1957 at 25*s*.

CONTENTS

As in the first edition, with the following additions: Barber's Shop [as "Comedy for Marionettes" in *The Wooden Pegasus*]—The White Owl [as "The Owl," in *Collected Poems*, 1930]—Cacophony for Clarinet [revised from *Collected Poems*, 1930]—One O'Clock [as "Great Snoring and Norwich" in *The Wooden Pegasus*]—Rain [revised from *Collected Poems*, 1930]—Fantasia for Mouth-Organ [revised from *Bucolic Comedies*]—Elegy for Dylan Thomas [from *Poetry*, November 1955]

EA50   THE POCKET POETS   1960

First edition

[*Within a border*]

THE POCKET POETS | [*swelled rule*] | EDITH SITWELL | [*device*] | [*swelled rule*] | LONDON: VISTA BOOKS

184 × 112 mm.

48 pp.: [1] half-title; [2] "The Pocket Poets ..."; [3] title; [4] First published in 1960 ... Made and printed in Great Britain by Purnell

and Sons, Ltd., Paulton (Somerset) and London. © Edith Sitwell, 1960; 5 Contents; 6 acknowledgements; 7–48 text.

Decorated green flush paper boards. Printed in black and white on covers and in black on spine.

5000 copies printed. Published in October 1960 at 2s. 6d.

CONTENTS

(All from *Collected Poems*, 1957)

Mandoline—Aubade—From *The Sleeping Beauty*—Four in the Morning—Jodelling Song—Waltz—Popular Song—Scotch Rhapsody—The Peach Tree—Still Falls the Rain—Lullaby—Street Song—O Yet Forgive—Song: Once my Heart was a Summer Rose—Heart and Mind—Green Song—How Many Heavens . . .—Song: We are the Darkness in the Heat of the Day—O Bitter Love, O Death . . .—Most Lovely Shade—The Canticle of the Rose—Sailor, What of the Isles?—Elegy for Dylan Thomas

EA51   THE OUTCASTS   1962

a. *First edition*

Edith Sitwell | [*short swelled rule*] | THE | OUTCASTS | LONDON | MACMILLAN & CO LTD | 1962

215 × 138 mm.

32 pp.: [1] half-title; [2] "Other books by Dame Edith Sitwell . . ."; [3] title; [4] Copyright © Dame Edith Sitwell 1962 . . . Printed in Great Britain; [5] dedication; [6] blank; 7 Contents; [8] blank; 9–11 Preface; [12] blank; [13–14], 15–30 text, with erratum slip tipped to p. 26; [31] blank; [32] Printed by R. & R. Clark, Ltd., Edinburgh.

Cloth boards decorated in green, maroon and white. Trimmed edges. Lettered in white on upper cover, and in white and maroon on spine.

3000 copies printed. Published 30 August 1962 at 10s. 6d.

CONTENTS

Preface.

The Outcasts—The War Orphans [from *Atlantic Monthly*, November 1957]—Choric Song [from *The Listener*, 31 March 1960]—Praise We Great Men [from *The Listener*, 18 June 1959, and *Atlantic Monthly*, November 1959]—"His Blood Colours my Cheek" [from *The Month*,

May 1958]—The Yellow Girl [from *The Listener*, 29 January 1959]—
Song: Said the Bee to the Lion—A Girl's Song in Winter [from
Encounter, January 1962]—La Bella Bona Roba [from *The Listener*,
1 January 1959]—Prothalamium [from *Yorkshire Post*, 8 June 1961]

b. *First edition, American issue*

Edith Sitwell | *Music and Ceremonies* | THE VANGUARD
PRESS, INC. | NEW YORK | [*decoration: two candlesticks,
with lit candles*]

235 × 154 mm.

48 pp.: [i–ii] blank; [1] facsimile of author's signature; [2] "Other
books by Edith Sitwell"; [3] half-title; [4] blank; [5] title; [6] "Copyright ©, 1959, 1962, 1963, by Dame Edith Sitwell . . . Manufactured
in the United States of America by H. Wolff. Designed by Marshall
Lee"; [7] dedication; [8] blank; [9] Contents; [10] blank; 11–13
Preface; [14] blank; [15–16], 17–44 text; [45–46] blank.

Beige and cerise cloth spine, cerise paper boards. Scarlet end-papers.
Trimmed edges. Gilt lettered on spine, blind and gilt stamped on
upper cover.

CONTENTS

As in *The Outcasts*, with the following additions:

March Past—Two Raw Songs of Jack Straw, i. The Death of Prometheus; ii. At the Crossroads [from *London Magazine*, March 1959]—
Music and Ceremonies

EA52 THE QUEENS AND THE HIVE 1962

a. *First edition*

THE QUEENS | AND THE HIVE | BY | EDITH SITWELL |
LONDON | MACMILLAN & CO LTD | 1962

216 × 141 mm.

544 pp.: [i] half-title; [ii] "By the same author . . ."; [iii] title; [iv]
Copyright © Dame Edith Sitwell 1962 . . . Printed in Great Britain;
[v] dedication; vi Acknowledgments; vii Contents; viii Illustrations;
1–542 text, appendices, index, and: Printed by R. & R. Clark, Ltd.,
Edinburgh.

Sixteen plates tipped in.

Dark red buckram boards. Trimmed edges. Stamped in gilt on spine.

5000 copies printed. Published 30 August 1962 at 42*s*.

b. *First edition, American issue*

THE QUEENS | AND THE HIVE | BY | EDITH SITWELL | WITH ILLUSTRATIONS | [*device*] | *An Atlantic Monthly Press Book* | LITTLE, BROWN AND COMPANY | *Boston Toronto*

Note: This issue, printed in the United States, was published on 14 November 1962 at $7.50. 5000 copies were printed. The contents are exactly as in the first edition.

EA53   TAKEN CARE OF   1965

a. *First edition*

Edith Sitwell | [*short ornamental rule*] | TAKEN CARE OF | an autobiography | [*device*] | HUTCHINSON OF LONDON

226 × 146 mm.

192 pp.: [1] half-title; [2] caption to frontispiece; [3] title; [4] "Hutchinson & Co (Publishers) Ltd . . . First published 1965. © Philip B. Frere, M.C., and Francis T. Sitwell 1965. This book has been set in Bembo, printed in Great Britain on Antique Wove paper by The Anchor Press, Ltd., and bound by Wm. Brendon & Son Ltd., both of Tiptree, Essex"; [5] dedication; [6] blank; [7] Acknowledgements; [8] blank; [9]–10 Contents; [11] Illustrations; [12] blank; [13] Preface, and note; [14] blank; [15–17], 18–192 text and index.

Frontispiece tipped in and eight plates sewn in.

Oatmeal buckram boards. Top edge royal blue, others trimmed. Reproduction of obituary on end-papers. Gilt lettered on spine with black panels.

3000 copies printed. Published 5 April 1965 at 30s.

CONTENTS

Includes part or the whole of the following: "Coming to London" [from *London Magazine*, April 1957]; "Dylan the Impeccable," "Hazards of Sitting for my Portrait," "A Visit to Lawrence" [from *The Observer*, 13–27 November 1960]; "Pride" [from *Sunday Times*, 17 December 1961]; "Our Childhood was Hell," "A Man with Red Hair," "Old Friends and Others" [from *Sunday Times*, 21 March–4 April 1965]; "When I Was Young and Uneasy" [from *Atlantic Monthly*, March 1965]; "Cast of Characters" [from *The Reporter*, 8 April 1965]; and "Pavel Tchelitchew" [from EB53]

b. *First edition, American issue*

TAKEN CARE OF | *THE AUTOBIOGRAPHY OF* | EDITH
SITWELL | [*short swelled rule*] | *ATHENEUM* | NEW YORK |
1965

237 × 136 mm.

256 pp.: [a–b] blank; [i] half-title; [ii] blank; [iii] title; [iv] acknowledge-
ments, and "Copyright © 1965 by Philip B. Frere M.C. and Francis
T. Sitwell . . . Library of Congress catalog card number 65–10912.
Manufactured in the United States of America by Kingsport Press,
Inc., Kingsport, Tennessee. Designed by Harry Ford. First printing
March 1965"; [v] dedication; [vi] publishers' acknowledgement;
[vii] preface; [viii] blank; [ix] Contents; [x] blank; xi–xii Illustrations;
[1–2], 3–239 text and index; [240] blank; [241–242] note on Edith
Sitwell.

Frontispiece tipped in, eight leaves of plates sewn in.

Red and blue buckram boards. Top edge yellow, others trimmed.
Orange end-papers. Gilt stamped on spine and upper cover.

10,000 copies printed. Published 28 April 1965 at $5.95. (The date of
"first printing" on p. [iv] is the month in which the book was ready at
the binder.)

CONTENTS

The text is as in the first edition, but the illustrations are largely new.

EA54   SELECTED POEMS   1965

First edition

SELECTED POEMS | OF | Edith Sitwell | [*decoration*] | *Chosen
with an introduction* | *by John Lehmann* | MACMILLAN |
London · Melbourne · Toronto | 1965

171 × 113 mm.

152 pp.: [i] half-title; [ii] "By the same author . . ."; [iii] title; [iv]
"Poems and notes: Copyright © Dame Edith Sitwell 1957, 1959,
1962, 1963. Introduction and selection: Copyright © John Lehmann
1965 . . . Printed in Great Britain by Richard Clay (The Chaucer
Press), Ltd., Bungay, Suffolk"; v–vi Contents; vii–viii Acknowledgments; 9–32 Introduction; 33–148 text and notes; 149–150 Index of
first lines; [151–152] blank.

Glossy paper covers, unsewn. Trimmed edges. Printed on covers in red and black and with a photograph of the author.

10,000 copies printed. Published 15 July 1965 at 6s. as "Papermac P113."

CONTENTS

BOOKS EDITED BY AND WITH CONTRIBUTIONS BY EDITH SITWELL
(EB1–EB61)

EB1 WHEELS [FIRST CYCLE] 1916

a. *First edition*

[*See Plate III*]

84 pages. 200 × 138 mm.

Yellow cloth spine, yellow paper boards. Untrimmed edges. Printed in black on spine and upper cover.

500 copies printed by Rogers and Broome, Oxford. Published by B. H. Blackwell 13 December 1916 at 2s. 6d.

CONTENTS

Edited by Edith Sitwell. Text by Edith Sitwell, pp. 35–53:

Processions—Gaiety—Thaïs in Heaven—A Lamentation (from 'Saul')—Antic Hay [revision of "Antic Dance" in *Twentieth Century Harlequinade*]—The Drunkard [from *The Mother*]—The Mother [from *The Mother*]—The King of China's Daughter—Nebuchadnezzar [by Edith and Osbert Sitwell]

b. *Second edition*

Note: A second edition (of which 500 copies were printed) was published on 14 April 1917 at 2s. 6d. It has 96 pages, bound in red cloth spine and black paper boards. The contents are as in the first edition, with the addition of a Preface, "In Bad Taste" [anonymous, by Osbert Sitwell] and press notices of the first edition.

EB2 WHEELS, SECOND CYCLE 1917

First edition

[Similar to Plate III, except that the title reads WHEELS: A SECOND CYCLE, and the authors are Sacheverell Sitwell,

III.   Title-page of *Wheels* [EB1] (reduced)

Arnold James, Iris Tree, Sherard Vines, Edith Sitwell, E. W. Tennant, Helen Rootham, Osbert Sitwell, Aldous Huxley; the date is 1917]

120 pages. 192 × 140 mm.

Black cloth spine, white paper boards printed in red, black and green. Untrimmed edges. White paper labels, printed in black, on spine and upper cover.

750 copies printed by Rogers and Broome, Oxford. Published by B. H. Blackwell 4 December 1917 at 2s. 6d.

CONTENTS

Edited by Edith Sitwell; text by Edith Sitwell, pp. 76–90:

From the Balcony. Lagoons—From the Balcony—Multitudes

A Histrion, from "Women in War-Time"

Two Orchard Poems. I. The Satyr in the Periwig—II. The Muslin Gown

A Scene from 'Saul,' an unfinished play—Messalina at Margate—The County Calls

EB3   NEW PATHS 1917–1918   1918

a. *First edition, special copies*

NEW PATHS | VERSE · PROSE · PICTURES | 1917–1918 | Edited by | C. W. BEAUMONT AND M. T. H. SADLER | Decorated by | ANNE ESTELLE RICE | [*decoration*] | LONDON | C. W. BEAUMONT | 75 CHARING CROSS ROAD W.C.2

176 pages, and frontispiece. 221 × 172 mm.

Buff paper boards. Untrimmed edges. Printed in blue on upper cover, decorated on upper and lower covers, and a white paper label on the spine.

(i) 30 copies printed. Published in July 1918 at 30s., signed by the artist and with an additional coloured frontispiece.

(ii) 100 copies printed. Published in July 1918 at 15s., not signed but numbered.

[In addition, six unnumbered copies on Japanese vellum were printed for presentation and are so inscribed in the publisher's autograph.]

CONTENTS

"Weathercocks" by Edith Sitwell, p. 66

b. *First edition, ordinary copies*

Note : These are as the special copies, above, but are on ordinary paper and have no certificate of limitation. "Probably 1000" copies (according to the publisher) were printed. The ordinary copies were published in July 1918 at 7s. 6d.

EB4 WHEELS, THIRD CYCLE 1919

First edition

[Similar to Plate III, except that the title reads WHEELS: A · THIRD · CYCLE, and the authors are Iris Tree, Sherard Vines, Sacheverell Sitwell, Arnold James, Aldous Huxley, Osbert Sitwell, A. D. L. de Guevara, and Edith Sitwell, whose name appears round the axle of the revolving wheel: no date]

104 pages. 190 × 142 mm.

Pictorial end-papers, printed in red, by Don Alvaro de Guevara.

Black cloth spine, white paper boards with a design by Laurence Atkinson printed in red and black. Untrimmed edges. White paper label, printed in black, pasted to spine. Two-colour decoration, and text, printed on upper cover.

1000 copies printed by Rogers and Broome, Oxford. Published by B. H. Blackwell 20 January 1919 at 4s. 6d.

CONTENTS

Edited by Edith Sitwell; text by Edith Sitwell, pp. 81–97:

Sugar for the Birds. I, Singerie—II, The Avenue—III, The Blackamoor Goes to Hell [from *Saturday Westminster Gazette*, 7 December 1918]—IV, Switchback—V, Falsetto Song

Stopping Place—Myself on the Merry-go-Round [from *Clowns'*
Houses]—Apricot Jam [has phrases and images from "Déjeuner
sur l'Herbe," in *Clowns' Houses*]—Song from "The Queen of
Palmyria" [*sic*]—Two Nocturnes. I, Vacuum; II, "Et l'on Entend
à peine leurs Paroles"

EB5 WHEELS, FOURTH CYCLE 1919

First edition

[Similar to Plate III, except that the title reads: WHEELS
1919 FOURTH CYCLE, and the authors are Osbert Sitwell,
Aldous Huxley, Sacheverell Sitwell, Arnold James, Alvaro
Guevara, Iris Tree, Wilfid [*sic*] Owen, Sherard Vines, and
Edith Sitwell, whose name appears round the axle of the
wheel; the wheel is revolving at speed]

104 pages. 181 × 135 mm.

Pictorial end-papers by William Roberts.

Black cloth spine, white paper boards. Trimmed edges. White paper
label, printed in black, pasted to spine. Coloured decoration printed
on upper cover.

1000 copies printed by Rogers and Broome, Oxford. Published by
B. H. Blackwell 2 November 1919 at 6s.

CONTENTS

Edited by Edith Sitwell; text by Edith Sitwell, pp. 77–92:

Materialism: or, Pastor takes the restaurant car for Heaven

Nine Bucolic Poems. 1. What the Goosegirl said about the Dean
[from *Coterie*, no. 2]—2. The Girl with the Lint-white locks [from
Saturday Westminster Gazette, 30 August 1919]—3. By Candlelight
[from *Coterie*, no. 2]—4. Variations on an old nursery rhyme [from
Clowns' Houses]—5. Serenade Bergamesque [as "Serenade" in *The
Mother*]—6. Clown's Houses [from *Twentieth Century Harlequinade*]—7. Miss Nettybun and the Satyr's Child [from *Saturday
Westminster Gazette*, 11 January 1919]—8. Queen Venus and the
Choir-Boy [from *Saturday Westminster Gazette*, 5 January 1919]—
9. "Tournez, Tournez, Bon [*sic*] Chevaux de Bois" [from *Coterie*,
no. 2]

EB6 A MISCELLANY OF POETRY 1919 1919

First edition

[*Within a decorated border*]

A MISCELLANY | OF POETRY–1919– | Edited by W Kean
Seymour. | With decorations by Doris Palmer. | [*decora-
tion*] | Cecil Palmer and Hayward.

136 pages. 184 × 120 mm.

Blue cloth spine, yellow cloth boards. Trimmed edges. Lettered in
blue on upper cover and on paper labels on the spine.

Published in December 1919 at 5s.

CONTENTS (BY EDITH SITWELL)

Eventail—The Lady with the Sewing Machine [from *Art and Letters*
February 1919]—Portrait of a Barmaid [from *Cambridge Magazine*
April 1919]—Solo for Ear-Trumpet [from *Saturday Westminster
Gazette* 5 April 1919] (pp. 114–117)

EB7 WHEELS, FIFTH CYCLE 1920

First edition

[Similar to Plate III, except that the title reads WHEELS 1920
FIFTH CYCLE, and the authors are Aldous Huxley, John
Adams, Sherard Vines, McTavish Cohen, Geoffrey Cook-
son, Alan Porter, W. Kean Seymour, Wyndham Lewis,
Osbert Sitwell, Sacheverell Sitwell and Edith Sitwell, whose
name appears round the axle of the wheel; the new publisher's name, Leonard Parsons, appears on the rim]

128 pages. 182 × 120 mm.

Pictorial end-papers by Gino Severini.

Black cloth spine, white paper boards with a design by Gino Severini,
printed in brown, red and blue on the upper cover. Trimmed edges.
White paper label, printed in black, pasted to spine.

Published in November 1920 at 6s. (The printers, Richard Clay and Sons Ltd., no longer have detailed records of this book.)

CONTENTS

Edited by Edith Sitwell; text by Edith Sitwell, pp. 94–116:

The Toilette of Myrrhine

Eight more Bucolic Poems. 1. Evening [revised from *Saturday Westminster Gazette*, 10 April 1920]—2. The five musicians—3. King Cophetua and the Beggar Maid [from *Saturday Westminster Gazette*, 31 July 1920]—4. Clown Argheb's Song—5. Fleecing Time [from *Saturday Westminster Gazette*, 4 December 1920]—6. The Higher Sensualism [from *Athenaeum*, 14 May 1920]—7. Falsetto Song [*not* as "Falsetto Song" in *Wheels 3*]—8. The Fat Woman

A Tragedy of Reaction, and R.I.P. Topsy Jones [E. B. C. Jones]

EB8 WHEELS, SIXTH CYCLE 1921

First edition

"WHEELS" | 1921. | (Sixth Cycle.) | EDITED BY | EDITH SITWELL. | LONDON: C. W. DANIEL, LTD., | Graham House, Tudor Street, E.C.4.

64 pages. 207 × 135 mm.

Black cloth spine, white paper boards. Trimmed edges. White paper label, printed in black, pasted on spine. Coloured decoration and black lettering on upper cover.

Published in November 1921 at 3s. 6d. (Publishers' records destroyed in 1941.)

CONTENTS

Edited by Edith Sitwell; text by Edith Sitwell, pp. 43–54:

Two Bucolic Poems. 1. On the vanity of human aspirations [from *Athenaeum*, 21 January 1921]—2. Green Geese

Fantasia for Mouth-Organ—Early Spring

EB8*A*   A MISCELLANY OF POETRY   1922
1920–1922

First edition

A Miscellany of Poetry | 1920–1922 | *Edited by* | *William Kean Seymour* | *London* | JOHN G. WILSON | 350 *Oxford Street.* | *W.* 1

224 pages. 186 × 126 mm.

Yellow cloth spine, blue paper boards. Trimmed edges. Gilt lettered on spine. White paper label on upper cover.

1500 copies printed. Published in December 1922 at 6*s*.

CONTENTS

Poor Martha [from *Spectator*, 22 April 1922]—Braga's Serenata [from *Weekly Westminster Gazette*, 18 November 1922], by Edith Sitwell, pp. 157–160

EB9   JOB LE PAUVRE   1923

a. *First edition, special copies*

Jean de BOSSCHÈRE | Job le Pauvre | *With English translation* | Avec un portrait par | —Wyndham Lewis— | traduction des poèmes | en anglais, et quatorze |— —gravures noires— — | John Lane The Bodley Head Limited | London, 1922

136 pages (including end-papers), and 15 plates. 202 × 149 mm.

Shiny black paper boards, untrimmed edges. (There may have been a paper label on the spine, but I have not seen one.)

50 numbered and signed copies printed, 12 of them with the plates hand-coloured by the author, and all with a duplicate set of plates tipped in. Probably published in February 1923 [*sic*], at 30*s*.

CONTENTS

"Absolvez-moi, Seigneur, si dans ma peine," translated by Edith Sitwell (pp. 112–114)

b. *First edition, ordinary copies*

Note: These differ from the special copies only in that they are not numbered or signed, do not have a duplicate set of plates, and were bound in matt black paper boards with a paper label on the spine. 450 copies were printed. Published in London 8 March 1923 at 15*s*., but copies are also found with the imprint: Collection d'Art "La Cible," Jacques Pavolozky & Cie, Éditeurs, 13, rue Bonaparte, Paris. I do not know how many were thus published, when, or at what price. According to the certificate of limitation on p. [iv], 500 copies in all were printed, including the 50 special copies.

EB10   YEA AND NAY   1923

First edition

YEA AND NAY | *A Series of Lectures and Counter-Lectures* | *given at the London School of Economics* | *in aid of the Hospitals of London* | PUBLISHERS | LONDON: BREN-TANO'S LTD. | NEW YORK: BRENTANO'S INC.

208 pages, and 8 plates. 184 × 120 mm.

Fawn cloth boards. Trimmed edges. Gilt lettered on spine and upper cover.

Published in London in December 1923 at 6*s*. (Publishers and printers no longer have any records of publication.)

CONTENTS

"Poetry and Modern Poetry" by Edith Sitwell, pp. 76–88. (Lecture delivered 8 May 1923.)

EB10*A*   THE BEST SHORT STORIES   1925
                   OF 1924

a. *First edition*

The Best | Short Stories of 1924 | I: English | [*device*] | *Edited by* | Edward J. O'Brien *and* John Cournos | London | Jonathan Cape Ltd

384 pages. 190 × 124 mm.

Blue cloth boards. Trimmed edges. Lettered in white on spine and covers.

Published in early 1925 at 7s. 6d. (The publishers no longer have details of publication.)

CONTENTS

"Undergrowth" by Edith Sitwell [from *The Golden Hind*, January 1924], pp. 278–293

b. *First edition, American copies*

Note: Copies were imported and published by Small, Maynard and Co., and later taken over by Dodd, Mead Co.

EB11   MEDDLESOME MATTY   1925

a. *First edition*

[*Within a rectangular border*]
MEDDLESOME | MATTY | AND · OTHER · POEMS · FOR · INFANT · MINDS | *by* | JANE & ANNE TAYLOR | *With an introduction by* | EDITH SITWELL | *Illustrated by* Wyndham Payne | [*coloured decoration*] | LONDON | *Published by* John Lane | The Bodley Head Limited | *in Vigo Street* . 1925.

68 pages. 218 × 141 mm.

Buff cloth spine, pictorial paper boards. Untrimmed edges. White paper label on upper cover, lettered in black up the spine.

Published 4 December 1925 at 6s. (Publishers and printers no longer know the printing number.)

CONTENTS

"Introduction" by Edith Sitwell, pp. vii–xii

b. *First edition, American copies*

Note: 1500 copies, with their imprint, were imported by The Viking Press, New York. Published in 1926 (date unknown) at $1.75.

First edition

JOY STREET POEMS | *By* ROSE FYLEMAN, MARIAN ALLEN, | EDITH SITWELL, ETC. | *Illustrated by various Artists* | OXFORD: BASIL BLACKWELL

28 pages. 209 × 168 mm.

Grey paper boards. Lettered in blue on upper cover, with a coloured illustration pasted on.

Published 21 June 1927 at 1*s.*, in the "Continuous Stories" series. (Neither printers nor publishers now know how many copies were printed.)

CONTENTS (BY EDITH SITWELL)

March for a Toy Soldier [from *No. 1 Joy Street*]—Dirge for a Gollywog [from *No. 1 Joy Street*]—The Little Musical Box [from *No. 1 Joy Street*]—Funny Loo [from *No. 2 Joy Street*] (pp. 8–15)

EB13   THE LEGION BOOK   1929

a. *First edition*

[I have not seen a copy of this edition. The following description is from *The Curwen Press Miscellany*, edited by Oliver Simon, 1931, p. 129: "The Legion Book. Edited by Captain Cotton Minchin. Privately printed. Royal 4to. Full vellumized pigskin (hand-sewn flexible covers, laced in boards.) 100 copies held in the gift of H.R.H. The Prince of Wales." Apparently later editions—see below—were all abridged from this. The printers have no further information, nor a copy.]

b. *Second edition*

THE | LEGION | BOOK | [*short swelled rule*] | EDITED BY | CAPTAIN H. COTTON MINCHIN | [*short swelled rule*] | [*engraving*] | LONDON | PRIVATELY PRINTED | 1929

270 pages. 311 × 240 mm.

Red buckram boards. Top edge gilt, others trimmed. Gilt lettered on spine. Issued in grey slip case with label.

600 numbered copies (500 for sale), signed by the editor, were printed. Published in June 1929 at 105*s.*

"The Scotch Rhapsody from 'Façade'" by Edith Sitwell, pp. 181–182

c. *First unlimited and first American printings*

Note: Ordinary printings were published in London by Cassell (1 October 1929 at 21s.) and in New York by Doubleday, Doran & Co., Inc. (22 November 1929 at $3.00). The poem by Edith Sitwell in both cases is as in the second edition.

EB14 TRADITION AND EXPERIMENT 1929

First edition

TRADITION AND | EXPERIMENT | IN PRESENT-DAY LITERATURE | ADDRESSES DELIVERED | AT THE CITY LITERARY | INSTITUTE | 1929 | OXFORD UNIVERSITY PRESS | LONDON: HUMPHREY MILFORD

224 pages. 193 × 128 mm.

Rough green cloth boards. Untrimmed edges. Gilt lettered on spine and upper cover.

2000 copies printed. Published 25 November 1929 at 7s. 6d.

CONTENTS

"Experiment in Poetry" by Edith Sitwell, pp. 74–97. (Lecture delivered 5 February 1929)

EB15 LIFAR EXHIBITION CATALOGUE 1930

First edition

[*Cover*] LA COLLECTION DE PEINTURES | DE NOS JOURS | APPARTENANT À | M. SERGE LIFAR | [*ornament*] | ARTHUR TOOTH & SONS, LTD. | 155, NEW BOND STREET, W.1

16 pages. 253 × 186 mm.

Blue paper wrappers, stapled. Untrimmed edges. Upper cover printed in black, as above.

Published for the exhibition, held from 16–27 September 1930.

(Messrs. Tooth write: "At this date it is impossible to say how many copies were printed and sold.")

Note: The prefaces did not appear in the catalogue of the same exhibition in Paris.

CONTENTS

"Preface (1)" by Edith Sitwell, [p. 3]

EB16   THE PLEASURES OF   1930–32
                    POETRY

a. *"First series", First edition*

THE | PLEASURES OF POETRY | A CRITICAL ANTHO-
LOGY | BY | EDITH SITWELL | *FIRST SERIES* | MILTON
AND THE AUGUSTAN AGE | DUCKWORTH | 3 Henrietta
Street, London | 1930

244 pages. 184 × 125 mm.

Smooth orange cloth boards. Trimmed edges. Gilt lettered on spine. 2000 copies printed. Published in November 1930 at 6s.

CONTENTS

Introduction (dated June–August 1930)—Anthology

"Second series", First edition

THE | PLEASURES OF POETRY | A CRITICAL ANTHO-
LOGY | BY | EDITH SITWELL | *SECOND SERIES* | THE
ROMANTIC REVIVAL | DUCKWORTH | 3 Henrietta Street,
London | 1931

276 pages. 184 × 125 mm.

Smooth orange cloth boards. Trimmed edges. Gilt lettered on spine. 2000 copies printed. Published in May 1931 at 6s.

CONTENTS

Introduction (dated January–March 1931)—Anthology

THE | PLEASURES OF POETRY | A CRITICAL ANTHO-
LOGY | BY | EDITH SITWELL | *THIRD SERIES* | THE
VICTORIAN AGE | DUCKWORTH | 3 Henrietta Street,
London | 1932

212 pages. 184 × 125 mm.

Smooth orange cloth boards. Trimmed edges. Gilt lettered on
spine.

2000 copies printed. Published in October 1932 at 6*s.*

CONTENTS

Introduction (undated)—Anthology

b. *First edition, American copies*

The PLEASURES *of* POETRY | A CRITICAL ANTHOLOGY |
BY EDITH SITWELL | [*ornament*] | FIRST [SECOND,
THIRD] SERIES | MILTON | AND THE | AUGUSTAN AGE |
[THE | ROMANTIC | REVIVAL] [THE | VICTORIAN | AGE] |
[*two short rules*] | W.W. NORTON & COMPANY, INC. | NEW
YORK

Note: 500 sets, with cancel titles, were imported, and the issue was
published 27 August 1934 at $2.00 per volume. The binding was
rough orange cloth boards, with top edge yellow, gilt lettered on the
spine. The contents are as in EB16a.

c. *Second edition*

THE | PLEASURES OF POETRY | A CRITICAL ANTHO-
LOGY | BY | EDITH SITWELL | DUCKWORTH | 3 Henrietta
Street, London | 1934

Note: 2000 copies were printed of this one-volume edition, which was
published in September 1934 at 8*s.* 6*d.* The contents are as in the first
edition, except for the correction of misprints.

PROSE POEMS FROM
'*LES ILLUMINATIONS*'

First edition

PROSE POEMS | FROM | *LES ILLUMINATIONS* | OF |
ARTHUR RIMBAUD | PUT INTO ENGLISH BY | HELEN
ROOTHAM | WITH AN | INTRODUCTORY ESSAY | BY |
EDITH SITWELL | LONDON | FABER & FABER LIMITED |
24 RUSSELL SQUARE

112 pages. 222 × 142 mm.

Orange cloth boards. Top edge blue, others untrimmed. Gilt
lettered on spine.

Published 17 October 1932 at 7s. 6d. (Publishers and printers say
"printing numbers not known.")

CONTENTS

"Arthur Rimbaud, an essay" by Edith Sitwell, pp. 9–49

TEN CONTEMPORARIES

First edition

TEN CONTEMPORARIES | NOTES TOWARD THEIR DE-
FINITIVE BIBLIOGRAPHY | by JOHN GAWSWORTH |
with a Foreword by | VISCOUNT ESHER | [*rule*] | [*device*] |
[*rule*] | and original essays by— | LASCELLES ABER-
CROMBIE | HERBERT E. PALMER | GEORGE EGERTON |
SIR RONALD ROSS | STEPHEN HUDSON | EDITH SIT-
WELL | WILFRID GIBSON | ROBERT NICHOLS | RHYS
DAVIES | M. P. SHIEL | LONDON | ERNEST BENN LIMITED

224 pages. 184 × 121 mm.

Royal blue cloth boards. Trimmed edges. Gilt lettered on spine.

Published in June 1932 at 7s. 6d. (Neither publishers' nor printers'
records survive.)

CONTENTS

"Some Notes on my Own Poetry" by Edith Sitwell (dated January
1932), pp. 199–203

"The Works of Edith Sitwell" by John Gawsworth, pp. 204–220

EB19   SACHEVERELL SITWELL: 1936
        COLLECTED POEMS

First edition

[*For description of the book, see* SA29]

CONTENTS

"The Poems of Sacheverell Sitwell," by Edith Sitwell, pp. 15–50.
[Contains passages from ch. VI of *Aspects of Modern Poetry*, 1934]

EB20   TWELVE MODERN PLAYS   1938

First edition

TWELVE | MODERN PLAYS | *Selected by* | JOHN HAMPDEN |
DUCKWORTH | 3 HENRIETTA STREET, LONDON, W.C.2

312 pages. 169 × 111 mm.
Smooth blue cloth boards. Trimmed edges. Gilt lettered on spine.
1500 copies printed. Published November 1938 at 3*s*. 6*d*., as no. 66 in
the "New Readers Library." (Received in the British Museum, 28
October 1938.)

CONTENTS

"The Last Party: a Radio Play" by Edith Sitwell, pp. 287–312

EB21   EDITH SITWELL'S   1940
            ANTHOLOGY

First edition

EDITH SITWELL'S | ANTHOLOGY | LONDON | VICTOR
GOLLANCZ LTD | 1940

812 pages. 183 × 127 mm.
Light blue cloth boards. Trimmed edges. Gilt lettered on spine.
5000 copies printed. Published 29 January 1940 at 7*s*. 6*d*.

CONTENTS

Some Notes at Random [partly taken from the introductions to *The
Pleasures of Poetry*, 1930–32]—Text of anthology

First edition

LOOK! THE SUN | *Edited by* | EDITH SITWELL | LONDON |
VICTOR GOLLANCZ LTD | 1941

384 pages. 182 × 123 mm.

Blue cloth boards. Trimmed edges. Gilt lettered on spine.

3500 copies printed. Published 29 September 1941 at 8*s*. 6*d*.

CONTENTS

Editor's note—Text of anthology

EB23   MAIDEN VOYAGE   1943

a. *First edition*

[*Engraved title, within a decorative border*]

MAIDEN | *VOYAGE* | *BY* | *DENTON* | *WELCH* | *ROUT-
LEDGE* | *LONDON* | *MCMXLIII*

312 pages. 183 × 122 mm.

Smooth buff cloth boards. Trimmed edges. Lettered in buff and red
on spine. Drawings by author on end-papers.

2000 copies printed. Published 7 May 1943 at 10*s*. 6*d*.

CONTENTS

"A Foreword" by Edith Sitwell, p. vii

b. *First edition, American issue*

Note: This issue, printed in America, was published by L. B. Fischer
Publishing Corporation 16 March 1945 at $2.75. "About 4000"
copies were printed, according to the publishers. The contents are as
in the first edition.

PLANET AND
GLOW-WORM

First edition

PLANET AND | GLOW-WORM | *A Book for the Sleepless* |
COMPILED BY | EDITH SITWELL | LONDON | MACMILLAN
& CO. LTD | 1944

96 pages. 189 × 124 mm.
Smooth navy-blue cloth boards. Trimmed edges. Gilt lettered on
spine.
5000 copies printed. Published 31 March 1944 at 6s.

CONTENTS

Foreword (dated Renishaw, 1943)—Text of anthology

RONALD BOTTRALL:
SELECTED POEMS
First edition

SELECTED POEMS | BY RONALD BOTTRALL | WITH A
PREFACE BY | EDITH SITWELL | *PL* | EDITIONS POETRY
LONDON

64 pages. 184 × 121 mm.
Brown cloth boards. Edges trimmed. Gilt lettered on spine.
2500 copies printed. Published November 1946 at 4s. 6d.

CONTENTS

"Preface" by Edith Sitwell, pp. vii–x. [This preface was reprinted in
The Collected Poems of Ronald Bottrall, published by Sidgwick and
Jackson on 27 November 1961 (pp. vii–x). 1000 copies printed]

DEMETRIOS CAPETANAKIS

a. First edition

DEMETRIOS | CAPETANAKIS | A GREEK POET IN ENG-
LAND | [*device*] | JOHN LEHMANN | LONDON | 1947

184 pages, and one plate. 215 × 135 mm.

Smooth dark blue cloth boards. Trimmed edges. Gilt lettered on spine.

Published in May 1947 at 10s. 6d. (Neither publishers nor printers have records of the numbers printed. Copies were later remaindered in the same binding.)

CONTENTS

"The Poetry of Demetrios Capetanakis" by Edith Sitwell, pp. 35–41 [from *New Writing and Daylight*, Autumn 1947]

b. *First edition, American copies*

Note: "About 500" copies of the first edition were imported, according to the publishers, with a cancel title. Published by The Devin-Adair Company under the title "The Shores of Darkness" in 1949 at $2.75. The contents are as in the first edition.

EB27   T. S. ELIOT, A SYMPOSIUM   1948

First edition

T. S. ELIOT | A symposium from Conrad Aiken, Luciano Anceschi, | [*17 lines of contributors' names*] | Compiled by Richard March and Tambimuttu | PL | Editions Poetry London | 1948

260 pages. 216 × 139 mm.

Buff linen boards. Top edge brown, others trimmed. Gilt lettered on two brown panels on the spine.

2500 copies printed. Published in September 1948 at 10s. 6d.

CONTENTS

"For T. S. Eliot" by Edith Sitwell, pp. 33–34

EB28   SLEEP IN A NEST OF FLAMES   1949

First edition

[*Red*] SLEEP IN A NEST OF FLAMES | [*black*] BY | CHARLES HENRI FORD | WITH A FOREWORD BY EDITH SITWELL |

"Extase, cauchemar, sommeil dans | un nid de flammes." |
Rimbaud | [*red rule*] | [*black*] A NEW DIRECTIONS BOOK

64 pages. 258 × 157 mm.

Pale green paper boards. Trimmed edges. Black paper labels, lettered in gilt, on spine and upper cover. Paper board slip-case, with label.

600 copies printed by Walter Cantz of Stuttgart, but according to the publishers only 300 copies were available for publication. Published by New Directions, Norfolk, Conn., in 1949 at $2.50.

CONTENTS

"Some notes on the poetry of Charles Henri Ford" by Edith Sitwell, pp. 9–13

EB29   A BOOK OF THE WINTER   1950

a. *First edition*

A BOOK | OF THE WINTER | Compiled by | EDITH SIT-WELL | LONDON | MACMILLAN & CO. LTD | 1950

100 pages. 191 × 125 mm.

Smooth maroon cloth boards. Trimmed edges. Gilt lettered on spine.

5000 copies printed. Published 8 September 1950 at 7s. 6d.

CONTENTS

Text of anthology

b. *First edition, American issue*

[*Double-page title*]

a | Book | of the | Winter | *Compiled by* | Edith Sitwell | [*rose*] | *New York* THE VANGUARD PRESS, INC. | [*decoration*]

128 pages. 235 × 151 mm.

Light grey cloth spine, black paper boards. Leading edge blue, others trimmed. Lilac end-papers. Blind-stamped on upper cover, and lettered in white, silver and blue down spine.

4500 copies printed. Published in December 1951 at $3.00.

As in the first edition, with the addition of "Preface, to my American readers" (pp. 15–21)

EB30   THE AMERICAN GENIUS   1951

[*Within a border of type ornaments*]

THE | AMERICAN | GENIUS | An Anthology of Poetry | with Some Prose | Selected with | a Preface by | EDITH SITWELL | [*star*] | 1951 | London: John Lehmann

208 pages. 217 × 136 mm.

Blue cloth boards. Trimmed edges. Stamped in gilt and black on spine.

Published on 22 February 1951 at 12s. 6d. (Publishers no longer have records of the printing number; some copies were later remaindered in the same binding.)

CONTENTS

Preface—Text of anthology—Notes

EB31   WILLIAM WALTON: FAÇADE   1951

First edition

To Constant Lambert | FAÇADE | AN ENTERTAINMENT | *with Poems by* | EDITH SITWELL | *and Music by* | WILLIAM WALTON | OXFORD UNIVERSITY PRESS | Music Department | 44 CONDUIT STREET, LONDON, W.1 | New York: Toronto: | 114 Fifth Avenue   480 University Avenue

112 pages. 252 × 178 mm.

Buff stiff paper wrappers. Trimmed edges. Lettered in black on pink and buff panels on upper, and in black on lower cover.

2000 copies printed. Published 26 July 1951 at 16s.

CONTENTS

[Poems by Edith Sitwell—all as in *Façade & other Poems*, 1950, unless otherwise stated]

Hornpipe—En Famille—Mariner Man—Long Steel Grass—Through Gilded Trellises—Tango-Pasodoblè [as "Tango—I Do Like to be Beside the Seaside"]—Lullaby for Jumbo—Black Mrs. Behemoth—Tarantella [from *Façade*, June 1926—EA6 (d)—and otherwise unpublished]—[Song of] A Man from a Far Countree—By the Lake—Country Dance—Polka—Four in the Morning [revised from all previous versions]—Something Lies beyond the Scene—Valse [as "Waltz"]—Jodelling Song—Scotch Rhapsody—Popular Song—Fox Trot: Old Sir Faulk—Sir Beelzebub

EB32   SOCIETY FOR TWENTIETH   1952
CENTURY MUSIC: PROGRAMME

First edition

[*Cover; in black within a red border*]

ROYAL FESTIVAL HALL | General Manager: T. E. Bean | THE SOCIETY | FOR TWENTIETH | CENTURY MUSIC | President: Sir William Walton | Tuesday, 8th July, 1952 | *Price One Shilling*

36 pages. 238 × 175 mm.

Grey paper wrappers. Stapled. Trimmed edges. Lettered on upper and lower covers.

"Probably 1500–2000 copies", according to the Royal Festival Hall, printed. Sold as programmes on 8 July 1952 at 1s.

CONTENTS

Programme Note by Edith Sitwell, pp. 17–18—"Façade" Poems, reprinted from *Façade & other Poems*, 1950

EB33   A BOOK OF FLOWERS   1952

First edition

A BOOK OF | FLOWERS | COMPILED BY | EDITH SITWELL | HON D LITT (Leeds) HON D LITT (Durham) | HON D LITT (Oxford) | LONDON | MACMILLAN & CO. LTD | 1952

24 pages. 217 × 138 mm.

Mauve cloth boards. Top edge mauve, others trimmed. Gilt lettered on spine.

3000 copies printed. Published 5 September 1952 at 18s.

CONTENTS

The anthology includes "The Orange-Tree: a bird's song," which is as "A Bird's Song" in *Selected Poems* (1952)

EB34　POETRY AND CHILDREN　1952

First edition

[*Cover; printed in green*]

County Council | of the | West Riding of Yorkshire | Education Committee | [*swelled rule*] | Poetry | and Children | [*swelled rule*] | Woolley College | 21st October–27th October | 1952

12 pages. 228 × 151 mm.

Rough cream paper wrappers, sewn with green thread. Upper cover printed as above.

120 copies printed by Edmund Arnold of Leeds in October 1952 for private distribution to members of the course, which was organised by Leonard Clark, H.M.I.

CONTENTS

"Foreword" by Edith Sitwell, p. 3

EB35　SO LATE INTO THE NIGHT　1952

First edition

[*Red*] SO LATE | INTO THE NIGHT | [*black*] [*star*] | FIFTY LYRICS | 1944–1948 | by | SYDNEY GOODSIR SMITH | [*star*] | *With a Preface by* | EDITH SITWELL | [*four stars*]| LONDON | PETER RUSSELL | 1952

72 pages. 216 × 139 mm.

Grey unprinted paper wrappers. Stapled. No end-papers. Trimmed edges.

500 numbered copies printed for sale. (A few additional copies were circulated to the press; these were unnumbered and marked.) Published in November 1952 at 8s. 6d.

CONTENTS

"Preface" by Edith Sitwell, pp. 7–8

EB36   CASSELL'S ENCYCLOPAEDIA   1953
OF LITERATURE

a. *First edition*

CASSELL'S | ENCYCLOPAEDIA | OF | LITERATURE | EDITED BY | S. H. STEINBERG | IN TWO VOLUMES · VOLUME I [II] | [*device*] | CASSELL & COMPANY LTD | LONDON

Two volumes, 2120 pages. 240 × 156 mm.

Blue buckram boards. Trimmed edges. Gilt lettered and blind-stamped on spine.

13,600 sets printed. Published 22 October 1953 at 84s. per set.

CONTENTS

"Poetry" by E[dith] S[itwell], vol. 1, pp. 423–433

b. *First edition, American issue*

Note: 1400 sets, printed in the United States, were issued under the title of "Cassell's Encyclopaedia of World Literature." Published by Funk & Wagnalls Company, New York, in April 1954 at $25.00 per set. The contents are as in the first edition.

EB37   ENGLISH MORNING   1953

First edition

English Morning | and other poems | [*swelled rule*] | LEONARD CLARK | With a preface by | EDITH SITWELL | HUTCHINSON | Stratford Place | London

88 pages. 211 × 138 mm.

Grey paper boards. Trimmed edges. Gilt lettered on upper cover. 1500 copies printed. Published 26 October 1953 at 10s. 6d.

CONTENTS

"Preface" by Edith Sitwell, pp. xi–xii

EB38　　　　THE FOURTEENTH　　　　1954
　　　　　　　　OF OCTOBER

First edition (of introduction)

BRYHER | [*rule*] | The | Fourteenth of | October | COLLINS | ST JAMES'S PLACE LONDON | 1954

228 pages. 196 × 130 mm.

Black and white cloth boards. Trimmed edges. Gilt lettered on spine. 5000 copies printed. Published 1 November 1954 at 10s. 6d.

CONTENTS

"Introduction" by Dame Edith Sitwell, pp. [i–iii]. [This introduction is not in the American edition of this book, published in 1952]

EB39　　EZRA POUND AT SEVENTY　　1956

First edition

[*The booklet printed in sepia throughout*]

Ezra Pound | AT SEVENTY — — — — — — — — —

16 pages. 121 × 89 mm.

Printed paper covers, as above. Stapled. Trimmed edges.

Not published for sale. 15,150 copies printed in 1956, of which 5800 were distributed through bookshops and the remainder by the publishers, New Directions.

CONTENTS

A message from Dame Edith Sitwell, pp. 12–13

First edition

DYLAN THOMAS | A Bibliography | BY | J. ALEXANDER
ROLPH | FOREWORD BY | DAME EDITH SITWELL |
Illustrated with | *sixteen pages of plates* | LONDON: J. M.
DENT & SONS LTD | NEW YORK: NEW DIRECTIONS

128 pages, and 16 plates. 212 × 138 mm.

Smooth brown cloth boards. Top edge red, others trimmed. Gilt
lettered on spine and on red panel on spine.

1500 copies printed, 1200 for Dent and 300 for New Directions.
Published in London 5 July 1956 at 45s., in New York 9 September
1956 at $8.50.

CONTENTS

"The Young Dylan Thomas" by Dame Edith Sitwell, pp. xiii–xv

EB41   AMERICAN WRITING TODAY   1957

First edition

[*Decoration*] AMERICAN | WRITING | TODAY | *Its Inde-*
pendence | *and Vigor* | Edited by ALLAN ANGOFF | [*de-*
vice] | *Washington Square* | *New York University Press* | *1957*

456 pages. 202 × 137 mm.

Blue cloth boards. Trimmed edges. Gilt lettered on spine and upper
cover.

5000 copies printed. Published 4 March 1957 at $4.50.

CONTENTS

"The Rising Generation" by Edith Sitwell, pp. 3–8 [from *Times
Literary Supplement*, 17 September 1954]

EB42   UNION STREET   1957

First edition

UNION STREET | *POEMS BY* | CHARLES CAUSLEY | *With*

a Preface by | EDITH SITWELL | [*device*] | RUPERT HART-DAVIS | SOHO SQUARE LONDON | 1957

96 pages. 203 × 129 mm.

Blue and green patterned paper boards. Trimmed edges. Lettered in red and black on spine, and on a framed panel on upper cover.

1000 copies printed. Published 22 March 1957 at 12s. 6d.

CONTENTS

"Preface" by Edith Sitwell, pp. 8–10

EB43   COMING TO LONDON   1957

First edition

COMING TO | LONDON | *by* William Plomer, Leonard Woolf, V. S. | Pritchett, George Barker, J. B. Priestley | Elizabeth Bowen, Geoffrey Grigson | John Middleton Murry, Christopher | Isherwood, Alan Pryce-Jones | William Sansom, Jocelyn | Brooke, Rose Macaulay |*and* Edith Sitwell | [*device*] | PHOENIX HOUSE LTD | LONDON

176 pages. 183 × 114 mm.

Red cloth boards. Top edge yellow, others trimmed. Silver stamped on spine.

5000 copies printed. Published 23 September 1957 at 12s. 6d.

CONTENTS

"Coming to London" by Edith Sitwell, pp. 167–176 [from *London Magazine*, April 1957]

EB44   SELECTED POEMS AND NEW   1958

a. *First edition, ordinary copies*

Selected Poems | and New | JOSÉ GARCIA VILLA | INTRODUCTION BY | DAME EDITH SITWELL | [*device*] | McDOWELL, OBOLENSKY | NEW YORK

256 pages. 233 × 155 mm.

Black cloth boards. Top edge red, others trimmed. Lettered in gilt on upper cover and spine.

2450 copies printed. Published 1 August 1958 at $5.00.

"Preface" by Dame Edith Sitwell, pp. ix–xiv.

b. *First edition, special copies*

[A limited issue of fifty copies signed by the author was published on the same date. The contents are as in the ordinary copies.]

EB45   THE ATLANTIC BOOK OF   1958
BRITISH AND AMERICAN POETRY

a. *First edition*

[Within a double-rule border]

The Atlantic Book | *of* | British and American | *Poetry* | [*rule*] | Edited by | DAME EDITH SITWELL | [*rule*] | [*device*] | *An Atlantic Monthly Press Book* | *Boston* · Little, Brown and Company · *Toronto*

1136 pages (in one volume). 231 × 154 mm.

Blue buckram boards. Top edge blue, others trimmed. Blind-stamped on upper cover, gilt stamped on spine with a light blue panel.

10,000 copies printed. Published 12 November 1958 at $12.50.

Introduction (dated London, June 1958)—text of anthology.

b. *First edition, English issue*

[Within a double-rule border]

The Atlantic Book | *of* | British and American | *Poetry* | [*rule*] | Edited by | DAME EDITH SITWELL | [*rule*] | [*device*] | LONDON | VICTOR GOLLANCZ LTD | 1959

1136 pages (in two volumes). 229 × 152 mm.

Blue cloth boards. Trimmed edges. Gilt stamped on spines with red panels.

4500 sets printed. Published 5 November 1959 at 63s.

CONTENTS

As in the first edition, Boston, 1958

EB46   HOMMAGE A ROY CAMPBELL   1958

First edition

HOMMAGE | A | ROY CAMPBELL | F.-J. TEMPLE * ROB LYLE * RICHARD | ALDINGTON * LAWRENCE DURRELL* | ALAN PATON * EDITH SITWELL * | MAURICE OHANA * ALISTER KER- | SHAW * CILETTE OFAIRE * ARMAND | GUIBERT * UYS KRIGE * WYNDHAM | LEWIS * HENRI CHABROL * CHARLES | DE RICHTER * | FREDERIC MISTRAL, | NEVEU * CATHERINE ALDINGTON * F. | DE FREMINVILLE | * * * | CHOIX DE POÈMES, TRADUITS | PAR ARMAND GUIBERT | 1958

148 pages, and 5 plates. 188 × 140 mm.

Pictorial wrappers. Untrimmed edges. Printed in black on sepia on upper cover and in black on spine.

700 copies printed. Published December 1958 at Montpellier by Société Cevenole du Mercou in their "Editions de la Licorne."

CONTENTS

["Roy Campbell" by] Edith Sitwell, pp. 47–51

EB47   POEMS OF OUR TIME   1959

First edition (of Modern Supplement)

POEMS OF OUR TIME | 1900–1960 | ORIGINAL EDITION CHOSEN BY | RICHARD CHURCH, C.B.E. | AND | MILDRED

BOZMAN | MODERN SUPPLEMENT CHOSEN BY | DAME
EDITH SITWELL, D.LITT. | [*device*] | LONDON J. M.
DENT & SONS LTD | NEW YORK E. P. DUTTON &
CO INC

384 pages. 181 × 117 mm.

Blue cloth boards. Top edge orange, others trimmed. Gilt stamped
on spine.

Published 5 June 1959 at 9s. 6d., as a revised edition of no. 981 of
"Everyman's Library." (The publishers decline to say how many
copies were printed.)

CONTENTS

"Preface to the Modern Supplement" (dated 1959) by Edith Sitwell,
pp. v–vii; Section V: "1946–   " (chosen by Edith Sitwell), pp.
313–335.

EB48   ADVENTURES OF THE MIND   1959

a. *First edition*

[I have been unable to see a copy of this edition, edited by Richard
Thruelsen and John Kobler, with an introduction by Mark van Doren.
It was published in New York by Alfred A. Knopf, Inc., on 21
September 1959 at $4.50, and 25,000 copies were printed. It contains
the same piece by Edith Sitwell as in the English issue, reprinted from
Saturday Evening Post, 15 November 1958.]

b. *First edition, English issue*

ADVENTURES | OF | THE MIND | [*rule*] | *Edited by Richard
Thruelsen and John Kobler* | INTRODUCTION BY | *Mark
Van Doren* | [*device*] | LONDON | VICTOR GOLLANCZ
LTD | 1960

296 pages. 216 × 139 mm.

Blue cloth boards. Trimmed edges. Gilt lettered on spine.

Published 25 January 1960. (The publishers decline to say how many copies were printed.)

CONTENTS

"The Poet's Vision" by Edith Sitwell, pp. 107–120

EB49 COLLECTED POEMS, VOLUME 3 1960

First edition

The | *Collected Poems of* | ROY CAMPBELL | VOLUME 3 | [TRANSLATIONS] | *with a Foreword by Edith Sitwell* | THE BODLEY HEAD | *LONDON*

144 pages. 216 × 138 mm.

Red cloth boards. Trimmed edges. Gilt lettered on spine with black panel.

2500 copies printed. Published 21 August 1960 at 18*s.*

CONTENTS

"Foreword " by Edith Sitwell, pp. 5–7

EB50 SWINBURNE: A SELECTION 1960

a. *First edition*

[*In three ornamental red- and black-bordered panels*]

SWINBURNE | *A Selection* | [*ornaments*] | COMPILED AND | WITH AN INTRODUCTION | BY | Dame Edith Sitwell | [*ornaments*] | WEIDENFELD AND NICOLSON | *20 New Bond Street · London W 1*

296 pages. 217 × 131 mm.

Grey cloth boards. Top edge red, others trimmed. Grey-blue endpapers. Stamped in gilt on red panel on spine.

2000 copies printed. Published 16 September 1960 at 25*s.*

"Introduction" by Edith Sitwell, pp. 1–51; text of selection, pp. 53–284

b. *First edition, American copies*

[*In three ornamental red- and black-bordered panels*]

SWINBURNE | *A Selection* | [*ornaments*] | COMPILED AND | WITH AN INTRODUCTION | BY | Dame Edith Sitwell | [*ornaments*] | HARCOURT, BRACE AND COMPANY | *New York*

296 pages. 216 × 132 mm.

Grey paper boards, blue cloth spine. Top edge maroon, others trimmed. Blind-stamped on upper cover, gilt lettered on spine.

3000 copies imported. Published 6 November 1960 at $5.75

As in English copies, above

EB51   DYLAN THOMAS   1960

First edition

Dylan Thomas: | The Legend and the Poet | A COLLECTION OF BIOGRAPHICAL | AND CRITICAL ESSAYS | EDITED BY | E. W. TEDLOCK | [*device*] | HEINEMANN | LONDON MELBOURNE TORONTO

296 pages. 215 × 139 mm.

Brown cloth boards. Trimmed edges. Silver lettered on spine and blind-stamped on lower cover.

3000 copies printed. Published 14 November 1960.

"Comment on Dylan Thomas" by Edith Sitwell, pp. 148–150 [from *The Critic*, Autumn 1947]

First edition (of introduction)

JAMES PURDY | Color of Darkness | ELEVEN STORIES |
AND A NOVELLA | Introduction by Dame Edith Sitwell |
[*device*] | J. B. LIPPINCOTT COMPANY | PHILADELPHIA
AND NEW YORK | 1961

192 pages. 204 × 135 mm.

Flush stiff paper boards. Unsewn. Printed in blue and green on black
on spine and upper cover, in black on white on lower cover.

10,000 copies printed. Published 24 April 1961 at $1.65, as no. KB 25
of the "Keystone Books."

CONTENTS

"Introduction" by Dame Edith Sitwell, pp. 9–14 (here first published);
"Color of Darkness" and "63: Dream Palace" by James Purdy (first
published 1956, 1957)

EB53   COLLECTION OF WORKS   1961
BY PAVEL TCHELITCHEW

First edition

CATALOGUE OF | The Collection of Works by | Pavel
Tchelitchew | *the property of* | DAME EDITH SITWELL,
D.B.E. | INCLUDING | Portrait of Dame Edith Sitwell |
A Self-portrait and Masks in wax and wire | ALSO | A
Series of Still Lifes | Ballet Designs and Figure Studies
| AND | Studies for Oil Paintings of the Period 1928–1939 |
ALSO | The Green Venus | WHICH WILL BE SOLD BY
AUCTION | BY MESSRS | SOTHEBY & CO. | [*five lines about
the auctioneers*] | DAY OF SALE, WEDNESDAY 13 DECEM-
BER 1961 | [*five lines about the sale, etc.*]

24 pages, and (in illustrated copies) 14 plates. 246 × 184 mm.

Green wrappers (illustrated copies); yellow wrappers (unillustrated
copies). Sewn. Trimmed edges. Covers printed in black.

About 3520 illustrated and 1528 unillustrated copies printed.

Distributed from mid-November 1961 as catalogue for the auction sale on 13 December 1961.

CONTENTS

"Pavel Tchelitchew" by Edith Sitwell, pp. 5–8

EB54   INTO THE TENTH DECADE   1962

First edition

Into the 10th Decade | Tribute to Bertrand Russell | [five lines of manuscript reproduced in red]

38 pages. 283 × 226 mm.

Glossy white paper wrappers. Stapled. Trimmed edges. Photograph of Bertrand Russell reproduced on upper cover.

2599 copies printed for the concert held for Bertrand Russell's 90th birthday in the Royal Festival Hall, London, 19 May 1962; 512 copies sold at the concert.

CONTENTS

A message from Edith Sitwell, p. [37]

EB55   THE UNCONSCIOUS   1962
               BEFORE FREUD

First edition (of foreword)

The | Unconscious | before Freud | [rule] | LANCELOT LAW WHYTE | *With a Foreword by* EDITH SITWELL | *[device] |* TAVISTOCK PUBLICATIONS

240 pages. 215 × 137 mm.

Slate-green cloth boards. Trimmed edges. Silver stamped on spine.

3000 copies printed. Published 24 October 1962 at 25s.

CONTENTS

"Foreword" by Edith Sitwell, pp. v–vi. (This foreword was not in the American edition published in 1960 by Basic Books, Inc.)

First edition

[*Full-opening title, with reproduction of wood-cut over all the right-hand page below the first line*]

The Seven Deadly Sins | *Angus Wilson* | *Edith Sitwell* | *Cyril Connolly* | *Patrick Leigh Fermor* |`*Evelyn Waugh* | *Christopher Sykes* | *W. H. Auden* | Introduction by RAY-MOND MORTIMER | SUNDAY TIMES PUBLICATIONS LTD

100 pages. 215 × 135 mm.

Red cloth boards. Trimmed edges. Gilt lettered on spine.

Published in October 1962 at 15s. (The publishers no longer know the number of copies printed.)

CONTENTS

"Pride" by Edith Sitwell, pp. 14–22 [from *Sunday Times*, 17 December 1961]

First edition

Cecil Beaton | IMAGES [*repeated five times, overlapping*] | With a preface by | Dame Edith Sitwell | and an introduction by | Christopher Isherwood | WEIDENFELD AND NICOLSON | 20 NEW BOND STREET LONDON W.1

64 pages. 248 × 186 mm.

Black cloth boards. Top edge red, others trimmed. Red end-papers. Gilt lettered on spine.

Published September 1963 at 27s. 6s.

CONTENTS

"Preface" by Edith Sitwell, p. [5]

First edition

[*Within an ornamental border*]

Mightier Than The Sword | THE P.E.N. HERMON OULD |
MEMORIAL LECTURES | *1953–1961* | *With a Foreword* | *by*
| *C. V. Wedgwood* | *Contributors* | CHARLES MORGAN
BERTRAND RUSSELL | J. B. PRIESTLEY EDITH SITWELL
| A. L. ROWSE ISAIAH BERLIN | C. V. WEDGWOOD |
LONDON | MACMILLAN & CO LTD | NEW YORK · ST
MARTIN'S PRESS | 1964

160 pages. 217 × 138 mm.

Red cloth boards. Trimmed edges. Gilt lettered on upper cover and
spine.

2000 copies printed. Published in London at 21*s*. on 6 August 1964
and in New York at $4.25 on 21 January 1965.

CONTENTS

"Young Poets" by Edith Sitwell, pp. 55–76. (The 1957 Hermon
Ould Memorial Lecture, delivered in London on 15 May 1957)

EB59   PORTRAIT OF A JUDGE   1964

First edition

HENRY CECIL | [*asterisk*] | Portrait of a Judge | AND
OTHER STORIES | [*device*] | *London* | MICHAEL JOSEPH

204 pages. 197 × 131 mm.

Black cloth boards. Trimmed edges. Gilt and white stamped on
spine.

10,000 copies printed. Published 7 September 1964 at 16*s*.

CONTENTS

Note by Edith Sitwell, p. 7

a. *First edition*

[*Full-opening title; left-hand page printed yellow on black, right-hand page black on white*]

FACE TO ꟻɔAꟻ | Edited and introduced by HUGH BURNETT | Portraits by FELIKS TOPOLSKI | [*device*] Jonathan Cape · 30 Bedford Square. W.C.1

96 pages. 261 × 246 mm.

Black cloth spine, printed paper boards. Trimmed edges. End-papers decorated by Topolski. Printed in colour on boards, gilt lettered on spine.

Published 29 October 1964 at 63s. (The publishers decline to divulge the printing number.)

CONTENTS

Interview of Edith Sitwell by John Freeman, from the television broadcast on 6 May 1959 in the series "Face to Face," pp. 18–21

b. *First edition, American issue*

Note: An issue, printed in the United States, was published by Stein and Day, Publishers, New York, in April 1965 at $10.

5300 copies were printed. The publishers say that, apart from the dust wrapper, the "book was exactly the same as the British edition."

EB61 THE JUDGEMENT SEAT 1965

First edition

𝕿𝖍𝖊 | 𝕵𝖚𝖉𝖌𝖊𝖒𝖊𝖓𝖙 𝕾𝖊𝖆𝖙 | 𝖇𝖞 | 𝕾𝖈𝖍𝖆𝖗𝖒𝖊𝖑 𝕴𝖗𝖎𝖘 | 𝕴𝖓𝖙𝖗𝖔= 𝖉𝖚𝖈𝖙𝖎𝖔𝖓 𝖇𝖞 | 𝕯𝖆𝖒𝖊 𝕰𝖉𝖎𝖙𝖍 𝕾𝖎𝖙𝖜𝖊𝖑𝖑 | [*decoration*] RALPH FLETCHER SEYMOUR | *PUBLISHER* | *1965*

84 pages (including back end-papers). 228 × 153 mm.

Purple plastic-covered boards. Trimmed edges. Gilt lettered on upper cover.

Presumably published in Chicago in 1965, but I have been unable to discover any information from book-trade bibliographies or from the publisher.

CONTENTS

"Introduction" by Edith Sitwell (dated February 1956), pp. xiii–xvi.

EC1 "Drowned Suns," *Daily Mirror*, no. 2928, p. 9, 13 March 1913.

EC2 "Song: Tell me, Where is Sorrow Laid," *Daily Mirror*, no. 3007, p. 7, 13 June 1913.

EC3 "Love in Autumn," *Daily Mirror*, no. 3093, p. 9, 22 September 1913.

EC4 "In Remembrance," *Daily Mirror*, no. 3095, p. 7, 24 September 1913.

EC5 "Serenade," *Daily Mirror*, no. 3146, p. 9, 22 November 1913.

EC6 "From an Attic Window," *Daily Mirror*, no. 3184, p. 7, 7 January 1914.

EC7 "Song: When Daisies White and Celandine," *Daily Mirror*, no. 3191, p. 7, 15 January 1914.

EC8 "Lullaby," *Daily Mirror*, no. 3563, p. 7, 26 March 1915.

EC9 "Selene," *Daily Mirror*, no. 3584, p. 7, 20 April 1915.

EC10 "Beggarman Blind," *Daily Mirror*, no. 3616, p. 7, 27 May 1915.

EC11 "Water Music," *Daily Mirror*, no. 3788, p. 7, 14 December 1915.

EC11A "Minstrels," *The Egoist*, v. 5, no. 10, pp. 133–134, November–December 1918.

EC12 "The Blackamoor Goes to Hell," *Saturday Westminster Gazette*, v. 52, no. 7946, p. 12, 7 December 1918.

EC13 "Miss Nettybun and the Satyr's Child," *Saturday Westminster Gazette*, v. 53, no. 7974, p. 13, 11 January 1919.

EC14 "The Lady with the Sewing Machine," *Art and Letters*, v. 2, no. 1, p. 8, [February 1919]. [There are two states of this issue, the earlier bearing "Winter 1918–19" on front cover.]

EC15 "Solo for Ear-Trumpet," *Saturday Westminster Gazette*, v. 53, no. 8046, p. 5, 5 April 1919.

EC16 "Portrait of a Barmaid," *Cambridge Magazine*, v. 8, no. 27, p. 584, 12 April 1919.

EC17 "Hymns of Hate," *Daily Herald*, no. 1049, p. 8, 4 June 1919. [Review of *Any Soldier to his Son* by George Willis.]

EC18 "Interlude," *The Monthly Chapbook*, no. 1, p. 23, July 1919. [There were two printings of this issue, the earlier having advertisements printed on orange—not yellow—paper.]

EC19 "Queen Venus and the Choir-Boy," *Saturday Westminster Gazette*, v. 54, no. 8121, p. 14, 5 July 1919.

EC20 "The Girl with the Lint-White Locks," *Saturday Westminster Gazette*, v. 54, no. 8167, p. 9, 30 August 1919.

EC21 "What the Goose-Girl Said about the Dean," "Tournez, Tournez, bons Chevaux de Bois," "By Candlelight," *Coterie*, no. 2, pp. 38–40, September 1919.

EC22 "Mandoline," *Art and Letters*, v. 2, no. 4, pp. 145–146, Autumn 1919.

EC23 "At the Fair: the Ape sees the Fat Woman," *Saturday Westminster Gazette*, v. 54, no. 8215, p. 13, 25 October 1919.

EC24 "At the Fair; I: Springing Jack, II: The Ape watches 'Aunt Sally,'" *Coterie*, no. 3, pp. 40–41, December 1919.

EC25 "Mandoline," *The Living Age*, v. 303, no. 3935, p. 630, 6 December 1919.

EC26 "Among the Dark and Brilliant Leaves," *The Living Age*, v. 304, no. 3942, p. 247, 24 January 1920. [As EC23.]

EC27 "Two Country Suck-a-Thumbs," "Pedagogues & Flower Shows," *Art and Letters*, v. 3, no. 2, pp. 3–5, Spring 1920.

EC28 "Sir Rotherham's Ride," *Saturday Westminster Gazette*, v. 55, no. 8355, p. 11, 10 April 1920.

EC29 "The Higher Sensualism," *Athenaeum*, 14 May 1920.

EC30 "Bank Holiday, I & II," "Small Talk, I," "Dansons la Gigue," *Oxford and Cambridge Miscellany*, pp. 9–11, [6] June 1920.

EC31 "En Famille," *The Chapbook*, no. 13, pp. 18–19, July 1920.

EC32 "King Cophetua and the Beggar-Maid," *Saturday Westminster Gazette*, v. 56, no. 8450, p. 11, 31 July 1920.

EC33 "Aubade," *Saturday Westminster Gazette*, v. 56, no. 8503, p. 12, 2 October 1920.

EC34 "Fleecing Time," *Saturday Westminster Gazette*, v. 56, no. 8557, p. 13, 4 December 1920.

EC35 "On the Vanity of Human Aspirations," *Athenaeum*, no. 4734, pp. 63–64, 21 January 1921.

EC36 "On the Vanity of Human Aspirations," *Literary Digest*, v. 68, no. 8, p. 36, 19 February 1921.

EC37 "Herodiade," *Saturday Westminster Gazette*, v. 58, no. 6, p. 10, 20 August 1921.

EC38 "Serenade for Two Cats and a Trombone," *Saturday Westminster Gazette*, v. 58, no. 8, p. 11, 3 September 1921.

EC39 "The Doll," *Form*, v. 1, no. 1, pp. 30–31, October 1921 [Issued in limited and ordinary editions.]

EC40 "Recent Poetry," *The Sackbut*, v. 2, no. 4, p. 38, October 1921. [Reviews of *The Farmer's Bride* by Charlotte Mew; *The Chapbook*, no. 10; and *Cranks*.]

EC41 "Reviews," *The Sackbut*, v. 2, no. 6, p. 38, December 1921. [Review of *Poems* by Marianne Moore.]

EC42 "Poems for Music, chosen by Edith Sitwell," *The Sackbut*, v. 2, no. 6, December 1921. [Two poems chosen by Edith Sitwell.]

EC43 "Poor Martha," *Spectator*, v. 128, p. 495, 22 April 1922.

EC44 "New Publications," *The Sackbut*, v. 2, no. 11, p. 35, June 1922. [Review of *The Eton Candle* edited by Brian Howard.]

EC45 "Readers and Writers," *The New Age*, new series, v. 31, no. 10, pp. 119–120, 6 July 1922. [First of a series of 11 general literary essays.]

EC46 "Readers and Writers," *The New Age*, new series, v. 31, no. 11, pp. 133–134, 13 July 1922.

EC47 "Readers and Writers," *The New Age*, new series, v. 31, no. 12, pp. 148–149, 20 July 1922.

EC48 "Readers and Writers," *The New Age*, new series, v. 31, no. 13, p. 161, 27 July 1922.

EC49 "New Publications," *The Sackbut*, v. 3, no. 1, pp. 31–32, August 1922. [Review of *The Chapbook*, May 1922, and *Public School Verse, 1920–21*.]

EC50 "Readers and Writers," *The New Age*, new series, v. 31, no. 14, pp. 171–172, 3 August 1922.

EC51 "Readers and Writers," *The New Age*, new series, v. 31, no. 15, pp. 184–185, 10 August 1922.

EC52 "Readers and Writers," *The New Age*, new series, v. 31, no. 16, p. 196, 17 August 1922.

EC53 "Readers and Writers," *The New Age*, new series, v. 31, no. 17, pp. 210–211, 24 August 1922.

EC54 "Readers and Writers," *The New Age*, new series, v. 31, no. 18, p. 222, 31 August 1922.

EC55 "Readers and Writers," *The New Age*, new series, v. 31, no. 19, p. 236, 7 September 1922.

EC56 "Readers and Writers," *The New Age*, new series, v. 31, no. 21, p. 261, 21 September 1922.

EC57 "Rain," *Weekly Westminster Gazette*, v. 1, no. 33, p. 20, 30 September 1922.

EC58 "Braga's Serenata," *Weekly Westminster Gazette*, v. 1, no. 40, p. 16, 18 November 1922.

EC59 "Promenade Sentimentale," *Spectator*, v. 129, p. 727, 18 November 1922.

EC60 "Winter," "Spring," *English Review*, v. 36, no. 3, pp. 201–204, March 1923.

EC61 "Winter," *Rhythmus*, v. 1, no. 3, pp. 48–51, March 1923.

EC62 "Rain," *The Living Age*, v. 316, no. 4105, p. 610, 10 March 1923.

EC63 "Cacophony for Clarinet," "By the Lake," *The Chapbook*, no. 37, pp. 13–14, May 1923.

EC64 "Daphne," *Spectator*, v. 130, p. 799, 12 May 1923.

EC65 "Advice to Young Poets," *Weekly Westminster Gazette*, v. 2, no. 65, pp. 16–17, 12 May 1923.

EC66 "Miss Stein's Stories," *The Nation and Athenaeum*, v. 33, no. 15, p. 492, 14 July 1923. [Review of *Geography and Plays*.]

EC67 "Some Books of Verse," *Weekly Westminster Gazette*, v. 2, no. 75, pp. 18–19, 21 July 1923. [Reviews.]

EC68 "The Gardener, from 'The Princess in the Sleeping Wood,'" *The Nation and Athenaeum*, v. 34, no. 4, p. 154, 27 October 1923.

EC69 "La Rousse, from The Sleeping Princess," *Oxford Outlook*, v. 5, no. 24, pp. 110–111, November 1923.

EC70 "March for a Toy Soldier," "Dirge for a Gollywog," "The Little Musical Box," *No. 1 Joy Street*, pp. 96–100, [9 November] 1923.

EC71 "Aubade," *Spectator*, v. 131, p. 993, 22 December 1923.

EC72 "Undergrowth," *The Golden Hind*, v. 2, no. 6, pp. 5–7, 10–16, January 1924. [Standard edition, and Edition-de-Luxe of 75 signed copies.]

EC73 "Song from 'The Sleeping Beauty,'" *The Nation and Athenaeum*, v. 34, no. 22, p. 765, 1 March 1924.

EC74 "Mademoiselle Richarde," *Spectator*, v. 132, p. 504, 29 March 1924.

EC75 "Chanson Gris," *Vogue* [London], v. 63, no. 8, p. 46, late April 1924.

EC76 "Yesterday," *The Nation and Athenaeum*, v. 35, p. 177, 10 May 1924.

EC77 "Colonel Fantock," *Spectator*, v. 132, p. 880, 31 May 1924.

EC78 "Yesterday," *The Literary Digest*, v. 81, no. 10, p. 40, 7 June 1924.

EC79 "The Country Cousin," *Vogue* [London], v. 64, no. 4, p. 32, late August 1924.

EC80 "Jane Austen and George Eliot," *Vogue* [London], v. 64, no. 4, pp. 32, 72, late August 1924.

EC81 "Song from 'The Sleeping Beauty,'" *The Literary Digest*, v. 82, no. 6, p. 34, 9 August 1924.

EC82 "Funny Loo," *No. 2 Joy Street*, p. 134, [1 September] 1924.

EC83 "Three Women Writers," *Vogue* [London], v. 64, no. 7, pp. 81, 114, early October 1924. [Katherine Mansfield, Gertrude Stein, Dorothy Richardson.]

EC84 "On an Autumn Evening spent in reading Cowper," *The Fortnightly Review*, new series, v. 116, pp. 558–559, October 1924.

EC85 "Pleasure Gardens," *The Nation and Athenaeum*, v. 36, no. 8, p. 297, 22 November 1924.

EC86 "Four in the Morning," *Vogue* [London], v. 64, no. 12, p. 33, late December 1924.

EC87 "Three Poor Witches," *Spectator*, v. 133, p. 1022, 27 December 1924.

EC88 "The Man with the Green Patch," *The Criterion*, v. 3, no. 10, pp. 244–248, January 1925.

EC89 "Some Observations on Women's Poetry," *Vogue* [London], v. 65, no. 5, pp. 59, 86, early March 1925.

EC89*A* "Criticism and Modern Poetry," *The Cambridge Review*, v. 46, no. 1146, pp. 502–503, 10 June 1925.

EC90 "Cendrillon and the Cat," *Vogue* [London], v. 66, no. 2, p. 29, late July 1925.

EC91 "The Criticism of Poetry," *Saturday Review of Literature*, v. 2, no. 7, pp. 117–118, 12 September 1925.

EC92 "The Work of Gertrude Stein," *Vogue* [London], v. 66, no. 7, pp. 73, 98, early October 1925.

EC93 "The Scandal," *The Nation and Athenaeum*, v. 38, no. 12, p. 437, 19 December 1925.

EC94 "Valse Maigre, 1843," *Vogue* [London], v. 66, no. 12, p. 42, late December 1925.

EC95 [Review], *The New Criterion*, v. 4, no. 2, pp. 390–392, April 1926. [Review of *The Making of Americans* by Gertrude Stein.]

EC96 "Poème: An Interview with Mars" (from "The Childhood of Cendrillon"), *Commerce*, Cahiers Trimestriels, cahier VII, pp. 113–123, Printemps 1926. [With a French translation by M. V. Larbaud.]

EC97 "My Brother's Book," *Weekly Dispatch*, no. 6519, p. 7, 10 October 1926. [Review of *Before the Bombardment* by Osbert Sitwell.]

EC98 "Who are the Sitwells—and why do they do it?," *Weekly Dispatch*, no. 6524, p. 8, 14 November 1926.

EC99 "A New Poet," *The Nation and Athenaeum*, v. 40, no. 14, pp. 514–515, 8 January 1927. [Review of *Poems* by Peter Quennell.]

EC99*A* "Good and Bad Literature: spiritual adventures among the arts," *T.P.'s and Cassell's Weekly*, v. 7, no. 176, p. 659, 12 March 1927.

EC99*B* "What Modern Poetry Needs," *T.P.'s and Cassell's Weekly*, v. 7, no. 177, p. 709, 19 March 1927.

EC100 "Our Family Ghost," *Weekly Dispatch*, no. 6550, p. 2, 15 May 1927.

EC100*A* "When is Poetry a Crime?," *Daily Mirror*, no. 7369, p. 4, 27 June 1927.

EC100*B* "Face- or Mind-lifting," *The London Magazine*, v. 59, no. 204, pp. 377–379, October 1927.

EC101 "My Awkward Moments," *Daily Mail*, no. 9822, p. 10, 15 October 1927.

EC102 "The Dog," *The Nation and Athenaeum*, v. 42, no. 2, p. 117, 22 October 1927.

EC103 "How Fame Looks to a Poetess," *Literary Digest*, v. 95, no. 5, p. 29, 29 October 1927. [Being part of EC101.]

EC104 "Panope," *The New Republic*, v. 54, no. 690, p. 16, 22 February 1928.

EC104*A* "Modern Poetry [1]," *Time & Tide*, v. 9, no. 13, pp. 308–309, 30 March 1928.

EC104*B* "Modern Poetry: a few remarks on Sitwellism," *Time & Tide*, v. 9, no. 14, pp. 332–333, 6 April 1928.

EC105 "The Peach Tree," *Saturday Review of Literature*, v. 4, p. 775, 21 April 1928.

EC105*A* "People who are Cruelly Kind," *Daily Mail*, no. 10020, p. 10, 5 June 1928.

EC106 "Must the World be so Noisy?," *Sunday Express*, p. 9, 24 June 1928.

EC107 "People I Annoy," *Daily Mail*, no. 10037, p. 12, 25 June 1928.

EC108 "A Poet of Fiery Simplicity," *T.P.'s Weekly*, v. 10, p. 598, no. 254, 8 September 1928. [Review of *The Heart's Journey* by Siegfried Sassoon.]

EC109 [*See* EC104*A–B*]

EC110 "Are there still Bohemians?," *Daily Chronicle*, no. 20790, p. 8, 31 October 1928.

EC111 "Modern Values," *Spectator*, v. 141, no. 5243, pp. 950–951, 22 December 1928.

EC112 "The Bat," *Time & Tide*, v. 10, p. 7, 4 January 1929.

EC113 "The Cherry Tree," *Time & Tide*, v. 10, p. 34, 11 January 1929.

EC113*A* [Answer to a questionnaire, "Confessions"], *The Little Review*, v. 12, no. 2, pp. 75–76, May 1929.

EC114 "The Poems of Charlotte Mew," *Time & Tide*, v. 10, p. 755, 21 June 1929.

EC115 [*Deleted.*]

EC116 "Oh, to be in Scarborough, now that August's here," *Daily Express*, no. 9141, p. 8, 17 August 1929.

EC117 [Review], *The Criterion*, v. 9, no. 34, pp. 130–134, October 1929. [Review of Charlotte Mew's *The Farmer's Bride* and *The Rambling Sailor*.]

EC118 "The Charwoman (London Types)," *Time & Tide*, v. 10, no. 42, pp. 1233–1234, 18 October 1929.

EC118*A* "The Ghost whose Lips were Warm," *Échanges*, no. 1, pp. 74–76, Décembre 1929.

EC119 "Who wants Poets now?," *Evening News*, no. 15076, p. 8, 25 April 1930.

EC119*A* "Modernist Poets," *Échanges*, no, 3, pp. 77–91, June 1930.

EC120 "Life's Tyrannies—and my gospel of happiness," *Evening News*, no. 15456, p. 8, 16 July 1931.

EC121 "Stories of Beau Nash," *Evening News*, p. 11, 13 May 1932.

EC122 "Don't Become a Standard Person," *Yorkshire Weekly Post*, no. 1848, p. 9, 4 June 1932.

EC123 "Why Worry about your Age?," *Yorkshire Weekly Post*, no. 1855, p. 9, 23 July 1932.

EC124 "Miss Sitwell presents a Genius," *The Graphic*, v. 121, no. 3059, p. 133, 28 July 1933. [On Pavel Tchelitchew.]

EC125 "Is our Civilization a Benefit?," *Time & Tide*, v. 14, no. 37, p. 1086, 16 September 1933.

EC125*A* "A Word to the 'Poetry Contractors,' " *Morning Post*, no. 50410, p. 10, 15 January 1934.

EC126 "Poets wise—and otherwise," *Morning Post*, no. 50453, p. 10, 6 March 1934.

EC127 "The Truth about Blood Sports," *Sunday Referee*, no. 2999, p. 10, 24 February 1935.

EC128 "Some Notes on my Own Poetry," *London Mercury*, v. 31, no. 185, pp. 448–454, March 1935.

EC129 "Twentieth Century Justice through a Camera Lens," *Sunday Referee*, no. 3001, p. 13, 10 March 1935.

EC130 "Here is a Dickens of our Time," *Sunday Referee*, no. 3003, p. 12, 24 March 1935. [On the novels of Walter Greenwood.]

EC131 "It is fear that breeds War," *Sunday Referee*, no. 3005, p. 12, 7 April 1935.

EC132 "People I Meet in the Train," *Sunday Referee*, no. 3007, p. 10, 21 April 1935.

EC133 "What do we Mean by Liberty?," *Sunday Referee*, no. 3009, p. 12, 5 May 1935.

EC134 "What is Slavery?," *Sunday Referee*, no. 3011, p. 12, 19 May 1935.

EC135 "Prelude," *London Mercury*, v. 32, no. 188, pp. 108–110, June 1935.

EC136 "Let's scrap Parliament," *Sunday Referee*, no. 3013, p. 12, 2 June 1935.

EC137 "Testament of a Young Man," *Time & Tide*, v. 16, pp. 1548–1549, 26 October 1935. [Review of *World Without Faith* by John Beevers.]

EC138 "A Correspondence on the Young English Poets, between Edith Sitwell and Robert Herring," *Life and Letters To-Day*, v. 13, no. 2, pp. 16–24, December 1935.

EC139 "Gangsters, Fraudulent Financiers, War-Mongers, Sneak-Motorists . . .," *Sunday Referee*, p. 12, 26 January 1936.

EC140 "Of Calamancoes, Shalloons, Garlets, Tabbeys & a hundred others," *Harper's Bazaar* [London], v. 13, no. 5, pp. 60, 90, February 1936.

EC141 "Four New Poets," *London Mercury*, v. 33, no. 196, pp. 383–390, February 1936. [Reviews of William Empson, Ronald Bottrall, Dylan Thomas and Archibald MacLeish.]

EC142 "Making Faces at the World," *Sunday Referee*, p. 12, 23 February 1936.

EC143 "Two Songs: Come, my Arabia . . .; My desert has a noble sun for heart," *Caravel* [Majorca], no. 5, p. [8], March 1936.

EC144 "Mustard and Cress," *Sunday Referee*, p. 2, 19 April 1936.

EC145 "(Dis)pleasures of Bickering," *Good Housekeeping*, v. 29, no. 3, pp. 24–25, 131, May 1936.

EC146 "The Late Miss Sitwell (Auto-obituary III)," *The Listener*, 29 July 1936.

EC147 "A Head of Feather and a Heart of Lead," *Harper's Bazaar* [London], v. 14, no. 5, pp. 56, 70, August 1936.

EC148 "Quintessence," *Harper's Bazaar* [London], v. 15, no. 3, pp. 52–53, 112–113, December 1936.

EC149 "A New Poet: achievement of Mr. Dylan Thomas," *Sunday Times*, no. 5927, p. 9, 15 November 1936. [Review of *Twenty-Five Poems*.]

EC150 "H. G. Wells," *Sunday Referee*, p. 12, 27 December 1936.

EC151 "That English Eccentric, Edith Sitwell," *Sunday Referee*, p. 14, 3 January 1937.

EC152 "I Like to wear Dramatic Clothes," *Daily Express*, no. 11693, p. 15, 8 November 1937.

EC153 "Precious Stones and Metals," *Harper's Bazaar* [London], v. 19, no. 5, pp. 68–69, 82, February 1939.

EC154 [Review], *Life and Letters To-day*, v. 23, no. 27, pp. 239–241, November 1939. [Review of *The Turning Path* by Ronald Bottrall.]

EC155 "On a Night of Full Moon," *Harper's Bazaar* [New York], no. 2734, pp. 84, 139, 1 March 1940. [The same as EC153.]

EC156 "Lullaby," *Times Literary Supplement*, Spring books supplement, p. i, 16 March 1940.

EC157 "Any Man to Any Woman," *Life and Letters To-Day*, v. 25, no. 32, pp. 35–36, April 1940.

EC158 [Review], *Life and Letters To-Day*, v. 27, no. 38, pp. 57–59, October 1940. [Review of *A.B.C.'s* by Charles Henri Ford.]

EC159 "Song: We are the rootless flowers in the air," *Life and Letters To-Day*, v. 27, no. 39, p. 128, November 1940.

EC160 "Street Song," "The Youth with the Red-Gold Hair," "Ragged Serenade: Beggar to Shadow," *Life and Letters To-Day*, v. 28, no. 41, pp. 48–51, January 1941.

EC161 "Poor Young Simpleton," "Song: Once my heart was a summer rose," *Life and Letters To-Day*, v. 30, no. 49, pp. 198–202, September 1941.

EC162 "Still Falls the Rain," *Times Literary Supplement*, p. 427, 6 September 1941.

EC163 "Any Man to Any Woman," *Vice Versa*, v. 1, nos. 3–5, p. 41, January 1942.

EC164 "Bread of Angels," *Times Literary Supplement*, p. 177, 4 April 1942.

EC165 "The Poet's Sister," *Spectator*, v. 168, p. 445, 8 May 1942. [Review of *Journals* of Dorothy Wordsworth.]

EC166 "Some Notes on Poetry," *Tribune*, no. 303, p. 18, 16 October 1942.

EC167 "A Mother to her Dead Child," *Times Literary Supplement*, p. 526, 24 October 1942.

EC168 "Green Song," *Life and Letters To-Day*, v. 35, no. 64, pp. 132–135, December 1942.

EC169 "Notes on Shakespeare," *View*, 3rd series, no. 1, pp. 16–18, 36, April 1943.

EC170 "Anne Boleyn's Song," *Times Literary Supplement*, p. 200, 24 April 1943.

EC171 "A Sleepy Tune," *Adam*, year XVI, no. 182, pp. 1–2, May 1943.

EC172 "Heart and Mind," *Times Literary Supplement*, p. 298, 19 June 1943.

EC173 "Lecture on Poetry since 1920," *Life and Letters To-Day*, v. 39, no. 75, pp. 70–97, November 1943.

EC174 "Invocation," *New Writing and Daylight*, pp. 7–9, Winter 1943–44.

EC175 "O Bitter Love, O Death," *Times Literary Supplement*, p. 32, 15 January 1944.

EC176 "Lo, this is she that was the world's desire," *Life and Letters To-Day*, v. 40, no. 79, pp. 133–135, March 1944.

EC177 "Holiday," *Times Literary Supplement*, p. 176, 8 April 1944.

EC178 "Why not Like Poetry?," *Woman's Journal*, v. 34, no. 200, pp. 10–11, 56, June 1944.

EC179 "Heart and Mind," *Atlantic Monthly*, v. 174, no. 1, p. 61, July 1944.

EC180 "The Poetry of Demetrios Capetanakis," *New Writing and Daylight*, pp. 44–50, Autumn 1944.

EC181 "Girl and Butterfly," *Penguin New Writing* 20, pp. 93–96, 1944.

EC182 "A Song at Morning," *Horizon*, v. 10, no. 60, p. 372, December 1944.

EC183 [Review], *Horizon*, v. 11, no. 61, pp. 70–73, January 1945. [Review of *Noblesse Oblige* by James Agate.]

EC184 "Fanfare for Elizabeth," *Harper's Bazaar* [New York], no. 2803, p. 30, July 1945.

EC185 "From 'Fanfare for Elizabeth,'" *Life and Letters To-Day*, v. 46, pp. 13–27, 98–107, 152–166; v. 47, pp. 6–17; July, August, September, October 1945.

EC186 "Eurydice," *Horizon*, v. 12, no. 68, pp. 77–80, August 1945.

EC187 "The Two Loves," *New Writing and Daylight*, pp. 15–17, 1945.

EC188 "Some Notes on 'King Lear,'" *New Writing and Daylight*, pp. 77–89, 1945.

EC189 "The Poet Laments the Coming of Old Age," *Orion* [*I*], pp. 28–29, 1945.

EC190 "A Song of the Cold," *Penguin New Writing* 23, pp. 52–56, 1945.

EC191 "A Sleepy Tune," *View*, series V, no. 6, pp. 4–5, January 1946.

EC192 "Some Notes on Shakespeare," *View*, series V, no. 6, pp. 8–9, January 1946.

EC193 "Some Notes on Shakespeare," *View*, v. 6, no. 3, pp. 15, 25, May 1946.

EC194 "Mary Stuart to James Bothwell: casket letter no. 2," *Penguin New Writing* 27, pp. 22–23, Spring 1946.

EC195 "A Note on 'Measure for Measure,'" *The Nineteenth Century*, v. 140, no. 835, pp. 131–135, September 1946.

EC196 "Notes from a Poet's Notebook," *View*, [v. 6, no. 6], pp. 24–26, Fall [October] 1946.

EC197 "'Iago,'" *New Writing and Daylight*, pp. 141–151, 1946.

EC198 "Early Spring," *Orion III*, pp. 59–61, 1946.

EC199 "A Simpleton," *Horizon*, v. 16, no. 90, p. 6, July 1947.

EC200 "Hymn to Venus (from 'A Canticle of the Rose')," *Poetry London*, v. 3, no. 11, pp. 31–34, September–October 1947.

EC201 "Comment on Dylan Thomas," *The Critic*, v. 1, no. 2, pp. 17–18, Autumn 1947.

EC202 "William Blake," *Spectator*, p. 466, 10 October 1947. [Review of *Fearful Symmetry* by Northrop Frye and *Selected Poems* edited by Denis Saurat.]

EC203 "Dirge for the New Sunrise," *Orion IV*, pp. 26–27, 1947.

EC204 "The Bee-Keeper," *Penguin New Writing* 32, pp. 25–27, 1947.

EC205 "The Coat of Fire," *Horizon*, v. 17, no. 100, pp. 236–238, April 1948.

EC206 "Of the Clowns and Fools of Shakespeare," *Life and Letters To-Day*, v. 57, no. 129, pp. 102–109, May 1948.

EC207 "Chain-Gang: penal settlement," *Sunday Times*, no. 6534, p. 3, 4 July 1948.

EC208 "A Note on Hamlet," *Tribune*, no. 611, pp. 23–24, 25 September 1948.

EC209 "A Simpleton," *Harper's Bazaar* [New York], no. 2842, p. 200, October 1948.

EC210 "Poetry of Miss Bowes-Lyon," *New Statesman and Nation*, v. 36, p. 306, 9 October 1948.

EC211 "Song: Now that fate is dead and gone," *Orpheus I*, pp. 27–28, 1948.

EC212 "Some Notes on the Making of a Poem," *Orpheus I*, pp. 69–75, 1948.

EC213 "The Canticle of the Rose," *Wake*, no. 7, pp. 23–25, 1948.

EC214 "Dirge for the New Sunrise," "The Bee-Keeper," "Early Spring," *Quarterly Review of Literature*, v. 4, no. 3, pp. 231–237, 1948.

EC215 "The Song of Dido," *Botteghe Oscure*, quaderno II, p. 268, 1948.

EC216 "Villa's Poetry," *The Literary Apprentice* [Manila], pp. 64–66, 1948–1949.

EC217 "Out of School," *Atlantic Monthly*, v. 183, no. 6, pp. 37–38, June 1949.

EC218 "Out of School," *Horizon*, v. 20, no. 116, pp. 77–80, August 1949.

EC219 "On My Poetry," *Orpheus II*, pp. 103–119, 1949.

EC220 "Medusa's Love Song," *Penguin New Writing* 38, pp. 9–11, 1949.

EC221 "A Vindication of Pope," *Sunday Times*, no. 6598, p. 3, 2 October 1949. [Review of *New Light on Pope* by Norman Ault.]

EC222 "Street Acrobat," *Arena*, no. 1, pp. 4–6, [Autumn 1949].

EC223 "Macbeth," *Atlantic Monthly*, v. 185, no. 4, pp. 43–48, April 1950.

EC224 "King Lear," *Atlantic Monthly*, v. 185, no. 5, pp. 57–62, May 1950.

EC225 "A Song of the Dust," *Penguin New Writing* 40, pp. 9–12, 1950.

EC226 "Whitman and Blake," *Proceedings of the American Academy of Arts and Letters and the National Institute of Arts and Letters*, 2nd series, no. 1, pp. 52–58, 1951.

EC227 "Gardeners and Astronomers," *Times Literary Supplement*, special supplement: The mind of 1951, p. iii, 24 August 1951.

EC228 "Prometheus' Love Song," *The Listener*, v. 47, no. 1216, 19 June 1952.

EC229 "Bagatelle," *The Listener*, v. 48, no. 1232, p. 586, 9 October 1952.

EC230 "Two Songs," *Atlantic Monthly*, v. 191, no. 2, p. 46, February 1953.

EC231 "The April Rain," *Atlantic Monthly*, v. 191, no. 4, p. 53, April 1953.

EC232 "The April Rain," *Times Literary Supplement*, no. 2672, p. 246, 17 April 1953.

EC233 "From 'The Road to Thebes': II: Interlude; III: The Night Wind," *New World Writing* 3, pp. 170–173, May 1953.

EC234 "The Love of Man, the Praise of God," *New York Herald-Tribune Book Review*, section 6, pp. 1, 14, 10 May 1953. [Review of *Collected Poems* of Dylan Thomas.]

EC235 "Sailor, What of the Isles?," *The Listener*, v. 49, no. 1258, p. 607, 9 April 1953.

EC236 "Sailor, What of the Isles?," *Atlantic Monthly*, v. 191, no. 6, p. 53, June 1953.

EC237 "The Queen of Scotland's Reply to a Reproof from John Knox," *New Statesman and Nation*, v. 45, no. 1163, p. 738, 20 June 1953.

EC238 "The Road to Thebes [I]," *Atlantic Monthly*, v. 192, no. 1, pp. 48–50, July 1953.

EC239 "Two Songs: A Mi-Voix; An Old Song Re-sung," *Encounter*, v. 1, no. 1, pp. 34–35, October 1953.

EC240 [A Telegram], *Adam*, year XXI, no. 238, p. ii, 1953.

EC241 "Dylan Thomas," *Atlantic Monthly*, v. 193, no. 2, pp. 42–45, February 1954.

EC242 "Down among the Glamour Girls," *Sunday Graphic*, no. 2037, p. 4, 25 April 1954.

EC243 "A Young Girl's Song," *London Magazine*, v. 1, no. 4, pp. 13–14, May 1954.

EC244 "The Rising Generation," *Times Literary Supplement*, special supplement: American Writing To-Day, p. i, 17 September 1954.

EC245 "Fruits and Flowers on a Poet's Vine," *The Saturday Review*, v. 38, no. 25, p. 19, 18 June 1955. [Review of *Selected Poems* of Roy Campbell.]

EC246 "A Tidy, Natural Taste," *The Saturday Review*, v. 38, no. 28, p. 14, 9 July 1955. [Review of *Birthdays from the Ocean* by Isabella Gardner.]

EC247 "Of what Use is Poetry?," *The Reader's Digest* [New York], pp. 101–104, August 1955. [Re-published in the following editions of the journal: English–Canadian (August 1955),

Australian, British (both September 1955), German, Portuguese (both October 1955), Spanish (November 1955), Finnish, French-Canadian (both March 1956).]

EC248 "Elegy for Dylan Thomas," *Poetry*, v. 87, no. 2, pp. 63–67, November 1955.

EC249 "Why I Look the Way I Do," *Sunday Graphic*, no. 2117, p. 6, 4 December 1955.

EC250 "The Last Days of Queen Mary the First," *Vogue* [London], v. 112, no. 2, pp. 82–83, 145, February 1956.

EC251 "In Praise of Jean Cocteau," *London Magazine*, v. 3, no. 2, pp. 13–15, February 1956.

EC252 "Dylan Thomas: tragic American visits," *Sunday Times*, no. 6936, p. 5, 22 April 1956. [Review of *Dylan Thomas in America* by John Malcolm Brinnin.]

EC253 "Sweet-Brier Leaves," *Sunday Times*, no. 6977, p. 7, 3 February 1957. [Review of *The Player's Boy* by Bryher.]

EC254 "What is Genius?," *Everybody's*, p. 31, 2 March 1957.

EC255 "Coming to London," *London Magazine*, v. 4, no. 4, pp. 39–44, April 1957. [No. 14 of a series by various writers.]

EC256 "Poets of Delight: Gordon Bottomley and Ralph Hodgson," *Sunday Times*, no. 6990, p. 4, 5 May 1957. [Great Writers Rediscovered Series, 5.]

EC257 "The Priest and the Plague," *Sunday Times*, no. 6996, p. 6, 16 June 1957. [Review of *Henry Morse* by Philip Caraman.]

EC258 "The Progress of a Poet," *Sunday Times*, no. 7008, p. 8, 8 September 1957. [A recorded interview.]

EC259 "The War Orphans," *Atlantic Monthly*, v. 200, no. 5, p. 78, November 1957.

EC260 "Roy Campbell," *Poetry*, v. 92, no. 1, pp. 42–48, April 1958.

EC261 "His Blood colours my cheek," *The Month*, new series, v. 19, no. 5, pp. 261–262, May 1958.

EC262 "Better Bye and Bye," *Sunday Times*, no. 7050, p. 7, 29 June 1958. [Review of *The Shaping Spirit* by A. Alvarez.]

EC263 "The Death of a Giant," *London Magazine*, v. 5, no. 11, pp. 11–12, November 1958.

EC263*A* "The Poet's Vision (Adventures of the Mind, 14)," *Saturday Evening Post*, pp. 29 and 126–128 and 130, 15 November 1958.

EC264 "Preface to Ezra Pound," *The Yale Literary Magazine*, v. 126, no. 5, pp. 42–44, December 1958. [Partly from *Atlantic Book of British and American Poetry*, 1958.]

EC265 "La Bella Bona Roba," *The Listener*, v. 61, no. 1553, p. 14, 1 January 1959. [Reprinted in *The Guinness Book of Poetry 1958/59* (Putnam, 1960) and in *New Poems 1960* (Hutchinson, 1960).]

EC266 "The Yellow Girl," *The Listener*, v. 61, no. 1557, p. 207, 29 January 1959. [Reprinted in *New Poems 1960*.]

EC267 "At the Cross-Roads," *London Magazine*, v. 6, no. 3, pp. 11–12, March 1959.

EC268 "Of Wrath and Writers," *Lilliput*, v. 45, no. 5, pp. 41–42, November 1959.

EC269 "Praise We Great Men," *The Listener*, v. 61, no. 1577, p. 1058, 18 June 1959; and *Atlantic Monthly*, v. 204, no. 5, p. 97, November 1959. (Poem read by the author at the Royal Festival Hall, 10 June 1959.)

EC269A "Sadist at Large," *Sunday Times*, no. 7137, p. 18, 28 February 1960. [Review of *Ritual in the Dark* by Colin Wilson.]

EC270 "Choric Song," *The Listener*, v. 63, no. 1618, p. 576, 31 March 1960.

EC271 "A Visit to Lawrence. (Personal Encounters, 1)," *The Observer*, p. 25, 13 November 1960.

EC272 "Dylan the Impeccable. (Personal Encounters, 2)," *The Observer*, p. 24, 20 November 1960.

EC273 "Hazards of Sitting for my Portrait. (Personal Encounters, 3)," *The Observer*, p. 24, 27 November 1960.

EC273A "Prothalamium," *Yorkshire Post*, no. 35472, wedding supplement, p. 1, 8 June 1961.

EC274 "Pride. (The Seven Deadly Sins, no. 2)," *Sunday Times*, no. 7231, p. 19, 17 December 1961. [Reprinted in *The Seven Deadly Sins*, Sunday Times, 1962.]

EC275 "A Girl's Song in Winter," *Encounter*, v. 18, no. 1, p. 41, January 1962.

EC276 "The Two Cultures," *Spectator*, no. 6977, p. 331, 16 March 1962. [A note.]

EC277 "Young William Walton comes to Town," *Sunday Times*, no. 7244, p. 40, 18 March 1962.

EC278 "The Young Ones?," *Daily Express*, no. 19352, p. 5, 17 August 1962.

EC279 "The Yellow Girl," *Atlantic Monthly*, v. 210, no. 5, p. 64, November 1962.

EC280 "When I was Young and Uneasy," *Atlantic Monthly*, v. 215, pp. 159–165, March 1965.

EC281 "Our Childhood was Hell," *Sunday Times*, no. 7401, pp. 21–22, 21 March 1965.

EC282 "A Man with Red Hair," *Sunday Times*, no. 7402, pp. 22–23, 28 March 1965.

EC283 "Old Friends and Others," *Sunday Times*, no. 7403, p. 22, 4 April 1965.

EC284 "Cast of Characters: a Bloomsbury memoir," *The Reporter*, v. 32, no. 7, pp. 43–45, 8 April 1965.

EDITH SITWELL: BOOKS
ANNOUNCED BUT NOT
PUBLISHED (ED1–ED3)

ED1 "Sitwells' Omnibus." Announced: ". . . begins running early in October" in *At the House of Mrs. Kinfoot*, September 1921, and as appearing "shortly" in *Dr. Donne and Gargantua, Canto the First*, October 1921.

ED2 "Le Canard à Chaud." Announced as "in preparation" in *Troy Park*, 1925.

ED3 "William Blake, a selection, edited by Edith Sitwell." Announced as a forthcoming volume in the series, on wrappers of *The Chiltern Library*, published by Messrs. John Lehmann, ca. 1950.

EE1 *Poème: an Interview with Mars.* With a translation by Valéry Larbaud. Paris: *Commerce*, cahier VII, pp. 113–123, Printemps 1926.

EE1*A Le Pêcher* [*The Peach Tree*]. Translated by G. Lasselin. *Le Fantôme aux Lévres vivantes* [*The Ghost whose Lips were Warm*]. Translated by Pierre d'Exideuil and Félix W. Crosse. *Échanges*, no. 1, pp. 74–81, Décembre 1929.

EE1*B Poètes Modernes.* Translated by Marianne Lams. *Échanges*, no. 3, pp. 92–107, June 1930.

EE2 *Victoria, Drottning av England, Kejsarinna av India.* Translated by Hans Langlet. Stockholm: Hökerberg, 1936.

EE3 *Victoria von England.* Translated by C. F. W. Behl. Berlin: Wolfg. Krüger, 1937.

EE4 *La Reine Victoria.* Translated by Jean Talva. Paris: Gallimard, 1938.

EE5 *Le Cœur et l'Esprit; Chanson: O amer Amour, O Mort.* Translated by Erica Farrare. *Toujours tombe la Pluie.* Translated by M. Bofourie. Paris (Algiers): *Fontaine*, nos. 37–40, pp. 417–420 (561–564), 1944. [All reprinted in *Aspects de la Littérature anglaise (1918–1945)*, edited by Kathleen Raine and Max-Pol Fouchet; Paris: Fontaine, 1947.]

EE6 *Chanson Verte.* Translated by Marie Laure. Paris: Confluences, 1946.

EE7 *Las Mujeres Inglesas.* (Anonymous translation.) Buenos Aires: Espasa-Calpe, [1946].

EE8 *Fanfare für Elisabeth.* Translated by Margaret Rauchenberger. Köln: Schaffrath, 1947.

EE9 *Corazion y Pensamiento* [*Heart and Mind*]. Translated by Charles David Ley. *Acanto*, v. 3, pp. [10–11], Marzo 1947.

EE10 *El Coronel Fantock.* Translated by Silvina Ocampo. *Sur*, año XV, pp. 401–409, Julio–Octubre 1947.

EE11 *Canción Callejera [Street Song]*. Translated by Ricardo Baeza. *Sur*, año XV, pp. 411–413, Julio–Octubre 1947.

EE12 *Il Canto di Didone [Dido's Song]*. Translated by A. G. Roma. *Botteghe Oscure*, quaderno II, supplement, "Poeti Inglesi e Americani," p. 28, 1948.

EE13 *Fanfare for Elisabeth*. Translated by Per Lange. København: Gyldendal, 1949.

EE14 *La Regina Vittoria*. Translated by Margherita Santi Farina. Milano: Longanesi, 1949.

EE15 *Ich lebe unter einer schwarze Sonne*. Translated by Hilda Mentzel and Paulheinz Quack. Düsseldorf: Schwann, 1950.

EE16 *Fanfare pour Elizabeth*. Translated by Denise Van Moppès. Paris: Albin Michel, 1953.

EE17 *Sotto il Sole Nero*. Translated by Ferdinanda Invrea. Milano, Roma: Bompiani, 1954.

EE18 *Genshi Jidai No Sambusaku [Three Poems of the Atomic Age]*. Translated by Yônosuke Suzuki. Tokyo: Kokobun-sha, 1955.

EE19 *Fanfare za Elizabeta*. Translated by Dr. Josip Ritig. Zagreb: Kultura, 1955.

EE20 *Cae la Lluvia Aún [Still Falls the Rain]*. Translated by Esteban Pujals. *Nuestro Tiempo* (3rd year, no. 20), February 1956.

EE21 *Mroczny Spiew [Dark Song]*. In: *Antologia Liryki Angielskiej 1300–1950*. London: Veritas Foundation Publication Centre, 1958.

EE22 *Der Schatten des Kain*. Translated by Erich Fried. *Neue Rundschau*, v. 74, no. 4, pp. 551–557, 1963.

EE23 *Gedichte*. With German translations by Christian Enzensberger, Erich Fried, Werner Vordtriede. Frankfurt a.M.: Insel-Verlag, 1964.

EE24 *Poesie dell'era atomica [Three Poems of the Atomic Age]*. Translated by Lina Angioletti. Milan: Del Duca, 1964.

EE25 *Los Siete Pecados capitale [Pride]*. Translated by Marta I. Guastavino. Buenos Aires: Compañia general Fabril editora, 1964.

EE26 *Elizabeth Zensôkyoku [Fanfare for Elizabeth]*. Translated by Izumi Keiko. Tokyo: Bunshûdô, 1966.

EDITH SITWELL: MUSICAL SETTINGS
(EF1–EF14)

EF1 *Façade*, by William Walton (1922; see EA6, &c.).

EF2 *Daphne, Through Gilded Trellises, Old Sir Faulk*, by William Walton, being his "Three Songs" (1932).

EF3 *The Sleeping Beauty, a masque*, by Leighton Lucas (1936).

EF4 *The King of China's Daughter*, by Arthur Duff, in "A Broadside," new series, no. 4 (Cuala Press, Dublin, 1937).

EF5 *The King of China's Daughter*, by Michael Head, in his "Five Songs" (1939).

EF6 *The Weeping Babe*, for soprano and unaccompanied chorus, by Michael Tippett (1945; see EA37).

EF7 *O Yet Forgive*, a song, by Elisabeth Lutyens.

EF8 *Gold Coast Customs*, for speakers, men's chorus and orchestra, by Humphrey Searle (1949).

EF9 *The Shadow of Cain*, for speakers, men's chorus and orchestra, by Humphrey Searle (1952).

EF10 *Still Falls the Rain*, by Benjamin Britten, being his "Canticle III" for tenor, horn and pianoforte (1956).

EF11 *The English Eccentrics*, opera by Malcolm Williamson. Libretto by Geoffrey Dunn, based on Edith Sitwell's book (1964).

EF12 *A Young Girl*, a song, by Malcolm Williamson (1964).

EF13 *The King of China's Daughter*, a song, by Arthur Veal (1965).

EF14 *The Canticle of the Rose*, for unaccompanied mixed chorus, by Humphrey Searle (1966).

EDITH SITWELL: RECORDINGS
(EG1–EG10)

EG1 *Façade*, recitation, with music by William Walton. (Recited by the author and Constant Lambert.) (Decca Records, AK 991–992.)

EG2 *Façade*, read by the author, with chamber orchestra conducted by Frederick Prausnitz. (Columbia Records [New York], sets ML 2047 and MM-829, released 2 May and 9 May 1949.)

EG3 "Still Falls the Rain," "Heart and Mind," "The Bee-Keeper," read by the author. (Harvard Vocarium Records P-1210, P-1211 [H.F.S.I. 281, 283], recorded for non-commercial distribution in 1950.)

EG4 Excerpts from *A Poet's Notebook* and *The Canticle of the Rose*, read by the author. ("Columbia Literary Series," set DSL-190, DSL-190E, released 5 October 1953, by Columbia Records in New York.)

EG5 *Façade*, recited by the author and Peter Pears, with the English Opera Group Ensemble, conducted by Anthony Collins. (Decca Records, set LXT 2977, released October 1954; issued in the U.S.A. by London Records.)

EG6 "Dirge for the New Sunrise," "The Canticle of the Rose," "Harvest," "The Peach Tree," "A Bird's Song," "Song: Once my Heart was a Summer Rose," "Gardeners and Astronomers," "A Song at Morning," "Said King Pompey," "Green Flows the River of Lethe-O," "The Coat of Fire," "Green Song," read by the author. (Library of Congress, Washington, D.C.; recorded 31 March 1955, but not hitherto issued.)

EG7 "Edith Sitwell reading her own Poems." ("The Wind's Bastinado," "Trio for Two Cats and a Trombone," "Said King Pompey," "Spinning Song," "Green Flows the River of Lethe-O," "Serenade: Any man to any woman," "Tattered Serenade," "Street Song," "An Old Woman," "The Youth with the Red-Gold Hair," "A Sylph's Song," "Most Lovely Shade," "The Queen of Scotland's Reply to a Reproof from John Knox,"

"Who shall have my Fair Lady," "The Bee-Keeper," "Dido's Song," "The Canticle of the Rose," "Gardeners and Astronomers," "Sailor, What of the Isles?," "Song of Queen Anne Boleyn," "At Cockcrow," "Song: Where is all the Bright Company gone?".) (Caedmon Publishers, New York; record TC 1016, issued August 1955.)

EG8 "Still Falls the Rain," read by the author. (Caedmon Publishers, "Caedmon Treasury of Modern Poets," TC 2006, issued late Fall 1956 in New York and March 1960 in London.)

EG9 "Most Lovely Shade," "Scotch Rhapsody," "When Sir Beelzebub," read by the author. (Jupiter Recordings, London, "Jupiter Anthology of 20th Century Poetry, part I," JUR–OOA1, issued September 1958.)

EG10 "Lullaby," "Dirge for the New Sunrise," "Heart and Mind," "Scotch Rhapsody," read by the author. (Jupiter Recordings, JEP OOC 1, issued December 1959.)

SIR OSBERT SITWELL, Bt.

BOOKS WRITTEN BY OSBERT SITWELL
(OA1–OA58)

OA1   TWENTIETH CENTURY   1916
              HARLEQUINADE

[*For description, see* EA2]

CONTENTS (BY OSBERT SITWELL)

Therefore is the Name of it called Babel [as "Babel" in *The Times*, 11
May 1916]—Twentieth Century Harlequinade—The Lament of the
Mole-Catcher

OA2   THE WINSTONBURG LINE   1919

First edition

[*On a drawing*]

THE | WINSTONBURG | LINE | 3 SATIRES | BY OSBERT |
SITWELL | [*heavy double rule at foot of drawing*] | LONDON
HENDERSONS 66 CHARING CROSS ROAD

218 × 172 mm.

20 pp.: [1] half-title; [2] acknowledgments; [3] title; [4] blank; 5–19
text; [20] advertisements.

Orange paper wrappers, sewn. Untrimmed edges. Printed in black
on upper and lower covers.

Printed by Strangeways, printers, London. Published in September
1919 at 6*d*.

CONTENTS

A Certain Statesman [from *Daily Herald*, 22 July 1919]—More about
Morale [from *Daily Herald*, 28 July 1919]—The Governess of Europe
[from *The Nation*, 5 July 1919]

a. *First edition*

Argonaut and | Juggernaut | BY | OSBERT SITWELL | LONDON | Chatto & Windus | 1919

183 × 127 mm.

136 pp.: [i] half-title; [ii] blank; [iii] title; [iv] "All rights reserved"; [v] dedication; [vi] acknowledgments; [vii], viii–ix prefatory poem; [x] blank; [xi]–xii Contents; [1–3], 4–123 text; [124] "Printed by Billing and Sons, Ltd., Guildford, England."

Grey cloth boards. Top edge grey, others untrimmed. White paper label, lettered in black, pasted on spine.

1000 copies printed. Published 30 October 1919 at 5s.

CONTENTS

How shall we rise to greet the dawn? [prefatory poem; as "Panorama" in *The Nation*, 16 November 1918]

Book I, The Phoenix-Feasters. Prelude [not as "Prelude" in *Wheels 1*] —The Silence of God—Adventure—Dusk—Sailor-Song—The Dance—Why Should a Sailor Ride the Sea?—Cornucopia—Song: Our Hidden Voices—Prospect Road [from *Wheels 2*]

Book II, Green-Fly. War-Horses—Church-Parade [from *Art and Letters*, Winter 1918–19]—At the House of Mrs. Kinfoot—Green-Fly—De Luxe (1. Hymn, 2. Nursery Rhyme [from *The Monthly Chapbook*, July 1919])

Book III, Promenades. Nocturne [as "Prelude" in *Wheels 1*]—The Lament of the Mole-Catcher [from *Twentieth Century Harlequinade*] —The Beginning [revised from *Wheels 1*]—The End [revised from *Wheels 1*]—Fountains [revised from *Wheels 2*]—Song of the Fauns [from *Wheels 3*]—A Sculptor's Cruelty [from *Colour*, May 1918]—Pierrot Old [from *Wheels 1*]—Night [from *Wheels 1*]— From Carcassonne—Progress [from *Wheels 1*]—The Return of the Prodigal [from *Wheels 2*]—London Squares [from *Wheels 3*]— Tears [from *Wheels 1*]—Clavichords [from *Wheels 3*]—Promenades [from *Wheels 2*]—Clown Pondi—Lausiac Theme [from *Art and Letters*, Spring 1919]—Metamorphosis [from *Wheels 3*]— The Gipsy Queen [from *Wheels 2*]—Black Mass [revised from *Wheels 1*]—Pierrot at the War [revised from *New Paths 1917–1918*] —Spring Hours [from *Cambridge Magazine*, 3 May 1919]

Book IV, War Poems. Therefore is the Name of it called Babel [from *Twentieth Century Harlequinade*]—Twentieth Century Harlequinade [from *Twentieth Century Harlequinade*]—This Generation [from *Wheels 3*]—Sheep-Song [from *The Nation*, 12 October 1918]—The Poet's Lament—Judas and the Profiteer [from *Cambridge Magazine*, 14 December 1918]—Rhapsode [from *The Nation*, 27 October 1917]—The Modern Abraham [from *The Nation*, 2 February 1918]—The Trap [from *The Nation*, 11 May 1918]—The Eternal Club [from *The Nation*, 10 August 1918]—Heaven—The Blind Pedlar—World-Hymn to Moloch—Armchair [revised from *Wheels 2*]—Ragtime [from *Wheels 2*]—Peace Celebration—The Next War [from *The Nation*, 21 September 1918]

b. *First edition, American issue*

Argonaut and | Juggernaut | by | Osbert Sitwell | [*device*] | New York | Alfred · A · Knopf | 1920

Note: This issue, printed in America, was published in 1920, but the publishers no longer have any details of publication. Bound in green cloth boards, linen spine; device blind-stamped on upper cover, spine lettered in green. The contents are as in 0A3a.

0A4   AT THE HOUSE OF   1921
                    MRS. KINFOOT

At the House of | *Mrs. Kinfoot* | *Consisting of Four Satires* | *BY* | *Osbert Sitwell* | *With Two Drawings by* | *WILLIAM ROBERTS* | *THE FAVIL PRESS* | *Kensington* | 1921

182 × 126 mm.

16 pp.: [1] half-title; [2] dedication; [3] title; [4] Contents; [5], 6–14 text; [15] "This Edition, which is privately printed, is limited to 101 Copies, of which 25 Copies are reserved by the Author. This Copy is No. ...." [in ink, with author's autograph signature], advertisements; [16] "Printed by Philip Sainsbury & Charles Birnstingl at The Favil Press, Peel Street, Kensington. September, MCMXXJ" [device].

Two designs by William Roberts printed in black, repeated on both end-papers.

Blue marbled paper wrappers. Untrimmed edges. White paper label, lettered in black, pasted on upper cover.

101 stated copies printed (76 for sale). Privately published in September 1921. (Five extra unnumbered copies printed for printer's file and copyright purposes.)

CONTENTS

At the Foot of the Ladder [revised from "At the House of Mrs. Kinfoot" in *Argonaut and Juggernaut*]—Malgré Soi [as "Malgré Lui" in *Wheels 5*]—P.S.—Paradise Regained.

oA5   WHO KILLED COCK-ROBIN?   1921

First edition

Who Killed Cock-Robin? | Remarks on Poetry, on its criticism, | and, as a sad warning, the story of | EUNUCH ARDEN. | BY OSBERT SITWELL. | LONDON: C. W. DANIEL, LTD. | Graham House, Tudor Street, E.C.4 | 1921.

16 leaves, in two gatherings, unsigned. 208 × 141 mm.

32 pp.: [1] title; [2] "In preparation . . ."; [3] Contents; [4] quotations; 5–32 text. (Erratum slip pasted to bottom of p. 26; and either on p. 32 or on the verso of the free back end-paper is a printer's stamp: "H. Howes & Co. Ltd. Printers. 62A, Southwark St., London, S.E.")

Yellow paper wrapper printed in red and black on upper cover pasted to spine, but loose over boards. Trimmed edges.

Published in December 1921, at 2s. (Later issues have the wrapper pasted down on boards, and are trimmed flush to 188 × 137 mm.; some lack the printer's stamp at the back. Publisher's records destroyed in 1941.)

oA6   OUT OF THE FLAME   1923

a. *First edition*

OUT OF THE FLAME | BY | OSBERT SITWELL | LONDON | GRANT RICHARDS LTD. | 1923

211 × 141 mm.

96 pp.: [1] half-title; [2] "By the same author . . ."; [3] title; [4] "Printed in Great Britain at The Mayflower Press, Plymouth. William Brendon & Son, Ltd.,"; 5–6 Contents, acknowledgments; [7–8], 9–95 text; [96] blank.

Frontispiece tipped in (photograph of Frank Dobson's bust of the author).

Smooth green cloth boards. Trimmed edges. Orange paper label, lettered in black, pasted on spine.

Published in June 1923 at 6s. (Printers' records lost in the war 1939–45.)

CONTENTS

BOOK I: OUT OF THE FLAME—

Two Mexican Pieces. 1. Song: How jolly are the dwarfs [revised from *Wheels 6*]—2. Maxixe [from "Matchiche" in *Wheels 6*]

Out of the Flame [last 46 lines as "Orpheus" in *The Nation*, 24 March 1923; also includes "Alone" from *Spectator*, 23 June 1923]

Two Dances. 1. Country Dance [from *Weekly Westminster Gazette*, 3 March 1923]—2. Fox-Trot: When Solomon met the Queen of Sheba [from *Form*, January 1922]

Two Garden Pieces. 1. Neptune in Chains [as "Le Notre" in *Spectator*, 23 April 1921]—2. Fountains [from *Spectator*, 16 July 1921—not as "Fountains" in *Argonaut and Juggernaut*]

Parade [revised from *Spectator*, 27 August 1921]—English Gothic [revised from *Wheels 4*]—The Backward Child [from *English Review*, April 1922]—Nursery Rhyme: The Rocking Horse [from *Saturday Westminster Gazette*, 4 September 1920]

Two Mythological Poems. 1. The Jealous Goddess [from *Spectator*, 14 January 1922]—2. Bacchanalia [from *Saturday Westminster Gazette*, 12 November 1921]

BOOK II: SING PRAISES: SATIRES—

Explanation: Subtlety of the Serpent

De Luxe. 1. Mrs. Freudenthal consults the Witch of Endor [8 lines omitted from *Wheels 5* version]—2. Night Thoughts [the 8 lines from above]—3. The War-Horse Chants—4. A Touch of Nature—5. Youth at the Prow, and Pleasure at the Helm—6. The Manner—7. The Open Door—8. Introducing—9. Malgré Soi [revised from *At the House of Mrs. Kinfoot*]—10. Paradise Regained [from *At the House of Mrs. Kinfoot*]

Five Portraits and a Group. 1. The General's Wife Refuses [revised from "Song of a General's Wife" in *The Apple*, January 1920]— 2. Aux Bords de la Mer [from *The Nation*, 29 October 1921]—3. Giardino Pubblico [from *The Nation*, 17 September 1921]—4. Ultimate Judgment [from *The Nation*, 28 August 1920]—5. An Old-Fashioned Sportsman—[6]. The Group: English Tea-Rooms

Sunday Afternoon [revised from *Art and Letters*, Winter 1920]— Corpse Day [from *Wheels 4*]

b. *First edition, American copies*

OUT OF THE FLAME | BY | OSBERT SITWELL | NEW [*device*] YORK | GEORGE H. DORAN COMPANY

Note: "260/520 copies" (according to the publishers' ledger) were imported, with a cancel title. Bound in brown paper boards, maroon cloth spine, orange labels on spine and upper cover. Published 24 April 1925. The contents are as in 0A6a.

oA7   TRIPLE FUGUE   1924

a. *First edition*

[*Type-ornaments between two rules*] | TRIPLE FUGUE | *By* | OSBERT SITWELL | [*two rules*] | LONDON | GRANT RICHARDS LIMITED | ST MARTIN'S STREET | [*type-ornaments between two rules*]

187 × 124 mm.

328 pp.: [1] half-title; [2] blank; [3] title; [4] "Printed in Great Britain by The Riverside Press Limited, Edinburgh. 1924"; 5 Preface; [6] blank; 7 Contents; [8] blank; [9] quotation; [10] blank; [11–12], 13–310, [311] text; [312] blank; [313–314], 315–327 "Appendix, some press opinions"; [328] blank.

Black cloth spine, orange patterned paper boards. Top edge black, others trimmed. Orange paper label, lettered in black, pasted on spine.

Published 16 June 1924 at 7s. 6d. (See G. F. Sims (Rare Books) Catalogue 46 [1960], item 572.) (Printers' records do not survive.)

Low Tide—Friendship's Due—The Greeting—His Ship comes Home—The Machine Breaks Down [from *English Review*, December 1922]—Triple Fugue—Appendix: some press opinions

b. *First edition, American issue*

[*Type-ornaments between two rules*] | TRIPLE FUGUE | *By* | OSBERT SITWELL | [*two rules*] | NEW [*device*] YORK | GEORGE H. DORAN COMPANY | [*type-ornaments between two rules*]

Note: This issue, printed in America, was published 20 February 1925 at $2.50. Bound in blue cloth boards, gilt lettered on spine and upper cover. The contents are the same as in the first edition, except that the "Appendix" is omitted—though included in the list of contents.

oA8　　　　DISCURSIONS　　　　1925

a. *First edition*

DISCURSIONS | ON | TRAVEL, ART AND LIFE | BY | OSBERT SITWELL | [*ornament*] | LONDON | GRANT RICHARDS LTD. | ST. MARTIN'S STREET | MDCCCCXXV

222 × 141 mm.

312 pp.: [1] half-title and dedication; [2] "By Osbert Sitwell . . ."; [3] title; [4] "Printed in Great Britain by The Riverside Press Limited, Edinburgh"; 5 Preface; [6] blank; 7 Contents; [8] blank; 9–10 List of illustrations; [11–12], 13–310 text; [311–312] blank.

Twenty-one plates tipped in singly.

Smooth orange cloth boards. Top edge gilt, fore edge trimmed, tail edge untrimmed. Gilt stamped on spine and upper cover.

Published in April 1925 at 15s. (Printers' records do not survive.)

CONTENTS

Includes the following periodical publications, all revised: "Lecce," from *The Nation*, 27 May–3 June 1922—"Puglia," from *The Nation*,

9–16 September 1922—"La Certosa di Padula," from *Weekly West-minster Gazette*, 5–12 August 1922—"Catania," from *The Chapbook*, 39, 1924—"A German Eighteenth Century Town," from *The Criterion*, July 1924—"Fiume," from *The Nation*, 1 January 1921

b. *First edition, American copies*

DISCURSIONS | ON | TRAVEL, ART AND LIFE | BY | OSBERT SITWELL | [*ornament*] | NEW [*device*] YORK | GEORGE H. DORAN COMPANY

Note: An unknown number of copies, with two cancel leaves, was imported. Grey-green paper boards, dark green cloth spine, with two paper labels. Published 11 September 1925 at $6.00. The contents are as A8a.

0A9   POOR YOUNG PEOPLE   1925

[*For description, see* EA10]

CONTENTS (BY OSBERT SITWELL)

Long Winter, 12 Songs. The Sword and the Herb—New Magic—"Then are the Woods so Empty"—"Perhaps–when the Owl at Night . . ?"—Superstition—And Science—Winter the Huntsman—Danse Macabre—Out in the Garden—The Fledgeling—"Which is the Triton true?"—The Gardener

0A10 BEFORE THE BOMBARDMENT 1926

a. *First edition*

BEFORE THE | BOMBARDMENT | BY | OSBERT SITWELL | AUTHOR OF "DISCURSIONS," "TRIPLE FUGUE," | "OUT OF THE FLAME," "ARGONAUT AND JUGGERNAUT," ETC. | "Is it Winter the Huntsman | Who gallops through his iron glades, | Cracking his cruel whip | To the gathering shades?" | DUCKWORTH | 3 HENRIETTA STREET, LONDON, W.C. | 1926

186 × 123 mm.

320 pp.: [1] half-title; [2] blank; [3] title; [4] "All rights reserved . . .
Printed in Great Britain"; [5] dedication; [6] blank; 7 Contents; [8]
blank; 9–10 Preface; 11–320 text, and imprint: "Bristol: Burleigh Ltd.,
at the Burleigh Press."

Smooth orange cloth boards. Top edge blue, others untrimmed.
Lettered in blue on spine and upper cover.

3000 copies printed. Published 4 October 1926 at 7s. 6d.

b. *First edition,* American issue

Before the Bombardment | *By* | *Osbert Sitwell* | "Is it Winter
the Huntsman | Who gallops through his iron glades, |
Cracking his cruel whip | To the gathering shades?" | [*de-
vice*] | *NEW YORK* | GEORGE H. DORAN COMPANY

Note: This issue, printed in America, was published 29 October 1926
at $2.50. Smooth crimson cloth boards, lettered in black on the spine
and upper cover. The contents are as in the first edition.

OA11   WINTER THE HUNTSMAN   [1927]

First edition

THE NEW BROADSIDE | [*decoration in black, red and blue-
grey*] | WINTER THE HUNTSMAN | [*text: 20 lines*] | [*de-
coration in same colours*] | *The Poem by Decorations by* |
Osbert Sitwell Edward Bawden | THE POETRY BOOKSHOP |
38 GREAT RUSSELL STREET, LONDON | *Made and Printed
in England* | *No. 17* | *The Westminster Press*

Folio half-sheet. 434 × 194 mm.

British Museum copy received 9 February 1927. Published as No. 17
of "The New Broadside." (Printers' records do not survive.)

CONTENTS

First separate publication of the poem; text as in *Poor Young People*

a. *First edition, ordinary copies*

[*Within a double rule border*]

England Reclaimed | A Book of Eclogues | [*rule*] | By | Osbert Sitwell | [*two rules*] | Duckworth | 3 Henrietta Street, London | 1927

228 × 141 mm.

100 pp.: [1] half-title; [2] "By Osbert Sitwell . . ."; [3] title; [4] "First Published 1927. All Rights Reserved"; 5 preface; [6], 7–8 Dedication; 9–11 Introduction; [12] blank; 13–14 Contents; 15–99 text and appendix; [100] "Made and Printed in Great Britain by Hazell, Watson & Viney Ld., London and Aylesbury."

Smooth orange boards. Top edge trimmed, others untrimmed. Gilt lettered on spine.

1500 copies printed. Published 20 October 1927 at 7s. 6d.

CONTENTS

Dedication, to Edith

Introduction [first fifty lines as "When first the poets sung" in *Harper's Monthly Magazine*, July 1927]

Prologue

Tom—Mrs. Hague [from *Vogue*, early December 1926]—Five drawings of Mr. Hague. 1. In the park, 2. In the potting-shed, 3. In the hothouses, 4. The spell, 5. Discordant dawn

Mary-Anne [from *Vogue*, late April 1927]

Mr. and Mrs. Nutch. 1. Mrs. Nutch—2. Mr. Nutch [both from *Vogue*, late August 1926]—3. Mrs. Nutch, Mr. Noyes and Myself—4. Mrs. Nutch in her arm-chair

Moping Fred. 1. Moping Fred—2. In a nutshell—3. The survival of the fittest

Mr. and Mrs. Goodbeare. 1. Elegy for Mr. Goodbeare—2. A talk with Mr. Goodbeare—3. Mr. and Mrs. Goodbeare [from *Saturday Review of Literature*, 24 September 1927]—4. Mr. Goodbeare at work —5. Mr. Goodbeare's cottage

Mr. and Mrs. Southern. Mrs. Southern, 1. Mrs. Southern's enemy— 2. What she liked—3. Twilight [all from *New Republic*, 4 January

1928]—Mr. Samuel Southern, 1. Portrait of Mr. Southern through the ages—2. In the market garden—3. No flowers by request—4. Conquering white—5. Under the camellia tree

Phoebe Southern. 1. Phoebe Southern—2. Silver lances—3. After the flower show

Luke Kembley. 1. Luke Kembley—2. In September—3. And October

Mrs. Kembley. 1. "The Boulders"—2. Circles—3. Interior of "The Boulders"—4. Evening

Grand Finale: Symphony

b. *First edition, special copies*
[*Title as in ordinary copies.*]

238 × 154 mm.

100 pp.: as in ordinary copies, except p. [4]: "Of this edition of "England Reclaimed," on hand-made paper and signed by the author, 165 copies have been printed, of which 150 copies only are for sale throughout the world. No." [number and author's autograph signature]. "All Rights Reserved. Printed in Great Britain."

Buff buckram boards. Untrimmed edges. Gilt lettered on spine.

165 copies printed (150 for sale). Published 20 October 1937 at 25*s*.

CONTENTS

As in the ordinary copies

c. *First edition, American copies*
[*Within a rectangular border*]

England Reclaimed | A Book of Eclogues | [*rule*] | By | Osbert Sitwell | [*two rules*] | *Garden City New York* | DOUBLEDAY, DORAN & COMPANY, INC. | 1928

Note: 500/520 copies were imported, with two cancel leaves, and were bound in black cloth spine, green laid paper boards, with yellow and white paper labels. Published 27 February 1928 at $2.00. The contents are as in the ordinary copies of the first edition.

(Note that the book *England Reclaimed and Other Poems*, 1949, whose contents are dissimilar, is included later—see oA46.)

a. *First edition*

ALL AT SEA | A SOCIAL TRAGEDY | IN THREE ACTS | FOR FIRST-CLASS PASSENGERS ONLY | BY | Osbert and Sacheverell Sitwell | WITH A PREFACE ENTITLED | A FEW DAYS | IN AN AUTHOR'S LIFE | BY | Osbert Sitwell | DUCKWORTH | 3 HENRIETTA STREET, W.C. | 1927

220 × 142 mm.

200 pp.: [1] half-title; [2] blank; [3] title; [4] "All Rights Reserved"; [5] dedication; [6] blank; [7] "A Few Days in an Author's Life . . ."; [8] blank; 9–10 Contents; 11–106 text of *A Few Days in an Author's Life*; 107 Appendix; [108] blank; [109], 110–195 text of *All at Sea*; [196] blank; 197–199 Appendix, "Façade," by Ernest Newman; [200] "Made and Printed in Great Britain by Hazell, Watson & Viney Ld., London and Aylesbury."

Grained blue and white cloth boards. Top edge trimmed, others untrimmed. Lettered in white on spine.

1500 copies printed. Published 28 November 1927 at 8*s.* 6*d.*

CONTENTS

Preface: A Few Days in An Author's Life (by Osbert Sitwell)

All at Sea (by Osbert and Sacheverell Sitwell)

Appendix: "Façade" (by Ernest Newman)

Note: "First-Class Passengers Only" was performed at the Arts Theatre Club London, on 28 November 1927, with the parts of the Sitwells played by the Sitwells.

b. *First edition, American copies*

ALL AT SEA | A SOCIAL TRAGEDY | IN THREE ACTS | FOR FIRST-CLASS PASSENGERS ONLY | BY | Osbert and Sacheverell Sitwell | WITH A PREFACE ENTITLED | A FEW DAYS | IN AN AUTHOR'S LIFE | BY | Osbert Sitwell | GARDEN CITY, NEW YORK | DOUBLEDAY, DORAN & COMPANY, INC. | 1928

Note: 400 copies were imported, with a cancel title. Light blue cloth spine, marbled paper boards. Paper label pasted on spine. Published 11 May 1928 at $2.50. The contents are as in OA13a.

a. *First edition, ordinary copies*

[*Within a rule border*]

The People's Album | of London Statues | [*rule*] | *Described by* | Osbert Sitwell | *Drawn by* | Nina Hamnett | [*rule*] | Duckworth | 3 Henrietta Street, London | 1928

256 × 173 mm.

196 pp.: [1] half-title; [2] blank; [3] title; [4] "All rights reserved. Printed in Great Britain at The Westminster Press, 411A Harrow Road, London, W.9"; [5] dedications; [6] blank; 7 Contents; 8 quotation; 9–12 Foreword; 13–131 [with 64 unnumbered pages interpolated] text and drawings; [132] device, and printer's imprint repeated.

32 line drawings by Nina Hamnett interpolated on integral but unnumbered pages.

Grey cloth boards. Top and fore edges trimmed, tail edge untrimmed. Lettered in black on spine and upper cover.

1500 copies printed. Published in November 1928 at 12s. 6d.

b. *First edition, special copies*

[*Title as in ordinary copies*]

262 × 182 mm.

196 pp.: [1] half-title; [2] certificate pasted on to page: "This edition of "The People's Album of London Statues," printed on Arnold's unbleached hand-made paper by The Westminster Press, is limited to one hundred and sixteen copies signed by the author and the artist, of which one hundred copies only are for sale throughout the world. No. . . ." [number, and artist's and author's autograph signatures]. (Thence as in ordinary copies.)

32 drawings, as in ordinary copies.

Cream buckram boards. Top edge gilt, others untrimmed. Gilt lettered on spine.

116 copies printed (100 for sale). Published in November 1928 at 42s.

CONTENTS

As in ordinary copies

a. *First edition*

The Man Who Lost | Himself | by | Osbert Sitwell | Duck-worth | 3 Henrietta Street, London | 1929

188 × 128 mm.

296 pp.: [i] half-title; [ii] "By Osbert Sitwell . . ."; [iii] title; [iv] "All Rights Reserved"; [v] dedication; [vi] "Caution to readers"; [vii]–viii Preface; [1], 2–288 text and appendix, and imprint: "Printed at The Chapel River Press, Kingston, Surrey".

Black cloth spine, orange patterned paper boards. Top edge orange, others trimmed. Gilt lettered on spine.

5000 copies printed. Published 24 October 1929 at 7s. 6d.

b. *First edition, American issue*

[*Red*] *The Man* | *Who Lost Himself* | [*black*] by | OSBERT SITWELL | *Published in New York by* | [*red*] COWARD-MCCANN, INC. | [*black*] IN THE YEAR 1930

Note: This issue, printed in America, has 320 pages in unsigned gatherings of eights. Smooth pale blue cloth boards, top edge maroon, lettered in maroon on spine and upper cover. 3000 copies printed. Published 26 February 1930 at $2.50. The contents are as in 0A15a.

0A16   MISS MEW   1929

First edition

[*Blue*] MISS MEW | [*black*] BY OSBERT SITWELL | STAN-FORD DINGLEY | THE MILL HOUSE PRESS | 1929

249 × 154 mm.

36 pp.: [1–8] blank; [9] title; [10] blank; [11] "One hundred and one copies of this book have been printed, of which thirty-five copies are reserved for the author. This is number" [in ink, with author's autograph signature];* [12] blank; [13–29] text; [30] "Printed by Robert Gathorne-Hardy and Kyrle Leng at the Mill House Press"; [31] author's advertisement for portrait poems; [32–36] blank.

Green cloth spine,* floral patterned paper boards. Untrimmed edges. Gilt lettered up spine.

101 copies printed (63 for sale).* Published 5 November 1929 at 7s. 6d.

CONTENTS

Elegy—A Feather Tapestry—Miss-Mew-Ad-Vincula—Miss Mew's Epoch—Miss Mew's Song of Perpetual Motion—Miss Mew's Window-Box [all from *The Nation and Athenaeum*, 17 September 1927, except the penultimate, from the same journal, 1 October 1927]

* *Note:* Of the 101 copies 35 were reserved for the author, and in addition the first three were special copies for the author and the two printer-publishers. These have red morocco spines, and on page 11 is printed "This is ——— ——'s copy," etc., instead of the number.

0A17   DUMB-ANIMAL   1930

a. *First edition, ordinary copies*

DUMB-ANIMAL | AND | OTHER STORIES | by | OSBERT SITWELL | DUCKWORTH | 3 Henrietta Street, W.C. 2 | 1930

190 × 127 mm.

368 pp.: [i] half-title; [ii] "By Osbert Sitwell . . ."; [iii] title; [iv] "All Rights Reserved"; [v] dedication; [vi] note; [vii] Contents; [viii] blank; [1], 2–360 text and appendix, and imprint: "Printed at The Chapel River Press, Kingston, Surrey".

Route map of the Mediterranean tipped in.

Magenta cloth boards. Top edge dark blue, others untrimmed. Gilt lettered on spine.

5000 copies printed. Published 16 October 1930 at 7s. 6d.

CONTENTS

Dumb-Animal [from *The Fortnightly*, 1 February 1930]—That Flesh is Heir to—Echoes [from *The Fortnightly*, August 1930]—The Love-Bird [from *Life and Letters*, January 1930]—Charles and Charlemagne —Alive-Alive Oh! [from *Life and Letters*, June 1930]—Happy Endings [see note]†

† *Note on "Happy Endings":* The author was sued for libel in respect of this story, and in March 1931 the remaining 691 copies of "the English edition" were withdrawn by the publishers. Thereafter the story has not been published in England, though it was included in the American issue.

b. *First edition, special copies*

[*Title as in ordinary copies.*]

193 × 130 mm.

368 pp.: [i] half-title; [ii] "By Osbert Sitwell . . ."; [iii] title; [iv] "This Edition, numbered and signed by the author and with a portrait of the author by Albert Rutherston, is limited to 110 copies. No." [in ink, with author's autograph signature]. "All Rights Reserved." (Thence as in ordinary copies, above.)

Frontispiece by Albert Rutherston (with tissue guard), and route map of the Mediterranean, tipped in.

Red buckram boards. Top edge gilt, others untrimmed. Gilt lettered on spine.

110 copies printed. Published 16 October 1930 at 42s.

CONTENTS

As in ordinary copies

c. *First edition, American issue*

OSBERT SITWELL | [*broken rule*] | DUMB-ANIMAL | AND | OTHER STORIES | [*two broken rules*] | PHILADELPHIA 1931 | J. B. LIPPINCOTT COMPANY

Note: This issue, printed in America, has 320 pages in unsigned gatherings of eights. Pale blue cloth boards, lettered in pale and dark blue on spine and upper cover. Published in 1931 at $2.50 (copyright date 8 April 1931). The publishers no longer have details of publication. The contents are as in the first edition.

oA18   COLLECTED   1931
SATIRES AND POEMS

a. *First edition, ordinary copies*

THE COLLECTED SATIRES | AND POEMS | OF | OSBERT SITWELL | DUCKWORTH | 3 Henrietta Street, W.C.2 | 1931

221 × 148 mm.

304 pp.: [i] half-title; [ii] "By Osbert Sitwell . . ."; [iii] title; [iv] "All Rights Reserved. Printed at The Chapel River Press for Gerald

Duckworth & Company, Ltd., London"; [v] Preface; [vi] blank; [vii], viii–xii Contents; [1–3], 4–292 text and indexes.

Smooth black cloth boards. Trimmed edges. Gilt lettered on spine. 2500 copies printed. Published 2 June 1931 at 8s. 6d.

CONTENTS

BOOK I— SATIRES

Introduction: Subtlety of the Serpent [revised from *Out of the Flame*]

Poems of the Last and the Next War [all from *Argonaut and Juggernaut*, unless otherwise stated]. Prefatory poem: The poet's lament [revised]—"Therefore is the Name of it Called Babel"—Sheep-Song [revised]—Judas and the Profiteer [revised]—Rhapsode—The Eternal Club—The Blind Peddlar—Armchair—The Modern Abraham—The Trap—Hymn to Moloch [as "World-Hymn to Moloch"]—Peace Celebration—Old-Fashioned Sportsmen [from "An Old-Fashioned Sportsman"]—Corpse-Day [both from *Out of the Flame*]—The Next War

Post-War Satires. Introduction: "How shall we rise to greet the dawn?" [revised from *Argonaut and Juggernaut*]—De Luxe (Nursery Rhyme) [from *Argonaut and Juggernaut*]—Mrs. Freudenthal consults the Witch of Endor [from *Out of the Flame*]—Night Thoughts [from *Out of the Flame*]—War-Horses [revised from *Argonaut and Juggernaut*]—Lullaby (The War-Horse Chants) [from "The War-Horse Chants" in *Out of the Flame*]—Youth at the Prow, and Pleasure at the Helm [from *Out of the Flame*]—The Manner [from *Out of the Flame*]—A Touch of Nature [from *Out of the Flame*]—Through the Window [part of "The Open Door" in *Out of the Flame*]—Green Fly [abridged from *Argonaut and Juggernaut*]—The Open Door [as the last part of this poem in *Out of the Flame*]—Introducing [from *Out of the Flame*]—At the House of Mrs. Kinfoot [from *Argonaut and Juggernaut*]—An Exception (The General's Wife Refuses) [as "The General's Wife Refuses" in *Out of the Flame*]—Malgrè Soi [from *Out of the Flame*]—Paradise Regained [from *Out of the Flame*]

Friday Evening, Saturday Afternoon, and Songs for Sunday at Home and Abroad. English Gothic (Friday Evening) [from *Out of the Flame*]—Promenades (Saturday Afternoon) [from *Argonaut and Juggernaut*]—Songs for Sunday: 1. Church-Parade [from *Argonaut and Juggernaut*]—2. Sunday Afternoon [from *Out of the Flame*]—3. Au Bord de la Mer [as "Aux Bords de la Mer" in *Out of the Flame*]—4. Ultimate Judgment [from *Out of the Flame*]—5.

Anglican Hymn in Foreign Parts [as "De Luxe: Hymn" in *Argonaut and Juggernaut*]—6. English Tea-Rooms [from *Out of the Flame*]—7. Giardino Pubblico [from *Out of the Flame*]

The Jolly Old Squire, or, Way-Down in Georgia. ["Note—This poem, . . . is here reprinted, with . . . very few alterations, almost as it appeared in the *Chapbook* . . . for September, 1922"]

BOOK II—POEMS

Winter the Huntsman [all from *Poor Young People*]. 1. The Sword and the Herb [abridged]—2. New Magic—3. "Then are the woods so empty?"—4. ". . . When the owl at night" [as "Perhaps . . . when the owl at night"]—5. Superstition—6. And Science—7. Winter the Huntsman—8. Danse Macabre—9. Out in the Garden—10. The Fledgeling—11. "Which is the Triton true?"—12. The Gardener

Out of the Flame [from *Out of the Flame*]

Three Mexican Pieces and Two Dances. 1. Dusk [from *Argonaut and Juggernaut*]—2. Song, How jolly are the dwarfs [from *Out of the Flame*]—3. Maxixe [from *Out of the Flame*]—Country Dance [from *Out of the Flame*]—Fox Trot: When Solomon met the Queen of Sheba [revised from *Out of the Flame*]

The Lumber Room, Two Garden Pieces, and Parade [all from *Out of the Flame*]. 1. Fountains—2. Neptune in Chains—Parade

Two Mythological Poems. 1. The Jealous Goddess [from *Out of the Flame*]—2. Jack in the Box: Fantasia [considerably revised from "The Backward Child" in *Out of the Flame*]

Two Poems from The Phoenix-Feasters [from *Argonaut and Juggernaut*]. 1. Cornucopia [revised and abridged]—2. Song, Our Hidden Voices [revised and abridged]

The Beginning [from *Argonaut and Juggernaut*]—The End [from *Argonaut and Juggernaut*]—Lausiac Theme [revised from *Argonaut and Juggernaut*]—Night [from *Argonaut and Juggernaut*]—From Carcassonne [from *Argonaut and Juggernaut*]

Three Nocturnes [from *Argonaut and Juggernaut*]. 1. The Valleys that we Knew in Sunlit Hours [revised from "Nocturne"]—2. An owl, horned wizard of the night [part of "Metamorphosis"]—3. The Milky Clouds, Dispersing [revision of part of "Spring Hours"]

Old Friends. 1. Elegy—2. A Feather Tapestry—3. Miss Mew-ad-Vincula—4. Miss Mew's Epoch—5. Miss Mew's Song of Perpetual Motion [revised and abridged]—6. Miss Mew's Window-Box [all from *Miss Mew*]

Major and Mrs. Postlethwaite [all from *The Nation and Athenaeum*, 8 December 1930]. 1. Prelude—2. Looking through one's old belongings—3. Major Postlethwaite—4. Brass Buttons—5. Other Times, Other Climes—6. Why?—7. Mrs. Postlethwaite—8. Winter

England Reclaimed, a Book of Eclogues [as the whole volume of *England Reclaimed*, 0A12]

b. *First edition, special copies*
[*Title as in ordinary copies*]

222 × 150 mm.

304 pp.: [i] half-title; [ii] "By Osbert Sitwell . . ."; [iii] title; [iv] "Of this edition of The Collected Satires and Poems of Osbert Sitwell, on handmade paper, numbered, and signed by the Author, 110 copies have been printed, of which 100 only are for sale. No." [in ink, with author's autograph signature]. "Printed at The Chapel River Press for Gerald Duckworth & Company, Ltd., London. All Rights Reserved." (Thence as in ordinary copies, above.)

Frontispiece tipped in, with tissue guard; being tinted photograph of Frank Dobson's bust of the author.

Buff buckram boards. Untrimmed edges. Gilt lettered on spine.

110 copies printed (100 for sale). Published 2 June 1931 at 63s.

CONTENTS
As in the ordinary copies

0A19   THREE-QUARTER LENGTH   1931
PORTRAIT OF
MICHAEL ARLEN

First edition

THREE-QUARTER LENGTH PORTRAIT | OF MICHAEL ARLEN | *By* | OSBERT SITWELL | *With a preface* | *The History of a Portrait* | *by the Author* | [star] | LONDON: WILLIAM HEINEMANN LIMITED | NEW YORK: DOUBLE-DAY, DORAN AND CO. INC.

260 × 200 mm.

24 pp.: [1–2] blank; [3] half-title; [4] "This edition is limited to five hundred and twenty copies, of which two hundred and fifty are for sale in Great Britain and Ireland, two hundred and fifty are for sale in the United States of America, and twenty are for presentation. This is No." [in ink, with author's autograph signature]; [5] title; [6] "Printed and bound in Great Britain at The Windmill Press, Kingswood, Surrey"; [7–13] Preface; [14] blank; [15–20] text; [21–24] blank.

Decorated initial printed in red on page 17.

Blue cloth spine, marbled cloth boards. Top edge gilt, others untrimmed. Gilt lettered up spine.

520 copies printed, 250 copies for publication in London on 29 June 1931 at 8s. 6d. and 250 copies for publication in New York on 30 July 1931 at $3.00.

CONTENTS

Pp. 7–13: Preface, The History of a Portrait—pp. 15–20: The Portrait

oA20   THREE-QUARTER-LENGTH   1931
           PORTRAIT OF THE
           VISCOUNTESS WIMBORNE

First edition

A Three-Quarter-length | Portrait of the | Viscountess | Wimborne | by | Osbert Sitwell | Christmas 1931

206 × 148 mm.

16 pp.: [i] blank; [ii] "Of this Poem 55 copies only have been printed by W. Lewis, M.A., at the University Press, Cambridge, and signed by the Author. No." [in ink, with author's autograph signature]; [iii] title; [iv] blank; 1–10 text; [11–12] blank.

Cream buckram boards. Untrimmed edges. Gilt lettered inside rule border on upper cover, gilt rule border on lower cover.

Privately printed (55 copies) for presentation, Christmas 1931. 57 copies were in fact printed, the two out of series copies being presented to the British Museum and Mr Thomas Balston.

a. *First edition, ordinary copies*

DICKENS | *BY* | OSBERT SITWELL | [*decoration: dolphin diving*] | **London** | *CHATTO & WINDUS* | 1932

187 × 122 mm.

60 pp.: [i–ii] blank; [iii] half-title; [iv] "The Dolphin Books . . ."; [v] title; [vi] "Printed in Great Britain by T. and A. Constable Ltd. at the University Press, Edinburgh. All Rights Reserved. First published 1932"; [vii] dedication; [viii] blank; [1], 2–47 text; [48] printer's imprint repeated; [49–52] publisher's advertisements tipped in.

Drawing on title by Edward Bawden.

Cream paper boards. Trimmed edges. Printed in sepia on spine and upper and lower covers, with drawings by Edward Bawden.

3000 copies printed. Published 18 February 1932 at 2s.

CONTENTS

Contains passages from "A Note on Charles Dickens" in *Week-End Review*, 21 November 1931

b. *First edition, special copies*

DICKENS | *BY* | OSBERT SITWELL | [*decoration: two boys riding a dolphin*] | **London** | *CHATTO & WINDUS* | 1932

207 × 137 mm.

56 pp.: [i] half-title; [ii] blank; [iii] "One hundred and ten copies of this special edition have been printed; one hundred are for sale. No." [in ink, with author's autograph signature]; [iv] blank; [v] title; [vi] "Printed in Great Britain by T. and A. Constable Ltd. at the University Press, Edinburgh. All Rights Reserved. First published 1932"; [vii] dedication; [viii] blank; [1], 2–47 text; [48] printer's imprint repeated.

Drawing on title by Edward Bawden.

Dark red cloth spine, black and white paper boards decorated by Edward Bawden. Top edge gilt, others untrimmed. Gilt lettered up the spine.

110 copies printed (100 for sale). Published 18 February 1932 at 15s.

As in ordinary copies, above

OA22   WINTERS OF CONTENT   1932

a. *First edition*

WINTERS   OF   CONTENT | MORE   DISCURSIONS
ON | TRAVEL, ART, AND LIFE | by | OSBERT SITWELL |
"Britons, you stay too long: | Quickly aboard bestow
you, | And with a merry gale | Swell your stretch'd sail |
With vows as strong | As the winds that blow you." |
DUCKWORTH | 3 HENRIETTA STREET, LONDON | 1932

221 × 139 mm.

296 pp.: [1] engraved half-title; [2] "By Osbert Sitwell . . ."; [3] title;
[4] "All Rights Reserved. Made and Printed in Great Britain By The
Camelot Press Limited, London and Southampton"; [5] dedication;
[6] blank; 8 [*sic:* i.e., 7] Contents; [8] Illustrations; [9–10], 11–291
text; [292] blank; 293–296 index.

Engraved half-title by Eric Ravilious, and 16 plates tipped in.

Orange cloth boards. Trimmed edges. Gilt lettered on spine.

2000 copies printed. Published June 1932 at 15*s*.

CONTENTS

Includes, slightly revised: "The Castel del Monte" [from *Architectural
Design and Construction*, January 1932]—"New Year in Bari" [from
Week-End Review, 2 January 1932]—"The Secrecy of Venice" [from
Week-End Review, 19 March 1932]—"Winter in Italy" [from *Week-
End Review*, 23 April 1932]

b. *First edition, American copies*

WINTERS OF CONTENT | MORE DISCURSIONS ON |
TRAVEL, ART, AND LIFE | by | OSBERT SITWELL |
"Britons, you stay too long: | Quickly aboard bestow you, |
And with a merry gale | Swell your stretch'd sail | With
vows as strong | As the winds that blow you." | PHILA-
DELPHIA | J. B. LIPPINCOTT COMPANY | 1932

Note: 500 copies imported, with a cancel title. Smooth brown cloth boards, top edge green, gilt lettered on spine. Published in 1932 at $3.50. The contents as in OA22a.

The book entitled *Winters of Content and other Discursions* (1950) is so very different that it is included separately—see OA49.

OA23 　　　MIRACLE ON SINAI　　　1933

a. *First edition*

MIRACLE ON SINAI | A SATIRICAL NOVEL | by | OSBERT SITWELL | "The Vision of Christ which thou dost see | Is my vision's chiefest enemy. | Yours is the healer of mankind, | Mine speaks in parables to the blind." | DUCK-WORTH | 3 Henrietta Street W.C. 2 | 1933

185 × 121 mm.

384 pp.: [1] half-title; [2] "By Osbert Sitwell . . ."; [3] title; [4] "First Published in 1933. All Rights Reserved. Made and Printed in Great Britain By The Camelot Press Ltd, London and Southampton"; [5] dedication; [6] Notice; [7] Contents; [8] blank; [9] note; [10] blank; [11–14], 15–382 text; [383–384] advertisements.

Blue cloth boards. Top edge blue, others trimmed. Gilt lettered on spine.

5000 copies printed. Published in October 1933 at 7s. 6d.

b. *First edition, American issue*

Miracle on Sinai | A SATIRICAL NOVEL | BY | OSBERT SITWELL | "The Vision of Christ which thou dost see | Is my vision's chiefest enemy. | Yours is the healer of mankind, | Mine speaks in parables to the blind." | [*device*] | NEW YORK | HENRY HOLT AND COMPANY

Note: 1500 copies of this issue were printed in America. It contained 352 pages, in eights. Smooth grey cloth boards, top edge red, lettered in red on spine and upper cover. Published 2 March 1934 at $2.00. The contents are as in OA23a.

c. *Second edition*

Miracle on Sinai | A SATIRICAL NOVEL | BY | OSBERT
SITWELL | [*quotations as in the first edition*] | [*device*] |
GERALD DUCKWORTH & CO., LTD. | 3 HENRIETTA
STREET, LONDON, W.C.2

272 pages. 185 × 125 mm.

Orange cloth boards. Trimmed edges. Lettered in purple on spine.
3000 copies printed. Published in October 1948 at 8s. 6d.

CONTENTS

New preface by the author on pp. ix–xiv; thence as in first edition.

OA24 BRIGHTON 1935

a. *First edition*

[*Within a blue border*]

BRIGHTON | [*blue*] *by* | [*black*] Osbert Sitwell and | Margaret
Barton | *London* | Faber and Faber Limited | *24 Russell
Square*

221 × 131 mm.

376 pp.: [1] half-title; [2] blank; [3] title; [4] "First Published in March
MCMXXXV by Faber and Faber Limited, 24 Russell Square, London
W.C.1. Printed in Great Britain by R. MacLehose and Company
Limited, The University Press, Glasgow. All Rights Reserved";
[5] dedication; [6] blank; 7–8 Preface; 9 Contents; [10] blank; 11
Illustrations; [12] blank; 13–373, [374] text, appendices, bibliography,
index, and printer's imprint repeated; [375–376] blank.

Sixteen plates tipped in.

Red cloth boards. Top edge gilt, others untrimmed. Gilt lettered on
spine, with green panels.

4720 copies printed. Published 14 March 1935 at 15s.

b. *First edition, American copies*

Note: I have not been able to see a copy of this issue; the following information has been kindly given me by the publishers, Messrs.

Houghton Mifflin Company. 750/780 copies imported in sheets, with a cancel title giving the Boston imprint. Red cloth, bristol boards, trimmed edges, gilt lettered on a metallic blue panel on the spine. Published 13 August 1935 at $4.00. The contents as in 0A24a.

0A25 PENNY FOOLISH 1935

First edition

PENNY FOOLISH | *A Book of* | *Tirades* | *&* | *Panegyrics* | *by* | OSBERT SITWELL | LONDON | MACMILLAN & COMPANY LTD | 1935

222 × 145 mm.

380 pp.; [i] half-title; [ii] "Macmillan & Co . . ."; [iii] title; [iv] "Copyright. Printed in Great Britain by R. & R. Clark, Limited, Edinburgh"; v Preface; vi–viii Contents; [1–2], 3–370, [371] text; [372] printer's imprint repeated.

Maroon cloth boards. Top edge maroon, others untrimmed. Gilt lettered on spine.

2000 copies printed. Published 17 September 1935 at 12s. 6d.

CONTENTS

The Best Years of Life [from *Daily Mail*, 30 December 1930]—On Private Schools—On Public Schools—On Anonymous Letters—Games: 1. As a Menace to the Country [from "Our strange amusements" in *Evening News*, 13 December 1929]—2. As a Pernicious Influence on the Individual [from "Why I don't Like Games" in *Daily Mail*, 15 November 1928]—On Broadening the Mind [as "Narrow your mind and be happy" in *Sunday Referee*, 1 July 1934]—In Praise of Indolence [from "In praise of laziness" in *Harper's Monthly Magazine*, August 1934 and *Sunday Referee* 20 May 1934]—Friends [from "Save me from my friends" in *Sunday Referee*, 17 June 1934]—Friends and Enemies [from *Evening News*, 15 June 1928]—The White Man's Burden [from *Sunday Referee*, 25 February 1934]—Rules for Being Rude [from "The Art of Being Rude" in *Sunday Referee*, 28 January 1934]—Hints on Life: 1. Manners—2. Success—Victorianism, an English disease—The Edwardians, the rich man's feast [from "The halcyon Edwardian day" in *Sunday Referee*, 29 April 1934]—On Progress [from "Looking forward in 1910" in *Sunday Referee*, 12 August 1934]—Let's All be Alike [from "Moderns who are all alike" in *Daily Telegraph*, 24 August 1933]—On Snobs—On Prigs—On Advice, its giving and receiving [from *Sunday Referee*, 4 February 1934]—On the Horror of Solitude [from "The necessity for solitude" in *Sunday Referee*, 22 April 1934]—On the Decay of Privacy—On Street Music [from "I would forbid street music" in *Sunday Referee*, 21 January 1934]—Arms and the Man [from "Are we muddling into war?" in *Sunday Referee*, 25 March 1934]—On Sex [from "Sex" in *Evening News*, 25 June 1930]—Out of Season [from "In season—and out" in *Sunday Referee*, 6 May 1934]—Encounter with the Oxford Group Movement [from "Caught by Buchmanites—in Canada" in *Sunday Referee*, 15 July 1934]—One or Two Lives [from "The double life" in *Sunday Referee*, 1 April 1934 and "The Lady with the Pink Feather" in *Harper's Magazine*, November 1934]—On Ghosts—The Ghost in the Green Mask [from "The ghost in the mask" in *Sunday Express*, 13 June 1926]—Holiday Conversations [from *Evening News*, 25 August 1930]—On the Effect of Minding One's Own Business—On English Food [from *Sunday Referee*, 13 May 1934]—On Health—On Gardening—On Cut Flowers [from "The abomination of cut flowers" in *Sunday Referee*, 8 April 1934]—On the Joys of a Telephone Exchange—On a Common Cold—On Words and their Meaning—On the Belittlement of the Great [from "Belittling the Great" in *Sunday Referee*, 11 March 1934]—Adult Franchise for Domestic Animals: the sad case of the pig—On Fogs [from "Englishmen love fogs" in *Sunday Referee*, 7 January 1934]—By Train—By Boat—America before the fall [from "How America 'got' me" in *Daily Express*, 24 February 1927]—Abroad [from "From Syracuse," *Week-End Review*, 17 January 1931]—Travellers' Tales [from *Week-End Review*, 28 February 1931]—Fortune Tellers [from "Pekin fortune-tellers" in *Sunday Referee*, 19 August 1934]—The Delights of Foreign Colonies [from "Self-Importance" in *Sunday Referee*, 11 November 1934]—The Summer Palace [from *Harper's Bazaar*, September 1934]—Dogs—Animals versus Children—Lewd sing Cuckoo [from "National birds" in *Sunday Referee*, 8 July 1934]—Portrait of Lawrence [from *Week-End Review*, 7 February 1931]—A Note on the Novel—Thackeray and *Vanity Fair* [from *Sunday Referee*, 27 May 1934]—Is Fascism British? [from "A Peer's war-time prophecies" in *Sunday Referee*, 4 March 1934]—Eighteenth-Century Details [from "A Forgotten England" in *Sunday Referee*, 11 February 1934]—Some Present Elements of Literary Corruption—The Arts of Reading and Writing, their future—On the Burning of Books as Private Pastime and National Recreation—Ta-Ra-Ra-Boom-De-Ay! the muse of Alfred Noyes [from *Spectator*, 14 June 1924]—On Prophets and Prophecy [from "Prophets of Evil are Popular" in *Sunday Referee*, 24 June 1934]—On Centenaries—More about Monkey Glands—The Ballet [from "The tenth muse" in *Harper's Bazaar*, June 1933]—On Interior Decorators and Decoration [from "For and against homes like aeroplanes" in *Sunday Referee*, 15 April 1934]—On Exhibitions [from "Of what use are these exhibitions?" in *Sunday Referee*, 14 January 1934]

oA26   MRS. KIMBER   1937

First edition

MRS. KIMBER | By | OSBERT SITWELL | With eight drawings by | MARY KESSELL | MACMILLAN & CO. LTD. | ST. MARTIN'S STREET | LONDON | 1937

216 × 171 mm.

24 pp.: [1] half-title; [2] drawing; [3] title; [4] "This Edition of *Mrs. Kimber* is limited to 500 copies. Copyright. Printed in Great Britain"; 5–23 text; [24] [*Device*]. "The Westminster Press, 411a Harrow Road, London W.9."

Eight drawings by Mary Kessell on text pages.

Tan paper boards. Trimmed edges (but a few advance copies may be found with edges untrimmed; these were used for subscription and travelling purposes). Cream paper label, printed in red and black, pasted on upper cover.

500 copies printed. Published 26 November 1937 at 8*s.* 6*d.*

CONTENTS

[All from *Week-End Review*, 2 July 1932.] 1. Invocation to Mrs. Kimber—2. Mrs. Kimber—3. Properties and Prospects—4. Day Dreams—5. Rough Weather—6. Colophon

oA27   THOSE WERE THE DAYS   1938

First edition

THOSE WERE | THE DAYS | *Panorama with Figures* | OSBERT SITWELL | LONDON | MACMILLAN | 1938

188 × 124 mm.

552 pp.: [i] half-title; [ii] blank; [iii] title; [iv] "Copyright. Printed in Great Britain by R. & R. Clark, Limited, Edinburgh"; v–vii Contents; viii note; [1–2], 3–544 text, and printer's imprint repeated.

Green cloth boards. Trimmed edges. Lettered in blue and gilt, with panels, on spine.

5000 copies printed. Published 1 March 1938 at 8*s*. 6*d*.

CONTENTS

Parts of Book I, Chapters II–III, are revised from "The Villa Angelica" in *Life and Letters To-day*, Winter 1935–36

Part of Book IV, Chapter III, is revised from "Paters' Match," in *Life and Letters To-day*, Winter 1937

Part of Book IV, Chapter IV, is revised from the version translated as "Epilog zum Roman" in *Deutsche Rundschau*, Okt.-Dez. 1928

oA28   TRIO   1938

[For description, see EA31]

CONTENTS (BY OSBERT SITWELL)

Pp. 1–45: Dickens and the Modern Novel [containing "a number of extracts from my book *Dickens*"]—pp. 49–93: The Modern Novel, its cause and cure [containing passages from "A Note on the Novel" in *Penny Foolish*]

(These lectures were delivered by the author on 18 and 21 October 1937, under the general title given above. The titles of the individual lectures were "Dickens, the Man and his Purpose" and "The Modern Novel, its Cause and Cure". See EA31 for details.)

oA29   ESCAPE WITH ME!   1939

a. *First edition*

ESCAPE | WITH ME! | AN ORIENTAL | SKETCH-BOOK | BY | OSBERT SITWELL | LONDON | MACMILLAN & CO. LTD | 1939

218 × 138 mm.

356 pp.: [i] half-title; [ii] blank; [iii] title; [iv] dedication . . . "Copyright. Printed in Great Britain by R. & R. Clark, Limited, Edin-

burgh"; v–vi Acknowledgements; vii–xii Preface; xiii–xiv Contents; xv Illustrations; [xvi] blank; 1–339, [340] text, index and printer's imprint repeated.

Sixteen single leaves of plates tipped in.

Green cloth boards. Trimmed edges. End-papers reproduced from Chinese wall-paper. Gilt lettered on the spine.

3000 copies printed. Published 7 November 1939 at 12s. 6d.

CONTENTS

Passages from the following articles are revised or reprinted in the book: "Summer Palace" [*Harper's Bazaar*, September 1934]—"Chinese Food" [*Harper's Bazaar*, July 1935]—"En Voyage" [*The Fortnightly*, August 1938]—"In Indo-China" [*The Queen*, 22 September 1938]—"Ports of Call" [*John O'London's*, 9 June 1938]—"Ancestral Hall of the Exalted Brave and Loyal" [*Life and Letters To-day*, July 1939]

b. *First edition, American issue*

ESCAPE | WITH ME! | AN ORIENTAL | SKETCH-BOOK | BY | OSBERT SITWELL | NEW YORK | HARRISON-HILTON BOOKS, INC. | 1940

Note: This issue, printed in America, contains 360 pages and is bound in light grey cloth boards, top edge blue, gilt lettered on spine with blue panel. Published in 1940 (copyright copy dated 17 July 1940). The contents are as in 0A29a.

c. *second edition*

ESCAPE | WITH ME! | OSBERT SITWELL | *A Travel Book* | [*device*] | PAN BOOKS LTD : LONDON

328 pages. 177 × 111 mm.

Pink glossy wrappers, printed in black and white and colour. Trimmed edges.

40,000 copies printed. Published in May 1948 at 2s. 6d.

CONTENTS

"Introduction, The Cherry Tree" (rewritten for this edition), pp. xiii–xix; thence as in the first edition but without illustrations.

a. *First edition*

OPEN THE DOOR! | *A volume of Stories* | *by* | OSBERT SITWELL | LONDON | MACMILLAN & CO. LTD | 1941

189 × 125 mm.

288 pp.: [i] half-title; [ii] acknowledgements; [iii] title; [iv] dedication ... "Copyright. Printed in Great Britain by R. & R. Clark, Limited, Edinburgh"; v Contents; [vi] Notice; 1–281, [282] text, and printer's imprint repeated.

Maroon cloth boards. Trimmed edges. Gilt lettered on spine.

3000 copies printed. Published 7 November 1941 at 7s. 6d.

CONTENTS

Death of a God [from *John O'London's*, 31 January 1941]—Defeat [from *Harper's Bazaar* (New York), May 1941]—The Man who Drove Strindberg Mad [from *Life and Letters To-day*, February 1941]—Pompey and Some Peaches, I and II [revised from *Yale Review*, March 1941]—Shadow Play—Lovers' Meeting—Touching Wood [from *Harper's Bazaar* (New York), 15 September 1938]—The Woman who Hated Flowers [from *Good Housekeeping*, September 1940]—Primavera—Plague-Cart before Horse [from *St. Martin's Review*, February 1940]—Champagne for the Old Lady [from *Bystander*, 25 November 1938, and *Harper's Bazaar* (New York), December 1938]—True Lovers' Knot [from *The Fortnightly*, August 1940]—The Messenger—Dead Heat [from "Neck and Neck" in *Harper's Bazaar* (New York), June 1939, and (London), October/November 1939]—Long Journey [from "Tuscan Ghost" in *John O'London's*, 2 August 1940]—Idyll through the Looking Glass [from *London Mercury*, November 1938] —The Glow-Worm [from *Life and Letters To-day*, August 1941]

b. *First edition, American issue*

[*Maroon*] *Open the Door!* | [*black*] A VOLUME OF STORIES BY | [*maroon*] *Osbert Sitwell* | [*black*] [*device*] | 1941 · SMITH & DURRELL · NEW YORK

Note: This issue, printed in America, contains 312 pages, and is bound in black cloth spine, pictorial maroon paper boards, lettered in mauve and gilt on the spine. Published in 1941 at $2.50 (copyright copy dated 6 December 1941). The contents are as in OA30a, but in a different order.

oA31   A PLACE OF ONE'S OWN   1941

First edition

A PLACE | OF ONE'S OWN | BY | OSBERT SITWELL |
LONDON | MACMILLAN & CO. LTD | 1941

187 × 122 mm.

80 pp.: [i] half-title; [ii] blank; [iii] title; [iv] "Copyright. Printed in
Great Britain by R. & R. Clark Ltd., Edinburgh"; [v] dedication;
[vi] blank; [vii] Note; [viii] blank; 1–70, [71] text, and printer's imprint repeated; [72] blank.

Cream paper boards. Trimmed edges. Lettered in red down the spine.

3000 copies printed. Published 12 December 1941 at 2s. 6d.

Note: A film was made of this book, with the author's collaboration.
It had the same title, was a "Gainsborough Picture" distributed by
Eagle-Lion Distributors Ltd., and was first shown in May 1945.

oA32   GENTLE CAESAR   [1943]

First edition

GENTLE CAESAR | *A Play in Three Acts* | BY | R. J. MIN-
NEY | AND | OSBERT SITWELL | LONDON | MACMILLAN
& CO. LTD | 1942

188 × 121 mm.

144 pp.: [i] half-title; [ii] "Books by Osbert Sitwell . . ."; [iii] title;
[iv] "Copyright. Printed in Great Britain by R. & R. Clark, Limited,
Edinburgh"; v–vi Preface; vii Characters; viii Scenes; 1–128, [129]
text, and printer's imprint repeated; [130–136] blank.

Blue cloth boards. Trimmed edges. Gilt lettered on spine.

2000 copies printed. Published 5 March 1943 at 6s.

oA33   SELECTED POEMS,   1943
        OLD AND NEW

First edition

SELECTED | POEMS | OLD AND NEW | by | OSBERT
SITWELL | DUCKWORTH | 3 Henrietta Street | LONDON,
W.C.2

184 × 122 mm.

164 pp.: [1] half-title; [2] "Works by Osbert Sitwell . . ."; [3] title; [4] "First published 1943. Printed in Great Britain by The Riverside Press, Edinburgh"; [5] Dedication; [6] acknowledgment; 7–11 Preface; 12–16 Contents; 17–163 text; [164] blank.

Yellow cloth boards. Trimmed edges. Lettered in red on spine.

3000 copies printed. Published in November 1943 at 7s. 6d.

CONTENTS

[Unless otherwise stated all poems are from *Collected Satires and Poems*, 1931]

Preface

Book I, Poems Old and New. The Vision [from *The Observer*, 14 May 1939]—To Charlotte Corday [from *The Observer*, 16 January 1940]—Fool's Song, I [from *The Observer*, 27 October 1940]—Fool's Song, II [from *Life and Letters To-day*, May 1941]—Journalist's Song [abbreviated from *Life and Letters To-day*, May 1941]—Personal Prejudice [from *Life and Letters To-day*, October 1940]—Life-Song [not from *Collected Satires and Poems*]—La Tour du Sorcier [from *The Observer*, 6 June 1937]—On the Coast of Coromandel [not from *Collected Satires and Poems*]—Three Mexican Pieces, 1. Dusk—2. Song, How Jolly are the Dwarfs—3. Maxixe

Two Poems from The Phoenix Feasters. 1. Cornucopia [revised]—2. Song, Our Hidden Voices

Fox Trot: When Solomon met the Queen of Sheba

Two Garden Pieces and Parade. 1. Fountain [revised from "Fountains"]—2. Neptune in Chains—3. Parade [revised]

Nocturne [as "Three Nocturnes—1"]—Lausiac Theme—From Carcassonne—Out of the Flame [revised]—Winter the Huntsman, 1–12—Night—The Beginning—The End

Book II, England Reclaimed, a Book of Eclogues, and Other Portraits. Dedication—Explanation [as "Introduction"]—Prologue—Tom—Mrs. Hague—Five Drawings of Mr. Hague—Mary-Anne—Mr. and Mrs. Nutch, 1–4—Moping Fred, 1. Moping Fred, 2. In a Nutshell—Mr. and Mrs. Goodbeare, 1. Elegy for Mr. Goodbeare, 2. Mr. and Mrs. Goodbeare, 3. Mr. Goodbeare at Work, 4. Mr. Goodbeare's Cottage—Mr. and Mrs. Southern, 1. Mrs. Southern's Enemy [abbreviated], 2. Twilight, 3. Mr. Southern in the Market Garden, 4. No Flowers by Request—Phoebe Southern, 1. Phoebe Southern, 2. Silver Lances [revised]—Mr. and Mrs. Kembley, 1. Luke Kembley in September, 2. And October, 3. Circles, 4. Interior of "The Boulders," 5. Evening—Grand Finale [abbreviated and revised]

Old Friends. Miss Mew, 1. A Feather Tapestry, 2. Miss Mew-Ad-Vincula, 3. Miss Mew's Window-Box—Mrs. Kimber, 1–6 [from *Mrs. Kimber*]

Book III, Satires. Church-Parade—Sunday Afternoon—Au Bord de la Mer—Ultimate Judgment—Anglican Hymn in Foreign Parts—English Tea-Rooms—Giardino Pubblico—English Gothic—Promenade [as "Promenades: Saturday Afternoon"]—A Touch of Nature

Book IV, Poems of the Last and the Next War. Introduction: How shall we rise to greet the dawn?—"Therefore is the Name of it Called Babel"—The Eternal Club [revised]—Arm-Chair—The Trap—Hymn to Moloch—Old-Fashioned Sportsmen—Corpse-Day—The Next War

0A34   LEFT HAND, RIGHT HAND!   1944

a. *First edition*

LEFT HAND, | RIGHT HAND! | [*three lines within a sepia border, with 14 sepia roses round it*] SIR | OSBERT | SIT-WELL|[*below the border*] *AN ATLANTIC MONTHLY PRESS BOOK* |LITTLE, BROWN AND COMPANY · BOSTON | 1944

215 × 142 mm.

348 pp.: [a–b] blank; [i] half-title; [ii] blank; [iii] title; [iv] "Copyright 1943, 1944, by Sir Osbert Sitwell. All rights reserved . . . First edition. Published May 1944 . . . Printed in the United States of America"; [v] Contents; [vi] blank; vii–xvi Introduction; [1–2], 3–327 text, appendices and index; [328] "Left Hand, Right Hand! was set in Janson by the J. S. Cushing Company; printed by the Rockwell and Churchill Press on paper made by the Tileston and Hollingsworth Company; bound in linen by the Riverside Bindery; and designed by Arthur Williams, April MCMXLIV." [*device*]; [329–330] blank.

Brown linen boards. Trimmed edges. Gilt stamped on upper cover and spine, with blue panels.

2000 copies printed. Published 10 May 1944 at $3.00.

CONTENTS

The following excerpts were published before the issue of the American and English editions respectively: "Left Hand, Right

Hand!," in *Atlantic Monthly*, January–May 1944—"The Sitwells as Children," in *Good Housekeeping*, May 1944—"Sitwell Settings," in *Good Housekeeping*, June 1944.

b. *First edition, English issue*
[*Within a double rule border*]
LEFT HAND | RIGHT HAND! | *An Autobiography by* | OSBERT SITWELL | VOL. I: THE CRUEL MONTH|LONDON| MACMILLAN & CO. LTD | 1945

215 × 138 mm.

288 pp.: [i] half-title; [ii] "List of works by Osbert Sitwell"; [iii] title; [iv] dedication . . . "Copyright. Printed in Great Britain by R. & R. Clark, Limited, Edinburgh"; v–xiii Introduction; xiv Acknowledgments; xv Contents; xvi List of illustrations; 1–271, [272] text, appendices, index and printer's imprint repeated.

12 plates tipped in, and folding "Line of Descent" tipped to back free end-paper.

Smooth scarlet buckram boards. Top edge black, others trimmed. Decorated end-papers. Gilt lettered on spine, with black panel.

20,000 copies printed. Published 27 March 1945 at 15*s*.

CONTENTS

As in the first edition, with the addition of illustrations and acknowledgments

0A35   SING HIGH! SING LOW!   1944

First edition
A Book of Essays | SING HIGH! | SING | LOW! | *By Osbert Sitwell* | LONDON | MACMILLAN & CO. LTD | 1944

214 × 135 mm.

200 pp.: [i] half-title; [ii] "List of works by Osbert Sitwell"; [iii] title; [iv] "Copyright. Printed in Great Britain by R. & R. Clark, Limited, Edinburgh"; v Acknowledgements; [vi] blank; vii Contents; [viii] blank; 1–188, [189] text, and printer's imprint repeated; [190] blank; [191–192] back paste-down end-paper.

Rust-red cloth boards. Trimmed edges. Gilt lettered on spine.

10,000 copies printed. Published 12 May 1944 at 10*s*. 6*d*.

Old Worlds for New [from *Life and Letters To-day*, April 1942]—The Conspiracy of Dwarfs [from *Daily Telegraph*, 10 August 1935]—The Banquets of Tantalus [revised and enlarged from "Notes on Stage Food" in *Wine & Food*, Winter 1937]—Save the Old School Tie [from "The Old School Tie" in *Lilliput*, July 1939]—The Red Folder [from *The Burlington Magazine*, April and May 1942]—Municipal Rhapsody: an Idyll—Still Life, 1. Dining-Room Piece [revised from "Far Away and Not so Long Ago" in *Wine & Food*, Winter 1942], 2. Box and Bottle [from *Life and Letters To-day*, February–May 1943] —A Rose by Any Other Name, being a discourse on the importance of bad art [revised from "An Author Kills a Country" in *Lilliput*, June 1940]—Roots of the Sole Arabian Tree [from "The Sole Arabian Tree" in *Times Literary Supplement*, 26 April 1941]—The Eye within the Ear [revised from "On the Relationship between Poetry and Painting" in *The Burlington Magazine*, February 1941]—The Art of Pavel Tchelitchew—Thomas Rowlandson [revised from *Thomas Rowlandson*, 0B11]—A Grain of Sand and a Grain of Salt [from "Notes on the Way" in *Time & Tide*, 7–14 September 1940]—Picnics and Pavilions [revised from "The Pleasures of Picnics" in *Good House-keeping*, June 1936, and "Water-Parties" in *Harper's Bazaar*, September 1936]—London [greatly revised from *Harper's Bazaar*, April 1944] —What it Feels Like to be an Author [from *Saturday Review of Literature*, 19 February 1944]

Note : Among the acknowledgements, p. v, is for permission to reprint from *The Boston Evening Transcript*. I have not been able to discover any article in that paper. The journal ceased publication in 1941, and a brief check through a microfilm copy was unsuccessful. Sir Osbert wrote: ". . . I don't think I ever had anything in the *Boston Evening Transcript*. I don't remember it."

0A36   A LETTER TO MY SON   1944

First edition

A | LETTER TO MY SON | BY | OSBERT SITWELL | HOME & VAN THAL LTD. | 1944

184 × 123 mm.

32 pp.: [1] half-title; [2] dedication; [3] title; [4] "First published 1944. . . . Printed in Great Britain by Morrison and Gibb Ltd., London and Edinburgh"; 5–32 text.

Dark blue cloth boards. Trimmed edges. Gilt lettered on upper cover. Published in August 1944 at 3s. 6d.

CONTENTS

Revised from *Horizon*, March 1943

oA37   THE TRUE STORY OF   [1946]
DICK WHITTINGTON

First edition

THE TRUE STORY OF | DICK WHITTINGTON | A CHRIST-MAS STORY FOR CAT-LOVERS | BY | OSBERT SITWELL | LONDON | HOME & VAN THAL LTD. | 3 CLIFFORD STREET. W.1

182 × 119 mm.

48 pp.: [1] half-title; [2] blank; [3] title; [4] "First Published 1945. . . . Printed by The Chaseton Press of H. Williams & Son Ltd., 222 Grays Inn Road, London, W.C.1"; [5] 6–48 text.

Terra-cotta cloth boards. Trimmed edges. Lettered in black on upper cover.

Published in February 1946 at 5s.

CONTENTS

Revised from *Horizon*, March 1945

oA38   THE SCARLET TREE   1946

a. *First edition*

THE | SCARLET TREE | [*three lines within a sepia border, with 14 sepia roses round it*] SIR | OSBERT | SITWELL | [*below the border*] AN ATLANTIC MONTHLY PRESS BOOK | LITTLE, BROWN AND COMPANY • BOSTON | 1946

215 × 142 mm.

392 pp.: [i] blank; [ii] "By Sir Osbert Sitwell . . ."; [iii] half-title; [iv] blank; [v] title; [vi] "Copyright 1946, by Sir Osbert Sitwell. All rights reserved . . . First edition. Published June 1946 . . . Printed in the United States of America"; [vii] Contents; [viii] blank; ix–x Introduction; [1–2], 3–381 text, appendices and index; [382] "The Scarlet

Tree was set in Janson by the J. S. Cushing Company; printed by the Rockwell and Churchill Press on paper made by the S. D. Warren Company; bound in linen by the Riverside Bindery; and designed by Arthur Williams. May MCMXLVI." [*Device.*]

Brown linen boards. Trimmed edges. Gilt lettered on upper cover and spine, with blue panels.

6000 copies printed. Published 20 June 1946 at $3.50.

CONTENTS

The following excerpts were published before the issue of the American and English editions: "A Victorian Boyhood," in *Atlantic Monthly*, February 1946—"A Hero for his Bed," in *Atlantic Monthly*, March 1946—"The Happiest Time of One's Life," in *Atlantic Monthly*, April 1946—"Father, Henry and I," in *Atlantic Monthly*, May 1946—"The Happiest Years," in *Town & Country*, April 1946—"To Grandmother's House we Go," in *Town & Country*, May 1946

b. *First edition, English issue*
[*Within a double rule border*]

THE SCARLET | TREE | BEING THE SECOND VOLUME OF | LEFT HAND, RIGHT HAND! | *An Autobiography by* | OSBERT SITWELL | LONDON | MACMILLAN & CO. LTD | 1946

215 × 138 mm.

328 pp.: [i] half-title; [ii] "List of works by Osbert Sitwell"; [iii] title; [iv] "Copyright. Printed in Great Britain by R. & R. Clark, Limited, Edinburgh"; [v] dedication, and quotation; [vi] Acknowledgements; vii Contents; viii List of illustrations; 1–318, [319] text, appendices, index, and printer's imprint repeated.

Five double leaves of plates sewn in, and two single leaves tipped in.

Smooth scarlet buckram boards. Top edge black, others trimmed. Decorated end-papers. Gilt lettered on spine, with black panel.

30,000 copies printed. Published 26 July 1946 at 15*s*.

CONTENTS

As in the first edition, with the addition of dedication, acknowledgements and illustrations.

First edition

Alive—Alive Oh! | *and other stories* | OSBERT SITWELL | [*device*] | PAN BOOKS LTD : LONDON

178 × 98 mm.

240 pp.: [1] half-title; [2] "First volumes in this series . . ."; [3] title; [4] "This collection first published 1947 by Pan Books Ltd . . ." [Acknowledgement]. "Made and printed in France by Imprimerie Paul Dupont, Paris"; 5–7 Author's note to this edition; [8] Contents; 9–239 text; [240] "336–7–47—imp. Paul Dupont, Paris.—C.O.L. 31–2567. Dépot légal: 3ᵉ trimestre 1947.—Nº. d'imp.: 1379."

Glossy blue paper wrappers. Trimmed edges. Printed in several colours on spine and upper and lower covers.

60,000 copies printed. Published in September 1947 at 1s. 6d., as Pan Book no. 19.

CONTENTS

Author's note to this edition—Charles and Charlemagne [from *Dumb-Animal*]—Alive–Alive Oh! [from *Dumb-Animal*]—The Greeting [from *Triple Fugue*]—Low Tide [from *Triple Fugue*]—That Flesh is Heir To . . . [from *Dumb-Animal*]

OA40   GREAT MORNING!   1947

a. *First edition*

GREAT | MORNING! | [*three lines within a sepia border, with 14 sepia roses round it*] SIR | OSBERT | SITWELL | [*below the border*] AN ATLANTIC MONTHLY PRESS BOOK | LITTLE, BROWN AND COMPANY · BOSTON | 1947

215 × 142 mm.

380 pp.: [i] blank; [ii] "By Sir Osbert Sitwell . . ."; [iii] half-title; [iv] blank; [v] title; [vi] "Copyright 1947, by Sir Osbert Sitwell. All rights reserved . . . First edition. Published October 1947 . . . Printed in the United States of America"; [vii] dedication; [viii] blank; ix–xv Introduction; [xvi] blank; [xvii] Contents; [xviii] blank; [1–2], 3–360 text, appendices and index.

Brown linen boards. Trimmed edges. Gilt lettered on upper cover and spine, with blue panels.

7500 copies printed. Published 8 October 1947 at $4.00.

CONTENTS

The following excerpts were published before the issue of the American and English editions respectively: "A Genius whose Jests were Dynamite," "Britain's greatest Soldier since Wellington," "When the Palace Band played the Wrong Tune," "Mrs. Asquith ruled in Downing St.," "The Gay Teen Age of the Century," "A War God slightly Gone to Seed," in *Daily Graphic*, 27 and 29 November, and 2, 4, 6 and 9 December 1946—"Before the War," in *The Cornhill*, Summer 1947—"Father and Son," in *Horizon*, July 1947—"The House of Mars Victoryall," in *Good Housekeeping*, July 1947— "Grooming for the Cavalry," "In the Tower of London," "Great Ladies of London," "The Golden Age of Opera," "How to Buy a Castle," in *Atlantic Monthly*, August–December 1947—"Oak and Olive," in *Orion IV*, 1947—"Pothooks in the Sand," in *Good Housekeeping*, October 1947—"Interludes and Diversions," in *The Cornhill*, Winter 1947/8.

b. *First edition, English issue*
[*Within a double rule border*]
GREAT | MORNING | BEING THE THIRD VOLUME OF | LEFT HAND, RIGHT HAND! | *An Autobiography by* | OSBERT SITWELL | LONDON | MACMILLAN & CO. LTD | 1948

215 × 142 mm.

336 pp.: [i] dedication; [ii] "List of works by Osbert Sitwell"; [iii] title; [iv] "Copyright. Printed in Great Britain"; [v] dedication; [vi] Acknowledgements; vii Contents; viii List of illustrations; 1–323, [324] text, appendices and index; [325] blank; [326] "Printed by R. & R. Clark, Ltd., Edinburgh"; [327–328] blank.

Six double leaves of plates sewn in.

Smooth scarlet buckram boards. Top edge black, others trimmed. Decorated end-papers. Gilt lettered on spine, with a black panel.

40,000 copies printed. Published 27 April 1948 at 15*s*.

As in the first edition, with the addition of acknowledgements and illustrations

oA41   THE NOVELS OF   1947
GEORGE MEREDITH

First edition

[*Cover:*]

THE ENGLISH ASSOCIATION | *Presidential Address* | *1947* | THE NOVELS OF | GEORGE MEREDITH | AND SOME NOTES ON THE | ENGLISH NOVEL | BY | SIR OSBERT SITWELL | Bart., LL.D. | *November* 1947

244 × 145 mm.

16 pp. (including cover): [i] cover-title; [ii] blank; [1], 2–12 text; [iii–iv, back cover] list of English Association pamphlets, and imprint: "Printed in Great Britain at the University Press, Oxford, by Charles Batey and published by Geoffrey Cumberlege, Oxford University Press, Amen House, London, E.C.4."

Grey paper wrappers, sewn. Trimmed edges. Printed in black as above.

3500 copies printed. Published 13 November 1947 at 2s. (One copy issued free to each member of the English Association, additional copies 1s. each.)

oA42   LAUGHTER IN THE   1948
NEXT ROOM

a. First edition

LAUGHTER | IN THE | NEXT ROOM | [*three lines within a sepia border, with 14 sepia roses round it*] SIR | OSBERT | SITWELL | [*below the border*] *AN ATLANTIC MONTHLY PRESS BOOK* | LITTLE, BROWN AND COMPANY · BOSTON | 1948

215 × 142 mm.

412 pp.: [i] blank; [ii] "By Sir Osbert Sitwell . . ."; [iii] half-title; [iv] blank; [v] title; [vi] "Copyright 1948, by Sir Osbert Sitwell. All rights reserved . . . First edition. Published October 1948 . . . Printed in the United States of America"; [vii] dedication; [viii] blank; [ix] Contents; [x] blank; [1-2], 3-400 text, appendices and index; [401] blank; [402] "Laughter in the Next Room was set in Janson by the J. S. Cushing Company; printed by the Rockwell and Churchill Press on paper made by the S. D. Warren Company; bound in linen by the Riverside Bindery; and designed by Arthur Williams. October MCMXLVIII." [*Device.*]

Brown linen boards. Trimmed edges. Gilt stamped on upper cover and spine, with blue panels.

11,500 copies printed. Published 5 October 1948 at $4.00.

CONTENTS

The following excerpts were published before the issue of the American and English editions respectively: "Laughter in the Next Room," in *Atlantic Monthly*, July–October 1948—"Bloomsbury in the 1920's," "Life with Sir George," "A Goddess in the Kitchen," in *Sunday Times*, 6, 13 and 27 February 1949—"Sir George," in *The Cornhill*, Spring 1949

b. *First edition, English issue*
[*Within a double rule border*]

LAUGHTER IN | THE NEXT | ROOM | BEING THE FOURTH VOLUME OF | LEFT HAND, RIGHT HAND! | *An Autobiography by* | OSBERT SITWELL | LONDON | MACMILLAN & CO. LTD | 1949

215 × 138 mm.

392 pp.: [i] half-title; [ii] "List of works by Osbert Sitwell"; [iii] title; [iv] "Copyright. Printed in Great Britain"; [v] dedication; vi Acknowledgements; vii Contents; viii List of illustrations; 1–380, [381] Text, appendices, index, and imprint: "Printed by R. & R. Clark, Ltd., Edinburgh"; [382–384] blank.

Four double leaves of plates sewn in, and four single leaves tipped in.

Smooth scarlet buckram boards. Top edge black, others trimmed. Decorated end-papers. Gilt lettered on spine, with black panel.

40,000 copies printed. Published 27 May 1949 at 18s.

CONTENTS

As in the first edition, with the addition of acknowledgements and illustrations

oA43   FOUR SONGS OF THE   1948
ITALIAN EARTH

First edition

[*Red*] FOUR SONGS | [*black*] *of the Italian Earth* | *by* SIR OSBERT SITWELL | [*rule*] | *Printed on* I*talian papers &* *published by* T*he Banyan Press* | *in November Mcmxlviii*

169 × 128 mm.

12 pp.: [1–2] blank; [3] title; [4] "Copyright 1948 Sir Osbert Sitwell"; [5–8] text; [9] [author's autograph signature]. "This is number [in red pencil] of an edition numbering 260 copies, of which only 175 are for sale."; [10–12] blank.

Rough red paper wrappers, sewn. Untrimmed edges. White paper label, lettered in black, pasted on panel on upper cover.

260 copies printed (175 for sale). Published November 1948 at $4.00.

CONTENTS

Four Songs of the Italian Earth—Spring Morning; Summer; Autumn; Winter [from *The Cornhill*, Spring 1948, and *American Scholar*, Winter 1948/49]

oA44   DEMOS THE EMPEROR   1949

a. *First edition, ordinary copies*

DEMOS | THE EMPEROR | A Secular Oratorio | BY | OSBERT SITWELL | LONDON | MACMILLAN & CO. LTD | 1949

245 × 154 mm.

32 pp.: [i–iv] blank; [v] half-title; [vi] blank; [vii] title; [viii] "Copy-right. Printed in Great Britain"; [ix] Introduction; [x] blank; 1–18, [19] text; [20] "Printed by R. & R. Clark, Ltd., Edinburgh"; [21–22] blank.

Yellow paper wrappers, sewn. Trimmed edges. Lettered in red on upper and lower covers, with decorations by H. Cowdell.

2000 copies printed. Published 26 April 1949 at 2s. 6d.

CONTENTS

Argument, The Squirrel with a Rose [as "A Rose in the Mouth," in *Sunday Times*, 8 December 1947, and *Atlantic Monthly*, January 1949]

Argument, Spoken Prologue [as the first ten lines of "The Invader," in *Penguin New Writing*, Autumn 1946, the whole argument being as "Prologue and Song," in *The Nation* (New York), 4 December 1948]

Demos the Emperor. [The following are from *Selected Poems* (1943—0A33): "To Charlotte Corday," "Fool's Song—II" (here as "Fool's Song—I"), "Journalist's Song," "Fool's Song—I" (here as "Fool's Song—II"). Also included are "Lines from 'Demos the Emperor,'" from *Life and Letters To-day*, September–October 1943]

b. *First edition, special copies*
[*Title and size as in ordinary copies*]

32 pp.: [i–iv] blank; [v] half-title; [vi] "Five Hundred numbered copies of this Edition have been signed by the Author. No. . . ." [in ink, with author's autograph signature]. (Thence as in ordinary copies, above.)

Binding as in ordinary copies. Issued in printed white envelope.

500 copies printed. Published 26 April 1949 at 8s. 6d.

CONTENTS

As in the ordinary copies

First edition

DEATH OF A GOD | *and Other Stories* | BY | OSBERT
SITWELL | LONDON | MACMILLAN & CO. LTD | 1949

191 × 126 mm.

256 pp.: [i] half-title; [ii] "Books by Osbert Sitwell . . ."; [iii] title;
[iv] "Copyright. Printed in Great Britain"; [v] dedication; [vi] note;
vii Contents; [viii] "Notice to Trespassers"; 1–246, [247] text, and:
"Printed by R. & R. Clark, Ltd., Edinburgh"; [248] blank.

Scarlet buckram boards. Top edge black, others trimmed. Lettered
in gold on spine, with a black panel.

10,000 copies printed. Published 4 November 1949 at 8*s*. 6*d*.

CONTENTS

[All from *Open the Door!* unless otherwise stated]
Death of a God—Defeat—The Man who Drove Strindberg Mad—
Pompey and Some Peaches, I and II—Shadow Play—Lovers' Meet-
ing—Touching Wood—The Woman who Hated Flowers—Prima-
vera—Plague-Cart before Horse—Champagne for the Old Lady—
True Lovers' Knot—The Messenger—Dead Heat—Long Journey—
Idyll through the Looking-Glass—The Glow-Worm—A Place of
One's Own [as *A Place of One's Own*, 1941]—Staggered Holiday
[from *English Story*, 3, 1942]

oA46   ENGLAND RECLAIMED AND   1949
                OTHER POEMS
First edition

ENGLAND | RECLAIMED | and Other Poems | [*three lines
within a sepia border, with 14 sepia roses round it*] SIR |
OSBERT | SITWELL | [*below the border*] AN ATLANTIC
MONTHLY PRESS BOOK | LITTLE, BROWN AND COM-
PANY · BOSTON | 1949

218 × 134 mm.

144 pp.: [a–b, i] blank; [ii] "By Sir Osbert Sitwell . . ."; [iii] half-title;
[iv] blank; [v] title; [vi] "Copyright 1948, 1949, by Sir Osbert Sitwell.

Brown linen boards. Trimmed edges. Lettered in gilt on upper cover
and spine, with blue panels.

1500 copies printed. Published 14 November 1949 at $2.75.

CONTENTS

[All poems as in *Selected Poems*, 1943, unless otherwise stated]

Introduction

Part I, ENGLAND RECLAIMED [as Book II of *Selected Poems*, but
omitting the "Dedication"; see 0A12]

Part II, FOREIGN PARTS. Three Mexican Pieces, 1. Dusk; 2. Song,
How Jolly are the Dwarfs; 3. Maxixe

On the Coast of Coromandel—From Carcassonne—Out of the Flame
—Four Italian Poems [as *Four Songs of the Italian Earth*]

Part III, POEMS OF THE WARS. To Charlotte Corday [revised, and in-
cluding part of "Prologue and Song" in *The Nation* (New York),
4 December 1948]—Fool's Song [as "Fool's Song—I"]—Personal
Prejudice—How Shall we Rise to Greet the Dawn?—"Therefore
is the Name of it Called Babel"—The Eternal Club—Arm-Chair—
The Trap—Hymn to Moloch—Old-Fashioned Sportsmen—
Corpse-Day—The Next War—Aspiring Ape [from *Times
Literary Supplement*, 6 January 1945, and *Atlantic Monthly*,
November 1949]

0A47   INTRODUCTION TO THE   1949
         CATALOGUE OF THE
           FRICK COLLECTION

First edition

INTRODUCTION | TO THE CATALOGUE OF THE | FRICK
COLLECTION | BY SIR OSBERT SITWELL | *Published on
the Founder's Centenary* | *19 December 1949* | [*sepia mono-
gram*] | REPRINTED FROM THE CATALOGUE

226 × 152 mm.

16 pp.: [1–2] blank; [3] title; [4] "Copyright 1949 by The Frick Art Reference Library, New York"; 5–12, [13] text; [14] blank; [15] "Designed and printed by Robert Haas at The Ram Press, New York, 1949."; [16] blank.

Orange paper wrappers, sewn. Trimmed edges. Lettered in black on upper cover.

Privately distributed, on or about 19 December 1949.

CONTENTS

"The Introduction" [from *The Catalogue of the Frick Collection*, vol. 1, 1949—see oB48]

Note: This Introduction was also reprinted in *A Description of the Catalogue of the Frick Collection*, by Paul Standard (Pittsburgh, 1949), of which 80 copies were distributed by the New York Public Library in May 1950.

oA48   NOBLE ESSENCES   1950

a. *First edition*

[*Within a double rule border*]

NOBLE ESSENCES | OR | COURTEOUS REVELATIONS | BEING A BOOK OF CHARACTERS | AND THE FIFTH AND LAST VOLUME OF | LEFT HAND, RIGHT HAND! | *An Autobiography by* | OSBERT SITWELL | LONDON | MAC-MILLAN & CO. LTD | 1950

215 × 138 mm.

336 pp.: [i] half-title; [ii] "List of works by Osbert Sitwell . . ."; [iii] title; [iv] "This book is copyright . . . Printed in Great Britain"; [v] dedication; [vi] quotation; vii–ix Acknowledgements; [x] blank; xi Contents; xii List of illustrations; 1–323, [324] text, appendices, index, and printer's imprint: "Printed by R. & R. Clark, Ltd., Edinburgh."

Two double leaves of plates sewn in, and eight single leaves tipped in.

Smooth scarlet buckram boards. Top edge black, others trimmed. Decorated end-papers. Gilt lettered on spine, with a black panel.

30,000 copies printed. Published 29 September 1950 at 21*s*.

The following parts were published before the issue of the London and Boston editions respectively: "A Reminiscence," in *A Celebration for Edith Sitwell* (1948)—"A Short Character of Sir Edmund Gosse," in *Horizon*, April 1942—"Ronald Firbank," in Ronald Firbank: *Five Novels*, 1949—"Wilfred Owen," in *Penguin New Writing* 27, Spring 1946, and *Atlantic Monthly*, August 1950—"Gabriele D'Annunzio," in *Atlantic Monthly*, September 1950, and *National & English Review*, August 1950; revised from *Discursions* (1925)—"Ada Leverson, Wilde, and 'Max,'" in *National & English Review*, September 1950— "A Short Character of Walter Richard Sickert," in *Orion II*, 1945, and *Atlantic Monthly*, October 1950—"A Character of the late W. H. Davies," in *Life and Letters To-day*, July–September 1942—"Two Portraits," in *Good Housekeeping*, September 1950—"A Short Character of Arnold Bennett," in *Orpheus I*, 1948

b. *First edition, American issue*

NOBLE | ESSENCES | *A BOOK OF CHARACTERS* | [*three lines within a sepia border, with 14 sepia roses round it*] SIR | OSBERT | SITWELL | [*below the border*] AN ATLANTIC MONTHLY PRESS BOOK | LITTLE, BROWN AND COMPANY · BOSTON | 1950

215 × 142 mm.

368 pp.: [i] blank; [ii] "By Sir Osbert Sitwell ..."; [iii] half-title; [iv] blank; [v] title; [vi] "Copyright 1950, by Sir Osbert Sitwell. All rights reserved ... First edition. Published October 1950 ... Printed in the United States of America"; [vii] dedication; [viii] blank; [ix] Contents; [x] blank; [1–2], 3–356 text, appendices and index; [357–358] blank.

Brown linen boards. Trimmed edges. Gilt lettered on upper cover and spine, with blue panels.

10,000 copies printed. Published 2 October 1950 at $4.50.

CONTENTS

As 0A48a, but without acknowledgements or illustrations

0A49 WINTERS OF CONTENT AND 1950
OTHER DISCURSIONS

First edition

WINTERS OF CONTENT | AND OTHER DISCURSIONS ON | MEDITERRANEAN ART AND TRAVEL | *by* | OSBERT SITWELL | "Britons, you stay too long: | Quickly aboard bestow you, | And with a merry gale | Swell your stretch'd sail | With vows as strong | As the winds that blow you." | [*device*] | GERALD DUCKWORTH & CO. LTD | 3 HENRIETTA STREET, LONDON, W.C.2

214 × 135 mm.

364 pp.: [1] half-title; [2] "Books by Osbert Sitwell"; [3] title; [4] "*Discursions* first published 1925 . . . *Winters of Content* first published 1932 . . . *Winters of Content and Other Discursions* first published 1950. All Rights Reserved. Made and printed in Great Britain by Ebenezer Baylis and Son, Ltd., The Trinity Press, Worcester, and London"; [5] dedication; [6] blank; [7] Contents; [8] List of illustrations; 9–22 Preface; [23–24], 25–362 text and index; [363–364] blank.

Two double leaves of plates sewn in, and five single leaves tipped in. Smooth scarlet buckram boards. Top edge black, others trimmed. Gilt lettered on spine, with a black panel.

3000 copies printed. Published in mid-November 1950 at 21*s*.

CONTENTS

[Preface:] "The book which follows includes *Winters of Content* almost in its entirety as first published, and to this core I have added a short story, 'Echoes,' from *Dumb-Animal*, and several of the chapters from *Discursions* that are concerned with the South of Italy and with Sicily—being 'King Bomba,' 'The Miracle,' 'Round Etna,' and 'Noto.'"

0A50 WRACK AT TIDESEND 1952

a. *First edition*

WRACK | AT TIDESEND | A BOOK OF BALNEARICS | *being* | *the second volume of* | ENGLAND RECLAIMED | *by* | OSBERT SITWELL | LONDON | MACMILLAN & CO. LTD | 1952

216 × 137 mm.

112 pp.: [i] half-title; [ii] "List of works by Osbert Sitwell"; [iii] title; [iv] "This book is copyright . . . Printed in Great Britain"; [v] dedication; [vi] blank; vii–viii Preface; ix–x quotations; xi–xii Prefatory Song; xiii–xvi Contents; 1–93, [94] text, and: "Printed by R. & R. Clark, Ltd., Edinburgh"; [95–96] blank.

Smooth scarlet buckram boards. Top edge black, others trimmed. Gilt lettered on spine, with a black panel.

3000 copies printed. Published 16 May 1952 at 10s. 6d.

CONTENTS

Doribell's Daughters; 4. Linda Doribell; 5. "Tim" Doribell; 6. Dora Doribell; 7. Laura Doribell; 8. "Tiny" Doribell—The Black Box, 1. Major Postlethwaite [revised from "Looking through one's old belongings," "Major Postlethwaite" and "Brass Button," in *Collected Satires and Poems*]; 2. Other Times, Other Climes [revised from *Collected Satires and Poems*]; 3. Mrs. Postlethwaite [revised from "Why?" and "Mrs. Postlethwaite"]; 4. Winter [revised]—Battling Mr. Better [as "Battling Mr. Fiddler," in *New Statesman and Nation*, 30 September 1950]—Local Press [from *New Statesman and Nation*, 30 September 1950]—Mrs. Crudeman—Felicity Crudeman—Mrs. Kimber, 1. Mrs. Kimber; 2. Properties and Prospects; 3. Day Dreams; 4. Rough Weather [all revised from *Mrs. Kimber*]—Mr. and Mrs. Travers [from *New Statesman and Nation*, 30 September 1950]—Summer Idyll, 1. Summer Idyll; 2. The Stables—Colonel Grindle, 1. Colonel Grindle; 2. It Depends how you See it—Colonel and Mrs. Nicodeme and Miss Hylda Nicodeme, 1. Mrs. Nicodeme; 2. Colonel Nicodeme; 3. Miss Hylda Nicodeme—The Great Nemo, 1. The Great Nemo; 2. The Voice [both from *World Review*, July 1951]—Municipal Idyll: a Dialogue [from *Times Literary Supplement*, 9 November 1951]—Mr. and Mrs. Eager—The Grey Man [from *Go*, August/September 1951]—The Count [from *Go*, August/September 1951]—Osmund Toulmin [from *Go*, August/September 1951]—Trippers [from *Go*, August/September 1951]—Old Charles—Urban Spring Song (a fragment)—Lament for Richard Rolston—Lady Holmandale—Miss Lukewell—What was your dream, Doctor Murricombe?—Grand Finale: Fireworks at the Winter Gardens

b. *First edition, American issue*

WRACK | AT TIDESEND | A Book of Balnearics | *being* | *the second volume of* | ENGLAND RECLAIMED | *by* | OSBERT SITWELL | [*device*] | 1953 | CAEDMON PUBLISHERS | NEW YORK

Note: This issue, printed in America, has 128 pages and is bound in patterned grey-green paper boards, grey cloth spine, gilt lettered on spine and upper cover. 3000 copies were printed, and the issue was published in October 1953 at $2.50. The contents differ from 0A50a in that: the Preface is revised; "Prefatory Song, The Innocent Sky" is omitted; and "Mr. Thuddock" is added [from "English Beach Memory: Mr. Thuddock," in *New Yorker*, 17 January 1953].

a. *First edition*

COLLECTED | STORIES | [*star*] | OSBERT SITWELL |
LONDON · 1953 | GERALD DUCKWORTH & CO. LTD |
MACMILLAN & CO. LTD

217 × 141 mm.

560 pp.: [i] half-title; [ii] "List of works by Osbert Sitwell"; [iii] title;
[iv] "This book is copyright ... Printed in Great Britain"; v–vi
Contents; vii–xviii Preface; 1–540, [541] text, and: "Printed by
R. & R. Clark, Ltd., Edinburgh"; [542] blank.

Sketch-map on p. 17.

Smooth red cloth boards. Top edge black, others trimmed. Gilt
lettered on spine, with a black panel.

5000 copies printed. Published 27 March 1953 at 25*s*.

CONTENTS

Defeat [from *Open the Door!*]—That Flesh is Heir to ... [from
Dumb-Animal]—Staggered Holiday [from *Death of a God*]—The
Love-Bird [from *Dumb-Animal*]—Primavera [from *Open the Door!*]
—Shadow-Play [from *Open the Door!*]—The Machine Breaks Down
[from *Triple Fugue*]—Dumb-Animal [from *Dumb-Animal*]—The
Glow-Worm [from *Open the Door!*]—His Ship comes Home [from
Triple Fugue]—Charles and Charlemagne [from *Dumb-Animal*]—
Plague-Cart before Horse [from *Open the Door!*]—Pompey and Some
Peaches, I and II [from *Open the Door!*]—Triple Fugue [from *Triple
Fugue*]—Idyll through the Looking-Glass [from *Open the Door!*]—
Champagne for the Old Lady [from *Open the Door!*]—Lovers'
Meeting [from *Open the Door!*]—The Woman who Hated Flowers
[from *Open the Door!*]—Low Tide [from *Triple Fugue*]—The Man
who Drove Strindberg Mad [from *Open the Door!*]—Death of a God
[from *Open the Door!*]—Long Journey [from *Open the Door!*]—
True Lovers' Knot [from *Open the Door!*]—The Messenger [from
Open the Door!]—Alive-Alive Oh! [from *Dumb-Animal*]—A Place
of One's Own [from *A Place of One's Own*]—Friendship's Due [from
Triple Fugue]—Touching Wood [from *Open the Door!*]—Dead Heat
[from *Open the Door!*]—"You Can Carry it, Mrs. Parkin" [from
Penguin New Writing 21, 1944]—The Greeting [from *Triple Fugue*]

b. *First edition, American issue*

COLLECTED | STORIES | [*star*] | OSBERT SITWELL | NEW
YORK | HARPER & BROTHERS PUBLISHERS

Note: This issue, printed in America, has 560 pages and is bound in
smooth green cloth boards, lettered in silver on the spine. 3000 copies
were printed, and the issue was published 12 November 1953 at $5.00.
The contents are as in OA51a.

OA52   THE FOUR CONTINENTS   1954

a. *First edition*

The Four Continents | BEING | MORE DISCURSIONS | ON
TRAVEL, ART | AND LIFE | BY | Osbert Sitwell | LONDON |
MACMILLAN & CO LTD | 1954

217 × 138 mm.

292 pp.: [i] half-title; [ii] "List of works by Osbert Sitwell"; [iii] title;
[iv] "This book is copyright . . . Printed in Great Britain"; [v] dedication; vi Acknowledgements; vii Contents; [viii] blank; ix–x Illustrations; 1–281, [282] text, and printer's imprint: "Printed by R. & R.
Clark, Ltd., Edinburgh."

16 plates tipped in.

Smooth scarlet buckram boards. Top edge black, others trimmed.
Gilt lettered on spine, with a black panel.

5000 copies printed. Published 16 July 1954 at 25*s.*

CONTENTS

Includes "Making a Bolt for It," from *Atlantic Monthly*, April 1951,
and *Lilliput*, September/October 1951

b. *First edition, American issue*

The Four Continents | BEING | MORE DISCURSIONS | ON
TRAVEL, ART | AND LIFE | BY | Osbert Sitwell | Drawings
by Daniel Maloney | Harper & Brothers Publishers | New
York

Note: This issue, printed in America, has 320 pages, and is bound in smooth orange cloth boards, rough grey cloth spine, and is lettered in orange on the spine. 4000 copies were printed and the issue was published 11 August 1954 at $4.00. The contents are as in OA52a, with the addition of the drawings (but without the plates).

OA53   ON THE CONTINENT   1958

First edition

ON THE CONTINENT | A BOOK OF INQUILINICS | *being* | *the third volume of* | ENGLAND RECLAIMED | *by* | OSBERT SITWELL | LONDON | MACMILLAN & CO LTD | 1958

216 × 137 mm.

128 pp.: [i] half-title; [ii] "List of works by Osbert Sitwell"; [iii] title; [iv] "Copyright © by Osbert Sitwell 1958. . . . Printed in Great Britain"; [v] dedication; [vi] blank; vii–viii Preface; ix–xiv Contents; 1–108, [109] text; [110] "Printed by R. & R. Clark, Ltd., Edinburgh"; [111–114] blank.

Smooth scarlet buckram boards. Top edge black, others trimmed. Gilt lettered on spine, with a black panel.

3000 copies printed. Published 20 March 1958 at 12s. 6d.

CONTENTS

The Courier—Villa l'Allegria, 1. Teresa [from *New Yorker*, 23 February 1957]; 2a. Doctor Ripoli; 2b. At Work; 3. A Day Out; 4. Il Capitano, the Fencing Master; 4a. Red Shirt [as "Il Capitano, the Fencing Master" in *New Yorker*, 23 February 1957]; 4b. The Treasure; 5. Jean Lovingay; 6. Umberto, the Gardener; 6a. Umberto; 6b. In the Winter—Four Songs of the Italian Earth: Old Peppino, the Peasant [from *Four Songs of the Italian Earth*, with one line added to "Summer"]—Life is a Great Adventure, 1. Mr. and Mrs. Tollpepper; 2. Mr. Tollpepper; 3. Mrs. Tollpepper; 4. The Groves of Love; 5. Life is a Great Adventure—The Villa Jernyngham, 1. The Villa Jernyngham; 2. The Two Porters; 3. Skirmishes with the Enemy; 4. What became of Buster?; 5. The Boston Lily; 5a. The Boston Lily; 5b. The Salon; 6. Miss Burtle; 6a. Miss Burtle; 6b. Passports to Safety; 6c. Postscript [nos. 1 and 5 from *Harper's Magazine*, February 1958]—Sir Hubald Ledbitter, 1. Sir Hubald Ledbitter; 2. Possessions; 3. An Inalienable

Heirloom—Archdeacon and Mrs. Sawnygrass, 1. Archdeacon Sawnygrass; 2. Mrs. Sawnygrass [both from *Harper's Magazine*, February 1958]; 3. The Harmonium—Mrs. Jenkinson Jonas, 1. Mrs. Jenkinson Jonas; 2. Gypsy of the Ritz; 3. The Sole Similarity— Mr. and Mrs. Prattle, 1. A Bibliophile; 2. Prattling Mrs. Prattle; 3. The Children—"W.D.," 1. "W.D."; 2. "Mrs. W.D."; 3. Snap Judgment —Milordo Inglese, 1. Milordo Inglese; 2. An Englishman's Home; 3. As an Old Man [all from *Atlantic Monthly*, July 1958]—"Little Miss Kitty," 1. Cultural Cuckoo; 2. Green Fingers—Countess Anastasia, 1. A Ghost; 2. Countess Anastasia; 3. A La Russe—Count Carlo Trovabene—Ivan—Mr. Algernon Braithwaite—Mr. Algernon Petre, 1. Mr. Algernon Petre; 2. Manikin; 3. Boxes—The Woman who Could Not Go Home—Donald McDougall, 1. Donald McDougall; 2. In the Early Morning; 3. Gino of the Bookshop—R. Muggeridge Moody—Emilio, 1. The Legionary; 2. In Action—Italian Tea-Rooms —Miss Ishmael—The Polish Villa, 1. The Polish Villa; 2. Outside; 3. Stanislas and Augustin—Leonora Starmore, 1. Leonora Starmore; 2. The Cave—Major Cameron and Miss Cairns [from *New Yorker*, 23 February 1957]—H.H. Princess Ernest, 1. Sunday; 2. Week-day— Madame de Maire, 1. Artistic; 2. The Voice; 3. Compliments; 4. Talk —Italian Streets, 1. Italian Streets; 2. The Grotto—Flowers, 1. A la Ville des Fleurs; 2. Old Angelo of the Posy Office; 3. Flower-Day at the Market—Antiques, 1. Countess Replica [from *Harper's Magazine*, February 1958]; 2. The Battonis, a. Signor Battoni; b. Introducing Mrs. Battoni; c. Old History; d. Mr. Battoni's collection; e. A Portrait; f. The Widower—Lending Library, 1. Spring comes to the Lending Library [from *New Yorker*, 23 February 1957]; 2. Drifting Conver-sation—Late Autumn at a Tuscan Castle, 1. By Day; 2. By Night— Spring Dawn, an Eclogue—Italian Beggars, 1. Beggars; 2. Luisa; 3. Gypsies, a. Gypsy Girl; b. Caravan; 4. Prospero, a. Prospero; b. Begging; c. The Daily Round; d. Dino—Competition, 1. The Nightingales; 2. The Neapolitan Singers; 3. Who Laughs Last— Grande Finale

0A54   FEE FI FO FUM!   1959

First edition

Fee Fi Fo Fum! | *A Book of Fairy Stories* | BY | OSBERT SITWELL | LONDON | MACMILLAN & CO LTD | 1959

191 × 124 mm.

256 pp.: [i] half-title; [ii] List of works by Osbert Sitwell; [iii] title;

[iv] Copyright © Osbert Sitwell 1959 . . .; [v] Author's Note; [vi] blank; vii Contents; [viii] blank; ix–xxi Preface; [xxii] blank; 1–230 text, and imprint: Printed by R. & R. Clark, Ltd., Edinburgh; [231–234] blank.

Smooth scarlet buckram boards. Top edge black, others trimmed. Gilt lettered on spine, with black panel.

5000 copies printed. Published 5 February 1959 at 15s.

CONTENTS

OA55   A PLACE OF ONE'S OWN,   1961
AND OTHER STORIES

First edition

A Place Of One's Own | AND OTHER STORIES | BY | [*swelled rule*] | OSBERT SITWELL | [*swelled rule*] | ICON BOOKS LIMITED

181 × 114 mm.

128 pp.: [1] half-title; [2] Printing history: All the stories in this volume . . . © 1959 by Sir Osbert Sitwell. Published as an Icon Book 1961 . . . Icon Books are published by Icon Books Ltd, 5 Royal Opera Arcade, Pall Mall, S.W.1, and are made and printed in Great Britain by Love and Malcolmson Ltd, London and Redhill, Surrey; [3] title; [4] blank; [5] Contents; [6] blank; 7–126 text; [127–128] blank.

Flush pictorial wrappers, designed by Fisk. Unsewn. Printed in red, black and white on yellow.

20,000 copies printed. Published September 1961 as Icon Book F3.

[All from *Collected Stories*, 1953]

A Place of One's Own—The Glow-Worm—Primavera—The Man who drove Strindberg Mad—Staggered Holiday—Charles and Charlemagne—Dead Heat

0A56　TALES MY FATHER TAUGHT　1962
ME

a. *First edition*

TALES MY | FATHER TAUGHT ME | An Evocation of Extravagant Episodes | [*short double rule*] | OSBERT SIT-WELL | [*device*] | HUTCHINSON OF LONDON

208 × 138 mm.

208 pp.: [1] half-title; [2] "By Osbert Sitwell . . ."; [3] title; [4] Hutchinson & Co . . . First published 1962. © Osbert Sitwell 1962. This book has been set in Bembo type face. It has been printed in Great Britain by The Anchor Press, Ltd., in Tiptree, Essex, on Antique Wove paper and bound by Taylor Garnett Evans & Co., Ltd., in Watford, Herts; [5] Acknowledgments; [6] blank; [7–8] Contents; [9] Illustrations; [10] blank; 11–206, [207] text & index; [208] blank.

Eight single leaves of plates tipped in.

Smooth green cloth boards. Top edge blue, others trimmed. Grey end-papers. Gilt lettered, with blue panel, on spine.

8000 copies printed. Published 12 February 1962 at 25s.

CONTENTS

Hortus Conclusus [from *On the Making of Gardens*, 1949]—All on a Summer's Afternoon—Cigarette Ends—Going for a Drive—Recollections of an Awkward Afternoon in Knightsbridge [from *London Magazine*, February 1958]—Catching the Bus—Henry Moat—Jezebel House and a Grand Piano—The Adventures of the Phantom Tax-Inspector—La Gallina—The Fountain—Ideas from the Bureau—[partly from "To Manage Parents" in *Vogue* [New York], 1 November 1961]—Looking Ahead—Unforgotten Feasts [as "Two Dinner Parties" in *Atlantic Monthly*, May 1960]—By Rail and Boat [from "Once, when travelling . . ." in *Vogue* [New York], 1 October 1961] —A Wink from the Great Beyond—Unusual Holidays [as "My

Father's Excursions and Alarms" in *The Reporter*]—Creating [from "Father and I" in *Atlantic Monthly*, August 1961]—Popularity [from *Vogue* [New York], July 1961, and [London], 1 February 1962]—Neapolitan Street Scene—Lord Henry—Music—Magic [partly from "Father and I" in *Atlantic Monthly*, August 1961]—The Rocking-horse—Making Bolt for It [from *The Four Continents*]—Thalia—The New Jerusalem [from "Father and I" in *Atlantic Monthly*, August 1961]

b. *First edition, American issue*

TALES MY | FATHER TAUGHT ME | An Evocation of Extravagant Episodes | [*short double rule*] | Sir Osbert Sitwell | WITH ILLUSTRATIONS | [*device*] | *An Atlantic Monthly Press Book* | LITTLE, BROWN AND COMPANY | *Boston Toronto*

Note: This issue, printed in the United States, was published on 5 June 1962 at $4.75. 5000 copies were printed. The contents are exactly as in the first edition.

oA57   POUND WISE   1963

a. *First edition*

OSBERT SITWELL | POUND WISE | [*short double rule*] | [*device*] | HUTCHINSON OF LONDON

209 × 140 mm.

320 pp.: [1] half-title; [2] "List of Works by Osbert Sitwell"; [3] title; [4] Hutchinson & Co . . . First published 1963. Copyright Osbert Sitwell. This book has been set in Bembo type face. It has been printed in Great Britain by The Anchor Press, Ltd., in Tiptree, Essex, on Antique Wove paper; [5] dedication; [6] blank; [7–8] Contents; [9] Introduction; [10] blank; 11–319, [320] text.

Frontispiece (from a portrait of the author by James Fosburg) tipped in.

Black cloth boards. Top edge blue, others trimmed. Grey end-papers. Gilt stamped on spine, with cerise panel.

5000 copies printed. Published 28 January 1963 at 25s.

What it Feels like to be an Author—Old Worlds for New—Dining-Room Piece [all from *Sing High! Sing Low!*]—Fortune-Tellers—The Summer Palace, 1935 [both from *Penny Foolish*]—Municipal Rhapsody: An Idyll (1920–40) [from *Sing High! Sing Low!*]—The Lady with the Pink Feather [part of "One or Two Lives" in *Penny Foolish*]—On Ghosts—The Ghost in the Green Mask—The Best Years of Life—On Private Schools—On Public Schools—Games, (1) and (2)—On Broadening the Mind—In Praise of Indolence—The White Man's Burden—Rules for Being Rude—The Edwardians, the Rich Man's Feast—On Progress—On Advice—On the Horror of Solitude—On the Decay of Privacy—On Sex—Out of Season—On a Common Cold—On Words and their Meaning—On the Belittlement of the Great—Adult Franchise for Domestic Animals—On Fogs—By Train—Dogs—Animals versus Children [all twenty-five from *Penny Foolish*]—On Statues in General [slightly revised from Chap. I of *The People's Album of London Statues*]—On Statues in London [revised from Chap. II of the same book]—Eighteenth Century Details [from *Penny Foolish*]—The Conspiracy of Dwarfs—The Banquets of Tantalus, 1942—Save the Old School Tie—A Rose by Any Other Name—The Eye within the Ear—The Art of Pavel Tchelitchew—A Grain of Sand and a Grain of Salt—London, 1943 [all eight from *Sing High! Sing Low!*]—A Bunch of Snowdrops [from *Sunday Times*, 25 December 1949]—A Letter to My Son [from the book of that title]

b. *First edition, American issue*

POUND WISE | [*short double rule*] | Sir Osbert Sitwell | [*device*] | *An Atlantic Monthly Press Book* | LITTLE, BROWN AND COMPANY | BOSTON TORONTO

Note: This issue, printed in the United States, was published on 9 September 1963 at $5.00. 5000 copies were printed. The contents are exactly as in the first edition.

0A58   POEMS ABOUT PEOPLE   1965

First edition

Poems about People | *or* | *England Reclaimed* | [*short ornamental rule*] | OSBERT SITWELL | [*device*] | HUTCHINSON OF LONDON

209 × 132 mm.

232 pp.: [1] half-title; [2] "List of works by Osbert Sitwell"; [3] title; [4] "Hutchinson & Co. (Publishers) Ltd . . . This edition first published 1965. © This edition Osbert Sitwell 1958, 1965. This book has been set in Bembo, printed in Great Britain on Antique Wove paper by The Anchor Press, Ltd., and bound by Wm. Brendon & Son Ltd., both of Tiptree, Essex"; [5] "Book I . . ."; [6] author's note; 7–8 "Dedication, To Edith"; 9–16 Contents; [17] Preface; [18] blank; 19–21 Introduction; [22] blank; [23–24], 25–231, [232] text.

Blue cloth boards. Trimmed edges. Pink end-papers. Gilt stamped on spine, with pink panel.

2000 copies printed. Published 22 November 1965 at 35s.

CONTENTS

Book I: England Reclaimed. [All poems as in *England Reclaimed*, 1927, unless otherwise stated]

Dedication, to Edith—Introduction—Prologue—Tom—Mrs. Hague —Five Drawings of Mr. Hague: 1. In the park, 2. In the potting-shed, 3. In the hothouses, 4. The Spell [much abbreviated], 5. Discordant dawn—Mary-Anne [much abbreviated]—Mr. and Mrs. Nutch: 1. Mrs. Nutch [abbreviated], 2. Mr. Nutch—Mr. and Mrs. Goodbeare: 1. Elegy for Mr. Goodbeare, 2. Mr. and Mrs. Goodbeare, 3. Mr. Goodbeare at work—Mr. and Mrs. Southern: 1. Mrs. Southern, 2. Mrs. Southern's enemy [these two poems being the whole of the original "Mrs. Southern's enemy"], 3. Twilight— Mr. Samuel Southern: 1. Portrait of Mr. Southern through the ages [much abbreviated], 2. No flowers by request, 3. Conquering white —Phoebe Southern: 1. Phoebe Southern, 2. Silver lances, 3. After the flower show—Luke Kembley: 1. In September, 2. And October —Mrs. Kembley: Evening—Grand Finale: Symphony [much abbreviated]

Book II: Wrack at Tidesend. [All poems as in *Wrack at Tidesend*, 1952, unless otherwise stated]

Introduction—Aubade: Dick, the Donkey-Boy—Lousy Peter: 1, Lousy Peter, 2. In the cold winter, 3. Frosty question—Chanson des Mouches—The Ballad of Sister Anne—The Three Miss Coltrums: 1. In the dog-cart, 2. Life—Mrs. Busk—Lady Sparrowe-bank, and Miss Sparrowebank: 1. Lady Sparrowebank's position, 2. Miss Sparrowebank's position—Mr. Harold Colbert and his sisters: 1. Mr. Harold Colbert, 2. In the autumn, 3. The Misses

Eurydice and Alberta Colbert—Miss Lopez—Say Ninety-Nine: 1. The Two Doctors, 2. Doctor Dougall, 3. Doctor Diggle, 4. Sea-anemone—Lord and Lady Romfort: 1. Villeggiatura (Trio for bailiff, housekeeper and gardener), 2. Golightly—Frieze of Doctors' Wives: 1. Mrs. Dougall, 2. Mrs. Humbleby, 3. Mrs. Grandestin, 4. Mrs. Frossart, 5. Mrs. Cropper, 6. Mrs. Chivers—The Woman who could not die—Mr. Linton, the lamplighter: 1. Mr. Linton, the lamplighter [abbreviated], 2. Rainy night, 3. In the summer—Miss Mew: 1. Past, 2. Miss Mew-ad-Vincula, 3. Miss Mew's window-box—Rosie—Mrs. Liversidge—Bishop Criddle—More Metopes: Frieze of vestry virgins: 1. Miss Criddle, 2. Miss Molly Criddle, 3. Canon Doribell's daughters, 4. Linda Doribell, 5. "Tim" Doribell, 6. Dora Doribell, 7. Laura Doribell, 8. "Tiny" Doribell—The Black Box: 1. Major Postlethwaite [abbreviated], 2. Other times, other climes [much abbreviated], 3. Winter—Battling Mr. Better —Local press—Felicity Crudeman—Mrs. Kimber: 1. Mrs. Kimber, 2. Day dreams, 3. Rough weather—Mr. and Mrs. Travers—Summer idyll: 1. Summer idyll, 2. The stables—Mrs. Nicodeme and Miss Hylda Nicodeme: 1. Mrs. Nicodeme, 2. Miss Hylda Nicodeme—The Great Nemo: 1. The Great Nemo, 2. The voice—Municipal Idyll: a dialogue—Mr. and Mrs. Eager—The Count—Osmund Toumin—Old Charles—Urban Spring Song (a fragment) —Lament for Richard Rolston—Lady Holmandale—What was your dream, Doctor Murricombe?—Grand Finale: Fireworks at the Winter Gardens [revised and abbreviated]

Book III: On the Continent. [All poems as in *On the Continent*, 1958, unless otherwise stated]

The Courier—Villa l'Allegria: 1. Teresa, 2. Doctor Ripoli, 3. Umberto, the gardener: (i) Umberto, (ii) In the winter—Life is a Great Adventure: 1. Mr. and Mrs. Tollpepper, 2. Mr. Tollpepper, 3. Mrs. Tollpepper, 4. The groves of love, 5. Life is a great adventure —The Villa Jernyngham: 1. The Villa Jernyngham, 2. Skirmishes with the enemy, 3. What became of Buster?, 4. The Boston Lily: (i) The Boston Lily, (ii) The salon, 5. Miss Burtle: (i) Passports to safety, (ii) Postscript—Archdeacon and Mrs. Sawnygrass: 1. Archdeacon Sawnygrass, 2. Mrs. Sawnygrass, 3. The harmonium —Mrs. Jenkinson Jonas: 1. Mrs. Jenkinson Jonas, 2. Gipsy of the Ritz, 3. The sole similarity—Mr. Pattle: a bibliophile—"W.D.": 1. "W.D.", 2. "Mrs. W.D."—Milordo Inglese: 1. Milordo Inglese, 2. An Englishman's home, 3. As an old man—"Little Miss Kitty": 1. Cultural cuckoo, 2. Green fingers—Countess Anastasia: 1. A ghost, 2. Countess Anastasia, 3. A La Russe—Count Carlo

Trovabene—Ivan—Mr. Algernon Braithwaite—Mr. Algernon Petre: 1. Mr. Algernon Petre, 2. Manikin, 3. Boxes—Donald McDougall: 1. Donald McDougall, 2. In the early morning, 3. Gino of the bookshop—Italian Tea-rooms—Miss Ishmael—Major Cameron and Miss Cairns—H.H. Princess Ernest: 1. Sunday, 2. Week-day—Madame de Maire: 1. Artistic, 2. The Voice, 3. Compliments, 4. Talk—Flowers: 1. Old Angelo of the Posy Office, 2. Flower-day at the market—Antiques: 1. Countess Replica, 2. The Battonis: (i) Signor Battoni, (ii) Introducing Mrs. Battoni, (iii) Old history, (iv) Mr. Battoni's collection, (v) A portrait, (vi) The widower—The Lending Library: 1. Spring comes to the lending library, 2. Goodbye Miss Visatelli—Italian Beggars: 1. Beggars, 2. Luisa—Gypsies: 1. Gypsy girl, 2. Caravan—Prospero: 1. Prospero, 2. Begging, 3. The daily round, 4. Dino—Competition: 1. The nightingales, 2. The Neapolitan singers, 3. Who laughs last—Grand Finale [slightly abbreviated and revised]

oB1 NEW PATHS 1917–1918 1918

[*For description, see* EB3]

CONTENTS

Pp. 67–69, "Song of the Fauns"—"Pierrot at the War" by Osbert Sitwell

oB2 THE PATHS OF GLORY 1919

First edition

The Paths of Glory | A Collection of Poems written | during the War 1914–1919 | EDITED BY | BERTRAM LLOYD | [*device*] | LONDON: GEORGE ALLEN & UNWIN LTD. | RUSKIN HOUSE, 40 MUSEUM STREET, W.C.I

120 pages. 174 × 109 mm.

Pale-blue paper boards. Untrimmed edges. Lettered in black on spine and upper cover.

Published 4 December 1919 at 3s.

CONTENTS

Pp. 108–111, "Sheep-Song" [from *The Nation*, 12 October 1918, but here revised]—"The Next War" [from *The Nation*, 21 September 1918]

oB2*A* THE ETON CANDLE 1922

First edition

THE ETON CANDLE | EDITED | BY | BRIAN HOWARD | VOLUME ONE | PRINTED IN MARCH, NINETEEN

HUNDRED AND | TWENTY-TWO, AT THE SAVILE PRESS
IN ETON, BY | SPOTTISWOODE, BALLANTYNE AND
COMPANY, LTD.

124 pages. 264 × 204 mm.

Pink paper boards. Trimmed edges. Lettered in yellow on upper cover.

Published in Spring 1922 at 2s. 6d.

CONTENTS

P. 57, "Aux bords de la mer" [from *The Nation and Athenaeum*, 29 October 1921]—"The jealous goddess" [from *Spectator*, 14 January 1922]

oB2*B*　　　ETHELBERT WHITE　　　1922

First edition

[*Cover*]

ETHELBERT WHITE | EXHIBITION | [*wood-engraving*] | THE | ST. GEORGE'S | GALLERY | Messrs. ARTHUR R. HOWELL | and F. HARRISON TATE, | 32a, GEORGE STREET, | NOVEMBER HANOVER SQ., LONDON, W.1 | 1922 MAYFAIR — — 2852

4 pages. 203 × 130 mm.

Grey wrappers, printed in black as above. Trimmed edges. Published for the exhibition, November 1922.

CONTENTS

P.1, "Ethelbert White", by Oswald [*sic*; corrected in ink] Sitwell.

oB2*C*　　A MISCELLANY OF POETRY　　1922
1920–1922

[*For description, see* EB8*A*]

CONTENTS

Pp. 161–164, "Giardino Publico" [*sic*] [from *The Nation and Athenaeum*, 17 September 1921]—"Bacchanalia" [from *Saturday Westminster Gazette*, 12 November 1921]

a. *First edition*

The Best | Short Stories of 1923 | I: English | [*device*] | *Edited by* | Edward O'Brien *and* John Cournos | Jonathan Cape | Eleven Gower Street, London

352 pages. 190 × 123 mm.

Blue cloth boards. Trimmed edges. Lettered in white on spine and upper cover.

Published in January 1924 at 7*s*. 6*d*. (The publishers no longer have details of publication.)

CONTENTS

Pp. 293–303, "The Machine Breaks Down" [from *English Review*, December 1922]

b. *First edition, American copies*

Note: Copies were imported and published by Small, Maynard and Co., and later taken over by Dodd, Mead Co.

oB3 CATALOGUE OF AN EXHIBITION 1925
OF ITALIAN ART

a. *First edition, unillustrated issue*

Burlington Fine Arts Club | [*two short rules*] | CATALOGUE OF AN EXHIBITION | OF | ITALIAN ART | OF THE | SEVEN-TEENTH CENTURY | [*ornament*] | LONDON | PRIVATELY PRINTED FOR THE BURLINGTON FINE ARTS CLUB | 1925

68 pages. 272 × 209 mm.

Blue paper boards. Trimmed edges. Lettered in black on upper cover.

Published for the exhibition in May 1925. (The printers no longer know the numbers printed nor of any priority between the issues.)

CONTENTS

Pp. [7], 8–15, "Pictures, introduction" by Osbert Sitwell

b. *First edition, illustrated issue*

BURLINGTON FINE ARTS CLUB | CATALOGUE | OF AN
EXHIBITION OF | ITALIAN ART | OF THE SEVENTEENTH
CENTURY | LONDON | PRIVATELY PRINTED FOR THE |
BURLINGTON FINE ARTS | CLUB | 1925

78 pages, including plates. 310 × 252 mm.

Maroon cloth boards, with bevelled edges. Trimmed edges. Gilt
lettered on spine and upper cover.

Published for the exhibition in May 1925.

CONTENTS

As in unillustrated issue, above

0B4 ETCHINGS BY QUEEN VICTORIA 1925
AND THE PRINCE CONSORT

First edition

[*Cover*]

Etchings by | [*red*] Her Majesty the late Queen Victoria |
and the Prince Consort | [*black*] also | Victorian Pictures
and Objets d'Art | [*illustration pasted on, within black frame*] |
[*red*] June 12th until July 3rd, 1925 | [*black*] THE BROOK
STREET ART GALLERY | 14, BROOK STREET, NEW BOND
STREET, | LONDON, W.I.

10 pages (including covers), and 4 plates. 255 × 187 mm.

White paper wrappers, stapled. Untrimmed edges. Printed on covers.

Published for the exhibition, 12 June–3 July 1925.

CONTENTS

Pp. 3–4, Preface by Osbert Sitwell

0B5   C. R. W. NEVINSON   1925

First edition

C. R. W. NEVINSON | [*device*] | LONDON: ERNEST BENN,
LTD. | 8 BOUVERIE STREET, E.C. 4 | 1925

68 pages. 248 × 185 mm.

Blue cloth spine, grey paper boards. Trimmed edges. Gilt lettered up spine.

Published 26 October 1925, at 8s. 6d., in the series "Contemporary British Artists," edited by Albert Rutherston. (Publishers' records were destroyed in the war of 1939–45.)

CONTENTS

"C. R. W. Nevinson" by O[sbert] S[itwell], pp. 7–31

0B5*A*   C. R. W. NEVINSON :   1925
                EXHIBITION CATALOGUE

First edition

ETHELBERT WHITE | [*wood-engraving*] | THE | ST. GEORGE'S | GALLERY | (ARTHUR R. HOWELL) | NOV. 32a, GEORGE STREET | HANOVER SQ., LONDON, W.I. | 1925. MAYFAIR — 2852

[The above description is quoted by the late Thomas Balston in a review in *The Library*, 5th series, v. 19, p. 331, 1964 (published 1968), with the statement that it contained a foreword by Osbert Sitwell. I have failed to find a copy of this catalogue.]

0B6   THOMAS LOWINSKY: 1926
             EXHIBITION CATALOGUE

First edition

CATALOGUE OF THE EXHIBITIONS | (1) Paintings and Drawings | by THOMAS LOWINSKY | (2) Paintings, Drawings and Designs | by ALBERT RUTHERSTON | ERNEST BROWN & PHILLIPS | THE LEICESTER GAL-LERIES | LEICESTER SQUARE, LONDON | FEBRUARY, 1926 | EXHIBITIONS NOS. 409–410

20 pages. 147 × 113 mm.

Grey paper wrappers, stapled. Untrimmed edges. Lettered in black on covers.

Published for the exhibition, February 1926.

CONTENTS

Pp. 7–9, "Thomas Lowinsky" by Osbert Sitwell

oB7 THE BIBLIOPHILE'S ALMANACK FOR 1927 1926

a. *First edition, ordinary copies*

[*Within an ornamental sepia border*]

THE BIBLIOPHILE'S | ALMANACK | FOR 1927 | [*star*] | *Edited by* | OLIVER SIMON & HAROLD CHILD | THE FLEURON | LONDON

92 pages. 186 × 123 mm.

Pale green paper wrappers, sewn. Trimmed edges. Lettered in sepia on upper cover, with red and blue decoration, and up the spine.

Published in September 1926 at 2s. 6d. (The Curwen Press no longer know how many copies were printed.)

CONTENTS

Pp. 19–23, "Festas" by Osbert Sitwell

b. *First edition, special copies*

[*Title as in ordinary copies*]

92 pages. 188 × 125 mm.

Blue buckram spine, grey pictorial and lettered paper boards. Untrimmed edges. Gilt lettered on the spine.

325 numbered copies printed (300 for sale). Published in September 1926 at 6s.

CONTENTS

As in ordinary copies

First edition

CATALOGUE OF THE EXHIBITIONS | (1) TEMPERA
PAINTINGS | BY EDWARD WADSWORTH | (2) PAINTINGS
OF CHILE | BY ALVARO GUEVARA | WITH A PREFATORY
NOTE | BY OSBERT SITWELL | ERNEST BROWN &
PHILLIPS | THE LEICESTER GALLERIES | LEICESTER
SQUARE, LONDON | NOVEMBER, 1926 | EXHIBITIONS
NOS. 420–421

20 pages. 147 × 113 mm.

Orange paper wrappers, stapled. Untrimmed edges. Lettered in black
on covers.

Published for the exhibition, November 1926.

CONTENTS

Pp. 11–14, "Alvaro Guevara" by Osbert Sitwell

oB9   THE WORKS OF   [1928]
RONALD FIRBANK, VOL. 1

First edition

THE WORKS OF | RONALD FIRBANK | VOL. 1 | INTRO-
DUCTION | By ARTHUR WALEY | BIOGRAPHICAL
MEMOIR | By OSBERT SITWELL | VAINGLORY | DUCK-
WORTH: LONDON | BRENTANO'S: NEW YORK | 1929

248 pages, and frontispiece. 218 × 142 mm.

Yellow buckram boards. Top edge blue, others untrimmed. Gilt
lettered on spine.

235 sets of five volumes printed (200 for sale). Published in December
1928 at 105s.

CONTENTS

Pp. 12–34, "Biographical Memoir" by Osbert Sitwell

EXHIBITION CATALOGUE

[*Cover*]

HOGARTH ROOM | [*within border*] CATALOGUE OF AN
EXHIBITION | OF PAINTINGS AND WATER- | COLOURS
BY ETHELBERT WHITE | WITH A PREFATORY NOTE BY |
OSBERT SITWELL | ERNEST BROWN & PHILLIPS |
(CECIL L. PHILLIPS OLIVER F. BROWN) | THE LEI-
CESTER GALLERIES | LEICESTER SQUARE, LONDON |
[*below the border*] EXHIBITION No. 478 APRIL, 1929

12 pages, and 4 plates. 147 × 113 mm.

Blue paper wrappers, stapled. Untrimmed edges. Lettered in black on covers.

Published for the exhibition, April 1929.

CONTENTS

Pp. 5–7, "The Seasons" by Osbert Sitwell

oB11   THOMAS ROWLANDSON   1929

First edition

FAMOUS WATER-COLOUR PAINTERS | VI — THOMAS
ROWLANDSON | INTRODUCTION BY | OSBERT SIT-
WELL | [*device*] | 1929 | "THE STUDIO" LIMITED | 44
LEICESTER SQ., LONDON, W.C. 2

28 pages. 295 × 242 mm.

Brick-red paper boards. Trimmed edges. White paper label, lettered in black, pasted on upper cover.

Published in August 1929 at 5*s.*, as no. VI of the series "Famous Water-Colour Painters." (Publishers' records destroyed in the war of 1939–45.)

CONTENTS

Pp. 1–10, Introduction by Osbert Sitwell

First edition

CARROLL CARSTAIRS | [*short rule*] | A | GENERATION |
MISSING | [*short rule*] | WITH A FOREWORD BY | *OSBERT
SITWELL* | [*device*] | [*short rule*] | *LONDON* | WILLIAM
HEINEMANN LTD.

222 pages. 184 × 121 mm.

Brown cloth boards. Trimmed edges. Blind-stamped on covers and
gilt lettered on spine.

2000 copies printed. Published 31 March 1930 at 5s.

CONTENTS

Pp. ix–xiii, "Foreword" by Osbert Sitwell

Note: The publishers say that there was at some date a 2-page cancel in
this book, but have no further details. I do not know if it affected the
foreword since I have not seen a copy with a cancel.

a. *First edition*

SOBER TRUTH | A Collection of Nineteenth-century
Episodes, | Fantastic, Grotesque and Mysterious | *Compiled
and edited by* | Margaret Barton and Osbert Sitwell | *With a
preface by* | OSBERT SITWELL | and Seventeen Illustrations |
DUCKWORTH | 3 Henrietta Street | London

280 pages, and 16 plates. 217 × 139 mm.

Yellow canvas boards. Trimmed edges. Gilt lettered on spine.

1500 copies printed. Published 1 April 1930 at 12s. 6d.

CONTENTS

Pp. 13–34: Preface, by Osbert Sitwell — pp. 35–280: The collection,
edited by Osbert Sitwell and Margaret Barton

b. *First edition, American copies*

SOBER TRUTH | A Collection of Nineteenth-century Epi-
sodes, | Fantastic, Grotesque and Mysterious | *Compiled and
edited by* | Margaret Barton and Osbert Sitwell | *With a pre-
face by* | OSBERT SITWELL | and Seventeen Illustrations |
NEW YORK | FREDERICK A. STOKES COMPANY | PUB-
LISHERS

Note: 500/520 copies were imported, but I have found only a rebound
copy. Published in 1930 at $3.50. The contents are as in 0B13a.

oB14   RONALD FIRBANK   1930

a. *First edition*

RONALD FIRBANK | A MEMOIR BY IFAN KYRLE FLET-
CHER | WITH PERSONAL REMINISCENCES BY | LORD
BERNERS, V. B. HOLLAND, | AUGUSTUS JOHN, R.A., AND
OSBERT SITWELL | *[drawing]* | WITH PORTRAITS BY |
ALVARO GUEVARA, AUGUSTUS JOHN, R.A., | WYNDHAM
LEWIS, AND CHARLES SHANNON, R.A. | DUCKWORTH |
3 HENRIETTA STREET, W.C. | 1930

152 pages, and 8 plates. 223 × 136 mm.
Black cloth boards. Trimmed edges. Gilt lettered up spine.
1500 copies printed. Published in November 1930 at 8*s.* 6*d.*

CONTENTS

Pp. 117–144, "Ronald Firbank" by Osbert Sitwell [revised from the
"Biographical Memoir" in *The Works of Ronald Firbank*, 0B9]

b. *First edition, American copies*

Note: About 250 copies were imported by Brentano's, New York,
with a cancel title dated 1932. Published at $2.50. The contents are as
in 0B14a.

oB15 LIFAR EXHIBITION CATALOGUE 1930

[For description, see EB15]

CONTENTS

Pp. [4–5], Preface (2) by Osbert Sitwell

oB16   RONALD ROSS   1931

First edition

RONALD ROSS | DISCOVERER AND CREATOR | *by* | R. L. MÉGROZ | *With a Preface by* | OSBERT SITWELL | LONDON | GEORGE ALLEN & UNWIN LTD | MUSEUM STREET

288 pages, and 4 plates. 216 × 138 mm.

Rough maroon cloth boards. Top edge maroon, others trimmed. Gilt lettered on spine. (A later binding was in smooth red cloth boards.)

1500 copies printed. Published 8 September 1931 at 10s. 6d.

CONTENTS

Pp. 9–10, Preface by Osbert Sitwell

oB17   VICTORIANA   1931

First edition

[*Within a heavy rule border*]

VICTORIANA | A SYMPOSIUM | OF VICTORIAN WISDOM | [*rule*] | edited, and compiled from many original sources, | by | MARGARET BARTON | AND | OSBERT SITWELL | [*rule*] | with a frontispiece in colour by | MAX BEERBOHM | and an introduction by | AUGUSTINE RIVERS | and a preface by | OSBERT SITWELL | [*rule*] | "And statesmen at her council met | Who knew the seasons when to take | Occasion by the hand, and make | The bounds of freedom wider yet." | [*rule*] | DUCKWORTH | 3 Henrietta Street, W.C.2 | 1931

160 pages, and frontispiece. 218 × 138 mm.

Yellow canvas boards. Trimmed edges. Gilt lettered on spine. (The publisher's name is lettered on the spine in more than one size, but no priority between bindings has been established.)

2000 copies printed. Published 12 March 1931 at 7s. 6d.

CONTENTS

Pp. 5–7: Introduction, by Augustine Rivers [Osbert Sitwell]—pp. 9–21: Preface, by Osbert Sitwell—pp. 23–157: the collection, edited by Margaret Barton and Osbert Sitwell.

oB18   BELSHAZZAR'S FEAST   1931

First edition

BELSHAZZAR'S FEAST | *for Mixed Choir, Baritone Solo and Orchestra* | *by* WILLIAM WALTON | *Text selected and arranged from the Holy Bible by* | OSBERT SITWELL | *German translation by* | Beryl de Zoete | *and* | Baronin Imma Doernberg | *Price* 3/– | OXFORD UNIVERSITY PRESS | Amen House, Warwick Square, London, E.C. 4

132 pages. 251 × 175 mm.

White paper wrappers, sewn. Trimmed edges. Printed in green and black on covers.

Published 15 September 1931 at 3s. [The publishers state: "It is not possible to distinguish between the first impression of this score and subsequent reprint, unless a search is made in each issue for any corrections . . ."]

CONTENTS

The text selected and arranged by Osbert Sitwell

First edition

GREEN THOUGHTS | By JOHN COLLIER with a Frontis- | piece by EDWARD WOLFE | and a Foreword by OSBERT | SITWELL | *Being No. 12 of the Furnival Books* | [*ornament*] | WILLIAM JACKSON (BOOKS) LTD | 18 TOOKS COURT, CHANCERY LANE, LONDON | 1932

[*Over this imprint is tipped a label*] THE *FURNIVAL BOOKS* ARE NOW PUBLISHED | BY JOINER & STEELE, LTD., 18 TOOKS COURT, | LONDON, E.C.4. — THE NAME 'WILLIAM JACKSON | (BOOKS) LTD.' HAS BEEN RETAINED ON | THE TITLE-PAGE IN ORDER THAT | THE SET OF TWELVE BOOKS | MAY BE TYPOGRAPHIC-ALLY | UNIFORM

60 pages, and frontispiece. 251 × 154 mm.

Tan buckram boards. Top edge gilt, others untrimmed. Gilt lettered up spine and on upper cover.

550 copies printed (500 for sale), all signed by the author. Published in March 1932 at 10s. 6d.

CONTENTS

Pp. 9–20, Foreword by Osbert Sitwell

oB20   SELECTED MODERN   1932
ENGLISH ESSAYS, SECOND SERIES

First edition

SELECTED | MODERN ENGLISH | ESSAYS | [*series device*] | *Second Series* | LONDON | OXFORD UNIVERSITY PRESS | HUMPHREY MILFORD

370 pages (including advertisements). 149 × 83 mm.

Smooth dark blue cloth boards. Top edge dark blue, others trimmed. Blind-stamped on upper cover, gilt and blind-stamped on spine.

5000 copies printed. Published 28 July 1932 at 2s., as no. 406 of "The World's Classics."

Pp. 295–298, "A Note on Charles Dickens" by Osbert Sitwell [from *Week-End Review*, 21 November 1931]

oB21   THE 'WEEK-END'   1932
CALENDAR

First edition

THE | 'WEEK-END' CALENDAR | *Edited by* | GERALD BARRY | *With decorations by* | JOHN ARMSTRONG | GEOFFREY BLES | 22 SUFFOLK STREET, PALL MALL | LONDON, S.W.1 | 1932

328 pages. 189 × 114 mm.

Blue cloth boards. Top edge blue, others trimmed. Gilt lettered on spine.

Published in December 1932 at 6s. (Publishers' records "destroyed by enemy action" in the war of 1939–45. The printers say 2170 copies were printed.)

CONTENTS

Pp. 32–34, "Portrait of Lawrence" by Osbert Sitwell [from *Week-End Review*, 7 February 1931]

oB21*A*   PAVEL TCHELITCHEW   1933

First edition

[*Cover; with pink vertical bars alongside first 6 lines*]

PAINTINGS | GOUACHES | DRAWINGS | by | [*pink:*] PAVEL | *TCHELITCHEW* | [*black:*] EXHIBITION | FEB. 23rd—MAR. 18th | 1933 | ARTHUR TOOTH & SONS, LTD. | 155 NEW BOND STREET, W.1

4 pages. 178 × 151 mm.

Stiff paper wrappers, upper cover printed as above. Trimmed edges. Published for the exhibition in February 1933.

CONTENTS

Pp. 1–2, "Foreword" by Osbert Sitwell

First edition

[*Within an ornamental border*]

Johnson's | England | An Account of the | *Life & Manners* | of his AGE | Edited by | A. S. TURBERVILLE | *Professor of Modern History in the* | *University of Leeds* | VOL. II | [*device*] | Clarendon Press Oxford | 1933

416 pages, and 59 plates. 228 × 144 mm.

Smooth dark-blue cloth boards. Trimmed edges. Gilt stamped on upper cover and spine, and blind-stamped on both covers.

5000 sets printed. Two uniform volumes published 23 November 1933 at 42s. the set.

CONTENTS

Pp. 1–40, "Taste" by Osbert Sitwell and Margaret Barton

oB23   LADY SYSONBY'S COOK BOOK 1935

First edition

Lady Sysonby's | *Cook Book* | *by* Ria Sysonby | *with an introduction by* | Osbert Sitwell | *and Decorations by* | Oliver Messel | Putnam | [*short swelled rule*] | Covent Garden London

328 pages; 10 plates as cancels. 186 × 123 mm.

Cream washable cloth boards. Trimmed edges. Printed in black on spine and upper cover.

Published in November 1935 at 7s. 6d.

CONTENTS

Pp. xi–xv, Introduction by Osbert Sitwell

oB24 THE ENGLISH COUNTRY HOUSE 1935

a. *First edition*

THE ENGLISH | COUNTRY HOUSE | *By* | RALPH DUT-TON | *With a Foreword by* | OSBERT SITWELL | *Illustrated*

from Photographs by | WILL F. TAYLOR | *and others* |
LONDON | B. T. BATSFORD LTD. | 15 NORTH AUDLEY
STREET, W.I.

160 pages (including 32 pages advertisements). 214 × 138 mm.

Tan cloth boards. Top edge yellow, others trimmed. Pictorial end-papers. Lettered in yellow on spine and upper cover.

8900 copies printed. Published in November 1935 at 7s. 6d. in "The British Heritage" series.

CONTENTS

Pp. v–vi, Foreword by Osbert Sitwell

b. *First edition, American copies*

Note: 1050 copies imported by Charles Scribner's Sons of New York, with their imprint added to the title. Published in 1936 at $3.00. Binding as above, but with SCRIBNERS substituted for BATSFORD on the spine. The contents as in oB24a.

oB25   THOMAS BABINGTON   1936
                      MACAULAY
First edition

[A postcard. The front reproduces in colour the painting—in the National Portrait Gallery—of Macaulay by Sir Francis Grant. Half the reverse is left for the address, and the other bears a brief text on Macaulay by Osbert Sitwell, and the imprint: "Printed for the National Portrait Gallery, London, by B. Matthews, Bradford, England."]

Published in 1936 by the National Portrait Gallery as no. 453 of its series of postcard reproductions.

oB26   TWO GENERATIONS   1940
First edition
[*Within a decorated border*]
TWO | *GENERATIONS* | *With a Preface,* | *and Edited, by* |
OSBERT SITWELL | **London** | *MACMILLAN & CO. LTD.* |
1940

348 pages, and 15 plates. 219 × 147 mm.

Green cloth boards. Trimmed edges. Gilt lettered on spine.

2000 copies printed. Published 24 September 1940 at 15s.

CONTENTS
Preface

The Dew, it Lyes on the Wood; being the reminiscences of Georgiana Caroline Sitwell, afterward Mrs. Campbell Swinton of Kimmerghame [partly previously published by Osbert Sitwell in *Life and Letters To-day*, February–August 1940]

Vestals and Vestries; being the Journal of Miss Florence Alice Sitwell [partly previously published by Osbert Sitwell in *Life and Letters To-day*, September 1935 and Winter 1936/37]

oB27   HERE'S RICHNESS!   1942

a. *First edition, ordinary copies*

HERE'S RICHNESS! | *AN ANTHOLOGY* | *OF AND BY* | JAMES AGATE | *WITH* | *A FOREWORD BY* | OSBERT SITWELL | "Ah!" said that gentleman [Mr. Squeers], | smacking his lips, "here's richness!" | *Nicholas Nickleby* | GEORGE G. HARRAP & CO. LTD. | LONDON TORONTO BOMBAY SYDNEY

272 pages. 198 × 134 mm.

Blue cloth boards. Trimmed edges. Lettered in pale pink on spine.

Published 30 April 1942 at 10s. 6d. (Neither publishers nor printers know the numbers printed.)

CONTENTS

Pp. 7–17, "Foreword" by Osbert Sitwell

b. *First edition, special copies*

[*Title and size as in ordinary copies, above*]

Blue morocco boards. Top edge gilt, others trimmed. Lettered in white on spine.

100 copies printed (90 for sale), numbered and signed by James Agate and Osbert Sitwell. Published 30 April 1942.

As in ordinary copies

oB28 COLLECTED POEMS OF 1943
W. H. DAVIES

First edition (of introduction)

COLLECTED POEMS | *of* | W. H. DAVIES | [*device*] | *Intro-duction by* | OSBERT SITWELL | JONATHAN CAPE | THIRTY BEDFORD SQUARE | LONDON

536 pages, and frontispiece. 193 × 121 mm.

Blue cloth boards. Trimmed edges. Silver stamped on spine.

4073 copies printed. Published 30 November 1943 at 8*s.* 6*d.*

CONTENTS

Pp. xxi–xxviii, Introduction by Osbert Sitwell

Note: Collected Poems of W. H. Davies first published 1942, but this "second impression" is the first to have the Introduction by Osbert Sitwell.

oB29 ECKINGTON SHOW 1944
PROGRAMME 1944

First edition

[*Cover*]

[*Within a drawing*] **Eckington War Comforts Committee** | (*Registered under the War Charities Act,* 1940 [*sic*] | A | HORTICULTURAL | AND RABBIT SHOW | to be held in the Park of | RENISHAW HALL | (By permission of Sir Osbert Sitwell, Bt.) | on | Saturday, August 12th, 1944 | To be opened by | C. H. MIDDLETON, Esq. | [*below drawing*] *Drawing by John Piper.* PROGRAMME 1/–.

40 pages. 217 × 138 mm.

White paper wrappers, stapled. Trimmed edges. Printed in black on covers.

Published at the show on 12 August 1944 at 1*s.*

P. 3, Preface by Sir Osbert Sitwell

Note: It is possible that there was a preface by Sir Osbert to the 1943 Eckington Show Programme; but no copy of this has been traced.

oB30   THE SITWELL COUNTRY: 1945
CATALOGUE

a. *First edition*

CATALOGUE | THE P.E.N. CLUB: Exhibition of Paintings and | Drawings by Contemporary Artists | THE SITWELL COUNTRY: Derbyshire | Domains, background to an Autobiography, and other Paintings and Drawings by | JOHN PIPER | With Preface by | Sir OSBERT SITWELL, Bart. | ERNEST BROWN & PHILLIPS, Ltd. | (Directors: CECIL L. PHILLIPS, OLIVER F. BROWN | PATRICK L. PHILLIPS) | THE LEICESTER GALLERIES | LEICESTER SQUARE, LONDON | JANUARY, 1945 | EXHIBITION NOS. 803–804

20 pages. 145 × 108 mm.

Salmon pink wrappers, stapled. Untrimmed edges. Lettered in black on covers.

Published for the exhibition in January 1945.

CONTENTS

Pp. 14–16, "Preface to John Piper's Exhibition" by Osbert Sitwell

Note: This exhibition was also shown at Chesterfield and Sheffield: Chesterfield [oB30b]: Exhibited at Chesterfield Public Library February 26–March 17, 1945, under the title "Derbyshire Mansions." The catalogue, printed for this showing, also contains "Preface to John Piper's Exhibition," pp. 2–3.

Sheffield [oB30c]: Exhibited at the Graves Art Gallery May 19–June 17, 1945, under the title "The Sitwell Country". The catalogue, printed for this showing, also contains "Preface to John Piper's Exhibition," pp. 2–3.

First edition

[*Society's shield & arms*] | THE FIRST TEN YEARS | BEING
AN ACCOUNT OF THE | ACTIVITIES OF THE SHEFFIELD |
PHILHARMONIC SOCIETY SINCE | THE DATE OF ITS
FORMATION, | 23rd AUGUST, 1935

32 pages. 212 × 138 mm.

Grey paper wrappers, stapled. Trimmed edges. Printed in black
with drawings on covers.

6200 copies printed. Published 17 July 1945 at 1s. 3d.

CONTENTS

Pp. 10–12, "A Tune in the Head" by Osbert Sitwell

First edition

[*Cover*]

[*With a drawing; in red*] 𝕰𝖈𝖐𝖎𝖓𝖌𝖙𝖔𝖓 𝖂𝖆𝖗 𝕮𝖔𝖒𝖋𝖔𝖗𝖙𝖘 𝕮𝖔𝖒-
𝖒𝖎𝖙𝖙𝖊𝖊 | (*Registered under War Charities Act, 1940*). | A |
HORTICULTURAL | AND RABBIT SHOW | to be held in the
Park of | RENISHAW HALL | (By permission of Sir Osbert
Sitwell, Bt.) | on | Saturday, August 11th, 1945 | To be
opened by | C. H. MIDDLETON, Esq. | [*black, below drawing*]
Drawing by John Piper. PROGRAMME 1/–.

36 pages (including covers). 212 × 138 mm.

White paper wrappers, stapled. Trimmed edges. Printed in black on
covers.

Published at the show on 11 August 1945 at 1s.

P. 3, Preface by Sir Osbert Sitwell

0B32*A*   STORIES OF THE FORTIES   1945

First edition

Stories of the | FORTIES | *edited by* | Reginald Moore | and | Woodrow Wyatt | Volume I | LONDON | NICHOLSON & WATSON

256 pages. 184 × 120 mm.

Orange cloth boards (copies also found in green cloth boards). Trimmed edges. Gilt lettered on spine.

Published in October 1945 at 8*s.* 6*d.*

CONTENTS

Pp. 9–21, "Staggered Holiday" by Osbert Sitwell [from *English Story*, [no.] 3, 1942]

0B33   THE HAPPY ROCK   1945

First edition

[Decorated title]

The Happy Rock | *[drawing]* | *A* | *Book* | *About* | *Henry Miller*

176 pages (printed in half-sheets on different coloured papers). 261 × 178 mm.

The first 750 copies bound in grey cloth spine, grey paper boards. Trimmed edges. Grey end-papers. Printed in red and black on upper cover.

3000 copies printed. 750 copies published by Bern Porter in Berkeley, California, 15 November 1945 at $5.00. (The remaining 2250 copies published 18 July 1947 at $5.00.)

P. 108, Cabled message from Osbert Sitwell

OB34   ECKINGTON SHOW   1946
              PROGRAMME 1946

First edition

[*Cover*]

[*Within a drawing*] ECKINGTON | 𝔥𝔬𝔯𝔱𝔦𝔠𝔲𝔩𝔱𝔲𝔯𝔞𝔩 � **Horticultural Rabbit and Poultry Society** | THE | Annual Show | will be held in | Renishaw Park | (By permission of Sir Osbert Sitwell, Bt.) | on | Saturday, August 10th, 1946 | To be opened by | GILLIE POTTER, ESQ. | [*below drawing*] *Drawing by John Piper.* PROGRAMME 1/–.

36 pages (including covers). 187 × 125 mm.

White paper wrappers, stapled. Trimmed edges. Printed in black on covers.

Published at the show on 10 August 1946 at 1*s*.

P. 3, Preface by Sir Osbert Sitwell

OB35   C. R. W. NEVINSON: 1947
              EXHIBITION CATALOGUE

First edition

CATALOGUE OF THE MEMORIAL | EXHIBITION OF PICTURES BY | C. R. W. NEVINSON, A.R.A. (1889–1946) | With a Preface by | SIR OSBERT SITWELL, BT. | ERNEST BROWN & PHILLIPS Ltd. | (Directors: Cecil L. Phillips, Oliver F. Brown | Patrick L. Phillips) | THE LEICESTER GALLERIES | LEICESTER SQUARE, LONDON | MAY–JUNE, 1947 | EXHIBITION NO. 858 | REYNOLDS & HOGARTH ROOMS

16 pages, and 2 plates. 145 × 108 mm.

Grey paper wrappers, stapled. Untrimmed edges. Printed in red on covers.

Published at the exhibition in May 1947.

CONTENTS

Pp. 3–5, "C. R. W. Nevinson" by Osbert Sitwell

oB36   A FREE HOUSE!   1947

First edition

A FREE HOUSE! | OR | THE ARTIST AS CRAFTSMAN | [*brief ornamental rule*] | BEING THE WRITINGS OF | WALTER RICHARD SICKERT | EDITED BY | OSBERT SITWELL | LONDON | MACMILLAN & CO. LTD | 1947

416 pages, and 17 plates. 217 × 138 mm.
Smooth green cloth boards. Trimmed edges. Gilt lettered on spine.
6000 copies printed. Published 24 June 1947 at 25*s*.

CONTENTS

The book edited by Osbert Sitwell, and including on pp. xiii–liv, "A short character of Walter Richard Sickert" by Osbert Sitwell [from *Orion II*, 1945]

oB37   THE BATTLE OF THE BOOKS   1947

[*Within a border*]

THE BATTLE | OF THE BOOKS | [*double rule*] | EDITED BY GERARD HOPKINS | [*double rule*] | [*eight lines of contributors' names, in two columns divided by a vertical rule:*] *Leonard Brooks   Alan S. Jackson* | *J. Foulis Clapperton   J. John Jarrold* | *Arthur Coleridge   Douglas Leighton* | *Rupert Hart-Davis   A. D. Peters* | *F. E. K. Foat   Sir Osbert Sitwell* | *Henry Green   Sir Stanley Unwin* | *John Hadfield   J. Murray Watson* | *John Hampden   P. S. J. Welsford* | *and a leader from* THE NEW STATESMAN | [*double rule*] | LONDON | ALLAN WINGATE

56 pages. 183 × 122 mm.

Brown paper wrappers, stapled. Trimmed edges. Lettered in white on covers.

10,000 copies printed. Published 18 July 1947 at 2s. 6d.

CONTENTS

Pp. 16–19, "The Present Difficulties of Authorship" by Sir Osbert Sitwell

oB38   ECKINGTON SHOW   1947
           PROGRAMME 1947

[*Cover*]

[*Within a drawing*] ECKINGTON | Horticultural, Rabbit and Poultry Society. | THE 6TH | Annual Show | will be held in | Renishaw Park | (By permission of Sir Osbert Sitwell, Bt.) | on | Saturday, August 9th, 1947 | To be opened by | sir OSBERT SITWELL | Bart. | [*below drawing*] Drawing by John Piper. Programme & Catalogue 2/6.

48 pages (including covers). 189 × 124 mm.

White paper wrappers, stapled. Trimmed edges. Printed in black on covers.

Published at the show on 9 August 1947 at 2s. 6d.

CONTENTS

P. 3, Preface by Sir Osbert Sitwell

oB39   A CELEBRATION FOR   1948
            EDITH SITWELL

First edition

A Celebration for | EDITH SITWELL | *edited by JOSE GARCIA VILLA* | *Direction* | SEVEN

144 pages. 235 × 151 mm.

White glossy paper wrappers, sewn. Trimmed edges. Printed in black on covers, with portrait of Edith Sitwell by Pavel Tchelitchew reproduced on upper cover. ("About 50 copies were hardbound for review and presentation" according to the publishers.)

"Under 1000 copies" printed, according to the publishers. Published "about April" 1948 at $1.50, as no. 7 in the series "Direction," by New Directions, Norfolk, Conn.

CONTENTS

Pp. 7–10, "A Reminiscence" by Sir Osbert Sitwell

oB40   ECKINGTON SHOW   1948
PROGRAMME 1948

First edition

[*Cover*]

[*Within a drawing*] Eckington Show Society. | THE 7TH | Annual Show | will be held in | Renishaw Park | (By permission of Sir Osbert Sitwell, Bt.) | on | Saturday, August 7th, 1948 | [*below drawing*] *Drawing by John Piper*. Programme & Catalogue 1/–.

56 pages (including covers). 185 × 124 mm.

White paper wrappers, stapled. Trimmed edges. Printed in black on covers.

Published at the show on 7 August 1948 at 1*s*.

CONTENTS

P. 3, Preface by Sir Osbert Sitwell

oB41   SACHEVERELL SITWELL: 1948
SELECTED POEMS

[*For description, see* sA49]

CONTENTS

Pp. v–x, "Preface" by Osbert Sitwell

First edition (of introduction)

BLEAK HOUSE | *By* | CHARLES DICKENS | *With Forty Illustrations by 'Phiz' | and an Introduction by* | SIR OSBERT SITWELL | [*sepia decoration*] | GEOFFREY CUMBERLEGE | OXFORD UNIVERSITY PRESS | *London   New York Toronto*

904 pages, and 40 plates. 183 × 122 mm.

Brown cloth boards. Top edge brown, others trimmed. Lettered in silver on spine.

10,000 copies printed. Published 25 November 1948 at 10s. 6d., in "The New Oxford Illustrated Dickens."

CONTENTS

Pp. v–xiv, "Introduction" by Osbert Sitwell

0B42*A*   SIR THOMAS BEECHAM: 1949
70th BIRTHDAY CONCERT

First edition

THE ROYAL ALBERT HALL | (*Manager:* C. S. Taylor) | MONDAY, 2nd MAY, 1949 | SIR THOMAS BEECHAM | 70th BIRTHDAY CONCERT | ROYAL PHILHARMONIC ORCHES-TRA | (Leader: DAVID MCCALLUM) | GORDON CLINTON | LUTON CHORAL SOCIETY | (Chorus Master: ARTHUR T. DAVIS) | CONDUCTOR: | SIR THOMAS BEECHAM, Bart. | Sponsored by | 𝕿𝖍𝖊 𝕯𝖆𝖎𝖑𝖞 𝕿𝖊𝖑𝖊𝖌𝖗𝖆𝖕𝖍 | IN AID OF THE FOUNDATION FUND OF | THE ROYAL PHILHAR-MONIC SOCIETY | *Honorary Management:* HAROLD HOLT LTD.

12 pages. 247 × 189 mm.

White paper wrappers, stapled. Trimmed edges. Printed in white, red and sepia on covers.

Published as the concert programme on 2 May 1949 at 1s.

Pp. 2–3, "Sir Thomas Beecham, an appreciation" by Sir Osbert Sitwell

oB43   TRAVELS THROUGH   1949
FRANCE AND ITALY

First edition (of introduction)

Travels through | France and Italy | [*short double rule*] | TOBIAS SMOLLETT | *With an introduction by* | OSBERT SITWELL | [*decoration*] | *London* | JOHN LEHMANN

304 pages. 184 × 122 mm.

Red cloth boards. Trimmed edges. Gilt stamped on spine.

Published in July 1949 at 8*s.* 6*d.*, as no. 30 in "The Chiltern Library." (Publishers and printers no longer have records of publication.)

CONTENTS

Pp. v–xi, Introduction by Osbert Sitwell

oB44   ECKINGTON SHOW   1949
PROGRAMME 1949

[*Cover*]

[*Within a drawing*] ECKINGTON SHOW SOCIETY | THE 8TH | Annual Show | will be held in | *Renishaw Park* | (By Permission of Sir Osbert Sitwell, Bt.) | on | Saturday, August 6th, 1949 | [*below drawing*] *Drawing by John Piper* PROGRAMME & CATALOGUE 1/–

60 pages (including covers). 197 × 131 mm.

White paper wrappers, stapled. Trimmed edges. Printed in black on covers.

Published at the show on 6 August 1949 at 1*s.*

CONTENTS

P. 3, Preface by Sir Osbert Sitwell [slightly revised from *Eckington Show Programme*, 1948]

a. *First edition*

Ronald Firbank | [*short swelled rule*] | FIVE NOVELS | VAL-
MOUTH | THE FLOWER BENEATH THE FOOT | PRANCING
NIGGER | CONCERNING THE ECCENTRICITIES | OF
CARDINAL PIRELLI | THE ARTIFICIAL PRINCESS |
With an introduction by | OSBERT SITWELL | [*device*] |
[*short swelled rule*] | Gerald Duckworth & Co. Ltd. | 3
Henrietta St., London, W.C.2

508 pages. 215 × 137 mm.

Smooth dark green cloth boards. Top edge dark green, others
trimmed. Gilt lettered on spine.

2350 copies printed. Published in October 1949 at 18*s*.

CONTENTS

Pp. vii–xxxi, Introduction by Osbert Sitwell [revised from "Ronald
Firbank" in I. K. Fletcher, *Ronald Firbank*, 1930]

b. *First edition, American copies*

Note: 3500 copies were imported by New Directions, Norfolk, Conn.,
with their imprint. Green cloth boards, trimmed edges, gilt lettered on
spine. Published in 1949 at $5.00. The contents as in oB45a.

oB46   DICTIONARY OF NATIONAL   1949
BIOGRAPHY 1931–1940

First edition

THE | DICTIONARY | OF | NATIONAL BIOGRAPHY |
Founded in 1882 by | GEORGE SMITH | [*short rule*] | 1931–
1940 | Edited by L. G. Wickham Legg | [*short rule*] | With
an Index covering the years 1901–1940 | in one alphabetical
series | OXFORD UNIVERSITY PRESS | LONDON:
GEOFFREY CUMBERLEGE | 1949

984 pages. 230 × 161 mm.

Dark blue cloth boards. Trimmed edges. Gilt lettered on spine.
5046 copies printed. Published 3 November 1949 at 50s.

CONTENTS

Pp. 784–785, "Sassoon, Sir Philip Albert Gustave David" by Osbert
Sitwell

0B47 ON THE MAKING OF GARDENS 1949

a. *First edition (of introduction), ordinary copies*

SIR GEORGE SITWELL | ON | THE MAKING | OF | GAR-
DENS | WITH AN INTRODUCTION BY | SIR OSBERT
SITWELL | AND DECORATIONS BY | JOHN PIPER |
[*small orange decoration*] | THE DROPMORE PRESS | 1949

140 pages. 230 × 147 mm.
Green buckram boards. Top edge green speckled, others untrimmed.
Gilt lettered on spine.
900 copies printed, numbered 101–1000. Published 14 November
1949 at 30s. (Sir George Sitwell's book was first published in 1909.)

CONTENTS

Pp. i–xiii, "Hortus Conclusus, my father in the garden" by Osbert
Sitwell

b. *First edition (of introduction), special copies*
[*Title and size as in ordinary copies, above*]

Full green morocco boards. Top edge gilt, others untrimmed. Gilt
stamped on spine and covers. Slip case.
100 copies printed, numbered 1–100, signed by Osbert Sitwell and
John Piper. Published 14 November 1949 at 63s.

CONTENTS

As in ordinary copies

c. *second edition* (*of introduction*)

SIR GEORGE SITWELL | [*short ornamental swelled rule*] |
ON THE MAKING | OF GARDENS | With an Introduction by
| SIR OSBERT SITWELL | [*short ornamental swelled rule*] |
New York: CHARLES SCRIBNER'S SONS | London:
GERALD DUCKWORTH & CO. LTD

96 pages, and 8 plates. 216 × 137 mm.

Green buckram boards. Top edge green, others trimmed. Gilt
lettered on spine.

960 copies printed for Duckworth, 1039 for Scribner's. Published in
May 1951 at 15*s*., and on 6 June 1951 at $3.75.

CONTENTS

The introduction is as in 0B47 a.–b.

oB48   THE FRICK COLLECTION   1949
CATALOGUE, Vol. I

First edition

[*Red decoration*] | [*black*] THE FRICK COLLECTION | AN
ILLUSTRATED CATALOGUE | OF THE WORKS OF ART
IN | THE COLLECTION OF | HENRY CLAY FRICK | WITH
AN INTRODUCTION BY SIR OSBERT SITWELL | VOLUME
ONE · PAINTINGS | TEXT | [*red decoration*] | PITTSBURGH |
PRINTED AT THE UNIVERSITY | 1949

328 pages [volume I]. 436 × 309 mm.

Terracotta buckram boards. Top edge gilt, others untrimmed. Gilt
lettered on spine and front cover.

175 sets of the first three volumes were given to libraries and institu-
tions throughout the world, from 1949. No sets were for sale. The
twelfth and last volume of the catalogue was issued in 1956.

CONTENTS

Pp. xxiii–xxviii, "Introduction" by Sir Osbert Sitwell (dated Renishaw, 30 June 1949). (The Introduction was also apparently included
in a prospectus, 8 pages, of the catalogue.)

First edition

[*Cover*]

[*Two lines within border*] HENRY WALTON | 1746–1813 |
[*below border*] H. BLAIRMAN & SONS LTD. | 16, GRAFTON
STREET, W.1 | HARROGATE: NEW YORK: | 12, Mont-
pellier Parade. 20, East 55th Street. | JULY 4th–25th. |
CATALOGUES 2/6. The entire proceeds will be given to
the Artists' | General Benevolent Institution.

8 pages (plus covers). 217 × 138 mm.

Cream stiff paper wrappers, stapled. Trimmed edges. Lettered in
black on front as above.

Published at the exhibition in London on 4 July 1950 at 2s. 6d.

CONTENTS

Pp. 1–4, "Henry Walton" [by Osbert Sitwell]

oB50   ECKINGTON SHOW   1950
          PROGRAMME 1950

First edition

[*Cover*]

[*Within a drawing*] ECKINGTON SHOW SOCIETY | THE
9TH | Annual Show | will be held in | RENISHAW PARK |
(*By permission of Sir Osbert Sitwell, Bt.*) | on | Saturday,
August 12th, 1950. | [*below drawing*] *Drawing by John
Piper.* PROGRAMME & CATALOGUE, 1/–.

52 pages (including covers). 197 × 131 mm.

White paper wrappers, stapled. Trimmed edges. Printed in black on
covers.

Published at the show on 12 August 1950 at 1s.

CONTENTS

P. 1, "Preface" by Sir Osbert Sitwell [revised from the 1948 and 1949
Eckington Show Programmes]

First edition

THE | SOMERSET | SEQUENCE | *by* | HORATIA DURANT |
with an introduction by | SIR OSBERT SITWELL | *LONDON* |
NEWMAN NEAME | 1951

224 pages, and 8 plates. 215 × 136 mm.

Blue cloth boards. Trimmed edges. Gilt lettered on spine and upper cover.

2000 copies printed. Published late September 1951 at 15*s*.

CONTENTS

Pp. 9–10, Introduction by Osbert Sitwell

oB51*A*   THE TATE GALLERY   1954–1958

[Osbert Sitwell was a Trustee of the Tate Gallery, London, from 1951 to 1958. With the other Trustees he signed the "Reports of the Trustees" for the years 1953–54, 1954–55, 1955–56, 1956–57 and 1957–58. Since these Reports were only in the most limited sense Osbert Sitwell's own work, no further description of them is given here.]

oB52   WINTER'S TALES, 1   1955

First edition

WINTER'S | TALES | [*within a wreath*] 1 | LONDON |
MACMILLAN & CO LTD | NEW YORK · ST MARTIN'S
PRESS | 1955

372 pages. 196 × 131 mm.

Blue cloth boards. Trimmed edges. Gilt lettered on spine.

7000 copies printed. Published 11 November 1955 at 16*s*.

CONTENTS

Pp. 253–302, "Follow M'Leader" by Osbert Sitwell, illustrated by H. Cowdell [from *Atlantic Monthly*, August 1952]

First edition (of introduction)

JOHN COLLIER | [*swelled rule*] | His Monkey | Wife | OR, MARRIED TO A CHIMP | "Till at last she set herself to man | Like perfect music unto noble words" | *Tennyson* | [*swelled rule*] | RUPERT HART-DAVIS | SOHO SQUARE LONDON | 1957

188 pages. 183 × 121 mm.

Blue cloth boards. Trimmed edges. Silver lettered on spine.

3500 copies printed. Published 20 September 1957 at 13s. 6d. (John Collier's book first published 1930.)

CONTENTS

Pp. 5–10, Introduction by Osbert Sitwell

oB54   EDMUND BLUNDEN, SIXTY-   1961
FIVE

First edition

EDMUND BLUNDEN | SIXTY-FIVE | NOVEMBER 1961 | HONG KONG

214 pages (including front free end-paper and plates). 231 × 165 mm.

White paper boards. Unsewn. Untrimmed edges. Lettered in red and gilt on spine and upper cover.

Published November 1961, by Hong Kong Cultural Enterprise Co. for the English Society, University of Hong Kong, as a special issue of *The Chimes*.

CONTENTS

[A message] "From Sir Osbert Sitwell," p. 169.

oB55   DAY'S AT THE MORN   1964

a. *First edition*

DAY'S AT | THE MORN | Samuel Chotzinoff | [*flourish*] | *Preface by Sir Osbert Sitwell* | HARPER & ROW, PUBLISHERS | New York · Evanston · London

[I have not seen a copy of this book; the transcription of the title above is from a facsimile. 6300 copies were printed; publication was on 7 October 1964 at $5.95. The contents are similar to oB56b, below, though the Preface in this issue appears on pp. ix–x.]

b. *First edition, English issue*

SAMUEL CHOTZINOFF | [*short swelled rule*] | Day's at the Morn | WITH A PREFACE BY | SIR OSBERT SITWELL | [*device*] | HAMISH HAMILTON | LONDON

320 pages. 215 × 135 mm.

Brick-brown cloth boards. Trimmed edges. Silver stamped on spine. Published 28 January 1965 at 25s. (The publishers decline to say how many copies were printed.)

CONTENTS

Pp. vii–ix, "Preface" by Osbert Sitwell

oB56   A WISER WOMAN?   1966

First edition

CHRISTABEL ABERCONWAY | A Wiser Woman? | [*ornamental rule*] | A BOOK OF MEMORIES | [*device*] | HUTCHINSON OF LONDON

176 pages, and 16 plates. 228 × 143 mm.

Green cloth boards. Top edge pink, others trimmed. Mosaic reproduced on grey end-papers. Gilt stamped on spine.

1500 copies printed. Published 17 October 1966 at 30s.

CONTENTS

Pp. 169–172, "A Three-Quarter Length Portrait of the Hon. Mrs. Henry McLaren" by Osbert Sitwell. (The first printing of this poem. Three copies, with the title "Portrait of Christabel," were produced in calligraphy by Rex Whistler in 1932; see Laurence Whistler and Ronald Fuller, *The Work of Rex Whistler*, 1960, p. 45.)

PERIODICAL CONTRIBUTIONS BY
OSBERT SITWELL (oC1–oC477)

oC1 "Babel," *The Times*, no. 41164, p. 9, 11 May 1916.

oC2 "The Beginning," "The End," "Progress," "Prelude," "Pierrot Old," "Night," "20th Century Harlequinade," "The Lament of the Mole-Catcher," "Tears," "Black Mass," *Wheels*, [*First Cycle*], pp. 9–28, [December] 1916.

oC2*A* "In Bad Taste" [anonymous], *Wheels*, [*First Cycle*], *second edition*, [April] 1917. (See EB1b.)

oC3 "An Airman's Dream" by 'Miles,' *Spectator*, v. 119, pp. 165–166, 18 August 1917.

oC4 "Rhapsode" by 'Miles,' *The Nation*, v. 22, no. 4, p. 126, 27 October 1917.

oC5 "Armchair," "Fountains," "Promenades," "Prospect Road," "Rag-Time," "The Gipsy Queen," "The Return of the Prodigal," "London," *Wheels, Second Cycle*, pp. v–vi, 9–22, [December] 1917.

oC6 "This Generation," *Everyman*, v. 11, no. 276, p. 372, 25 January 1918.

oC7 "The Modern Abraham" by 'Miles,' *The Nation*, v. 22, no. 18, p. 567, 2 February 1918.

oC8 "A Sculptor's Cruelty," *Colour*, v. 8, p. 84, May 1918.

oC9 "The Trap" by 'Centurion,' *The Nation*, v. 23, no. 6, p. 143, 11 May 1918.

oC10 "Green-Fly," *The Nation*, v. 23, no. 14, p. 366, 6 July 1918.

oC11 "The Eternal Club," *The Nation*, v. 23, no. 19, p. 499, 10 August 1918.

oC12 "The Next War" by 'Miles,' *The Nation*, v. 23, no. 25, p. 650, 21 September 1918.

oC13 "Judas," *To-Day*, v. 4, no. 20, p. 56, October 1918.

oC14 "The Turn of the Tide" by 'Miles,' *English Review*, v. 27, pp. 308–310, October 1918.

oC15 "Sheep-Song" by 'Miles,' *The Nation*, v. 24, no. 2, p. 45, 12 October 1918.

oC16 "Panorama" by 'Miles,' *The Nation*, v. 24, no. 7, p. 190, 16 November 1918.

oC17 [Election address], *Scarborough Evening News & Mercury*, 29 November 1918. [If this was also separately printed I have not found a copy.]

oC18 "Judas and the Profiteer," *Cambridge Magazine*, v. 8, no. 10, p. 240, 14 December 1918.

oC19 "London Squares," "Clavichords," "Metamorphosis," "This Generation," "Youth and Age," "Song of the Fauns," *Wheels, Third Cycle*, pp. 9–18, [January 1919].

oC20 "Te Deum," "Church Parade," *Art and Letters*, v. 2, no. 1, pp. 1–3, Winter 1918–1919 [i.e., February 1919]. [There are two states of this issue, the earlier bearing "Winter 1918–1919" on the front cover.]

oC21 "November," *Cambridge Magazine*, v. 8, no. 21, p. 472, 1 March 1919.

oC22 "Lausiac Theme," *Art and Letters*, v. 2, no. 2, pp. 56 and 59, Spring 1919.

oC23 "Spring Hours," *Cambridge Magazine*, v. 8, no. 30, 3 May 1919.

oC24 "De Luxe: nursery rhyme," *The Monthly Chapbook*, v. 1, no. 1, pp. 8–9, July 1919.

oC25 "The Governess of Europe" by 'Miles,' *The Nation*, v. 25, no. 14, p. 420, 5 July 1919.

oC26 "Corpse-Day" by 'Miles,' *Daily Herald*, no. 1088, p. 4, 19 July 1919.

oC27 "A Certain Statesman," *Daily Herald*, no. 1090, p. 4, 22 July 1919. [Published anonymously as the leading article.]

oC28 "More about Morale," *Daily Herald*, no. 1095, p. 4, 28 July 1919. [Published anonymously.]

oC29 "Wizardry," *Daily Herald*, no. 1110, p. 4, 14 August 1919. [Published anonymously.]

oC30 "Discords," *Art and Letters*, v. 2, no. 4, pp. 143–144, Autumn 1919.

oC31 "Eternal Club," "Sheep Song," *The Living Age*, v. 303, pp. 44–45, 4 October 1919.

oC32 "Shepherd Wind," *Saturday Westminster Gazette*, v. 54, no. 8203, p. 12, 11 October 1919.

oC33 "Corpse-Day," "English Gothic," "Nocturne," *Wheels, Fourth Cycle*, pp. 9–16, [November] 1919.

oC34 "Koltchakerie" by 'Q,' *Daily Herald*, no. 1188, p. 4, 13 November 1919.

oC35 "The New Legend," "Summer Wind," "What the Syren said to the Sea-Horse," *Coterie*, no. 3, pp. 28–34, December 1919.

oC36 "Discords," *The Living Age*, v. 303, no. 3937, p. 754, 20 December 1919.

oC37 "Song of a General's Wife," *The Apple*, v. 1, no. 1, pp. 33–34, first quarter 1920.

oC38 "Shaking Hands with Murder," *Daily Herald*, no. 1353, p. 4, 27 May 1920. [Published anonymously.] [Reprinted in *Poems of Revolt* (1924).]

oC39 "Our-Rough-Island-Story" by 'Miles,' *The Nation*, v. 27, no. 12, p. 374, 19 June 1920.

oC40 "Cornucopia," "At the House of Mrs. Kinfoot," "Malgré Lui" [reprinted as "Malgré Soi" in *The New Keepsake for 1921* (1920)], "From 'The Valley of the Giants,'" "Mrs. Freudenthal consults the Witch of Endor," *Wheels, Fifth Cycle*, pp. 9–11, 22–32, 1920.

oC41 "Winston's Jamboree," *Daily Herald*, no. 1417, p. 4, 10 August 1920. [Reprinted in *Poems of Revolt* (1924).]

oC42 "'How Easily Things Go Wrong!,'" by O. S., *Daily Herald*, no. 1422, p. 4, 16 August 1920. [Reprinted in *Poems of Revolt* (1924).]

oC43 "'Lady Adela,'" *Daily Herald*, no. 1430, p. 7, 25 August 1920. [Review of *Lady Adela* by Gerald Gould.]

oC44 "Ultimate Judgment," *The Nation*, v. 27, no. 22, p. 669, 28 August 1920.

oC45 "The Rocking-Horse," *Saturday Westminster Gazette*, v. 56, no. 8479, p. 7, 4 September 1920.

oC46 "Diversions of the Bourgeois, 1: Sunday Afternoon," *Art and Letters*, v. 3, no. 1, pp. 11–13, Winter 1920.

oC47 "Malgré Lui," *The Dial*, v. 69, no. 6, pp. 583–585, December 1920.

oC48 "Two Poems: Mrs. Freudenthal consults the Witch of Endor; Dead Man's Wood," *Poetry*, v. 17, no. 3, pp. 130–133, December 1920.

oC49 "Fiume" by O. S., *The Nation*, v. 28, no. 14, pp. 476–477, 1 January 1921.

oC50 "A Mexican Piece" by O. S., *The Nation*, v. 28, no. 16, p. 550, 15 January 1921.

oC51 "Maxixe," *Saturday Westminster Gazette*, v. 57, no. 8639, p. 10, 12 March 1921.

oC52 "Who's Who in Heaven," *The Nation and Athenaeum*, v. 28, p. 873, 19 March 1921.

oC53 "Le Notre; or, Neptune in Chains," *Spectator*, v. 126, p. 524, 23 April 1921.

oC54 "Fountains," *The Sackbut*, v. 2, no. 2, p. 28, July 1921.

oC55 "Fountains," *Spectator*, v. 127, p. 78, 16 July 1921.

oC56 "Parade," *Spectator*, v. 127, p. 268, 27 August 1921.

oC57 "Giardino Pubblico," *The Nation and Athenaeum*, v. 29, no. 25, p. 855, 17 September 1921.

oC58 "Fountains," *The Living Age*, v. 310, no. 4029, p. 794, 24 September 1921.

oC59 "Aux Bords de la Mer," *The Nation and Athenaeum*, v. 30, no. 5, p. 177, 29 October 1921.

oC60 "Two Mexican Pieces," *Wheels, Sixth Cycle*, pp. 5–9, 1921.

oC61 "Bacchanalia," *Saturday Westminster Gazette*, v. 58, p. 11, 12 November 1921.

oC62 "Fox-Trot: When Solomon met the Queen of Sheba," *Form*, v. 1, no. 3, pp. 104–105, January 1922. [This issue published in an ordinary edition and an Edition-de-Luxe of fifty signed copies.]

oC63 "Degas" by O. S., *The Nation and Athenaeum*, v. 30, no. 16, pp. 600–602, 14 January 1922. [Review of exhibition at the Leicester Galleries.]

oC64 "The Jealous Goddess," *Spectator*, v. 128, p. 49, 14 January 1922.

oC65 "The Backward Child," *English Review*, v. 34, pp. 301–303, April 1922.

oC66 "Sketches of Travel: Lecce," *The Nation and Athenaeum*, v. 31, nos. 9–10, pp. 305–306, 338–339, 27 May–3 June 1922.

oC67 "Maxixe," *Poetry*, v. 20, no. 3, pp. 126–127, June 1922. [Also in *The Living Age*, v. 314, no. 4069, p. 54, 1 July 1922.]

oC68 "Lecce," *The Living Age*, v. 314, no. 4074, pp. 338–342, 5 August 1922.

oC69 "La Certosa di Padula," *Weekly Westminster Gazette*, v. 1, nos. 25–26, pp. 8 and 12, 5–12 August 1922.

oC70 "Sketches of Travel: II, Puglia," *The Nation and Athenaeum*, v. 31, pp. 764–765 and 791–793, 9–16 September 1922.

oC71 "The Jolly old Squire; or, Way-Down in Georgia. Being the Prologue to a Mime-Drama," *The Chapbook*, no. 29, pp. 13–24, September 1922.

oC72 "The Machine Breaks Down," *English Review*, v. 35, no. 6, pp. 493–503, December 1922.

oC73 "Country Dance," *Weekly Westminster Gazette*, v. 2, no. 55, p. 19, 3 March 1923.

oC74 "Orpheus," *The Nation and Athenaeum*, v. 32, p. 951, 24 March 1923.

oC75 "Marching with the Band," *The Nation and Athenaeum*, v. 33, no. 9, p. 305, 2 June 1923.

oC76 "Alone," *Spectator*, v. 130, p. 1042, 23 June 1923.

oC77 "Poets and Poetry," *The Nation and Athenaeum*, v. 34, no. 3, p. 122, 20 October 1923. [Review of *The Art of Poetry* by W. P. Ker.]

oC78 "Walter de la Mare," *The Nation and Athenaeum*, v. 35, no. 4, pp. 118–120, 26 April 1924. [Review of *Walter de la Mare* by R. L. Mégroz.]

oC79 "Ta-Ra-Ra-Boom-De-Ay," *Spectator*, v. 132, pp. 962–963, 14 June 1924. [Review of *Songs of Shadow-of-a-Leaf* by Alfred Noyes.]

oC80 "The Empire Exhibition," *Vogue* [London], v. 63, no. 12, pp. 43–45, 90 and 92, late June 1924.

oC81 "A German Eighteenth-Century Town" [Bayreuth], *The Criterion*, v. 2, no. 8, pp. 433–447, July 1924.

oC82 "Catania," *The Chapbook*, no. 39, pp. 26–29, 1924.

oC83 "Art at Wembley: some remembered and forgotten masterpieces in the Palace of Art," *Vogue* [London], v. 64, no. 3, pp. 23–25, early August 1924.

oC84 "The London Group exhibition," *New Statesman*, v. 24, p. 110, 1 November 1924.

oC85 "Literarische Koterien in London" (übersetz. aus dem englischen Manuskript, Max Meyerfeld), *Die Literatur*, 27er. Jahrgang, heft 4, pp. 212–218, [December 1924]. [The original English has not been published.]

oC86 "The Problem of the Patron," *New Statesman*, v. 24, pp. 472–474, 31 January 1925.

oC87 "Reflections on the Royal Academy" by Osbert and Sacheverell Sitwell, *New Statesman*, v. 25, pp. 133–134, 16 May 1925.

oC88 "June Pot-Pourri," *New Statesman*, v. 25, pp. 337–338, 4 July 1925.

oC88*A* "The Courtauld Collection," *Apollo*, v. 2, no. 8, pp. 63–69, August 1925.

oC89 "P.P.S. and R.S.V.P.: Einsteinismo per le Danni," *Vogue* [London], v. 66, no. 6, pp. 58–59, 86 and 88, late September 1925.

oC90 "Situations Required," *The Chapbook*, no. 40, pp. 26–28, 1925.

oC90*A* "Les Poseuses [of Seurat]," *Apollo*, v. 3, no. 18, p. 345, June 1926.

oC91 "The Ghost in the Mask, a true story," *Sunday Express*, p. 8, 13 June 1926.

oC92 "In the Days of my Youth," *T.P.'s & Cassell's Weekly*, v. 6, no. 141, pp. 370 and 376, 10 July 1926.

oC93 "Mr. and Mrs. Nutch," *Vogue* [London], v. 68, no. 4, pp. 32 and 74, late August 1926.

oC94 "Imbecile Plays and Advertising Actors," *Weekly Dispatch*, no. 6515, p. 8, 12 September 1926.

oC95 "Mrs. Hague," *Vogue* [London], v. 68, no. 11, p. 77, early December 1926.

oC96 "How America 'got' me," *Daily Express*, no. 8371, p. 8, 24 February 1927.

oC97 "Mary Anne," *Vogue* [London], v. 69, no. 8, p. 54, late April 1927.

oC98 "When First the Poets Sung," *Harper's Monthly Magazine*, v. 155, pp. 148–149, July 1927.

oC99 "Miss Mew," *The Nation and Athenaeum*, v. 41, pp. 774–776, 17 September 1927.

oC100 "Mr. and Mrs. Goodbeare," *Saturday Review of Literature*, v. 4, p. 134, 24 September 1927.

oC101 "Miss Mew's Song of Perpetual Motion," *The Nation and Athenaeum*, v. 41, no. 26, p. 839, 1 October 1927.

oC102 "Mrs. Southern," *New Republic*, v. 53, no. 683, p. 193, 4 January 1928.

oC103 "Friends and Enemies," *Evening News*, p. 8, 15 June 1928.

oC104 "Epilog zum Roman 'Vor dem ersten Bombenabwerf,'" von Osbert Sitwell, deutsch von Max Meyerfeld, *Deutsche Rundschau*, Bd. 217, pp. 55–62, Oktober–Dezember 1928.

oC105 "Why I don't like Games," *Daily Mail*, no. 10160, p. 12, 15 November 1928.

oC106 "What I want most in 1929," *Daily Mail*, no. 10200, p. 8, 3 January 1929.

oC107 "What Osbert Sitwell likes about Yorkshire," *Yorkshire Post*, 25 May 1929.

oC108 "Statues, Mr. Epstein and the Public," *The Listener*, v. 1, no. 22, pp. 817–818, 12 June 1929.

oC109 "Canaletto," *The Studio*, v. 98, pp. 697–704, October 1929; and in *Creative Art*, v. 5, no. 4, pp. 697–704, October 1929.

oC110 "The Sitwells, by one of them (Osbert)," *Morning Post*, no. 49136, p. 10, 5 December 1929.

oC111 "Our Strange Amusements," *Evening News*, no. 14965, p. 8, 13 December 1929.

oC112 "The Love-Bird," *Life and Letters*, v. 4, no. 20, pp. 1–26, January 1930.

oC113 "Dumb-Animal," *The Fortnightly Review*, v. 127 (new series), pp. 184–190, 1 February 1930.

oC114 "Are we so much Cleverer?," *Evening News*, p. 9, 16 May 1930.

oC115 "Alive—Alive Oh!," *Life and Letters*, v. 4, no. 25, pp. 427–476, June 1930.

oC116 "Sex," *Evening News*, p. 7, 25 June 1930.

oC117 "Echoes," *The Fortnightly Review*, v. 128 (new series), pp. 195–204, August 1930.

oC118 "Theatre Slump will Do Good," *Evening News*, p. 6, 19 August 1930.

oC119 "Holiday Conversations," *Evening News*, p. 9, 25 August 1930.

oC120 "Major and Mrs. Postlethwaite," *The Nation and Athenaeum,* v. 48, no. 6, pp. 190–192, 8 November 1930. [Published anonymously.]

oC121 "Severini's Art," *The Observer,* no. 7280, p. 6, 7 December 1930. [Review of *Fleurs et Masques* by Gino Severini.]

oC122 "The Best Years of Life," *Daily Mail,* no. 10820, p. 6, 30 December 1930.

oC123 "From Syracuse," *Week-End Review,* v. 3, no. 45, pp. 69–70, 17 January 1931.

oC124 "Portrait of Lawrence," *Week-End Review,* v. 3, no. 48, pp. 173–174, 7 February 1931.

oC125 "Travellers' Tales," *Week-End Review,* v. 3, no. 51, pp. 302–303, 28 February 1931.

oC126 "My Ideal Dinner Party," *Good Housekeeping,* v. 19, no. 3, pp. 6–7 and 103, May 1931.

oC127 "Say What He Will," *Week-End Review,* v. 3, no. 68, pp. 952–953, 27 June 1931. ["First of a new series of personal notes to be contributed by Mr. Osbert Sitwell."]

oC128 "Say What He Will," *Week-End Review,* v. 4, no. 1, pp. 8–9, 4 July 1931.

oC129 "Say What He Will," *Week-End Review,* v. 4, no. 2, pp. 40–41, 11 July 1931.

oC130 "Say What He Will," *Week-End Review,* v. 4, no. 71, pp. 72–73, 18 July 1931.

oC131 "Say What He Will," *Week-End Review,* v. 4, no. 72, pp. 103–104, 25 July 1931.

oC132 "Say What He Will," *Week-End Review,* v. 4, no. 73, pp. 136–137, 1 August 1931.

oC133 "A Note on Charles Dickens," *Week-End Review,* v. 4, no. 89, pp. 643–644, 21 November 1931.

oC134 "Far Away and Long Ago," *Week-End Review,* v. 4, no. 91, pp. 706–707, 5 December 1931.

oC135 "Venice in December," *The Listener,* v. 6, no. 153, pp. 1055–1056, 16 December 1931.

oC135*A* "Is Christmas Christian or a Guzzling Feast?," *Action,* v. 1, no. 11, p. 6, 17 December 1931.

oC135*B* "The Castel del Monte," *Architectural Design and Construction,* v. 2, no. 3, pp. 104–107, January 1932.

oC136 "New Year in Bari," *Week-End Review*, v. 5, no. 95, pp. 7–8, 2 January 1932.

oC137 "The Secrecy of Venice," *Week-End Review*, v. 5, no. 106, pp. 354–356, 19 March 1932.

oC138 "Winter in Italy," *Week-End Review*, v. 5, no. 111, pp. 515–516, 23 April 1932.

oC139 "Mrs. Kimber," *Week-End Review*, v. 6, no. 121, pp. 7–9, 2 July 1932.

oC140 "The Collected Poems of D. H. Lawrence" [a review], *Week-End Review*, v. 6, no. 127, pp. 190–191, 13 August 1932.

oC141 "A Great Critic," *Week-End Review*, v. 6, no. 132, pp. 318–320, 17 September 1932. [Review of *Selected Essays* by T. S. Eliot.]

oC142 "The Slave of Time," *Week-End Review*, v. 6, no. 139, pp. 535–536, 5 November 1932.

oC143 "We are Hopeless Gramophonists" by Osbert and Sacheverell Sitwell, *Harper's Bazaar* [London], v. 7, no. 4, pp. 18–19 and 73, January 1933.

oC144 "Sicily," *Harper's Bazaar* [London], v. 7, no. 5, pp. 50–51 and 91, February 1933.

oC145 "The Tenth Muse," *Harper's Bazaar* [London], v. 8, no. 3, pp. 16–17 and 76, June 1933.

oC146 "Moderns who are All Alike," *Daily Telegraph*, no. 24418, p. 10, 24 August 1933.

oC147 "After Victoria," *Week-End Review*, v. 8, no. 190A, p. 414, 21 October 1933. [Review of *The Post-Victorians*.]

oC148 "The Musical Season," *Harper's Bazaar* [London], v. 9, no. 2, p. 50–51 and 104, November 1933.

oC149 "Autocriticisms, 8," *Week-End Review*, v. 8, no. 191, p. 462, 4 November 1933. [Review of *Miracle on Sinai*.]

oC150 "Englishmen Love Fogs," *Sunday Referee*, no. 2940, p. 6, 7 January 1934.

oC151 "Of What Use are these Exhibitions?," *Sunday Referee*, no. 2941, p. 6, 14 January 1934.

oC152 "I Would Forbid Street Music," *Sunday Referee*, no. 2942, p. 6, 21 January 1934.

oC153 "The Art of Being Rude," *Sunday Referee*, no. 2943, p. 9, 28 January 1934.

oC154 "On Advice: its giving and receiving," *Sunday Referee*, no. 2944, p. 6, 4 February 1934.

oC155 "A Forgotten England," *Sunday Referee*, no. 2945, p. 9, 11 February 1934.

oC156 "The White Man's Burden," *Sunday Referee*, no. 2947, p. 6, 25 February 1934.

oC157 "A Peer's War-time Prophecies," *Sunday Referee*, no. 2948, p. 10, 4 March 1934. [Review of *How to Lengthen our Ears* by Lord Harberton.]

oC158 "Belittling the Great," *Sunday Referee*, no. 2949, p. 6, 11 March 1934.

oC159 "Make War on Slums—not on Men!," *Sunday Referee*, no. 2950, p. 6, 18 March 1934.

oC160 "Are we Muddling into War?," *Sunday Referee*, no. 2951, p. 6, 25 March 1934.

oC160*A*. "The Double Life," *Sunday Referee*, no. 2952, p. 6, 1 April 1934.

oC161 "The Abomination of Cut Flowers," *Sunday Referee*, no. 2953, p. 11, 8 April 1934.

oC162 "For and Against Homes like Aeroplanes," *Sunday Referee*, no. 2954, p. 13, 15 April 1934.

oC163 "The Necessity for Solitude," *Sunday Referee*, no. 2955, p. 12, 22 April 1934.

oC164 "The Halcyon Edwardian Day," *Sunday Referee*, no. 2956, p. 6, 29 April 1934.

oC165 "In Season—and Out," *Sunday Referee*, no. 2957, p. 6, 6 May 1934.

oC166 "English Food," *Sunday Referee*, no. 2958, p. 6, 13 May 1934.

oC167 "Virtue of Laziness," *Sunday Referee*, no. 2959, p. 11, 20 May 1934.

oC168 "Thackeray and 'Vanity Fair,'" *Sunday Referee*, no. 2960, p. 11, 27 May 1934.

oC169 "Keep Your Temper," *Sunday Referee*, no. 2961, p. 6, 3 June 1934.

oC170 "The People without a Home," *Sunday Referee*, no. 2962, p. 10, 10 June 1934.

oC171 "Save me from my Friends," *Sunday Referee*, no. 2963, p. 17, 17 June 1934.

oC172 "Prophets of Evil are Popular," *Sunday Referee*, no. 2964, p. 12, 24 June 1934.

oC173 "Narrow your Mind and be Happy," *Sunday Referee*, no. 2965, p. 12, 1 July 1934.

oC174 "National Birds: the wicked cuckoo," *Sunday Referee*, no. 2966, p. 6, 8 July 1934.

oC175 "Caught by Buchmanites—in Canada," *Sunday Referee*, no. 2967, p. 10, 15 July 1934.

oC176 "Water, a luxury," *Sunday Referee*, no. 2969, p. 6, 29 July 1934.

oC177 "In Praise of Laziness," *Harper's Magazine*, v. 169, pp. 378–380, August 1934.

oC178 "The Strong School of Women Novelists," *Life and Letters*, v. 10, no. 56, pp. 536–541, August 1934.

oC179 "Germany Always: plus ça change," *Sunday Referee*, no. 2970, p. 6, 5 August 1934.

oC180 "Looking Forward in 1910—and the result today," *Sunday Referee*, no. 2971, p. 10, 12 August 1934.

oC181 "Pekin Fortune-tellers," *Sunday Referee*, no. 2972, p. 6, 19 August 1934.

oC182 "Summer Palace," *Harper's Bazaar* [London], v. 10, no. 6, pp. 62 and 69, September 1934.

oC183 "Mr. and Mrs. Goodbeare," *Saturday Review of Literature*, v. 4, no. 9, p. 134, 24 September 1934.

oC184 "Noto, a baroque city," *Architectural Review*, v. 76, pp. 129–130, October 1934.

oC185 "A Plea for Justice," *Sunday Referee*, no. 2980, p. 12, 14 October 1934.

oC186 "The Lady with the Pink Feather," *Harper's Magazine*, v. 169, pp. 762–764, November 1934.

oC187 "Self-Importance," *Sunday Referee*, no. 2984, p. 7, 11 November 1934.

oC188 "The Magic of London," *Sunday Referee*, no. 2986, p. 12, 25 November 1934.

oC189 "Our Patriotic Arms-Makers," *Sunday Referee*, no. 2987, p. 7, 2 December 1934.

oC190 "The Strong School of Women Novelists," *Saturday Review of Literature*, v. 11, no. 21, p. 339, 8 December 1934.

oC191 "A Lament to the Countryside that is Vanishing," *Sunday Referee*, no. 2989, p. 7, 16 December 1934.

oC192 "There's Romance in Beards," *Sunday Referee*, no. 2991, p. 10, 30 December 1934.

oC193 "My view of the B.B.C.," *Sunday Referee*, no. 2993, p. 10, 13 January 1935.

oC194 "Why do you live in a Flat?," *Sunday Referee*, no. 2995, p. 10, 27 January 1935.

oC195 "Do Bores sport Beards?," *Sunday Referee*, no. 2997, p. 6, 10 February 1935.

oC196 "Galas," *Harper's Bazaar* [London], v. 12, no. 3, pp. 70 and 95, June 1935.

oC197 "Fight this Good-Time Creed," *Sunday Referee*, no. 3015, p. 10, 16 June 1935.

oC198 "An Army for the League," *Sunday Referee*, no. 3017, p. 12, 30 June 1935.

oC199 "Chinese Food," *Harper's Bazaar* [London], v. 12, no. 4, pp. 26 and 93, July 1935.

oC200 "Hang the War-mongers," *Sunday Referee*, no. 3019, p. 10, 14 July 1935.

oC201 "The Ghost of Hyde Park," *Sunday Referee*, no. 3021, p. 10, 28 July 1935.

oC202 "Conspiracy of Dwarfs," *Daily Telegraph*, no. 25026, p. 10, 10 August 1935.

oC203 "I am Proud of England," *Sunday Referee*, no. 3023, p. 10, 11 August 1935.

oC204 "England has Faults—but can America Crow about this Record?," *Sunday Referee*, no. 3025, p. 6, 25 August 1935.

oC205 "Passages from the Journal of a Religious Aunt," *Life and Letters To-Day*, v. 13, no. 1, pp. 49–54, September 1935.

oC206 "The Spain of Somerset Maugham," *London Mercury*, v. 32, no. 191, pp. 485–486, September 1935. [Review of *Don Fernando*.]

oC207 "Our Traffic Muddle," *Sunday Referee*, no. 3027, p. 4, 8 September 1935.

oC208 "Patronage in Art Today—II," *The Listener*, v. 14, no. 348, pp. 419–421, 11 September 1935.

oC209 "Sanctions!," *Sunday Referee*, no. 3029, p. 10, 22 September 1935.

oC210 "General Conversation," *Nash's Pall Mall Magazine*, v. 96, no. 509, pp. 12 and 14–15, October 1935.

oC211 "Do we really want war?," *Sunday Referee*, no. 3031, p. 4, 6 October 1935.

oC212 "General Conversation," *Nash's Pall Mall Magazine*, v. 96, no. 510, pp. 8 and 10–11, November 1935.

oC213 "Half a League Onward," *Sunday Referee*, no. 3035, p. 7, 3 November 1935.

oC214 "General Conversation," *Nash's Pall Mall Magazine*, v. 96, no. 511, pp. 8 and 10–11, December 1935.

oC215 "Shops I Like," *Good Housekeeping*, v. 28, no. 4, pp. 22–23 and 181–182, December 1935.

oC216 "The Villa Angelica," *Life and Letters To-Day*, v. 13, no. 2, pp. 120–128, Winter 1935–36.

oC217 "If you had to Live in a Play or a Novel," *Strand Magazine*, v. 90, no. 2, p. 159, December 1935.

oC218 "General Conversation," *Nash's Pall Mall Magazine*, v. 96, no. 512, pp. 8 and 10–11, January 1936.

oC219 "The Chinese Exhibition," *Harper's Bazaar* [London], v. 13, no. 4, pp. 49 and 77–78, January 1936.

oC220 "General Conversation," *Nash's Pall Mall Magazine*, v. 96, no. 513, pp. 8 and 10–11, February 1936.

oC221 "General Conversation," *Nash's Pall Mall Magazine*, v. 96, no. 514, pp. 8 and 10–11, March 1936.

oC222 "General Conversation," *Nash's Pall Mall Magazine*, v. 97, no. 515, pp. 8 and 10–11, April 1936.

oC223 "General Conversation," *Nash's Pall Mall Magazine*, v. 97, no. 516, pp. 8 and 10–11, May 1936.

oC224 "The Pleasures of Picnics," *Good Housekeeping*, v. 29, no. 4, pp. 12–13 and 188–189, June 1936.

oC225 "General Conversation," *Nash's Pall Mall Magazine*, v. 97, no. 517, pp. 8 and 10–11, June 1936.

oC226 "The Conspiracy of the Dwarfs," *The Living Age*, v. 350, no. 4437, pp. 332–334, June 1936.

oC227 "Dinners in Different Countries," *Harper's Bazaar* [London], v. 14, no. 4, pp. 62 and 94, July 1936.

oC228 "General Conversation," *Nash's Pall Mall Magazine*, v. 97, no. 518, pp. 8 and 10–11, July 1936.

oC229 "Must we Fight for our Country?," *Sunday Referee*, p. 12, 12 July 1936.

oC230 "Wild Parties," *Sunday Referee*, p. 14, 26 July 1936.

oC231 "General Conversation," *Nash's Pall Mall Magazine*, v. 97, no. 519, pp. 8 and 10–11, August 1936.

oC232 "For the Custody of a Child," *Sunday Referee*, p. 14, 9 August 1936.

oC233 "Scarborough (The Yorkshire I Know)," *Yorkshire Post*, no. 27790, p. 8, 22 August 1936.

oC234 "This 'Team Spirit' Worship," *Sunday Referee*, p. 14, 23 August 1936.

oC235 "General Conversation," *Nash's Pall Mall Magazine*, v. 97, no. 520, pp. 8 and 10–11, September 1936.

oC236 "Water Parties," *Harper's Bazaar* [London], v. 14, no. 6, pp. 32 and 106, September 1936.

oC237 "Transfer Britain across the Atlantic," *Sunday Referee*, p. 14, 6 September 1936.

oC238 "General Conversation," *Nash's Pall Mall Magazine*, v. 98, no. 521, pp. 8 and 10–11, October 1936.

oC239 "Chinese Food," *Harper's Bazaar* [New York], no. 2688, pp. 172–173, October 1936.

oC240 "Democracy is a Luxury Now," *Sunday Referee*, p. 14, 4 October 1936.

oC241 "So Science Blunders On," *Sunday Referee*, p. 14, 25 October 1936.

oC242 "General Conversation," *Nash's Pall Mall Magazine*, v. 98, no. 522, pp. 8 and 10–11, November 1936.

oC243 "Mustard and Cress," *Sunday Referee*, p. 2, 8 November 1936.

oC244 "What it Feels like to be an Author," *News Chronicle*, no. 28252, p. 12, 13 November 1936.

oC245 "Make the Coronation a Free Show," *Sunday Referee*, p. 14, 22 November 1936.

oC246 "Giving and Receiving," *Harper's Bazaar* [London], v. 15, no. 3, p. 15, December 1936.

oC247 "General Conversation," *Nash's Pall Mall Magazine*, v. 98, no. 523, pp. 8 and 10–11, December 1936.

oC248 "Anything on Your Conscience?," *Sunday Referee*, p. 14, 13 December 1936.

oC249 "Abroad: more pages from the Journal of a Religious Aunt," *Life and Letters To-Day*, v. 15, no. 6, pp. 13–18, Winter 1936–37.

oC250 "General Conversation," *Nash's Pall Mall Magazine*, v. 98, no. 524, pp. 8 and 10–11, January 1937.

oC251 "Some Writing-paper, Please," *Harper's Bazaar* [London], v. 15, no. 5, pp. 58–59 and 97, February 1937.

oC252 "General Conversation," *Nash's Pall Mall Magazine*, v. 98, no. 525, pp. 8 and 10–11, February 1937.

oC253 "National Rat Week," *Cavalcade*, v. 3, no. 3, p. 44, 13 February 1937. [This was published in a letter from a reader, together with editorial comment; a law suit followed, in which Osbert Sitwell successfully claimed that there had been an infringement of copyright.]

oC254 "Easter in Greece," *Harper's Bazaar* [London], v. 15, no. 6, pp. 64–65, 108 and 110, March 1937.

oC255 "Pomp and Pageantry," *Nash's Pall Mall Magazine*, v. 99, no. 528, pp. 74–75, May 1937.

oC256 "Ode for the Coronation of Their Majesties, May 12, 1937," *Sunday Times*, no. 5952, Coronation supplement p. ii, 9 May 1937.

oC257 "La Tour du Sorcier," *The Observer*, no. 7619, p. 20, 6 June 1937.

oC258 "The Englishman's Credo," *Sunday Times*, no. 5967, p. 12, 22 August 1937.

oC259 "Ex-Libris," *Harper's Bazaar* [London], v. 16, no. 6, pp. 76 and 102, September 1937.

oC260 "Paters' Match," *Life and Letters To-Day*, v. 17, no. 10, pp. 86–97, Winter 1937.

oC261 "Notes on Stage Food," *Wine & Food*, no. 16, pp. 29–32, Winter 1937.

oC262 "The Englishman's Credo," *The Living Age*, v. 353, no. 4455, pp. 349–352, December 1937.

oC263 "Decoration from 1900 to 1925," *Harper's Bazaar* [London], v. 17, no. 5, pp. 66 and 86, February 1938.

oC264 "En Voyage: a memory," *The Fortnightly*, v. 144 (new series), pp. 172–183, August 1938.

oC265 "Bella Vista," *Harper's Bazaar* [London], v. 18, no. 5, pp. 52–53 and 79–80, August 1938.

oC266 "Reforms in the Air: questions and suggestions for the B.B.C.," *Sunday Times*, no. 6019, p. 12, 21 August 1938.

oC267 "Touching Wood," *Harper's Bazaar* [New York], no 2714, pp. 95, 115 and 117, 15 September 1938.

oC268 "In Indo-China," *The Queen*, v. 183, no. 4787, pp. 14–15 and 46, 22 September 1938.

oC269 "Touching Wood," *Harper's Bazaar* [London], v. 19, no. 1, pp. 79, 104 and 106, October 1938.

oC270 "The Heart of France," *The Observer*, no. 7689, p. 10, 9 October 1938. [Review of *Through French Windows* by David Horner.]

oC271 "Idyll through the Looking-Glass," *London Mercury*, no. 229, pp. 38–46, November 1938.

oC272 "Slogans," *The Star*, no. 15737, p. 2, 15 November 1938.

oC273 "Champagne for the Old Lady," *Bystander*, v. 140, no. 1823A, pp. 11–13, 25 November 1938.

oC274 "Champagne for the Old Lady," *Harper's Bazaar* [New York], no. 2717, pp. 74–75 and 123–124, December 1938.

oC275 "The Ghost of a City," *Architectural Review*, v. 85, no. 1, pp. 1–4, January 1939.

oC276 "A New Idea about Passports," *The Star*, no. 15853, p. 4, 1 April 1939.

oC277 "The Vision," *The Observer*, no. 7720, p. 26, 14 May 1939.

oC278 "Neck and Neck," *Harper's Bazaar* [New York], no. 2724, pp. 56 and 110–111, June 1939.

oC279 "Sir Philip Sassoon: an appreciation," *The Times*, no. 48324, p. 16, 6 June 1939.

oC280 "Ports of Call," *John o' London's*, v. 41, no. 1052, pp. 335–336, 9 June 1939.

oC281 "The Old School Tie," *Lilliput*, v. 5, no. 1, pp. 79–82, July [1939].

oC282 "Ancestral Hall of the Exalted Brave and Loyal," *Life and Letters To-Day*, v. 22, no. 23, pp. 30–44, July 1939.

oC283 "My Garden," *My Garden*, v. 17, no. 67, pp. 323–329, July 1939.

oC284 "Neck and Neck," *Harper's Bazaar* [London], v.21, no. 1, pp. 23 and 78–79, October–November 1939.

oC285 "A War to End Class War," *Spectator*, v. 163, pp. 678–679, 17 November 1939.

oC286 "Hints on Relaxing for Christmas," *Harper's Bazaar* [London], v. 21, no. 2, pp. 12–13, December 1939.

oC287 "Escape with Me," *Town & Country*, v. 95, no. 4208, pp. 24 and 55, January 1940.

oC288 "Mr. Piper's Brighton," *The Listener*, v. 23, no. 573, p. 38, 4 January 1940. [Review of his *Brighton Aquatints*.]

oC289 "To Charlotte Corday," *The Observer*, no. 7756, p. 4, 21 January 1940.

oC290 "Escape with Me," *Town & Country*, v. 95, no. 4209, pp. 40 and 90, February 1940.

oC291 "Plague-Cart before Horse," *St. Martin's Review*, no. 588, pp. 84–88, February 1940.

oC292 "Changes in Fifty Years: being extracts from the diary of Georgiana Sitwell, edited by Osbert Sitwell," *Life and Letters To-Day*, v. 24, no. 30, pp. 140–147, February 1940.

oC293 "Authors and the War," *The Author*, v. 50, no. 3, pp. 55–56, Spring 1940.

oC294 "Changes of fifty years . . .," *Life and Letters To-Day*, v. 25, no. 32, pp. 26–34, April 1940.

oC295 "Send the Public Schools to Germany," *Lilliput*, v. 6, no. 4, pp. 319–321, April 1940.

oC296 "Changes of fifty years . . .," *Life and Letters To-Day*, v. 25, no. 33, pp. 148–157, May 1940.

oC297 "An Author Kills a Country," *Lilliput*, v. 6, no. 6, pp. 469–471, June 1940.

oC298 "Changes of fifty years . . .," *Life and Letters To-Day*, v. 25, no. 34, pp. 246–257, June 1940.

oC299 "Yr. Obedient Servant," *Town & Country*, v. 95, no. 4214, pp. 26 and 69, July 1940.

oC300 "The True Lovers' Knot," *The Fortnightly*, v. 148 (new series), pp. 174–181, August 1940.

oC301 "Changes of fifty years . . .," *Life and Letters To-Day*, v. 26, no. 36, pp. 122–136, August 1940.

oC302 "Tuscan Ghost," *John o' London's*, v. 43, no. 1112, pp. 481–482, 2 August 1940.

oC303 "The Woman who Hated Flowers," *Good Housekeeping*, v. 38, no. 1, pp. 18–19 and 73–76, September 1940.

oC304 "Notes on the Way," *Time & Tide*, v. 21, no. 36, p. 902, 7 September 1940.

oC305 "Notes on the Way," *Time & Tide*, v. 21, no. 37, pp. 921–922, 14 September 1940.

oC306 "Lord Alington" [an appreciation], *The Times*, no. 48730, p. 7, 25 September 1940.

oC307 "Personal Prejudice," *Life and Letters To-Day*, v. 27, no. 38, pp. 36–37, October 1940.

oC308 "Vichy Vignette," *The Star*, no. 16319, p. 2, 1 October 1940.

oC309 "Fool's Song," *The Observer*, no. 7796, p. 4, 27 October 1940.

oC310 "Selections from Sitwell's Fables," *Life and Letters To-Day*, v. 27, no. 40, pp. 210–212, December 1940.

oC311 "Death of a God," *John o' London's*, v. 44, no. 1138, pp. 453–454, 31 January 1941.

oC312 "On the Relationship between Poetry and Painting," *Burlington Magazine*, v. 78, no. 455, pp. 47–48, February 1941.

oC313 "The Man who drove Strindberg Mad," *Life and Letters To-Day*, v. 28, no. 42, pp. 141–148, February 1941.

oC314 "Pompey and Some Peaches," *Yale Review*, v. 30, no. 3, pp. 531–548, March 1941.

oC315 "The Sole Arabian Tree," *Times Literary Supplement*, pp. 199 and 206, 26 April 1941.

oC316 "Defeat," *Harper's Bazaar* [New York], no. 2751, pp. 53 and 105, May 1941.

oC317 "Fool's Song, Journalist's Song, from 'Demos the Emperor,'" *Life and Letters To-Day*, v. 29, no. 45, pp. 148–151, May 1941.

oC318 "The English Scene during the Crimean War: being selections from the Journal of Louisa Lucy Hely-Hutchinson, afterwards Lady Sitwell, edited by . . . Osbert Sitwell," *Life and Letters To-Day*, v. 29, no. 46, pp. 208–224, June 1941.

oC319 "The New London—or, Sitwell's Utopia," *Harper's Bazaar* [London], v. 25, no. 4, pp. 48 and 58, July–August 1941.

oC320 "The Glow-Worm," *Life and Letters To-Day*, v. 30, pp. 121–137, August 1941.

oC321 "Set up a Ministry of Muddle," *Strand Magazine*, v. 102, no. 610, pp. 35–36, October 1941.

oC322 "My Favourite Gardens," *My Garden*, v. 23, no. 94, pp. 301–304, October 1941.

oC323 "Control the Food Controller!," *Strand Magazine*, v. 102, no. 611, pp. 153–154, November 1941.

oC324 "My First Poem," *Lilliput*, v. 10, no. 2, p. 144, February 1942.

oC325 "A Short Character of Sir Edmund Gosse," *Horizon*, v. 5, no. 28, pp. 243–266, April 1942.

oC326 "Old Worlds for New," *Life and Letters To-Day*, v. 33, pp. 19–31, April 1942.

oC327 "The Red Folder," *Burlington Magazine*, v. 80, nos. 469 and 470, pp. 85–90 and 115–118, April and May 1942.

oC328 "Shopping in China," *Strand Magazine*, v. 103, no. 618, pp. 24–26, June 1942.

oC329 "Elementary Notes on Strategy and Statecraft," *New Statesman and Nation*, v. 23 (new series), p. 403, 20 June 1942.

oC330 "Far Away and Not so Long Ago," *Wine & Food*, no. 34, pp. 54–63, Summer 1942.

oC331 "Staggered Holiday," *English Story*, [no.] 3, pp. 89–102, 1942.

oC332 "A Character of the late W. H. Davies," *Life and Letters To-Day*, v. 34, nos. 59–61, pp. 2–21, 81–91 and 156–171, July, August and September 1942.

oC333 "Still-Life: box and bottle [I]," *Life and Letters To-Day*, v. 36, no. 66, pp. 77–84, February 1943.

oC334 "Letter to My Son," *Horizon*, v. 7, no. 39, pp. 159–177, March 1943.

oC335 "Still-Life: box and bottle [II]," *Life and Letters To-Day*, v. 37, no. 68, pp. 13–21, April 1943.

oC336 [Deleted]

oC337 "Still-Life: box and bottle [III]," *Life and Letters To-Day*, v. 37, no. 69, pp. 56–68, May 1943.

oC338–346 [Deleted]

oC347 "Rheims in 1919," *Architectural Review*, v. 94, p. 25, July 1943.

oC348–351 [Deleted]

oC352 "Reviewing Reviewed," *The Author*, v. 53, no. 4, pp. 72–73, Summer 1943.

oC353–354 [Deleted]

oC355 "Lines from 'Demos the Emperor,'" *Life and Letters To-Day*, v. 38, no. 73, pp. 124–127, September 1943.

oC356 [Deleted]

oC357 "Vulgarity in Literature," *Times Literary Supplement*, p. 438, 11 September 1943.

oC358 [Deleted]

oC359 "Lines from 'Demos the Emperor,'" *Life and Letters To-Day*, v. 39, no. 74, pp. 2–8, October 1943.

oC360–366 [Deleted]

oC367 "Left Hand, Right Hand," *Atlantic Monthly*, v. 173, nos. 1–5, January, February, March, April and May 1944.

oC368 "What it Feels like to be an Author," *Saturday Review of Literature*, v. 27, no. 8, pp. 6–8, 19 February 1944.

oC369 "London," *Harper's Bazaar* [New York], no. 2788, pp. 86–87 and 138–139, April 1944.

oC370 "The Sitwells as Children," *Good Housekeeping*, v. 45, no. 5, pp. 18–19, 55 and 57, May 1944.

oC371 "Enchantment," *The Observer*, no. 7983, p. 3, 28 May 1944. [Review of *The Walls do not Fall* by H. D.]

oC372 "Sitwell Settings," *Good Housekeeping*, v. 45, no. 6, pp. 20–21, 53 and 55, June 1944.

oC373 "The State and the Arts," *The Author*, v. 54, no. 4, p. 53, Summer 1944.

oC374 "Lieutenant Rex Whistler" [an appreciation], *The Times*, no. 49928, p. 6, 7 August 1944.

oC375 "You Can Carry It, Mrs. Parkin," *Penguin New Writing*, no. 21, pp. 50–55, 1944.

oC376 "Osbert Sitwell reviews Mr. Agate," *Daily Express*, no. 13886, p. 2, 2 December 1944. [Review of his *Noblesse Oblige*.]

oC377 "Aspiring Ape," *Times Literary Supplement*, p. 8, 6 January 1945.

oC378 "Vestals and Vestries—a continuation, being further extracts from the Journal of Florence Alice Sitwell, edited by Osbert Sitwell," *Life and Letters To-Day*, v. 44, no. 90, pp. 67–81, February 1945.

oC379 "The True Story of Dick Whittington," *Horizon*, v. 11, no. 63, pp. 169–205, March 1945.

oC380 "Vestals and Vestries . . .," *Life and Letters To-Day*, v. 44, no. 91, pp. 133–146, March 1945.

oC381 "A Letter to My Son," *Atlantic Monthly*, v. 175, no. 4, pp. 90–96, April 1945.

oC382 "Vestals and Vestries . . .," *Life and Letters To-Day*, v. 45, no. 92, pp. 4–17, April 1945.

oC383 "A Short Character of Walter Richard Sickert," *Orion, II*, pp. 121–154, 1945.

oC384 "Vestals and Vestries . . .," *Life and Letters To-Day*, v. 45, no. 93, pp. 109–120, 122, 124 and 126, May 1945.

oC385 "A Victorian Boyhood," *Atlantic Monthly*, v. 177, no. 2, pp. 86–91, February 1946.

oC386 "A Hero for his Bed," *Atlantic Monthly*, v. 177, no. 3, pp. 61–65, March 1946.

oC387 "Golden Trio," *The Observer*, no. 8077, p. 3, 17 March 1946. [Review of *Three* by William Sansom.]

oC388 "The Happiest Years," *Town & Country*, v. 100, no. 4283, pp. 84–85, 148, 150, 152, 155–156 and 164, April 1946.

oC389 "The Happiest Time of One's Life," *Atlantic Monthly*, v. 177, no. 4, pp. 92–97, April 1946.

oC390 "Wilfred Owen," *Penguin New Writing*, no. 27, pp. 114–132, Spring 1946.

oC391 "To Grandmother's House we Go," *Town & Country*, v. 100, no. 4284, pp. 76–77, 135–136, 138 and 140–144, May 1946.

oC392 "Father, Henry and I," *Atlantic Monthly*, v. 177, no. 5, pp. 65–70, May 1946.

oC393 "The Future of Fiction," *New Writing and Daylight*, pp. 95–97, 1946.

oC394 "The Invader," *Penguin New Writing*, no. 29, p. 79, Autumn 1946.

oC395 "A Genius whose Jests were Dynamite," *Daily Graphic*, p. 5, 27 November 1946.

oC396 "Britain's Greatest Soldier since Wellington," *Daily Graphic*, p. 5, 29 November 1946.

oC397 "The True Story of Dick Whittington," *Town & Country*, v. 100, no. 4291, pp. 93–96, 282–284, 286 and 288–292, December 1946.

oC398 "When the Palace Band played the Wrong Tune," *Daily Graphic*, p. 5, 2 December 1946.

oC399 "Mrs. Asquith ruled in Downing Street," *Daily Graphic*, p. 5, 4 December 1946.

oC400 "The Gay Teen Age of the Century," *Daily Graphic*, p. 5, 6 December 1946.

oC401 "A War God slightly Gone to Seed," *Daily Graphic*, p. 5, 9 December 1946.

oC402 "The Last Master," *Strand Magazine*, v. 112, no. 674, pp. 68–70 and 109, February 1947.

oC403 "Queen Mary: a portrait," *The Observer*, no. 8139, p. 4, 25 May 1947.

oC404 "The House of Mars Victoryall," *Good Housekeeping*, v. 52, no. 1, pp. 4–6 and 90–101, July 1947.

oC405 "Father and Son," *Horizon*, v. 16, no. 90, pp. 17–49, July 1947.

oC406 "Before the War," *The Cornhill*, v. 162, no. 971, pp. 376–394, Summer 1947.

oC407 "Grooming for the Cavalry," *Atlantic Monthly*, v. 180, no. 2, pp. 43–48, August 1947.

oC408 "Oak and Olive: being pages from *Great Morning*," *Orion*, *IV*, pp. 74–88, 1947.

oC409 "In the Tower of London," *Atlantic Monthly*, v. 180, no. 3, pp. 42–48, September 1947.

oC410 "Pothooks in the Sand," *Good Housekeeping*, v. 52, no. 4, pp. 8–9 and 54–60, October 1947.

oC411 "Great Ladies of London," *Atlantic Monthly*, v. 180, no. 4, pp. 41–47, October 1947.

oC412 "The Golden Age of Opera," *Atlantic Monthly*, v. 180, no. 5, pp. 109–114, November 1947.

oC413 "Interludes and Diversions," *The Cornhill*, v. 163, no. 973, pp. 3–24, Winter 1947–8.

oC414 "How to Buy a Castle," *Atlantic Monthly*, v. 180, no. 6, pp. 86–91, December 1947.

oC415 "A Rose in the Mouth," *Sunday Times*, no. 6507, p. 4, 28 December 1947.

oC416 "Four Songs of the Italian Earth," *The Cornhill*, v. 163, no. 974, pp. 155–157, Spring 1948.

oC417 "First Day in the Old Home," *Vogue* [London], v. 104, no. 5, pp. 65, 102 and 108, May 1948.

oC418 "Laughter in the Next Room," *Atlantic Monthly*, v. 182, no. 1, pp. 73–84, July 1948.

oC419 "A Short Character of Arnold Bennett," *Orpheus*, *I*, pp. 83–95, 1948.

oC420 "Laughter in the Next Room," *Atlantic Monthly*, v. 182, no. 2, pp. 71–82, August 1948.

oC421 "Laughter in the Next Room," *Atlantic Monthly*, v. 182, no. 3, pp. 73–84, September 1948.

oC422 "Keats and Shelley," *Sunday Times*, no. 6545, p. 4, 19 September 1948.

oC423 "Laughter in the Next Room," *Atlantic Monthly*, v. 182, no. 4, pp. 73–84, October 1948.

oC424 "Rex Whistler's Art," *Sunday Times*, no. 6551, p. 3, 31 October 1948. [Review of *Rex Whistler* by Laurence Whistler.]

oC425 "Four Songs of the Italian Earth," *American Scholar*, v. 18, no. 1, pp. 50–53, Winter 1948–49.

oC426 "Prologue and Song," *The Nation* [New York], v. 167, no. 23, p. 636, 4 December 1948.

oC427 "A Rose in the Mouth," *Atlantic Monthly*, v. 183, no. 1, p. 35, January 1949.

oC428 "Bloomsbury in the 1920s," *Sunday Times*, no. 6564, p. 4, 6 February 1949.

oC429 "Life with Sir George," *Sunday Times*, no. 6565, pp. 4–5, 13 February 1949.

oC430 "A Goddess in the Kitchen," *Sunday Times*, no. 6567, p. 4, 27 February 1949.

oC431 "Sir George: extracts from an autobiography," *The Cornhill*, v. 163, no. 978, pp. 429–444, Spring 1949.

oC432 "Hail, Columbia," *Sunday Times*, no. 6573, p. 4, 10 April 1949.

oC433 "A Modern Figaro," *Sunday Times*, no. 6579, p. 3, 22 May 1949. [Review of *The Body* by William Sansom.]

oC434 "Drinking Song," "The Journalists," *Wake*, no. 8, pp. 57–58, 1949.

oC435 "Cities of America," *Sunday Times*, no. 6582, p. 6, 12 June 1949.

oC436 "Sir Thomas [Beecham] goes on Record," *Etude*, v. 67, no. 10, p. 13, October 1949.

oC437 "Aspiring Ape," *Atlantic Monthly*, v. 184, no. 5, p. 51, November 1949.

oC438 "The Influence of Literature on Life: a note on English literary fashions between the wars," *The Times Book Club Review*, no. 5, pp. 7–9, Winter 1949–50.

oC439 "A Bunch of Snowdrops," *Sunday Times*, no. 6610, p. 4, 25 December 1949.

oC440 "Remembrance of Christmases Past," *New York Times Magazine*, pt. 6, pp. 9 and 17, 25 December 1949. [Being the same as no. 439.]

oC441 "Gabriele d'Annunzio," *National & English Review*, v. 135, no. 810, pp. 205–209, August 1950. [In part revised from *Discursions*, Part III.]

oC442 "Wilfred Owen," *Atlantic Monthly*, v. 186, no. 2, pp. 37–42, August 1950.

oC443 "Two Portraits," *Good Housekeeping*, v. 58, no. 3, pp. 36 and 105–113, September 1950.

oC444 "Ada Leverson, Wilde, and 'Max,'" *National & English Review*, v. 135, no. 811, pp. 286–290, September 1950.

oC445 "Gabriele d'Annunzio," *Atlantic Monthly*, v. 186, no. 3, pp. 44–48, September 1950.

oC446 "Poems from a Sequence: Ballad of Sister Anne; Mr. and Mrs. Travers; Local Press; Battling Mr. Fiddler; Blind Girl; Miss Lopez," *New Statesman and Nation*, v. 40, no. 1021, p. 320, 30 September 1950.

oC447 "Walter Richard Sickert," *Atlantic Monthly*, v. 186, no. 4, pp. 46–50, October 1950.

oC448 "The True Story of Cinderella," *Saturday Book*, no. 10, pp. 25–56, [October] 1950.

oC449 "Making a Bolt for it," *Atlantic Monthly*, v. 187, no. 4, pp. 55–57, April 1951.

oC450 "Poems from Tidesend," *World Review*, no. 29 (new series), pp. 2–5, July 1951.

oC451 "The Woman who Could Not Die," *Poetry London*, no. 22, pp. 8–10, Summer 1951.

oC452 "Poems from Tidesend," *World Review*, no. 30 (new series), pp. 2–3, August 1951.

oC453 "At the Seaside, 1900: four new poems," *Go*, no. 3 (new series), [inset folder between pp. 28–39], August–September 1951.

oC454 "Constant Lambert," *New Statesman and Nation*, v. 42, no. 1069, pp. 225–226, 1 September 1951.

oC455 "Making a Bolt for it," *Lilliput*, v. 29, no. 3, pp. 45–50, September–October 1951.

oC456 "Municipal Idyll," *Times Literary Supplement*, p. 709, 9 November 1951.

oC457 "Follow m'Leader," *Atlantic Monthly*, v. 190, no. 2, pp. 21–31, August 1952.

oC458 "English Beach Memory: Mr. Thuddock," *New Yorker*, v. 28, no. 48, p. 88, 17 January 1953.

oC459 "Queen Mary," *Spectator*, no. 6509, p. 366, 27 March 1953.

oC460 "Through Five Reigns," *Sunday Times*, Coronation supplement p. iii, 31 May 1953.

oC461 "Towers," *Harper's Magazine*, v. 208, no. 1246, pp. 66–67, March 1954.

oC462 "Books of the Year," *Sunday Times*, no. 6972, p. 10, 30 December 1956. [On *The Bourbons of Naples* by Harold Acton.]

oC463 "Recollections from an English Childhood—Italy, 1900–1910," *New Yorker*, v. 33, no. 1, pp. 34–35, 23 February 1957.

oC464 "The Door Knocker: further notes on my father," *Atlantic Monthly*, v. 200, no. 5, pp. 185–189, November 1957.

oC465 "Recollections of an Awkward Afternoon in Knightsbridge," *London Magazine*, v. 5, no. 2, pp. 26–31, February 1958.

oC466 "Florence: At the Villa Jernyngham," *Harper's Magazine*, v. 216, pp. 68–71, February 1958.

oC468 "Milordo Inglese," *Atlantic Monthly*, v. 202, no. 1, pp. 46–49, July 1958.

oC469 "Books of the Year," *Sunday Times*, no. 7024, p. 4, 29 December 1957.

oC469A "My Father's Excursions and Alarms," *The Reporter*, v. 19, no. 4, pp. 37–39, 18 September 1958.

oC470 "Books of the Year," *Sunday Times*, p. 11, 28 December 1958.

oC471 "Jack and the Beanstalk," *Argosy*, v. 20, no 1, pp. 26–34, January 1959.

oC471*A* "Postscript: poem," *Good Housekeeping* [New York], v. 150, p. 130, January 1960.

oC472 "Two Dinner Parties," *Atlantic Monthly*, v. 205, no. 5, pp. 41–46, May 1960.

oC472*A* "Popularity," *Vogue* [New York], v. 138, no. 1, pp. 48 & 104, July 1961; and *Vogue* [London], v. 118, no. 2, pp. 64–65, 1 February 1962.

oC473 "Father and I," *Atlantic Monthly*, v. 208, no. 2, pp. 67–72, August 1961.

oC473*A* "Once, when travelling . . .," *Vogue* [New York], v. 138, no. 6, pp. 144 & 173, 1 October 1961.

oC473*B* "To Manage Parents . . .," *Vogue* [New York], v. 138, no. 8, pp. 138 & 172–173, 1 November 1961.

oC474 "New York in the Twenties," *Atlantic Monthly*, v. 209, no. 2, pp. 38–43, February 1962.

oC475 "Lord Abingdon and Lindsey" (a tribute), *The Times*, no. 55815, p. 14, 25 September 1963.

oC476 "Farewell to Carlyle Square," *Atlantic Monthly*, v. 213, no. 3, pp. 76–78, March 1964.

oC477 "The Magnasco Society," *Apollo*, v. 79, no. 5, pp. 378–381, May 1964. [Followed by the Society's exhibition catalogues reprinted.]

OSBERT SITWELL: BOOKS
ANNOUNCED BUT NOT PUBLISHED
(oD1–oD5)

oD1 "Sitwells' Omnibus." (See ED1.)

oD2 "A Study in Evolution, by Augustine Rivers." Announced in *Who Killed Cock Robin?*, 1921.

oD3 "A Comic History of the Squire-Archy, by Augustine Rivers." Announced in *Who Killed Cock-Robin?*, 1921. (But see oC71.)

oD4 "Fox-Trot, and other poems." Announced as "to be published shortly" in *Façade*, 1922.

oD5 "A Book of Characters: short stories and sketches." Announced as "in preparation" in *Out of the Flame*, 1923.

OSBERT SITWELL: TRANSLATIONS
(oE1–oE20)

oE1 *Nocturne.* Translated by Max Meyerfeld. In: *Britanniens neue Dichtung,* edited by Karl Arns and Paul Selver. Munster i. West.: Verlag Greve, 1923.

oE2 *Literarische Koterien in London.* Translated [from the manuscript] by Max Meyerfeld. *Die Literatur,* 27er Jhrg., pp. 212–218, Dezember 1924.

oE3 *Epilog zum Roman 'Vor dem ersten Bombenabwurf.'* Translated by Max Meyerfeld. *Deutsche Rundschau,* Bd. 217, Oktober–Dezember 1928, pp. 55–62.

oE4 *L'Homme qui se Perdit Lui-même.* Translated by Mme. Bourdieux. *Nouvelle Revue Française,* 1933.

oE5 *Amritsar* (peu abrégé). In: *La Domination de l'Angleterre sur L'Inde* by Reinhard Frank. Berlin: Deutsche Informationsstelle, 1940. [Translation of "Shaking Hands with Murder."]

oE6 *Amritsar* (etwas gekürzt). In: *Englands Herrschaft in Indien* by Reinhard Frank. Berlin: Deutsche Informationsstelle, 1940.

oE7 *Lettre à mon Fils* (Fragments). Translated by M. Bofourie. *Fontaine,* nos. 37–40, pp. 282–301 (426–445), 1944. [Reprinted in *Aspects de la Littérature anglaise (1918–1945)* edited by Kathleen Raine and Max-Pol Fouchet; Paris: Fontaine, 1947.]

oE8 *El Hombre que se Perdió a sí Mismo.* Translated by Pedro Fraga de Porto. Barcelona: José Janes, 1945.

oE8A *Thomas Rowlandson.* Translated by G. Jean-Aubry. *Le Portique* [Paris], no. 4, pp. 108–128, November 1946.

oE9 *El Arbol Escarlata* [fragment]. Translated by Elena Cruz. *Sur,* año XV, Julio–Octubre 1947, pp. 339–357.

oE10 *Lysmasken* [The Glow-Worm]. Translated by Torsten Blomkvist. *All Världens Berättare,* no. 6, 1947.

oE11 *Antes del Bombardeo.* Translated by Harry Leslie Reader and María Luisa Ubeda. Barcelona: José Janes, 1947.

oE12 *Gestalt und Zukunft des Romans* [The Future of Fiction]. Translated by Wilhelm Maria Lüsberg. *Berliner Hefter für geistiges Leben*, 3er Jhrg., heft 3, pp. 276–278, erstes Halbjahr 1948.

oE13 *Linke Hand, Rechte Hand: selbstbiographie, erste band.* Hamburg: Wolfg. Krüger, 1948.

oE14 *Venstre Haand, Højre Haand, en selvbiografi.* Translated by Margrethe van Rheden and Finn Brink Carlsen, poems by Kai Friis Møller. København: Gyldendal, 1948.

oE15 *Airs Graves, Airs Légers.* [*Sing High! Sing Low!*.] Translated by Madeleine T. Guéritte. Paris: Laffont, 1949.

oE16 *Blodets Røde Træ: en selvbiografi, andet bind.* Translated by Peter P. Rohde. København: Gyldendal, 1950.

oE17 *Vänster Hand, Höger Hand! en självbiografi.* Translated by Nils Homberg. Stockholm: Bonnier, 1950. [Abridgement of first two volumes of autobiography.]

oE18 *Forskudt Ferie* [Staggered Holiday]. Translated by Margrethe van Rheden. In: *40 Dage og 40 Nætter.* København: Hasselbachs, 1954.

oE19 *Marée Basse* [Low Tide]. Translated by J. Chambon-Gardet. *Les Oeuvres Libres*, nlle. série no. 114, Novembre 1955.

oE20 *I Quattro Continenti.* Translated by Marcella Hannau. Milano: Longanesi, 1955.

OSBERT SITWELL: MUSICAL SETTINGS
(oF1–oF3)

---

oF1 *Belshazzar's Feast*, by William Walton. (1931; see oB18.)

oF2 *Winter the Huntsman*, by Elisabeth Lutyens, a chamber cantata for chorus, trumpet, cello and pianoforte. (1934.)

oF3 *Winter the Huntsman*, by David Pedley, for SATB. (1966.)

OSBERT SITWELL: RECORDINGS
(oG1–oG4)

---

oG1 "To Charlotte Corday," "Fool's Song," "Journalist's Song," "Mary-Anne," "Mrs. Southern's Enemy," read by the author. (Harvard Vocarium Records P-1212, P-1213 [H.F.S.I. 285, 287], recorded in 1950 for non-commercial distribution.)

oG2 "Osbert Sitwell reading poetry from *Wrack at Tidesend, England Reclaimed* and *Selected Poems*." (Caedmon Publishers, New York; record TC 1013, issued Fall 1953.)

oG3 *Left Hand, Right Hand!*—introduction, and excerpts from chapters V–VI. ("Columbia Literary Series," set DSL-190, DSL-190E, released 5 October 1953, by Columbia Records [New York].)

oG4 "Subtlety of the Serpent," "Chanson des Mouches," "The Ballad of Sister Anne," "The Three Miss Coltrums," "A Rose in the Mouth," "Fool's Song," "Winter the Huntsman, 1–12," "Mr. and Mrs. Kembley, I–V," "Three Mexican Pieces," "Elegy for Mr. Goodbeare," "Mr. Hague," "Mrs. Kimber: invocation," read by the author. (Library of Congress, Washington, D.C.; recorded 31 March 1955, but not hitherto issued.)

SIR SACHEVERELL SITWELL, Bt.

BOOKS WRITTEN BY SACHEVERELL
SITWELL
(SA1–SA70)

SA1   THE PEOPLE'S PALACE   1918

First edition

[*Within a border*]

THE PEOPLE'S | PALACE | BY | SACHEVERELL SITWELL |
[*ornament*] | OXFORD | B. H. BLACKWELL, BROAD
STREET, | 1918

194 × 145 mm.

56 pp.: [1] half-title; [2] decoration; [3] title; [4] blank; [5] Contents;
[6] blank; 7–52, [53] text and publisher's imprint; [54–55] advertisements; [56] blank.

Decoration on p. 2.

Terracotta paper wrappers. Untrimmed edges. White paper labels,
printed in black, pasted on spine and upper cover.

400 copies printed at the Vincent Works. Published 15 June 1918 at
2s. 6d., as no. 22 of the "Adventurers All" series.

CONTENTS

Fountains—Pindar—Li-Tai-Pé [a different poem from "Li-Tai-Pé
Drinks and Drowns" in *Wheels 1*]—Brighton Pier—Fragment from
Sirens—Outskirts—Tahiti [from *Wheels 2*]—Barrel-Organs, 1. Prelude; 2. The Feathered Hat [both from *Wheels 2*]—The Moon [as
"The Nightingale" in *Wheels 2*]—"The Mayor of Murcia," 1. Soliloquy [from *Wheels 2*]; 2. The Speech [from *Wheels 2*]; 3. The Return;
4. The Festa; 5. The Home-Coming—Trumpets [from *Wheels 2*]
—"Psittachus eois Imitatrix Ales ab Indis" [from *The Egoist*, May
1918]—Trapeze-Song from "Perspectives"—"Whitsun"

First edition

𝕯𝖔𝖈𝖙𝖔𝖗 𝕯𝖔𝖓𝖓𝖊 𝖆𝖓𝖉 | 𝕲𝖆𝖗𝖌𝖆𝖓𝖙𝖚𝖆 | [*one line between two short rules*] FIRST CANTO | BY | *Sacheverell Sitwell* | WITH A DRAWING BY | WYNDHAM LEWIS | AT | THE FAVIL PRESS | KENSINGTON | A. 1921 D.

190 × 132 mm.

16 pp.: [1] half-title; [2] drawing; [3] title; [4] quotation; [5], 6–14 text; [15] "This Edition, which is privately printed, is limited to 101 Copies, of which 50" [crossed out in red ink, "21" substituted] "Copies are reserved by the Author. This Copy is No." [in red ink, with author's autograph signature in red ink]. [Advertisement]; [16] "Printed by Philip Sainsbury & Charles Birnstingl at The Favil Press, Peel Street, Kensington, London. October mcmxxj" [*device*].

Drawing on p. [2] by Wyndham Lewis.

Marbled paper wrappers, sewn. Untrimmed edges. White paper label, printed in black, pasted on upper cover.

101 copies printed (80 for sale). Privately issued in October 1921. (Five extra unnumbered copies printed for printer's file and copyright purposes.)

Note: There is an MS. correction in red ink on p. 9, line 24.

sA3   THE HUNDRED AND   1922
ONE HARLEQUINS

a. *First edition*

THE HUNDRED AND ONE HARLEQUINS | BY | SACHE-VERELL SITWELL | LONDON | GRANT RICHARDS LTD. | 1922

211 × 140 mm.

96 pp.: [1] half-title; [2] blank; [3] title; [4] "Printed in Great Britain at The Mayflower Press, Plymouth. William Brendon & Son, Ltd."; 5 Contents; [6] dedication; 7–96 text.

Lilac and crimson crash canvas boards. Trimmed edges. Cream paper label, lettered in brown, pasted on spine.

Published in July 1922 at 6s. (Printers' records lost in the war 1939–45.)

CONTENTS

Ten Serenades [the first as "Serenade (from 'Bird Actors')" in *Wheels 4*]—The Italian Air [being "The Italian Air" from *Wheels 4*, and 120 new lines; the whole revised from "The Italian Air" in *The Chapbook*, May 1922]—Fables [from *Wheels 3*]—Church and Stage [from *The Monthly Chapbook*, no. 1]—Valse Estudiantina [from *Wheels 4*]

From "The Hundred and One Harlequins". 1. A Pro's Landlady—2. At Breakfast—3. Reading the Paper—4. In the Train—5. At the Tailor's—6. On the Telephone—7. Portrait of Mr. Geo. F. M. Airey–a secretary [revised from "Portrait of a Harlequin" in *The Eton Candle*, 1922]—11[*sic*]. From a Hill-Top

The Hochzeit of Hercules—Et in Arcadia, Omnes (from "The Bird-Actors") [revised from *Wheels 5*]—Two Clowns' Psychology—First Variation on a Theme by George Peele [as "An Imitation" in *Wheels 6*]—Second Variation [as "Another Imitation" in *Wheels 6*]—Third Variation—Mrs. H. . . . . . or a Lady from Babel [from *Wheels 4*]—Week-Ends [from *Coterie 3*]—Extract from "Bird-Actors" [from *Art and Letters*, Winter 1918–1919]—Two Variations on Themes out of Zarathustra, 1. "Laughing Lions will come" [from *Wheels 5*]; 2. Parade Virtues for a Dying Gladiator [revised from *Wheels 6*]—Dr. Donne and Gargantua [as *Doctor Donne and Gargantua, First Canto*]—A March Past at the Pyramids [from *Art and Letters*, Winter 1920]—The Neptune Hotel

b. *First edition, American copies*

THE HUNDRED AND ONE HARLEQUINS | BY | SACHE-VERELL SITWELL | BONI AND LIVERIGHT | PUBLISHERS NEW YORK

Note: I have seen only a re-bound example of these copies. They were imported and published in 1922 (date unknown) at $1.75. The contents are as in sA3a.

First edition

Doctor Donne & Gargantua | Canto the Second | By | Sacheverell Sitwell | With two decorations by Gino Severini | The Favil Press, Kensington | London, 1923

221 × 148 mm.

20 pp.: [1] half-title; [2] blank; [3] title; [4] blank; [5] Synopsis; [6] quotation; [7], 8–18 text; [19] blank; [20] "Thirty-five copies of this book have been printed for the author in Caslon Old Face type, on a Columbian hand press, by Charles Birnstingl at The Favil Press, 24 Peel Street, Kensington, London, in June 1923." [*Device.*]

Decorations by Gino Severini on pp. 7 and 18.

Green paper boards. Untrimmed edges. Printed in black on upper cover.

35 copies printed for the author in June 1923. (Five extra copies printed for printer's file and copyright purposes.)

sA5   THE PARROT   [1923]

First edition

THE NEW BROADSIDE | The Parrot | [*coloured decoration*] | [*text: 4 lines*] | [*coloured decoration*] | From a Poem by Sacheverell Sitwell | Decorations by E. McKnight Kauffer | THE POETRY BOOKSHOP 35 DEVONSHIRE STREET | THEOBALDS ROAD W.C.1 | No. 4

Folio, half sheet. 429 × 188 mm.

Decorations by E. McKnight Kauffer.

Published as no. 4 of "The New Broadside." (Nos. 1–6 received at the British Museum on 13 December 1923.)

CONTENTS

The Parrot [from "Psittachus eois Imitatrix Ales ab Indis"]

a. *First edition*

Southern | Baroque Art | A Study of | Painting, Architecture and Music | in Italy and Spain of the | 17th & 18th Centuries | By | Sacheverell Sitwell | [*ornament*] | London | Grant Richards Ltd. | St Martin's Street | mdccccxxiv

220 × 144 mm.

320 pp.: [1] half-title; [2] blank; [3] title; [4] "Printed in Great Britain by The Riverside Press Limited, Edinburgh"; 5 Contents; [6] blank; 7 List of illustrations; [8] blank; 9–12 Introduction; [13–14], 15–319 text, index and bibliography; [320] blank.

Sixteen plates tipped in.

Smooth orange cloth boards, bevelled edges. Top edge gilt, others trimmed. Gilt stamped on spine and upper cover.

Published in February 1924 at 20s. (Printers' records do not survive.)

b. *First edition, American copies*

Southern | Baroque Art | A Study of | Painting, Architecture and Music | in Italy and Spain of the | 17th & 18th Centuries | By | Sacheverell Sitwell | [*device*] | New York | Alfred A. Knopf | mdccccxxiv

Note: Copies were imported and published in 1924 (the publishers have no records of publication) at $6.00. Bound in blue and yellow patterned paper boards, buff linen spine. Top edge yellow, others trimmed. Lettered in blue on the spine. The contents are as in sA6a.

c. *Second edition*

Southern | Baroque Art | A Study of | Painting, Architecture and Music | in Italy and Spain of the | 17th & 18th Centuries | By | Sacheverell Sitwell | [*ornament*] | London | Duckworth | 3 Henrietta St., W.C. | 1927

Note: This edition contains the whole text of the first edition, and also a "Preface to Second Edition" (dated 31 July 1927) on pp. 10–12. Published in January 1928 [*sic*] at 10s. 6d. 1500 copies were printed, but of these "about 1000" copies were bound with a cancel title and published in April or May 1931 in "Duckworth's Georgian Library," and are incorrectly described on the verso of the title as the "Third edition." (For the third edition, see below.)

d. *Third edition*

SOUTHERN BAROQUE ART | A Study of Painting, Architecture and | Music in Italy and Spain of the | 17th & 18th Centuries | by | SACHEVERELL SITWELL | DUCKWORTH | 3 HENRIETTA STREET | LONDON, W.C.2

Note: This, the true third edition, was published in 1930 in "The New Readers' Library" at 3s. 6d. 2000 copies were printed. A note on p. [5] explains that the whole of part IV, "Mexico," is omitted; and there are no illustrations.

sA7   THE THIRTEENTH CÆSAR   1924

a. *First edition*

THE THIRTEENTH CÆSAR | AND OTHER POEMS | BY | SACHEVERELL SITWELL | LONDON | GRANT RICHARDS LTD. | 1924

210 × 141 mm.

112 pp.: [1] half-title and dedication; [2] "By the same author . . ."; [3] title; [4] "Printed in Great Britain at The Mayflower Press, Plymouth. William Brendon & Son, Ltd."; 5–6 Contents; 7–112 text.

Yellow cloth boards. Trimmed edges. Brick-red paper label, lettered in black, pasted on spine. (Copies bound later have a green paper label.)

Published in October 1924 at 6s. (Printers' records lost in the war 1939–45.)

CONTENTS

Hortus Conclusus, 1. The Cherry Tree—2. The Gardener—3. Gardener's Song [from *Spectator*, 10 May 1924]—4. The Fruit-Gatherers—5. The Red-Gold Rain: orange tree by day—6. Orange Tree by Night [from *Spectator*, 12 July 1924]—7. Magnolia Tree—

8. Apple Tree—9. Snow and Wind—10. Eurydice—11. The Fiery
Torch [from *Vogue*, late May 1924]—12. The Golden Bell—
13. Complaint—14. Warning—15. The Island—16. Memory—
17. Fortune—18. Shadow—19. Dancer—20. The Venus of Bolsover Castle [from *A Miscellany of Poetry*, *1920–1922*]—21.
Variation on a Theme by Marlowe—22. Variation on a Theme by
Alexander Pope [from *The Criterion*, April 1924]—23. Daphne,
an adaptation from John Milton [from *The Criterion*, April 1924]—
24. Variation on a Theme by John Lely [from *The Criterion*, April
1924]—25. Finale

New Water Music—Two Water Songs, 1. The Sea God; 2. The
River God—The Paradise of Alexander—The Fisherman—Wind
as Husbandman—Gardener Trimming Hedges—On Hearing Four
Bands Play at once in a Public Square

Doctor Donne and Gargantua: Canto the Second [from the book]

The Rio Grande

The Santander Quartet in a Programme of Spanish Music, 1. In the
wine-shop—2. Moon and Cloud, or Sword and Cloak—3. The
Mirador—4. The Mirador (another version)—5. Telling Fortunes
—6. At Supper—7. Gipsy Song—8. Solo—9. Song with Bagpipe—
10. Village Band—11. The Statue of the Comendador—12. The
Comendador turns Burlador

Two Mirror Poems, 1. On a Name Scratched upon a Window [from
Spectator, 16 August 1924]—2. The Poet and the Mirror

The Thirteenth Cæsar, 1. The Opening of the Tomb—2. At the Bedside—3. As of Old—4. They are still with us—5. Last Will and
Testament

The Winter Walk—Bolsover Castle [from *The Chapbook*, March 1923]

Actor Rehearsing, 1. Prologue—2. At his Mirror—3. Rehearsal—
4. Performance

b. *First edition, American copies*

THE THIRTEENTH CÆSAR | AND OTHER POEMS | BY |
SACHEVERELL SITWELL | NEW [*device*] YORK | GEORGE
H. DORAN COMPANY

Note: 200/250 copies imported with a cancel title. Published 24 April
1925 at $2.00, bound in black cloth spine, grey veined paper boards,
with a buff paper label on spine and a green paper label on upper
cover. The contents as in sA7a.

First edition

[*For description, see* EA10.]

CONTENTS (BY SACHEVERELL SITWELL)

Twelve Poems, by Sacheverell Sitwell: The Myrtle Tree—The Names upon the Trees—Actæon—Song: A Creole Winter have I Found [from *The Decachord*, January–February 1925]—Selection—The Glass—Love-and the Sexton—Bitter Dawn—Rock-Carving—To a Statue—Donkey's Ears—The Mill

sA9   EXALT THE EGLANTINE   1926

First edition

EXALT THE EGLANTINE | AND OTHER POEMS | BY | SACHEVERELL SITWELL | DECORATED BY THOMAS LOWINSKY | [*drawing*] | LONDON | THE FLEURON | 1926

208 × 173 mm.

48 pp.: [i] "This edition is limited to 370 copies of which 350 are for sale. This is No." [in ink]; [ii] blank; [iii] half-title; [iv] blank; [v] title; [vi] "Printed and made in England at The Curwen Press, Plaistow for The Fleuron Ltd."; vii–viii Contents; 1–36 text; 37 Notes; [38–40] blank.

Nineteen drawings by Thomas Lowinsky.

Magenta cloth boards printed in ochre on covers only. Untrimmed edges. Gilt lettered up spine.

370 copies printed (350 for sale). Published in September 1926 at 21*s*. (Publishers' and printers' records do not survive.)

CONTENTS

Exalt the Eglantine. 1. Time and the Stag—2. The Ghost at the Window—3. The Playing-Cards—4. The House of Sun—5. Haunted—6. Feeding the Stag

The Maze—Doubt—Dying on Paper—Change in the Mirror—The Canal—An Equinox [from *Vogue*, October 1925]—The Mirror—Drift—In the Orchard—The Potting-Shed—The Bonfire on Boxing Day—The Great Harlequin

Studies on the Black Keys. 1. In the Corn—2. The Dark of Night—
3. Black Venus—4. Black Sonnet—5. Black Shepherdess
Blue Sonnet—The Candiote

sA10   ALL SUMMER IN A DAY   1926

a. *First edition*

[*Within a double rule border*]

All Summer in a Day | An Autobiographical Fantasia |
[*rule*] | By | Sacheverell Sitwell | [*two rules*] | Duckworth |
Henrietta Street, London | 1926

223 × 143 mm. (later bindings slightly shorter).

288 pp.: [1] half-title; [2] "By the same author . . ."; [3] title; [4] "All
Rights Reserved. Made and Printed in Great Britain by Hazell,
Watson & Viney Ld. London and Aylesbury"; 5 Contents; [6] de-
dication; 7–10 Preface; 11–287 text; [288] blank.

Smooth green cloth boards. Top edge gilt, others untrimmed. Blind-
stamped on upper cover, gilt lettered on spine. (Later bindings have
top edge plain.)

2500 copies printed. Published 21 October 1926 at 16s.

b. *First edition, American issue*

All Summer in a Day | *An Autobiographical Fantasia* |
by | Sacheverell Sitwell | *Author of* "Southern Barque [*sic*]
Art," "The Thirteenth Cæsar," | "The Hundred and
One Harlequins," etc., etc. | [*device*] | New York | *George
H. Doran Company*

Note: This issue, printed in the United States, was published 4
November 1926 at $3.50. Bound in pink patterned paper boards,
maroon cloth spine, with a label on the spine. The contents are as in
sA10a.

First edition

DOCTOR DONNE | AND GARGANTUA | CANTO THE
THIRD | By Sacheverell Sitwell | Decorated by Thomas
Lowinsky | [*decoration*] | Privately Printed | At the Shake-
speare Head Press | Stratford-upon-Avon | 1926

252 × 194 mm.

24 pp.: [1] blank; [2] decoration; [3] title; [4] "Sixty-Five Copies of
Doctor Donne & Gargantua, Canto the Third, have been printed, of
which Fifty are for sale"; 5–16 text; [17] decoration; [18–24] blank.

Decorations by Thomas Lowinsky on text pages.

Half black cloth, marbled paper boards. Untrimmed edges. Gilt
lettered on cloth on upper cover.

65 copies printed (50 for sale). Published in late 1926. (The Shakespeare Head Press write that they have neither records nor recollection
of this book.)

sA12 THE CYDER FEAST 1927

a. *First edition, ordinary copies*

[*Within a double rule border*]

The Cyder Feast | And Other Poems | [*rule*] | By | Sache-
verell Sitwell | [*two rules*] | Duckworth | 3 Henrietta Street,
London | 1927

222 × 143 mm.

96 pp.: [1] half-title; [2] "By the same author . . ."; [3] title; [4] "All
Rights Reserved"; 5 dedication; [6] blank; 7–8 Contents; 9–93 text
and notes; [94] "Made and Printed in Great Britain by Hazell, Watson
& Viney Ld. London and Aylesbury"; [95–96] blank.

Smooth blue cloth boards. Untrimmed edges. Gilt lettered on spine.

1000 copies printed. Published 2 June 1927 at 7s. 6d.

CONTENTS

New Poems for Hortus Conclusus. Song: O Hard Voluptuary—
1. Damson and Medlar—2. The Two Almond Trees—3. Pear

Tree—4. Plum Tree—5. Hawthorn—6. Apricot—7. Tulip Tree—
8. Paulovnia—9. Snowflowers—10. Lords and Ladies—11. Wall-
flowers—12. White Hyacinth—13. Kingcups—14. Dandelion—
15. Cowslips—16. Warning—17. Variation upon Old Lines on the
Harlequin, John Bologna—18. Derbyshire Bluebells, four variations upon William Brown of Tavistock—19. The Mulberry—
20. The Mulberry (second version)—21. Apple Song—22. Quince
—23. Variation on a Theme of Robert Herrick—24. Variation upon
a Couplet of Alexander Pope—25. Water-Song, an adaptation
from John Milton—[26] Countersong

The Renishaw Woods—Two Pastoral Poems, 1. The Cyder Feast—
2. The Chamber Idyll

Doctor Donne and Gargantua, Canto the Third [from the book]

Convent Thoughts in Cadiz [from *The Chapbook*, 1925]

Canons of Giant Art, Three Torsos. 1. The Farnese Hercules—2. The
Laocoon—3. The Hermes

b. First edition, special copies

[*Within a double-rule border*]

The Cyder Feast | And Other Poems | [*rule*] | By | Sache-
verell Sitwell | [*two rules*] | London: Duckworth | New
York: George H. Doran Coy. | 1927

245 × 162 mm.

96 pp.: [1] half-title; [2] blank; [3] title; [4] "Of this edition of 'The
Cyder Feast,' on hand-made paper and signed by the Author, 165
copies have been printed, of which 150 copies only are for sale
throughout the world." [Number in ink, with author's autograph
signature.] "All Rights Reserved. Printed in Great Britain." [Thence
as in ordinary copies, above.]

Buff buckram boards. Untrimmed edges. Gilt lettered on spine.

165 copies printed (150 for sale). 125 copies published in London
2 June 1927 at 25s., 25 copies in New York later.

CONTENTS

As in ordinary copies, above

c. *First edition, American ordinary copies*

[*Within a double-rule border*]

The Cyder Feast | And Other Poems | [*rule*] | By | Sacheverell Sitwell | [*two rules*] | New York | George H. Doran Company | 1927

Note: 500/520 copies imported, and bound in black cloth spine, beige patterned paper boards. Orange paper labels pasted on spine and upper cover. Published 30 September 1927 at $2.00. The contents as in sA12a–b.

sA13   GERMAN BAROQUE ART   1927

a. *First edition*

[*Blue*] GERMAN | BAROQUE ART | [*black*] BY | SACHEVERELL SITWELL | AUTHOR OF "SOUTHERN BAROQUE ART" | [*blue medallion*] | LONDON | DUCKWORTH | 3 HENRIETTA STREET | 1927

252 × 181 mm.

112 pp. (excluding illustrations): [1] half-title; [2] blank; [3] title; [4] "All rights reserved. Printed in Great Britain by The Riverside Press Limited, Edinburgh"; [5] dedication; [6] blank; 7–8 List of illustrations; 9–10 Preface; 11–102 text; 103–108 bibliography; 109 Acknowledgements; [110–112] blank.

Colour frontispiece tipped in; 48 plates following text.

Smooth red cloth boards. Top edge gilt, fore edge trimmed, tail edge untrimmed. Gilt stamped on spine and upper cover.

1000 copies printed. Published 10 November 1927 at 25*s*.

b. *First edition, American copies*

[*Blue*] GERMAN | BAROQUE ART | [*black*] BY | SACHEVERELL SITWELL | AUTHOR OF "SOUTHERN BAROQUE ART" | [*blue medallion*] | NEW YORK | GEORGE H. DORAN COMPANY | 1928

Note: 500/520 copies imported. Bound in beige buckram boards, with blue paper labels. Published 23 March 1928 at $6.00. The contents are as in sA13a.

[For description, see OA13*]*

CONTENTS

Pp. 109–195, "All at Sea, a social tragedy in three acts, for first-class passengers only," by Osbert and Sacheverell Sitwell

SA15   A BOOK OF TOWERS   1928

First edition

A | BOOK OF TOWERS | and | OTHER BUILDINGS | of SOUTHERN EUROPE | A Series of Dry-Points | Engraved | by | RICHARD WYNDHAM | With an Introduction | and Brief Descriptions | by | SACHEVERELL SITWELL | [*three stars*] | LONDON | Frederick Etchells & Hugh Macdonald | 1a Kensington Place, W.8 | 1928

297 × 197 mm.

120 pp.: [a–b] blank; [i] half-title; [ii] blank; [iii] engraved title; [iv] blank; [v] title, as above; [vi] "Printed and made in Great Britain"; vii Table of Contents; [viii] blank; ix–xii Introduction; 1–101, [102–103] text; [104] blank; [105] engraving, and: "Of this edition, printed in England by Spottiswoode, Ballantyne & Co. Ltd., on Zanders hand-made paper, 350 numbered copies are for sale, of which No. 1 has with it a complete additional set of plates, and Nos. 2 to 13 have with them 3 additional plates. The dry-points have been printed by Messrs. A. Alexander & Sons, Ltd. The typography and arrangement are by Frederick Etchells. This is Number" [in ink, with—in nos. 1–13—autograph signatures of author and artist]. "The copper plates have been destroyed"; [106] blank.

Engravings by Richard Wyndham.

Copy no. 1 : Full blue morocco. Untrimmed edges. Gilt stamped on upper cover and spine. In slip case, with additional plates in another slip case.

Copies nos. 2–13 : Vellum boards, blue morocco spine and corners. Untrimmed edges. Gilt stamped on upper cover and down spine. In slip case, with additional plates in another slip case.

Copies no. 14–350: Buff paper boards, forrel spine and corners. Untrimmed edges. Printed in black on upper cover, and gilt lettered down spine. In slip case.

350 copies printed. Published in June 1928, no. 1 at 50 guineas, nos. 2–13 at 10 guineas, nos. 14–350 at 3½ guineas.

SA16   AUGUSTAN BOOKS OF   1928
                ENGLISH POETRY

First edition

[*Within a border*]

THE AUGUSTAN BOOKS OF | ENGLISH POETRY |
SECOND SERIES NUMBER TWENTY-NINE | [*rule*] |
SACHEVERELL | SITWELL | [*rule*] | LONDON: ERNEST
BENN LTD. | BOUVERIE HOUSE, FLEET STREET

210 × 134 mm.

32 pp.: [i] title; [ii] "The Augustan Books . . ."; iii "Sacheverell Sitwell [by] Humbert Wolfe"; [iv] Contents; 5–30 text; 31 Bibliography; [32] "The Augustan Books . . . Printed in Great Britain by Billing and Sons, Ltd., Guildford and Esher."

No covers. Stapled. Trimmed edges.

Published in November 1928 at 6*d.* (Copies issued "in the early 1930's" had maroon linen wrappers pasted over front and back pages, with a window cut in front to show the author's name. The series was later transferred to Messrs. Eyre & Spottiswoode, but neither they nor Messrs. Benn have records of publication, nor do the printers now know how many copies were printed.)

CONTENTS

The Moon [from *The People's Palace*]—A Serenade [as "Serenade II" in *The Hundred and One Harlequins*]

On a Name Scratched upon a Window—Gipsy Song—Variation on a Theme by John Lely—Daphne, an adaptation from John Milton—Variation on a Theme by Alexander Pope—The Cherry Tree—The Golden Bell—The Venus of Bolsover Castle [all from *The Thirteenth Cæsar*]

The Maze—Haunted—Change in the Mirror—The Great Harlequin [all from *Exalt the Eglantine*]

Lines from "The Chamber Idyll"—Variation on a Theme by Robert Herrick—Variation on a Couplet by Alexander Pope—Damson and Medlar—The Two Almond Trees—Hawthorn—Paulownia—Derbyshire Bluebells—Kingcups—Cowslips [all from *The Cyder Feast*]

Two Songs. "My balm giver, my golden tree"—"This moment" [both previously unpublished]

sA17   THE GOTHICK NORTH   1929–30

a. *First edition, first volume*

The Gothick North | A Study of Mediaeval Life, Art, and Thought | [*star*] | The Visit of the Gypsies | by | Sacheverell Sitwell | Duckworth | 3 Henrietta Street, London | 1929

221 × 143 mm.

164 pp.: [i] half-title; [ii] "By the same author . . ."; [iii] title; [iv] "All rights reserved"; [v] Contents; [vi] List of illustrations; [vii] dedication; [viii] blank; [1], 2–5 Preface; [6] blank; 7–156 text and notes; printer's imprint: "Printed at The Chapel River Press, Kingston, Surrey".

Nine plates tipped in.

Smooth yellow cloth boards. Untrimmed edges. Gilt lettered on spine.

2500 copies printed. Published in April 1929 at 8*s.* 6*d.*

CONTENTS

"The Visit of the Gypsies," the first volume of *The Gothick North*

First edition, second volume

The Gothick North | A Study of Mediaeval Life, Art, and Thought | [*two stars*] | These Sad Ruins | by | Sacheverell Sitwell | Duckworth | 3 Henrietta Street, London | 1929

221 × 143 mm.

160 pp.: [i–ii] blank; [iii] half-title; [iv] "By the same author . . .", [v] title; [vi] "All rights reserved"; [vii] Contents; [viii] blank; 1–152

text and notes; printer's imprint: "Printed at The Chapel River Press, Kingston, Surrey."

Binding uniform with first volume.

2500 copies printed. Published in September 1929 at 8s. 6d.

CONTENTS

"These Sad Ruins," the second volume of *The Gothick North*

First separate edition, third volume

The Gothick North | A Study of Mediaeval Life, Art, and Thought | [*three stars*] | The Fair-Haired Victory | by | Sacheverell Sitwell | Duckworth | 3 Henrietta Street, London | 1930

221 × 143 mm.

152 pp.: [i] half-title; [ii] "By the same author . . ."; [iii] title; [iv] "All rights reserved"; [v] Contents; [vi] blank; [vii] List of illustrations; [viii] blank; 1–144 text, notes and index; printer's imprint: "Printed at The Chapel River Press, Kingston, Surrey."

Eight plates tipped in.

Binding uniform with first two volumes.

2500 copies printed. Published in January 1930 at 8s. 6d.

CONTENTS

"The Fair-Haired Victory," the third volume of *The Gothick North*. (This volume had in fact already been published in America—see below.)

b. *First complete edition*

[*Within a green border*]

THE GOTHICK NORTH | A STUDY OF | MEDIAEVAL LIFE, ART, AND THOUGHT | BY | SACHEVERELL SITWELL | WITH ILLUSTRATIONS | [*device*] | BOSTON AND NEW YORK | HOUGHTON MIFFLIN COMPANY | The Riverside Press Cambridge | 1929

235 × 163 mm.

472 pp.: [i] half-title; [ii] blank; [iii] title; [iv] "The Riverside Press, Cambridge, Massachusetts. Printed in the U.S.A."; [v] dedication; [vi] blank; [vii] Contents; [viii] blank; [ix] Illustrations; [x] blank; [1], 2–5 Preface; [6] blank; [xi] half-title of book I; [xii] blank; 7–155 text of book I; [156] blank; [xiii] half-title of book II; [xiv] blank; 157–308 text of book II; [xv] half-title of book III; [xvi] blank; 309–454 text of book III and index; [455–456] blank.

Nine plates tipped in.

Dark green cloth spine, blue paper boards. Trimmed edges. Decorated end-papers. Gilt lettered on spine.

2500 copies printed. Published 18 October 1929 at $5.00.

CONTENTS

Contains all three volumes of *The Gothick North*, and thus contains the first printing of "The Fair-Haired Victory." There are no textual differences in the two editions.

Note: 500 copies of a one-volume edition were published by Messrs. Duckworth in October 1938 at 8*s.* 6*d.* There were no alterations in the text.

sA18   TWO POEMS, TEN SONGS   1929

First edition

TWO POEMS, TEN SONGS | *BY* | *SACHEVERELL SITWELL* | *DUCKWORTH* | *3 Henrietta Street, London* | *1929*

242 × 190 mm.

32 pp.: [i] blank; [ii] "Of this edition of *Two Poems and Ten Songs*, signed by the author, 275 copies have been printed, of which 250 only are for sale throughout the world. This is Number . . ." [in ink, with author's autograph signature]. "All Rights Reserved"; [iii] half-title; [iv] blank; [v] title; [vi] "Printed in England at The Curwen Press, Plaistow"; [vii] Contents; [viii] blank; 1–32 text.

Black cloth spine, decorated paper boards. Untrimmed edges. Gilt lettered up the spine.

275 copies printed (250 for sale). Published 5 December 1929 at 15*s.*

The Lady and the Rooks

Two Irish Songs. 1. Saint Erc of Slane—2. The Hazels of Cantire

Eight Pieces. 1. The Swing—2. Prisoner—3. Song, My balm-giver, my golden tree [from *Augustan Books of English Poetry*]—4. Moment [as "This Moment" in *Augustan Books of English Poetry*]—5. Masque—6. The Sun-Bath—7. What's in a Name?—8. Popular Song Improved

Thoughts in a High Wind Sailing a Boat

SA19   DR DONNE & GARGANTUA,   1930
        THE FIRST SIX CANTOS

a. *First edition, ordinary copies*

SACHEVERELL SITWELL | [*swelled rule*] | DOCTOR DONNE & GARGANTUA | *THE FIRST SIX CANTOS* | LONDON | DUCKWORTH | 3 HENRIETTA STREET | 1930

252 × 159 mm.

80 pp.: [1] half-title; [2] blank; [3] title; [4] "Printed in Great Britain"; [5] dedication; [6] blank; [7] preface; [8] blank; 9–79, [80] text and notes; printer's imprint: "Cambridge: Printed by W. Lewis, M.A., at the University Press."

Blue-green cloth boards. Untrimmed edges. Gilt lettered on spine.

1000 copies printed. Published 26 June 1930 at 7s. 6d.

CONTENTS

"Doctor Donne & Gargantua, Cantos 1–6" [the first three as previously published separately, the last three hitherto unpublished]

b. *First edition, special copies*

SACHEVERELL SITWELL | [*swelled rule*] | DOCTOR DONNE & GARGANTUA | *THE FIRST SIX CANTOS* | LONDON | GERALD DUCKWORTH & COMPANY, LTD. | HOUGHTON MIFFLIN COMPANY | NEW YORK | 1930

252 × 159 mm.

80 pp.: [1] half-title; [2] blank; [3] title; [4] "Of this edition of *Doctor Donne and Gargantua* 215 numbered copies (of which 100 only are for sale in Great Britain and 100 in the U.S.A.) have been embellished with a frontispiece by Rex Whistler and signed by the author. No." [in ink, with author's autograph signature]. "Printed in Great Britain at the University Press, Cambridge, for Gerald Duckworth & Co., Ltd. London, and Houghton Mifflin Company, Boston, U.S.A., 1930." [Thence as in ordinary copies, above.]

Frontispiece by Rex Whistler tipped in, with tissue guard.

Blue cloth spine, decorated blue and white paper boards. Untrimmed edges. Gilt lettered up the spine.

215 copies printed (see Certificate, above). Published in London 26 June 1930 at 42s., and in New York 10 September 1930 at $10.00.

CONTENTS

As in ordinary copies, with frontispiece

sA20 BECKFORD AND BECKFORDISM 1930

First edition

BECKFORD AND | BECKFORDISM | *AN ESSAY* | BY | SACHEVERELL SITWELL | DUCKWORTH | 3 HENRIETTA STREET | LONDON, W.C. | 1930

222 × 142 mm.

40 pp.: [1] half-title; [2] "Of *Beckford and Beckfordism* 265 copies only have been printed by the Cambridge University Press, numbered, and signed by the Author. No." [in ink, with author's autograph signature]; [3] title; [4] "Printed in Great Britain"; [5] Note; [6] blank; 7–39 text; [40] "Printed by Walter [*device*] Lewis, M.A. at the University Press, Cambridge."

Brown linen boards. Untrimmed edges. Gilt lettered on spine.

265 copies printed. Published 5 December 1930 at 12s. 6d.

CONTENTS

"The following Essay was written in 1924 as preface to a proposed edition of William Beckford's Works." (Note on p. [5].)

a. *First edition, ordinary copies*

FAR FROM MY HOME | Stories : Long & Short | by | SACHEVERELL SITWELL | DUCKWORTH | 3 Henrietta Street, W.C.2 | 1931

188 × 129 mm.

320 pp.: [1] half-title; [2] "By Sacheverell Sitwell . . ."; [3] title; [4] "All rights reserved. Copyright in the U.S.A."; [5] dedication; [6] blank; [7] Contents; [8] blank; [9], 10–310 text; [311–317] advertisements; [318] "Made and printed in Great Britain By The Camelot Press Ltd, London and Southampton"; [319–320] blank.

Orange cloth boards. Top edge orange, others untrimmed. Gilt lettered on spine.

3000 copies printed. Published 14 May 1931 at 7s. 6d.

CONTENTS

A Change of Owners—The End of the Holidays—The Question at Bolingbroke Mansions—Annual Visit—Birds of a Feather—Innocent Enough—A Game of Red Indians—Hark! The Trumpet and the Drum!

b. *First edition, special copies*
[*Title as in ordinary copies, above*]

187 × 128 mm.

320 pp.: [1] half-title; [2] "By Sacheverell Sitwell . . ."; [3] title; [4] "Of this edition of *Far From My Home* 110 copies only have been printed by the Camelot Press on Abbey Mills paper, numbered, and signed by the Author. No." [in ink, with author's autograph signature]. "All rights reserved. Copyright in the U.S.A." [Thence as in ordinary copies, above.]

Frontispiece drawing by Pavel Tchelitchew tipped in with tissue guard.

Dark brick-red buckram boards. Top edge gilt, others untrimmed. Gilt lettered on spine.

110 copies printed. Published 14 May 1931 at 42s.

CONTENTS

As in ordinary copies, with frontispiece

First edition

SPANISH BAROQUE ART | *with buildings in Portugal,* *Mexico, and* | *other Colonies* | by | SACHEVERELL SITWELL | Author of | "Southern Baroque Art," "German Baroque Art," | etc. | DUCKWORTH | 3 Henrietta Street, W.C. 2 | 1931

222 × 139 mm.

112 pp.: [1] half-title; [2] "By Sacheverell Sitwell . . ."; [3] title; [4] "All rights reserved. Made and printed in Great Britain by The Camelot Press Ltd, London and Southampton"; [5] Contents; [6] Illustrations; [7] dedication; [8] acknowledgements; 9–11 Preface; [12] blank; 13–112 text and bibliography.

24 plates tipped in.

Smooth magenta cloth boards. Top and fore edges trimmed, tail edge untrimmed. Gilt stamped on spine and upper cover.

1500 copies printed. Published 18 June 1931 at 12s. 6d.

CONTENTS

Chapter III, "Mexico," replaces the fourth part of *Southern Baroque Art*, but is quite different (see sA6d)

sA23   MOZART   1932

a. *First edition*

MOZART | BY | SACHEVERELL SITWELL | WITH A FRONTISPIECE | PETER DAVIES LIMITED | 1932

181 × 129 mm.

192 pp.: [1] half-title; [2] blank; [3] title; [4] "First published in April 1932. Printed in Great Britain . . . by T. and A. Constable at the University Press, Edinburgh"; 5 Contents; [6] dedication; 7–191 text, bibliographical note and index; [192] blank.

Frontispiece tipped in.

Smooth black cloth boards. Top edge mauve, others trimmed. Gilt lettered on spine, with mauve panels.

2500 copies printed. Published 28 April 1932 at 5s.

b. *First edition, American issue*

MOZART | By | SACHEVERELL SITWELL | [*device*] | NEW
YORK | D. APPLETON AND COMPANY | 1932

191 × 132 mm.

196 pp.: [i] half-title; [ii] "Appleton Biographies . . ."; [iii] title; [iv]
"Copyright, 1932, by D. Appleton and Company . . . Printed in the
United States of America"; [v] dedication; [vi] blank; [vii] Contents;
[viii] blank; 1–184, [185] text, bibliographical note and index; [186–
188] blank.

Frontispiece tipped in.

Smooth black cloth boards. Top edge red, others trimmed. Gilt
lettered on spine, with red panels.

2500 copies printed. Published 19 August 1932 at $1.50 in the series
"Appleton Biographies."

CONTENTS

As in sA23a

sA24   CANONS OF GIANT ART   1933

First edition

CANONS OF GIANT ART | TWENTY TORSOS | IN HEROIC
LANDSCAPES | BY | SACHEVERELL | SITWELL | [*en-
graving*] | LONDON | FABER AND FABER | 24 RUSSELL
SQUARE

218 × 141 mm.

228 pp.: [1] half-title; [2] "Forthcoming books by Sacheverell Sitwell . . ."; [3] title; [4] "First published in May MCMXXXIII by
Faber and Faber Limited, 24 Russell Square, London W.C.1. Printed
in Great Britain at The Alcuin Press, Campden, Gloucestershire. All
Rights Reserved . . ."; [5] dedication; [6] blank; 7 Preface; [8] blank;
9 Contents; [10] blank; 11–225 text and notes; [226] printer's device;
[227–228] blank.

Wood-engraving by Enid Lacey on title.

Red cloth boards. Top edge silver, others untrimmed. Lettered in
silver on spine.

2000 copies printed. Published 25 May 1933 at 7s. 6d.

1. The Farnese Hercules [from *The Cyder Feast*]—2. (i) Landscape with the Giant Orion—3. (ii) Landscape with the Giant Orion—4. The Hermes of Praxiteles [as "The Hermes" in *The Cyder Feast*]—5. Fugal Siege—6. The Laocoon of El Greco [as "The Laocoon" in *The Cyder Feast*]—7. St. Maurice and the Theban Legion—8. Pastoral —9. Aeneas Hunting Stags upon the Coast of Libya—10. The Royal Hunt and Storm in the Forest—11. Agamemnon's Tomb—12. Bacchus in India—13. Krishna with the Milkmaids—14. The Bayadères—15. Battles of the Centaurs, i. Centaurs and Lapithae—16. ii. Fight in the House of Pholus—17. Cephalus and Procris—18. Upon an Image of Dante—19. Bohemond, Prince of Antioch—20. Grande Adagio: The Enchanted Palace

SA25   LISZT   1934

a. *First edition*

SACHEVERELL | SITWELL | [*within a calligraphic border*] LISZT | [*below border, a drawing of Liszt*] | LONDON | FABER & FABER

221 × 145 mm.

440 pp.: [i] half-title; [ii] blank; [iii] title; [iv] "First published in April MCMXXXIV by Faber and Faber Limited, 24 Russell Square, London W.C.I. Printed in Great Britain by R. MacLehose and Company Limited, The University Press, Glasgow. All rights reserved"; [v] dedication; [vi] blank; [vii] quotation; [viii] blank; ix Acknowledgement; [x] blank; xi–xviii Contents; xix–xx Illustrations; [1–2], 3–417, [418] text, appendices and index; [419–420] blank.

Sixteen plates tipped in, and drawings and cartoons in the text.

Smooth lilac cloth boards. Top edge silver, others untrimmed. Lettered in silver on spine.

Published 26 April 1934 at 15s. (The publishers say "printing numbers not known"; the printers say 1000 copies were printed.)

b. *First edition, American copies*

SACHEVERELL | SITWELL | [*within a border*] LISZT | [*below border, a decoration*] | Boston and New York | HOUGHTON MIFFLIN COMPANY | 1934

Note: 775 copies imported (according to Houghton Mifflin; the printers say "500 cancel titles were printed for Houghton Mifflin"). Bound in black cloth boards, lettered in silver on spine and upper cover. Published 4 September 1934 at $4.00. The contents are as in sA25a.

c. Second edition

SACHEVERELL SITWELL | [*swelled rule*] | LISZT | [*device*] | CASSELL & COMPANY LTD | LONDON

216 × 138 mm.

432 pp.: [i] half-title; [ii] "List of chief works by Sacheverell Sitwell"; [iii] title; [iv] "Cassell & Co. . . . Copyright, 1955, by Sacheverell Sitwell. First published . . . This revised edition 1955. Set in Bembo type and made and printed in Great Britain by William Clowes and Sons, Limited, London and Beccles. F.455"; [v] dedication; [vi] blank; [vii] quotation; [viii] blank; ix Contents; [x] blank; xi List of illustrations; [xii] blank; xiii–xxx New introduction to the revised edition; [1–2], 3–400 text, appendices, postscript and index; [401–402] blank. Seven plates tipped in.

Black cloth boards. Trimmed edges. Gilt lettered on spine.

1509 copies printed. Published 21 July 1955 at 30*s.*

CONTENTS

Text revised throughout. New illustrations.

d. Second edition, *American copies*

Note: 505 copies of the second edition, above, were imported and published in New York by the Philosophical Library.

sA26   TOUCHING THE ORIENT   1934

First edition

Touching the Orient | Six Sketches by | Sacheverell Sitwell | Duckworth | 3 Henrietta Street, London

216 × 137 mm.

96 pp.: [i–iv] front end-papers; [1] half-title; [2] "Books by Sacheverell Sitwell . . ."; [3] title; [4] "First published November 1934. All Rights Reserved. Made and Printed in Great Britain By The Camelot

Press Ltd, London and Southampton"; [5] dedication; [6] blank;
7 Contents; [8] blank; [9–10], 11–88 text; [v–viii] back end-papers.
Maroon cloth boards. Trimmed edges. Gilt lettered up spine.
1250 copies printed. Published 15 November 1934 at 5s.

CONTENTS

The Dinka ["preface to a poem not published yet"]—The Mosques of
Cairo—Relizane ["the first pages of a book on Morocco"]—Oran—
The Abbey of Nālāndā—The Kailasa of Ellora

sA27   A BACKGROUND FOR   1935
                 DOMENICO SCARLATTI

First edition

A Background | for | Domenico Scarlatti | 1685–1757 |
written for his | two hundred and fiftieth | anniversary | by |
Sacheverell | Sitwell | *London* | Faber and Faber Limited |
24 *Russell Square*

190 × 127 mm.
168 pp.: [1–2] blank; [3] half-title; [4] "By the same author . . ."; [5]
title; [6] "First published in May Mcmxxxv by Faber and Faber
Limited, 24 Russell Square London W.C.1. Printed in Great Britain
by R. MacLehose and Company Limited, The University Press,
Glasgow. All rights reserved"; [7] dedication; [8] blank; 9 Contents;
[10] blank; 11–168 text.
Frontispiece tipped in.
Blue cloth boards. Untrimmed edges. Gilt lettered on spine.
2000 copies printed. Published 9 May 1935 at 5s.

sA28   DANCE OF THE   1936
                 QUICK AND THE DEAD

a. *First edition*

DANCE OF THE QUICK | AND THE DEAD | An Entertain-
ment of the | Imagination | by | SACHEVERELL | SITWELL |
[*decoration*] | FABER AND FABER LIMITED | 24 Russell
Square | London

218 × 137 mm.

432 pp.: [i–ii] blank; [iii] half-title; [iv] blank; [v] title; [vi] "First published in October Mcmxxxvi by Faber and Faber . . . Printed in Great Britain by R. MacLehose and Company Limited, The University Press, Glasgow . . ."; [vii] dedication; [viii] blank; ix–xii Contents; xiii–xv Illustrations; [xvi] blank; [1–2], 3–413 text and index; [414–416] blank.

Fifteen plates tipped in.

Green cloth boards. Top edge gilt, others untrimmed. Gilt lettered on spine with black panel.

2575 copies printed. Published 1 October 1936 at 15s.

b. *First edition, American copies*

DANCE OF THE QUICK | AND THE DEAD | An Entertainment of the | Imagination | by | SACHEVERELL | SITWELL | [*decoration*] | HOUGHTON MIFFLIN COMPANY | Boston and New York | 1937

Note: 750/780 copies imported, with a cancel title. Bound in smooth red cloth boards, lettered in silver on black panel, with black decoration, on spine. Published 13 April 1937 at $4.25. Contents as in sA28a.

sA29   COLLECTED POEMS   1936

First edition

COLLECTED POEMS | SACHEVERELL SITWELL | With a long Introductory Essay | *by* | EDITH SITWELL | DUCKWORTH | 3 Henrietta Street, W.C.2 | 1936

195 × 129 mm.

596 pp.: [1] half-title; [2] "By Sacheverell Sitwell . . ."; [3] title; [4] "All Rights Reserved. Made and Printed in Great Britain by the Kemp Hall Press, Ltd. in the City of Oxford"; [5] dedication; [6] blank; 7 Preface; [8] blank; 9–14 Contents; 15–50 introduction; 51–593 text and indexes; [594–596] blank.

Black cloth boards. Trimmed edges. Gilt lettered on spine.

1500 copies printed. Published in November 1936 at 15s.

The Poems of Sacheverell Sitwell, by Edith Sitwell

Outskirts—"Psittachus eois Imitatrix Ales ab Indis"—Whitsun—
Pindar—Brighton Pier—Trapeze Song from "Perspectives"—
Trumpets—Fragment from "Sirens"—Li-Tai-Pé—The Moon—
Fountains—Tahiti—Barrel Organs, i. Prelude, ii. The Feathered
Hat [all from *The People's Palace*]

Mrs. H . . . or a Lady from Babel—Week-Ends—Church and Stage—
Fables—Valse Estudiantina—The Hochzeit of Hercules—Serenades [as "Ten Serenades"]—The Italian Air [all from *The Hundred
and One Harlequins*]

New Water Music—The Paradise of Alexander—Two Water Songs,
i. Sea God, ii. River God—Fisherman [as "The Fisherman"]—
Wind as Husbandman—Gardener Trimming Hedges [all from *The
Thirteenth Cæsar*]

Extract from "The Bird-Actors"—Et in Arcadia, Omnes—Two
Extracts from "The Hundred and One Harlequins," i. At Break-
fast, ii. In the Train—A March Past at the Pyramids—Two Varia-
tions on Themes out of Zarathustra, i. "Laughing Lions will
Come," ii. Parade Virtues for a Dying Gladiator [all from *The
Hundred and One Harlequins*]

At the Theatre, Once [as part of no. II of "Two Odes in Praise of
Popular Music" in *The Chapbook*, 1924]

Two Clowns' Psychology [from *The Hundred and One Harlequins*]

Actor Rehearsing—The Thirteenth Cæsar [both from *The Thirteenth
Cæsar*]

Grande Sicilienne

The Rio Grande—The Santander Quartet in a Programme of Spanish
Music [both from *The Thirteenth Cæsar*]

Convent Thoughts in Cadiz [from *The Cyder Feast*]

Dr. Donne and Gargantua, Cantos the First—the Sixth [from *Dr.
Donne & Gargantua, the First Six Cantos*]

Hortus Conclusus. 1. The Cherry Tree—2. The Gardener—3.
Gardener's Song—4. The Fruit Gatherers—5. The Red-Gold
Rain: orange tree by day—6. Orange Tree by Night [all from *The
Thirteenth Cæsar*]—7. The Two Almond Trees [from *The Cyder*

Feast]—8. Magnolia Tree—9. Apple Tree [both from *The Thirteenth Cæsar*]—10. Tuscan [from *The Fortnightly*, October 1936]—11. Damson and Medlar—12. Hawthorn—13. Paulownia—14. Snowflowers—15. White Hyacinths—16. Kingcups—17. Dandelion—18. Cowslips [all from *The Cyder Feast*]—19. Snow and Wind—20. Eurydice—21. Variation on a Theme by Marlowe—22. Variation on a Theme by Alexander Pope—23. Daphne–an adaptation from John Milton—24. Variation on a Theme by John Lely [all from *The Thirteenth Cæsar*]—25. Variation on a Theme by Robert Herrick [from *The Cyder Feast*]—26. First Variation on a Theme by George Peele—27. Second Variation—28. Third Variation [all from *The Hundred and One Harlequins*]—29–32. Four Variations upon William Browne of Tavistock [all from *The Cyder Feast*]—33. The Golden Bell—34. The Fiery Torch—35. Complaint—36. Warning—37. The Island—38. Memory—39. Fortune—40. Shadow—41. The Dancer—42. The Venus of Bolsover Castle [all from *The Thirteenth Cæsar*]—43. Derbyshire Bluebells [from *The Cyder Feast*]—44. Finale [from *The Thirteenth Cæsar*]

The Eckington Woods [as "The Renishaw Woods" in *The Cyder Feast*]—Bolsover Castle [from *The Thirteenth Cæsar*]—Exalt the Eglantine, 1–6 [from *Exalt the Eglantine*]—The Winter Walk [from *The Thirteenth Cæsar*]—Prisoner [from *Two Poems, Ten Songs*]—Song: My balm giver, my golden tree [from *Augustan Books of English Poetry*]—Thoughts in a High Wind, Sailing a Boat [from *Two Poems, Ten Songs*]

Two Mirror Poems. 1. On a Name Scratched upon a Window—2. The Poet and the Mirror [both from *The Thirteenth Cæsar*]

Change in the Mirror—The Maze—The Great Harlequin—Studies on the Black Keys (The Sleepy Hills of Tennessee), 1–5 [all from *Exalt the Eglantine*]

Three Nights in Fez [from *The London Aphrodite*, October 1928]—The Lady and the Rooks [from *Two Poems, Ten Songs*]—Two Pastoral Poems, 1. The Cyder Feast—2. The Chamber Idyll [both from *The Cyder Feast*]

Canons of Giant Art, Twenty Torsos in Heroic Landscapes. 1. Fugal Siege—2. Pastoral—3. Aeneas Hunting Stags upon the Coast of Libya—4. The Royal Hunt, and Storm in the Forest—5. Agamemnon's Tomb—6. Bacchus in India—7. Krishna with the Milkmaids—8. The Bayadères—9. Battles of the Centaurs, i. Centaurs and Lapithae—10. ii. Fight in the House of Pholus—11. Landscape with the Giant Orion—12. Landscape with the Giant Orion (second version)—13. The Hermes of Praxiteles—14. The Farnese Hercules—15. The Laocoon of El Greco—16. St. Maurice and the Theban Legion—17. Upon an Image of Dante—18. Bohemund, Prince of Antioch—19. Cephalus and Procris—20. Grande Adagio, the Enchanted Palace [all from *Canons of Giant Art*]

sA30 CONVERSATION PIECES 1936

a. *First edition*

[*Within a decorated border*]

CONVERSATION | PIECES | *A Survey of English Domestic Portraits* | *and their Painters* | By | SACHEVERELL SITWELL | With Notes on the Illustrations by | MICHAEL SEVIER | LONDON | B. T. BATSFORD LTD. | 15 NORTH AUDLEY STREET | MAYFAIR, W.1

245 × 186 mm.

160 pp.: [i] half-title; [ii] blank; [iii] title; [iv] "First Published November 1936. Made and Printed in Great Britain. Text by T. & A. Constable Ltd., Edinburgh, plates by Jarrold & Sons Ltd., Norwich"; [v] dedication; [vi] blank; vii Preface [dated November 1936—*see also second issue, below*]; viii Contents; 1–88 text; 89–114 Notes on the Illustrations, by Michael Sevier; 115–119 Index; [120] blank; [1–2], 3–31, [32] "A selected list of Batsford books" [list F. 3/34, printed by The Stanhope Press Ltd. Rochester].

54 leaves of plates.

Rough maroon cloth boards. Top edge maroon, others trimmed. Gilt stamped on spine and upper cover. (The first binding order was for 1500 copies; copies in later bindings have advertisement list G. 5/36.)

3000 copies printed. Published in November 1936 at 21*s*.

b. *First edition, second issue*

Note: In December 1936 an unknown number of copies of the original printing was bound and issued. These are identical with those described above, except that pp. vii–viii are a cancel with an additional note printed under the preface.

c. *First edition, American copies*

[*Within a decorated border*]

CONVERSATION | PIECES | *A Survey of English Domestic Portraits* | *and their Painters* | By | SACHEVERELL SIT-WELL | With Notes on the Illustrations by | MICHAEL SEVIER | NEW YORK | CHARLES SCRIBNER'S SONS | LONDON: B. T. BATSFORD LTD | 1937

Note: 350/375 copies imported. Bound as the first issue. Published 29 January 1937 at $8.50. Contents as in the first issue.

SA31   NARRATIVE PICTURES   1937

a. *First edition*

[*Within a decorated border*]

NARRATIVE | PICTURES | *A Survey of English Genre* | *and its Painters* | By | SACHEVERELL SITWELL | With Notes on the Illustrations by | MICHAEL SEVIER | LONDON | B. T. BATSFORD LTD. | 15 NORTH AUDLEY STREET | MAY-FAIR, W.1

245 × 184 mm.

160 pp.: [i] half-title; [ii] "Uniform with this Volume . . ."; [iii] title; [iv] "First Published November 1937. Made and Printed in Great Britain for the publishers . . . Text by T. & A. Constable Ltd., Edinburgh, plates by Jarrold & Sons Ltd., Norwich"; v Preface; vi Contents; 1–94 text; 95–118 Notes on the Illustrations, by Michael Sevier; 119–122 Index; [1–2], 3–30, [31–32] "A selected list of Batsford books" [list G. 3/37, printed by The Stanhope Press, Ltd., Rochester].

54 leaves of plates.

Rough brown cloth boards. Top edge brown, others trimmed. Gilt lettered on spine.

3000 copies printed. Published in November 1937 at 21*s*.

b. *First edition, American copies*

[*Within a decorated border*]

NARRATIVE | PICTURES | *A Survey of English Genre* | *and its Painters* | By | SACHEVERELL SITWELL | With Notes on the Illustrations by | MICHAEL SEVIER | NEW YORK | CHARLES SCRIBNER'S SONS | LONDON: B. T. BATSFORD LTD. | 1938

Note: 250/268 copies imported, with a cancel title and without the 32 pp. of advertisements. Binding similar to sA31a. Published 18 February 1938 at $8.50. The contents otherwise as in sA31a.

SA32   LA VIE PARISIENNE   1937

a. *First edition*

[*Within a calligraphic border*]

LA VIE | PARISIENNE | *A Tribute to Offenbach* | *by* | Sacheverell | Sitwell | FABER AND FABER | 24 Russell Square | London

188 × 122 mm.

112 pp.: [1–2] blank; [3] half-title; [4] blank; [5] title; [6] "First published in November Mcmxxxvii by Faber and Faber . . . Printed in Great Britain by R. MacLehose and Company Limited, The University Press, Glasgow. All rights reserved"; [7] dedication; [8] blank; 9–108 text; [109–112] blank.

Frontispiece tipped in.

Pink cloth boards. Trimmed edges. Lettered on spine in pink on a gilt-framed blue panel.

3000 copies printed. Published 4 November 1937 at 3s. 6d.

b. *First edition, American copies*

Note: 500/520 copies imported by Houghton Mifflin Company, with a cancel title. Bound in yellow cloth spine, grey cloth boards. Lettered in black on the spine. Published 1 March 1938 at $1.65. The contents as in sA32a

a. *First edition*

ROUMANIAN | JOURNEY | *By* | SACHEVERELL SITWELL |
Illustrated from Photographs | *by* | A. COSTA, | RICHARD
WYNDHAM, | AND OTHERS | LONDON | B. T. BATSFORD
LTD. | 15 NORTH AUDLEY STREET, W.1

209 × 136 mm.

128 pp.: [i] half-title; [ii] "Just Published . . ."; [iii] title; [iv] "First
Published, April 1938. Made and printed in Great Britain for the
publishers . . . by Morrison and Gibb Ltd., Tanfield, Edinburgh";
[v] dedication; [vi] "By the Same Author . . ."; vii Preface; viii Publisher's note; 1–120 text and index.

96 pages of plates sewn in, and two plates tipped in.

Blue cloth boards. Top edge blue, others trimmed. Map on end-
papers. Gilt lettered on spine.

4200 copies printed. Published in April 1938 at 8s. 6d.

b. *First edition, American copies*

Note: 770 copies were imported by Messrs. Scribner's of New York.
Published in 1938 at $3.50. I have not been able to find a copy, and
the publishers themselves do not have one or any information of this
issue. Presumably—like sA30 and sA31 above—there was a cancel
title to an otherwise identical book.

a. *First edition*

[*Within a red ornamental border*]

EDINBURGH | *by* | Sacheverell Sitwell | *and* | Francis Bam-
ford | [*short red swelled rule*] | Faber and Faber Limited | *24
Russell Square* | *London*

221 × 140 mm.

320 pp.: [1–2] blank; [3] half-title; [4] "Other books by Sacheverell
Sitwell . . ."; [5] title; [6] "First published in May Mcmxxxviii by

Faber and Faber Limited . . . Printed in Great Britain by R. MacLehose and Company Limited, The University Press, Glasgow. All rights reserved"; [7] dedication; [8] blank; 9 Preface; [10] blank; 11–14 Contents; 15–16 Illustrations; 17–319, [320] text, appendices and index.

Twelve plates tipped in.

Lilac cloth boards. Top edge pale blue, others trimmed. Gilt lettered, with a blue panel, on the spine. (See below.)

3500 copies printed. Published 19 May 1938 at 12s. 6d. (A later binding is of blue cloth, with no blue panel on the spine.)

b. *First edition, American copies*

[*Within a red ornamental border*]

EDINBURGH | *by* | Sacheverell Sitwell | *and* | Francis Bamford | [*short red swelled rule*] | Boston | Houghton Mifflin Company | 1938

Note : 750/780 copies imported, with a cancel title. Bound in red cloth spine, blue cloth boards. Lettered in blue on spine and upper cover. Published 31 January 1939 at $4.00. The contents as in sA34a.

sA35 GERMAN BAROQUE SCULPTURE 1938

First edition

German Baroque Sculpture | *by* | SACHEVERELL SITWELL | *With* 48 *Photographs by* | ANTHONY AYSCOUGH | *and* | Descriptive Notes by NIKOLAUS PEVSNER | DUCKWORTH | 3 Henrietta Street, London, W.C.2

248 × 183 mm.

96 pp. (excluding plates): [1] half-title; [2] blank; [3] title; [4] "First published in 1938. All rights reserved. Made and Printed in Great Britain by the Kemp Hall Press Ltd. in the City of Oxford"; 5 Contents; [6] blank; 7–8 List of illustrations; 9–28 Introduction; 29–47 The Brothers Asam; 49–84 Descriptive notes; 85–90 Bibliography; [91] blank; 92–95 Table of names and dates; [96] Note on plate 1.

48 plates bound in after text, with errata slip pasted to verso of plate 25.

Red cloth boards. Trimmed edges. Gilt lettered on spine.

1500 copies printed. Published in June 1938 at 21s.

Introduction by Sacheverell Sitwell—The Brothers Asam by Sacheverell Sitwell—Descriptive Notes by Nikolaus Pevsner

SA36   TRIO   1938

First edition

[*For description, see* EA31]

CONTENTS

Pp. 191–217, "Palladian England" by Sacheverell Sitwell—pp. 221–248, "George Cruikshank" by Sacheverell Sitwell

(These lectures were delivered by the author on 1 and 4 November 1937, under the general title of "Cruikshank and Palladian England"; the titles of the individual lectures were as above. See EA31 for details.)

SA37   THE ROMANTIC BALLET IN   1938
LITHOGRAPHS OF THE TIME

First edition

THE | ROMANTIC BALLET | *in* | *Lithographs of the Time* | *by* | CYRIL W. BEAUMONT | *and* SACHEVERELL SITWELL | [*red decoration*] | FABER AND FABER LIMITED | *24 Russell Square* | *London*

278 × 191 mm. (see below).

320 pp.: [1] half-title; [2] blank; [3] title; [4] "First published in November Mcmxxxviii by Faber and Faber Limited, 24 Russell Square, London W.C.1. Printed in Great Britain by R. MacLehose and Company Limited, The University Press, Glasgow. All Rights Reserved"; [5] dedication; [6] blank; 7–8 Preface; 9 Contents; 10 decoration; 11–17 Illustrations; [18] decoration; 19–141 text; [142] blank; [143], 144–306, [307] illustrations; [308] decoration; 309–316 indexes; [317–320] blank.

Reproductions of lithographs mounted on 81 leaves from p. 145 to p. 307, and decorations throughout.

Rose pink silk cloth boards, with fleur-de-lys pattern. Gilt lettered on spine, with lilac and blue panels. Blue end-papers. Black headband. (See below.)

1250 copies printed. Published 1 December 1938 at 50s. (A later binding has plain silver silk boards, pink headband and is slightly shorter.)

CONTENTS

Pp. 19–31, "Introduction" by Sacheverell Sitwell—pp. 33–55, "The Dancers of the Romantic Ballet" by Cyril W. Beaumont—pp. 57–101, "The Romantic Ballet" by Sacheverell Sitwell—pp. 103–141, "Lithographs of the Romantic Ballet: an annotated catalogue" by Cyril W. Beaumont

sA38   OLD FASHIONED FLOWERS   1939

First edition

[Engraved title in colour, tipped in]

OLD FASHIONED | FLOWERS | *by* | *Sacheverell* | *Sitwell* | *Illustrated by* | *John Farleigh* | *[printed]* LONDON | COUNTRY LIFE LIMITED

246 × 182 mm.

206 pp. (including title-leaf): [i] half-title; [ii] "First published 1939. Printed in Great Britain at The Curwen Press, Plaistow, E.13"; [iii] title; [iv] blank; [v] Contents; [vi] blank; [vii] List of plates; [viii] dedication; [ix–x], 1–193 text and index; [194–196] blank.

Twelve plates by John Farleigh (including the title) tipped in.

Brick-red cloth boards. Trimmed edges. Lettered in white on upper cover and gilt lettered on spine.

2500 copies printed. Published 4 October 1939 at 15s.

sA39   MAURETANIA   1940

First edition

MAURETANIA | WARRIOR, MAN, AND WOMAN | by | SACHEVERELL SITWELL | DUCKWORTH | 3 Henrietta Street, London, W.C.

216 × 137 mm.

328 pp.: [i] half-title; [ii] "By the same author ..."; [iii] title; [iv] "First published 1940. All rights reserved. Printed in Great

Britain by Billing and Sons Ltd., Guildford and Esher"; [v] quotations; [vi] dedication; vii–viii Contents; ix List of illustrations; x blank; 11–328 text and index.

Sixteen plates tipped in.

Smooth yellow cloth boards. Top edge dark blue, others trimmed. Map on front end-papers. Lettered in yellow on a dark-blue panel on the spine.

1500 copies printed. Published in April 1940 at 15s.

sA40   POLTERGEISTS   1940

a. *First edition*

POLTERGEISTS | *An Introduction and Examination* | *followed by* | *Chosen Instances* | [star] | SACHEVERELL | SITWELL | *with decorations by* | *Irene Hawkins* | *and silhouettes by* | *Cruikshank* | [decoration] | FABER AND FABER LIMITED | *24 Russell Square* | *London*

217 × 138 mm.

420 pp.: [1–2] blank; [3] half-title; [4] "Also by Sacheverell Sitwell . . ."; [5] title; [6] "First published in June Mcmxl by Faber and Faber Limited, 24 Russell Square London W.C.I. Printed in Great Britain by R. MacLehose and Company Limited, The University Press, Glasgow. All rights reserved"; [7] dedication; [8] blank; 9–10 "The Drum" by Edith Sitwell; 11 "The Cauld Lad o' Hilton"; [12] blank; 13 note; [14] blank; 15–16 Contents; 17–24 Foreword; 25–419 text and index; [420] blank.

Decorations throughout by Irene Hawkins and Cruikshank.

Black cloth boards. Top edge green, others trimmed. Gilt lettered on spine.

2130 copies printed. Published 11 July 1940 at 15s.

b. *First American edition*

[University Books, Inc., published an edition of "about 4000 copies" in September 1959 at $5.75. Contents as in sA40a].

First edition

Sacred & Profane | [*in decorated initials*] LOVE | *by* | *Sacheverell Sitwell* | *Faber and Faber Limited* | *24 Russell Square* | *London*

217 × 141 mm.

336 pp.: [i] half-title; [ii] "By the same author . . ."; [iii] title; [iv] "First published in November Mcmxl by Faber and Faber Limited, 24 Russell Square, London W.C.I. Printed in Great Britain by the Chiswick Press Ltd. London. All rights reserved"; [v] dedication; [vi] blank; vii Preface; [viii] blank; ix–xiv Contents; xv Illustrations; [xvi] blank; [1–2], 3–317 text and index; [318–320] blank.

Eight plates tipped in, and engravings on several pages.

Pink cloth boards. Top edge silver, others trimmed. Lettered in silver on spine, with a red panel.

2850 copies printed. Published 7 November 1940 at 15*s*.

First edition

VALSE DES FLEURS | *A Day in St. Petersburg* | *and a Ball at the Winter Palace* | *in 1868* | *by* | SACHEVERELL | SITWELL | FABER AND FABER LIMITED | 24 Russell Square | London

188 × 120 mm.

152 pp.: [1–2] blank; [3] half-title; [4] "By the same author . . ."; [5] title; [6] "First published in July Mcmxli by Faber and Faber Limited, 24 Russell Square, London W.C.I. Printed in Great Britain by R. MacLehose and Company Limited, The University Press, Glasgow. All rights reserved"; [7] dedication; [8] blank; 9–151 text; [152] blank.

Frontispiece tipped in.

Lilac cloth boards. Trimmed edges. Lettered in silver down the spine, on a silver-framed maroon panel.

2000 copies printed. Published 24 July 1941 at 5*s*.

First edition

[*Wavy rule*] | *Sacheverell Sitwell* | [*wavy rule*] | PRIMITIVE
SCENES | AND | FESTIVALS | [*drawing by Irene Hawkins*]
| [*wavy rule*] | Faber and Faber | [*wavy rule*]

215 × 140 mm.

296 pp.: [i] half-title; [ii] "By the same author ..."; [iii] title; [iv]
"First published in Mcmxlii by Faber and Faber Limited ... Printed
in Great Britain by R. MacLehose and Company Limited, The
University Press, Glasgow ..."; [v] dedication; [vi] blank; vii–x
Contents; xi–xii Illustrations; [1–2], 3–283 text and index; [284] blank.
Sixteen plates tipped in.

Green cloth boards. Top edge grey, others trimmed. Lettered in
silver on spine, with red panels.

3000 copies printed. Published 19 February 1942 at 21s.

sA44   THE HOMING OF THE WINDS   1942

First edition

THE HOMING OF THE WINDS | and other passages in
prose | by | SACHEVERELL SITWELL | FABER AND
FABER LIMITED | 24 Russell Square | London

188 × 121 mm.

160 pp.: [1] half-title; [2] "Some books by Sacheverell Sitwell"; [3]
title; [4] "First published in September Mcmxlii by Faber and Faber
Limited, 24 Russell Square, London W.C.I. Printed in Great Britain
by Western Printing Services Ltd. Bristol. All Rights Reserved ...";
5–8 Contents and Acknowledgements; 9–158 text; [159–160] blank.

Yellow cloth boards. Trimmed edges. Lettered in blue on spine.

4000 copies printed. Published 9 September 1942 at 3s. 6d., in
"Sesame Books" series.

CONTENTS

Pp. 11–13, "A Sketch of the Scarborough Sands," "from an unpublished study, *The Bond Street Beau*"—and extracts from previously
published books by Sacheverell Sitwell

First edition

Sacheverell Sitwell | [*swelled rule*] | SPLENDOURS | *and* |
MISERIES | [*decoration*] | *Faber and Faber Ltd* | *24 Russell*
Square | *London*

220 × 139 mm.

264 pp.: [1] half-title; [2] "By the same author . . ."; [3] title; [4]
"First published in Mcmxliii by Faber and Faber Limited, 24 Russell
Square, London W.C.1. Printed in Great Britain by R. MacLehose
and Company Limited, The University Press, Glasgow. All rights
reserved"; 5–6 Contents; 7–8 Illustrations; 9–263 text and index;
[264] blank.

Sixteen plates tipped in.

Yellow cloth boards. Top edge blue, others untrimmed. Lettered in
silver on spine and decorated in silver on upper cover.

3000 copies printed. Published 17 December 1943 at 18*s*.

sA46   BRITISH ARCHITECTS   1945
              AND CRAFTSMEN

a. *First edition*

BRITISH | ARCHITECTS AND | CRAFTSMEN | *A Survey of*
Taste, Design, and | *Style during Three Centuries* | 1600 to
1830 | *by* | SACHEVERELL SITWELL | *With* 200 *Illustra-*
tions | *from Photographs, Prints and Drawings* | [*decoration*] |
LONDON | B. T. BATSFORD LTD. | 15 North Audley Street,
W.I | and at Malvern Wells, Worcestershire

219 × 148 mm.

204 pp.: [i] half-title; [ii] "Books by Sacheverell Sitwell"; [iii] title;
[iv] dedication and: "First Published, Spring, 1945. Made and
Printed in Great Britain for the Publishers . . . at The Aberdeen
University Press Ltd."; v Contents; vi Preface; vii Acknowledgment;
[viii] Illustrations; 1–196 text, index and printer's imprint repeated.

96 pages of plates sewn in, four plates tipped in, and drawings on
pages throughout.

Red cloth boards. Top edge red, others trimmed. Gilt lettered on spine.

7200 copies printed. Published in June 1945 at 21*s*.

b. *Second edition*
[*Title as in first edition*]

221 × 150 mm.

204 pp.: [i] half-title; [ii] "Books by Sacheverell Sitwell"; [iii] title; [iv] dedication and: "First Published, Spring 1945. Second Edition, revised, Winter 1945–6. Made and Printed" [as first edition]; v Contents; vi Preface, Note to the Second Edition; vii Acknowledgment and Postscript. (Thence as in first edition.)

Illustrations as in first edition, with two plates differently sewn and alteration to fig. 100.

Binding as in first edition.

2100 copies printed. Published in February 1946 at 21*s*.

CONTENTS

Revisions on pp. v–vi and in the text

c. *Second edition, American copies*

BRITISH | ARCHITECTS AND | CRAFTSMEN | *A Survey of Taste, Design, and* | *Style during Three Centuries* | 1600 to 1830 | *by* | SACHEVERELL SITWELL | *With* 200 *Illustrations* | *from Photographs, Prints and Drawings* | [*decoration*] | NEW YORK | CHARLES SCRIBNER'S SONS | LONDON: B. T. BATSFORD LTD | 1946

Note: Imported and published 28 October 1946 at $6.00. Similar binding and identical contents to sA46b above. Messrs. Batsford say 1450 copies imported, Messrs. Scribner's say 1000/1050 copies. This is the first American issue of the book.

d. *Third edition*
[*Title and size as in* sA46b]

204 pp.: [i] half-title; [ii] "Books by Sacheverell Sitwell"; [iii] title; [iv] dedication and: "First Published, Spring 1945. Second Edition,

revised, Winter 1945–6. Third Edition, with further revisions, Winter 1946–7. Made and Printed in Great Britain for the publishers ... at The Aberdeen University Press Ltd."; v Contents; vi Preface, Note to the Second Edition and Note to the Third Edition; vii continuation of Note to the Third Edition, and Acknowledgment. [Thence as in earlier editions.]

Illustrations as in sA46b.

Binding as in sA46a–b.

6400 copies printed. Published January 1947 at 21s.

CONTENTS

Revisions on pp. vi–vii and in the text

e. *Fourth edition*

BRITISH | ARCHITECTS AND | CRAFTSMEN | *A Survey of Taste, Design and* | *Style during Three Centuries* | 1600 to 1830 | *by* | SACHEVERELL SITWELL | *With* 200 *Illustrations* | *from Photographs, Prints and Drawings* | [*decoration*] | B. T. BATSFORD Ltd. | LONDON - NEW YORK - TORONTO | SYDNEY

220 × 150 mm.

204 pp.: [i] half-title; [ii] blank; [iii] title; [iv] dedication and: "First Published, Spring 1945. Second Edition, revised, Winter 1945–6. Third Edition, with further revisions, Winter 1946–7. Fourth Edition, Spring 1948. Made and Printed in Great Britain at The University Press, Aberdeen, for the Publishers ..."; v Contents; vi–vii Preface, Note to the Fourth Edition, Acknowledgment. [Thence as in earlier editions.]

Illustrations as in sA46(b).

Binding similar to sA46(a–b).

8300 copies printed. Published in February 1949 at 21s.

CONTENTS

Revisions on pp. vi–vii and in the text

f. *Fifth edition*

BRITISH ARCHITECTS | AND CRAFTSMEN | *A Survey of Taste, Design and* | *Style during Three Centuries* | 1600 to

1830 | SACHEVERELL SITWELL | [*drawing; caption:*] | The Mausoleum of Nicholas Hawksmoor | in the grounds of Castle Howard, York | PAN BOOKS LTD : LONDON

177 × 110 mm.

320 pp.: [1] half-title; [2] note on cover photographs; [3] title; [4] "First published 1945 ... This revised edition published 1960 by Pan Books ...," dedication, and "Printed in Great Britain by Cox & Wyman Ltd., London, Fakenham and Reading"; [5] Contents; [6–8] lists of illustrations; [9] Preface to the First Edition; [10–11] Note to the Fourth Edition; [12] Acknowledgment; [13–14] Preface to the Pan Edition; 15–319, [320] text, appendix, and index.

Twelve plates inserted between sections and twelve drawings in the text.

Pictorial paper wrappers. Unsewn. Trimmed edges. Printed in black, white and colours on covers and yellow spine (see below).

25,000 copies printed. Published 13 May 1960 at 5s. (In November 1963 10,000 copies of the original printing were re-bound in a different cover and published at the same price.)

CONTENTS

New preface, revisions in the text. Fewer illustrations.

sA47   THE HUNTERS AND   1947
                 THE HUNTED

a. *First edition*

THE HUNTERS | AND THE HUNTED | BY | SACHEVERELL SITWELL | LONDON | MACMILLAN & CO. LTD | 1947

213 × 138 mm.

324 pp.: [i] half-title; [ii] blank; [iii] title; [iv] "Copyright. Printed in Great Britain"; v Foreword; [vi] dedication; vii Contents; [viii] blank; ix List of illustrations; [x] blank; 1–313, [314] text and printer's imprint: "Printed by R. & R. Clark, Limited, Edinburgh."

Sixteen plates tipped in.

Smooth blue cloth boards. Top edge blue, others trimmed. Gilt lettered on spine.

8500 copies printed. Published 14 March 1947 at 15s.

b. *First edition, American issue*

THE HUNTERS | AND THE HUNTED | BY | SACHEVERELL
SITWELL | NEW YORK | THE MACMILLAN COMPANY |
1948

Note: This issue, printed in America, was published 10 February 1948
at $4.00. Bound in blue cloth boards, lettered in white on the spine.
3752 copies printed. Contents as in sA47a.

sA48 THE NETHERLANDS [1948]

a. *First edition*

THE | NETHERLANDS | *A Study of some aspects of* | *Art,*
Costume and Social Life | By | SACHEVERELL SITWELL |
B. T. BATSFORD LTD. | LONDON NEW YORK | TORONTO
SYDNEY

213 × 139 mm.

176 pp.: [i] half-title; [ii] "Batsford Books on Foreign Countries . . .";
[iii] title; [iv] dedication and: "Made and printed in Great Britain by
The Darien Press Ltd., Edinburgh, for the publishers . . ."; v–v [i.e.,
v–vi] Author's acknowledgment; vii Publishers' acknowledgment;
viii Contents; 1–168 text, index and printer's imprint repeated.

Sixteen double leaves of plates sewn in, and nine single leaves and a
folding map tipped in.

Orange cloth boards. Top edge orange, others trimmed. Pictorial
end-papers. Gilt lettered on spine.

8900 copies printed. Published in London in April [1948] at 18s., and
1255 additional copies published later in New York.

b. *Second edition*
[*Within a border*]

THE | NETHERLANDS | *A Study of some aspects of* | *Art,*
Costume and Social Life | *By* | Sacheverell Sitwell | B. T.
BATSFORD LTD | LONDON NEW YORK | TORONTO
SYDNEY

213 × 139 mm.

176 pp.: [i] half-title; [ii] "Books on the Countries of Europe . . .";
[iii] title; [iv] dedication and: "First published . . . 1948. Second

315

Edition, revised . . . 1952. Made and printed in Great Britain by The Darien Press Ltd., Edinburgh. for the publishers . . ."; v–vi Author's acknowledgment, and Note to Second Edition. [Thence as in first edition.]

Illustrations as in first edition.

Binding as in first edition, but with plain end-papers.

6000 copies printed. Published in London 27 March 1952 at 18s.

CONTENTS

Revisions on p. vi and in the text

sA49   SELECTED POEMS   1948

First edition

SELECTED POEMS | *by* | SACHEVERELL SITWELL | *with a Preface by* OSBERT SITWELL | [*device*] | GERALD DUCK-WORTH & CO. LTD. | 3 HENRIETTA STREET, LONDON, W.C.2

184 × 122 mm.

192 pp.: [i] half-title; [ii] blank; [iii] title; [iv] "*Collected Poems* first published 1936. This Selection first published 1948. All rights reserved." [Dedication]. "Printed in Great Britain by Billing and Sons Ltd., Guildford and Esher. F8680"; v–x Preface; xi–xiii Contents; [xiv] Acknowledgement; 15–190 text; 191–192 index.

Smooth blue cloth boards. Trimmed edges. Gilt lettered on spine.

3000 copies printed. Published in October 1948 at 8s. 6d.

CONTENTS

Preface by Osbert Sitwell

[Poems all from *Collected Poems*, 1936, unless otherwise stated]

Group I. The Rio Grande, and four poems from "The Santander Quartet": In the Wine Shop—Telling Fortunes—At Supper—Gypsy Song

Group II. Two Variations on Themes out of Zarathustra, 1. "Laughing Lions will Come"—2. Parade Virtues for a Dying Gladiator

Group III. Et in Arcadia, Omnes (extract from "The Bird-Actors")

Group IV. Actor Rehearsing

Group V. Fisherman—Wind as Husbandman

Group VI. From *Canons of Giant Art*. 1. Fugal Siege—2. Pastoral—3. Agamemnon's Tomb—4. From "Battles of the Centaurs: Centaurs and Lapithae"—5. The Farnese Hercules—6. Fragment from "Bohemund, Prince of Antioch"

Group VII. *The People's Palace*. Trumpets—Outskirts—"Psittachus eois Imitatrix Ales ab Indis"—Pindar—Brighton Pier—Li-Tai-Pé—The Moon—Tahiti—Barrel Organs—Mrs. H ... or a Lady from Babel—Week-Ends—Valse Estudiantina

Group VIII. Extracts from *The Thirteenth Cæsar*. The Opening of the Tomb—At the Bedside—As of Old

Group IX. Serenades. 1. Sigh soft, sigh softly [as "Serenade I"]—2. Open your Window [as "Serenade III"]—2. I see no breath upon the window's water [as "Serenade IV"]—Hortus Conclusus. Cherry Tree—Gardener's Song—The Red-Gold Rain, i. Orange Tree by Day, ii. Orange Tree by Night—Damson and Medlar—Dandelion—Cowslips—Variation on a Theme of Robert Herrick—Complaint—Warning—The Island—Derbyshire Bluebells—Fortune—Shadow

Group X. A March Past at the Pyramids

Group XI. Two Mirror Poems. 1. On a Name Scratched upon a Window—2. The Poet and the Mirror

Group XII. Part II from "New Water Music"

Group XIII. Studies on the Black Keys. 1. The Dark of Night—2. Black Sonnet—3. Black Shepherdess

Two Pastoral Poems. The Cyder Feast—Chamber Idyll

Group XIV [Previously unpublished, and dated July 1947]. White Rose—The Lime Avenue—The Sick Man—The Mezquita—Outside Dunsandle

SA50   MORNING, NOON AND   1948
        NIGHT IN LONDON

First edition

MORNING, NOON | AND NIGHT IN | LONDON | BY | SACHEVERELL SITWELL | LONDON | MACMILLAN & CO. LTD | 1948

218 × 140 mm.

96 pp.: [i] half-title; [ii] blank; [iii] title; [iv] "Copyright. Printed in Great Britain"; v List of plates; [vi] dedication; 1–85, [86] text and note; [87] "Printed by R. & R. Clark, Ltd., Edinburgh"; [88–90] blank.

Eight plates tipped in.

Yellow cloth boards. Trimmed edges. Gilt lettered on spine.

5000 copies printed. Published 12 November 1948 at 12s. 6d.

SA51   THEATRICAL FIGURES   1949
IN PORCELAIN

[*Within a decorated border*]

SACHEVERELL | SITWELL | THEATRICAL | FIGURES | IN | PORCELAIN | GERMAN | 18th CENTURY | WITH AN INTRODUCTION | BY | WILLIAM KING | THE CURTAIN PRESS | LONDON | 1949

186 × 125 mm.

64 pp.: [1] half-title; [2] blank; [3] title; [4] "Editor, Lionel Carter, Art Editor, Joan Hassall. Acknowledgements . . . Made and Printed in Great Britain by Staples Press Limited, St. Albans, Herts. Block by Tessa Process Co. Ltd."; [i] blank; [ii] plate, tipped on; 5–[6] Introduction; 7–43, [44] text; [iii–xviii] plates; [xix] blank; [xx] advertisement.

One colour plate tipped on and sixteen pages of half-tone plates, the first two tipped in as C8 cancellans, the last fourteen with the advertisement leaf forming the last section; black and white scraperboard drawings by Joan Hassall on text pages.

3000 copies bound in paper boards. Trimmed edges. Design by Joan Hassall printed in sepia on green on upper cover, and white-lettered on spine.

2000 copies bound in stiff white paper wrappers. Else as above.

5000 copies printed. Published in June 1949 as no. 9 of "The Masque," at 5s. (boards) and 3s. 6d. (wrappers). A slip-case was issued for nos. 7–9 of the series.

a. *First edition*

SPAIN | [*short swelled rule*] | Sacheverell Sitwell | [*short swelled rule*] | B. T. BATSFORD LTD | LONDON · NEW YORK · TORONTO · SYDNEY

216 × 137 mm.

160 pp.: [i] half-title; [ii] "Books on the Countries of Europe"; [iii] title; [iv] dedication and: "First published, 1950. Made and printed in Great Britain by William Clowes and Sons Ltd, London and Beccles, for the publishers . . ."; v–vii Preface and Acknowledgment; viii Contents; ix–xii Introduction; 1–148 text, maps and index.

17 double leaves of plates sewn in, two plates tipped in and maps on pp. 138–141.

Dark blue cloth boards. Top edge dark blue, others trimmed. Gilt lettered on spine.

10,000 copies printed. Published in April 1950 at 16s.

CONTENTS

Includes "The Gipsy Caves at Guadix" from *Journal of the Gipsy Lore Society*, January–April 1950

b. *Second edition*

[*Title and size as in first edition*]

160 pp.: [i] half-title; [ii] "Books on the Countries of Europe"; [iii] title; [iv] dedication and: "First published 1950. Second edition, 1951. Made and printed in Great Britain by William Clowes and Sons Ltd, London and Beccles, for the publishers . . ."; v–vii Preface and Acknowledgment; viii Contents; ix–xii Introduction and Preface to Second Edition; 1–148 text, maps and index.

Illustrations as in first edition.

Grey cloth boards. Top edge green, others trimmed. Gilt lettered on spine. (Some copies have top edge blue.)

10,000 copies printed. Published 13 August 1951 at 16s.

Revisions on p. xii and in the text

c. *Third edition*

[*Within a rectangular rule*]

Spain | SACHEVERELL SITWELL | [*device*] | B. T. BATS-
FORD LTD LONDON

172 × 111 mm.

204 pp.: [1] half-title; [2] blank; [3] title; [4] "First published 1950,
Fourth impression 1955, Paperback edition 1961. Revised Edition
© Sacheverell Sitwell, 1961. Printed and bound in the Netherlands by
the Hooiberg Printing Company, Epe . . ."; [5] dedication; [6] blank;
7 Contents; 8 Acknowledgment; 9–10 List of illustrations; 11–15
Introduction; [16] blank; 17–203 text, maps and index; [204] blank.

Sixteen plates inserted between sections, maps on pp. [192–195].

Pictorial glossy wrappers. Unsewn. Printed in green and white on
covers and spine.

35,000 copies printed. Published 1 September 1961 at 5s.

CONTENTS

Text revised. [Includes, in part 3 of chapter 2, material from *Truffle
Hunt*, 1953]

SA53 CUPID AND THE JACARANDA 1952

First edition

CUPID AND | THE JACARANDA | BY | SACHEVERELL
SITWELL | LONDON | MACMILLAN & CO. LTD | 1952

216 × 140 mm.

324 pp.: [i] half-title; [ii] "List of Chief Works by Sacheverell Sitwell";
[iii] title; [iv] "This book is copyright . . . Printed in Great Britain";
v–vi Contents; 1–316, [317] text and printer's imprint: "Printed by
R. & R. Clark, Ltd., Edinburgh"; [318] blank.

Red cloth boards. Top edge lilac, others trimmed. Gilt lettered on
spine.

3000 copies printed. Published 30 May 1952 at 24s.

First edition

TRUFFLE | HUNT | *with* | SACHEVERELL SITWELL | ROBERT HALE LIMITED | 63 Old Brompton Road London S.W.7

215 × 137 mm.

320 pp.: [i] half-title; [ii] "By the Same Author . . ."; [iii] title; [iv] "First published 1953. Made and printed in Great Britain by William Clowes and Sons, Limited, London and Beccles"; [v] dedication; [vi] blank; vii Author's foreword; [viii] note; ix–x Illustrations; 1–303 text; [304] blank; 305–310 Contents.

Frontispiece tipped in and six double leaves of plates sewn in.

Grey cloth boards. Trimmed edges. Lettered in red on spine.

4750 copies printed. Published 21 October 1953 at 24*s*.

CONTENTS

The paragraphs by Sacheverell Sitwell in the *Sunday Times* from 12 November 1950 to 23 September 1951, under the title "People and Memories," are here reprinted in revised and extended form. "Two Japanese Landscape Gardens by the Monk Soami" is also reprinted from *Life and Letters*, December 1945.

a. *First edition, ordinary copies*

[*Red*] FINE | BIRD | BOOKS | 1700–1900 | [*black*] By | Sacheverell Sitwell | Handasyde Buchanan | and James Fisher | [*red*] COLLINS & VAN NOSTRAND | LONDON 1953 NEW YORK

490 × 336 mm.

128 pp.: [i] engraved half-title; [ii] "This Edition has been made and designed for William Collins, 14 St James's Place, London, and D. Van Nostrand Company, Inc., New York, by George Rainbird and Ruari McLean at 8 Wyndham Place, London, W.1. The plates have been printed in 8-colour photo-litho offset and collotype monochrome by Van Leer of Amsterdam. The text pages have been set in Mono-type Bembo and printed by The Chiswick Press of London. The

binding has been executed by Mansell of London. 295 numbered copies have been printed on Pannekoek mould made paper and 2000 copies on Gelderland mill paper"; [iii] title; [iv] blank; [v] Contents; vi–vii Plates and Acknowledgements; [viii] Illustrations; [1], 2–118 text; 119–120 index.

Six double leaves and four single leaves of plates sewn in, and monochrome illustrations on text pages.

Terracotta buckram spine and corners, marbled paper boards. Trimmed edges. Gilt lettered on spine.

2000 copies printed. Published in London and New York 26 October 1953 at 12 guineas and $50.00.

CONTENTS

Pp. 1–45, "Fine Bird Books" by Sacheverell Sitwell; pp. 47–116, "The Bibliography" by Handasyde Buchanan and James Fisher

b. *First edition, special copies*

[*Title, size and illustrations as in ordinary copies*]

128 pp.: As in ordinary copies, except p. [ii]: ". . . Gelderland mill paper. This is number" [in ink, with authors' autograph signatures].

Quarter crimson leather, marbled paper boards. Trimmed edges. Reproductions of feathers on end-papers. Gilt lettered on spine. Red and white headband. Slip case of crimson cloth and marbled paper boards.

295 copies printed. Published in London and New York 26 October 1953 at 20 guineas and $85.00.

CONTENTS

As in ordinary copies, above

sA56   SELECTED WORKS   1953

First edition

Selected Works of | *Sacheverell Sitwell* | [*decoration*] | THE BOBBS-MERRILL COMPANY, INC. | Publishers | Indianapolis New York

215 × 144 mm.

408 pp.: [1] half-title; [2] blank; [3] title; [4] "Copyright, 1953, by Sacheverell Sitwell. Printed in the United States of America. Library of Congress Catalog Card Number: 53–10551. First Edition"; [5] Acknowledgments; [6] blank; [7] Contents; [8] blank; 9–23 Introduction; [24] blank; 25–406 text; [407–408] blank.

Frontispiece tipped in.

Rough red cloth boards. Trimmed edges. Gilt lettered on spine and upper cover.

3000 copies printed. Published 28 October 1953 at $4.00.

CONTENTS

Introduction—Excerpts from *Dance of the Quick and the Dead*—*Splendours and Miseries*—*Sacred and Profane Love*—*Spain*—*Mauretania*—*Roumanian Journey*—*Primitive Scenes and Festivals*—*Southern Baroque Art*

Note: This is a totally different book from the *Selected Works* published in London in 1955—see sA59.

SA57   PORTUGAL AND MADEIRA   1954

First edition

PORTUGAL | AND MADEIRA | *By* | *Sacheverell Sitwell* | [*device*] | London | B. T. BATSFORD LTD

216 × 138 mm.

242 pp. (including plates): [1] half-title; [2] "By the same author . . ."; [3] blank; [4] frontispiece; [5] title; [6] "First published 1954. Made and printed in Great Britain by William Clowes and Sons, Limited, London and Beccles, for the publishers . . ."; [7] dedication; [8] blank; 9–11 Preface; [12] blank; 13 Contents; [14] Acknowledgment; 15–17 List of illustrations; [18] map; 19–242 text, plates and index.

Twenty-four plates on art paper bound in, frontispiece tipped in; all included in the pagination.

Smooth green cloth boards. Top edge green, others trimmed. Gilt lettered on spine.

9000 copies printed. Published 23 September 1954 at 18*s.*

a. *First edition, ordinary copies*

[*Red*] OLD | GARDEN ROSES | [*black*] Part One | [*short red rule*] | [*black*] By Sacheverell Sitwell | & James Russell | with 8 reproductions from paintings | by Charles Raymond | and a Foreword by | Graham Thomas | [*short red rule*] | [*black*] London | GEORGE RAINBIRD LTD | *in association with* | COLLINS, 14 ST JAMES'S PLACE, LONDON | 1955

427 × 308 mm.

52 pp.: [1] title; [2] [*device*]. "*Old Garden Roses* is the first book published by George Rainbird Ltd, under the direction of Sacheverell Sitwell, Sir Alfred Beit, Bt, Ruari McLean and George Rainbird, at 8 Wyndham Place, London W.1. The colour plates have been printed in 8-colour photo-litho-offset by Van Leer of Amsterdam. The text has been set in 18-point Monotype Caslon Old Face and printed by The Chiswick Press, London. Copies numbered 1 to 160 are signed by the artist and authors, printed on 'Amstel' Special mould-made paper and bound in quarter vellum by Edward Hiscox of London. Copies numbered 161 to 2160 are printed on 'Gelderland' white cartridge and bound by Mansell of London. This is Copy No." [in ink]; [3] Contents and Colour Plates; [4] dedication; 5–8 List of Subscribers; 9 Foreword; 10 blank; 11–12 Authors' preface; 13–52 text.

Eight leaves sewn in reproducing paintings by Charles Raymond.

Plain green paper boards. Trimmed edges. Pink paper label, gilt lettered, pasted on upper cover.

2000 copies printed. Published 27 June 1955 at 7 guineas.

CONTENTS

Pp. 13–41, "Old Roses" by Sacheverell Sitwell; pp. 42–52, "The History of Old Garden Roses" by James Russell

b. *First edition, special copies*

[*Title, size and illustrations as in ordinary copies*]

52 pp.: As in ordinary copies, but with artist's and authors' autograph signatures after "This is Copy No." [number] on p. [2].

Vellum spine and corners, decorated paper boards. Top edge gilt, others trimmed. Gilt stamped on corners and spine. Decorated end-papers. Binder's stamp inside lower cover. Slip case of green cloth boards.

160 copies printed. Published 27 June 1955 at 15 guineas.

CONTENTS

As in ordinary copies

sA59   SELECTED WORKS   1955

First edition

SELECTED | WORKS | *of* | SACHEVERELL SITWELL | ROBERT HALE LIMITED | 63 Old Brompton Road London S.W.7

215 × 137 mm.

320 pp.: [i] half-title; [ii] "By the same author . . ."; [iii] title; [iv] "First published 1955. Made and printed in Great Britain by William Clowes and Sons, Limited, London and Beccles"; v Contents; [vi] blank; vii–viii List of illustrations, Acknowledgments; ix–xx Introduction; 1–300 text.

Frontispiece tipped in, and four double leaves of plates sewn in.

Grey cloth boards. Trimmed edges. Lettered in red on spine.

2500 copies printed. Published 23 November 1955 at 24s.

CONTENTS

Introduction—*La Vie Parisienne* [complete]—Extracts from *Primitive Scenes and Festivals, Splendours and Miseries, Dance of the Quick and the Dead, Touching the Orient, Sacred & Profane Love, A Background for Domenico Scarlatti* and *Roumanian Journey*

Note: This is a totally different book from the *Selected Works* published in Indianapolis in 1953—see sA56.

sA60   DENMARK   1956

a. *First edition*

DENMARK | *By* | *Sacheverell Sitwell* | [*device*] | London | B. T. BATSFORD LTD

216 × 137 mm.

168 pp. (including plates): [1] half-title; [2] "By the same Author"; [3] blank; [4] frontispiece; [5] title; [6] "First published 1956. Printed and bound in Great Britain by William Clowes and Sons, Limited, London and Beccles, for the publishers . . ."; [7] dedication; [8] blank; 9–13 Preface and Postscript; [14] blank; 15 Contents; 16 Acknowledgments; 17–18 List of illustrations; 19–168 text, plates and index. Six double leaves of plates sewn in and included in the pagination.

Pink cloth boards. Top edge pink, others trimmed. Gilt lettered on spine.

4175 copies printed. Published 26 April 1956 at 21s.

b. *First edition, American copies*

Note: 525 copies were imported and published by Messrs. Hastings House in New York in 1956. I have not been able to see a copy, and Messrs. Hastings House said in 1957 they were unable to give any information about these copies, nor did they retain a file copy.

sA61 GREAT FLOWER BOOKS 1956

a. *First edition, ordinary copies*

GREAT FLOWER | BOOKS | 1700–1900 | A Bibliographical Record of two Centuries | of finely-illustrated Flower Books | by Sacheverell Sitwell | & Wilfrid Blunt | The Bibliography edited by | Patrick M. Synge | [*in black, within a green border*] London | COLLINS | 1956

493 × 342 mm.

104 pp.: [i] half-title; [ii] blank; [iii] title; [iv] "*Great Flower Books* has been made and designed for William Collins, 14 St. James's Place, London SW 1 by Rainbird, McLean Ltd at 8 Wyndham Place, London W 1. The Plates have been printed in 8-colour photo-litho-offset and monochrome collotype by Van Leer of Amsterdam. The text pages have been set in Monotype Garamond and printed by Meijer of Wormeveer . . . 295 numbered copies have been printed on 'Amstel' special mould-made paper and 1750 copies on 'Gelderland' white cartridge. The binding of the numbered copies has been executed by the Wigmore Bindery, London. The unnumbered copies have been bound by Mansells of London"; [v] Contents; [vi] decoration; vii–x Plates; 1–94 text and index.

One double leaf and 36 single leaves of plates tipped in, and black and white illustrations on text pages.

Green buckram spine and corners, green marbled paper boards. Trimmed edges. Gilt lettered on spine.

1750 copies printed. Published 24 September 1956 at 12 guineas.

CONTENTS

Pp. 1–15, "The Romance of the Flower Book" by Sacheverell Sitwell

b. *First edition, special copies*
[*Title, size and illustrations as in ordinary copies*]

104 pp.: As in ordinary copies, except p. [iv]: ". . . Mansells of London. This copy is number" [in ink, with authors' autograph signatures].

Green morocco spine, green marbled paper boards. Trimmed edges. Decorated end-papers. Gilt lettered on spine. Slip case of green cloth and marbled paper boards.

295 copies printed. Published 24 September 1956 at 20 guineas.

CONTENTS

As in ordinary copies

sA62 ARABESQUE AND HONEYCOMB 1957

a. *First edition*

ARABESQUE | AND | HONEYCOMB | *by* | SACHEVERELL SITWELL | ROBERT HALE LIMITED | 63 Old Brompton Road London S.W.7

229 × 151 mm.

256 pp.: [i] half-title; [ii] "By the same Author . . ."; [iii] title; [iv] "© Sacheverell Sitwell, 1957. Made and printed in Great Britain by William Clowes and Sons, Limited, London and Beccles"; [v] dedication; [vi] blank; vii–x Contents; xi–xii List of illustrations; xiii–xxviii Introduction; [xxix] blank; [xxx–xxxi] map; [xxxii] blank; 1–224 text and index.

Six double leaves of plates sewn in, four single leaves tipped in, and map on pp. xxx–xxxi.

Grey cloth boards. Trimmed edges. Lettered in red on spine.

3500 copies printed. Published 30 October 1957 at 35*s*.

CONTENTS

Most or all of each of the following periodical publications are included: "The Blue Mosque," *Sunday Times*, 5 August 1956—"In the Steps of Alexander," *Sunday Times*, 26 August 1956—"A Look at Teheran and Isfahan," *The Listener*, 4 October 1956—"Nuptials of the East and West," *The Listener*, 18 October 1956—"The Friday Mosque," *The Selective Eye*, 1956/1957

b. *First edition, American copies*

ARABESQUE | AND | HONEYCOMB | *by* | SACHEVERELL SITWELL | RANDOM HOUSE [*device*] NEW YORK

Note: 3500 copies were imported by Random House, Inc., and published 25 March 1958 at $6.00. The contents are as in sA62a.

SA63   MALTA   1958

First edition

By Sacheverell Sitwell | MALTA | & Tony Armstrong Jones | B. T. BATSFORD LTD. [*device*] LONDON

282 × 211 mm.

144 pp.: [i] half-title; [ii] blank; [iii] title; [iv] © Sacheverell Sitwell and Tony Armstrong Jones, 1958. First published, 1958. Made and printed in Great Britain by William Clowes and Sons Ltd, London and Beccles. Collotype plates by L. Van Leer and Co. Ltd., London and Amsterdam . . .; v dedication; [vi] blank; vii–viii Preface, and Postscript; ix Contents; x–xi List of Illustrations; [xii] map of Malta and Gozo; 1–76 text; [77–124] Illustrations; [125–126], 127–131 Index; [132] blank.

Photographs by Tony Armstrong Jones on pp. [77–124]; map on p. [xii].

Blue cloth boards. Top edge blue, others trimmed. Gilt lettered on spine.

3000 copies printed. Published 38 October 1958 at 40*s*.

sA64   JOURNEY TO THE ENDS OF   1959
TIME, Vol. I

a. *First edition*

SACHEVERELL SITWELL | [*star*] | JOURNEY | TO THE
ENDS | OF TIME | [*star*] | VOLUME ONE | LOST IN THE
DARK WOOD | [*device*] | CASSELL · LONDON

217 × 137 mm.

496 pp.: [i] half-title; [ii] blank; [iii] "By the same author . . ."; [iv]
blank; [v] title; [vi] Cassell & Company . . . © Sacheverell Sitwell,
1959. First published, 1959. Made and printed in Great Britain by
William Clowes and Son, Limited, London and Beccles. F459; [vii]
dedication; viii quotation from Dante; ix–x Contents; xi–xx A Note
of Explanation; 1–475 text; [476] blank.

Black cloth boards. Trimmed edges. Lettered in silver on spine.

3041 copies printed. Published 11 June 1959 at 35*s*.

b. *First edition, American copies*

SACHEVERELL SITWELL | [*star*] | JOURNEY | TO THE
ENDS | OF TIME | [*star*] | VOLUME ONE | LOST IN THE
DARK WOOD | [*device*] | RANDOM HOUSE | NEW YORK

Note: 2000 copies were imported, and were published on 18 August
1959 at $7.50. The contents are exactly as in sA64a

sA65   BRIDGE OF THE BROCADE   1959
SASH

a. *First edition*

BRIDGE | OF THE BROCADE SASH | *Travels and Observa-
tions in Japan* | [*ornamental rules*] | SACHEVERELL SIT-
WELL | WEIDENFELD AND NICOLSON | 7 CORK STREET
LONDON W1

242 × 152 mm.

316 pp.: [1] half-title; [2] blank; [3] title; [4] © 1959 by Sacheverell
Sitwell. Printed in Great Britain by C. Tinling & Co. Ltd., Liverpool,

London and Prescot. R.6574; [5]–6 Contents; [7]–8 Illustrations; [9] Acknowledgments; [10] dedication; 11–14 Introduction; 15–314 text; [315–316] blank.

Eight double leaves of plates sewn in and four single leaves tipped in.

Maroon cloth boards. Top edge maroon, others trimmed. Pink endpapers. Silver lettered on spine.

3000 copies printed. Published 12 December 1959 at 36s.

CONTENTS

Includes part of "A Note on Two Japanese Landscape Gardens by the Monk Soami" (pp. 101 *et seq.*) from *Life and Letters To-Day*, December 1945

b. *First edition, American copies*

[4500 copies were imported (according to the English publishers; "about 5,500" copies according to the American publishers) by The World Publishing Company, New York. The price was $8.50 and the date of publication was 22 March 1960.]

sA66 GOLDEN WALL AND MIRADOR 1961

a. *First edition*

GOLDEN WALL | AND MIRADOR | *From England to Peru* | SACHEVERELL SITWELL | '*Let observation with extensive view,* | *Survey mankind from China to Peru;* | *Remark each anxious toil, each eager strife,* | *And watch the busy scene of crowded life.*' | Dr Johnson, *The Vanity of Human Wishes* | WEIDENFELD AND NICOLSON | 20 NEW BOND STREET LONDON W1

242 × 152 mm.

292 pp.: [i] half-title; [ii] "Also by Sacheverell Sitwell . . ."; [iii] title; [iv] © 1961 by Sacheverell Sitwell. Printed in Great Britain by C. Tinling & Co. Ltd., Liverpool, London and Prescot. 17/6228; [1–2] Contents; [3–4] Illustrations; [5] dedication; [6] blank; [7–9] Introduction; [10] blank; 11–286 text and index; [287–288] blank.

Eight double leaves of plates sewn in and four single leaves tipped in.

Brown cloth boards. Top edge brown, others trimmed. Yellow end-papers. Lettered in silver on the spine.

3500 copies printed. Published 12 May 1961 at 36s.

CONTENTS

Includes "Cuzco" from *Geographical Magazine*, May 1961

b. *First edition, American copies*
[*Full-opening title*]
Sacheverell Sitwell | [*decorated capitals:*] GOLDEN WALL AND MIRADOR | Travels and Observations in Peru | [*device*] | CLEVELAND AND NEW YORK THE WORLD PUBLISHING COMPANY

242 × 204 mm.

292 pp.: [i] half-title; [ii–iii] title; [iv] Published by The World Publishing Company . . . Library of Congress Catalog Card Number: 61–12015. First edition. GBWP. Copyright © 1961 by Sacheverell Sitwell . . . Printed in Great Britain. [Thence as in English copies.]

Illustrations as in English copies.

Rough buff cloth boards. Top edge pink, others trimmed. Pale orange end-papers. Orange and red head- and tail-bands. Decorations in pink and black on spine and upper cover, lettered in black on spine.

3500 copies (according to the English publishers; "about 4400" copies according to the American publishers) imported. Published 14 August 1961 at $7.50.

sA67   THE RED CHAPELS OF   1962
              BANTEAI SREI

a. *First edition*

THE RED CHAPELS | OF BANTEAI SREI | *And Temples in Cambodia, India, Siam and Nepal* | SACHEVERELL SIT-WELL | WEIDENFELD AND NICOLSON | 20 NEW BOND STREET LONDON WI

242 × 155 mm.

240 pp.: [1] half-title; [2] "Also by Sacheverell Sitwell . . ."; [3] title; [4] © 1962 by Sacheverell Sitwell. [Dedication]. Printed in Great

Britain by C. Tinling & Co. Ltd., Liverpool, London and Prescot. 17/6228; [5–6] Contents; [7–8] Illustrations; [9–10], 11–239 text; [240] blank.

Eight double leaves of plates sewn in and four single leaves tipped in.

Dark red cloth boards. Top edge dark red, others trimmed. Pink end-papers. Gilt lettered on spine.

3000 copies printed. Published 19 October 1962 at 42s.

b. *First edition, American copies*

(An American issue was published by Obolensky, New York, in 1963, under the title of *Great Temples of the East*. It had 284 pages, and the price was $4.00.)

sA68   MONKS, NUNS AND   1965
MONASTERIES

a. *First edition*

Sacheverell Sitwell | MONKS, NUNS AND | MONASTERIES | WEIDENFELD AND NICOLSON | 20 NEW BOND STREET LONDON WI

246 × 177 mm.

220 pp.: [i] half-title; [ii] blank; [iii] title; [iv] "© 1965 by Sacheverell Sitwell. Text printed in Great Britain by Morrison and Gibb Limited, London and Edinburgh. Illustrations printed by Jarrolds of Norwich"; [v] dedication; [vi] blank; [vii] Contents; [viii] blank; [ix], x–xiii Illustrations; [xiv] Acknowledgements; 1–205 text and index; [206] blank.

Eight colour plates tipped in, twenty-four double leaves of black-and-white plates sewn in.

Brown cloth boards. Trimmed edges. Photograph reproduced on end-papers. Gilt lettered on spine.

4000 copies printed. Published 23 September 1965 at 63s.

b. *First edition, American copies*

Sacheverell Sitwell | MONKS, NUNS AND | MONASTERIES | [*device*] | HOLT, RINEHART AND WINSTON | NEW YORK CHICAGO SAN FRANCISCO

Note: 10,000 copies imported. Apart from the title leaf and the lettering on the spine, they are identical with the first edition. Published
26 October 1965 at $12.50.

sA69   SOUTHERN BAROQUE   1967
                    REVISITED
a. *First edition*

SOUTHERN | BAROQUE | REVISITED | SACHEVERELL
SITWELL | WEIDENFELD AND NICOLSON | 5 WINSLEY
STREET LONDON WI

247 × 176 mm.

320 pp. (including 24 black-and-white plates): [i] half-title; [ii] caption
to frontispiece; [iii] title; [iv] "© 1967 by Sacheverell Sitwell.
Phototypeset by BAS Printers Limited, Wallop, Hampshire. Text
printed in Great Britain by Loew and Brydone (Printers) Ltd. Illustrations printed by Jarrold and Sons Ltd, Norwich"; [v] dedication;
[vi] blank; [vii] Contents; [viii] blank; [ix], x–xiii List of illustrations,
and Acknowledgments; [xiv] quotation; 1–306 text, black-and-white
plates, Appendix and index.

Two colour plates tipped in, three double leaves of colour plates
sewn in. (For black-and-white plates see above.)

Fawn cloth boards. Trimmed edges. Illustration in blue on end-
papers. Gilt lettered on spine.

4000 copies printed. Published 12 October 1967 at 63s.

b. *First edition, American copies*

BAROQUE | AND | ROCOCO | SACHEVERELL SITWELL |
G. P. PUTNAM'S SONS | 200 MADISON AVENUE NEW
YORK

Note: 7500 copies imported. Published 12 October 1967 at $12.95.
The contents are as in sA69a.

sA70   GOTHIC EUROPE   1969

a. *First edition*

𝕲𝖔𝖙𝖍𝖎𝖈 | 𝕰𝖚𝖗𝖔𝖕𝖊 | [*short rule*] | SACHEVERELL | SITWELL |

333

WEIDENFELD & NICOLSON | 5 WINSLEY STREET
LONDON WI

247 × 177 mm.

208 pp.: [i] half-title; [ii] caption to frontispiece; [iii] title; [iv] "SBN
297 17810 5. © 1969 by Sacheverell Sitwell. Designed by John
Wallis . . . Printed in Great Britain by The Camelot Press Ltd,
London and Southampton"; [v] dedication; [vi] blank; [vii] Contents;
[viii] blank; ix–xiii List of illustrations; [xiv] blank; xv–xvi Preface;
[1–2], 3–192 text and index.

Eight colour plates tipped in, forty-eight leaves of black-and-white
plates sewn in between sections.

Brown buckram boards. Trimmed edges. Monochrome reproduction
of painting on end-papers. Gilt lettered on spine.

3500 copies printed. Published 17 July 1969 at 70s.

b. *First edition, American copies*

𝕲𝖔𝖙𝖍𝖎𝖈 | 𝕰𝖚𝖗𝖔𝖕𝖊 | [*short rule*] | SACHEVERELL | SITWELL |
[*device*] | HOLT, RINEHART AND WINSTON | NEW YORK
CHICAGO SAN FRANCISCO

Note: 6000 copies imported. Apart from the title leaf, and the
lettering on the spine, they are identical with the first edition. Published
2 October 1969 at $11.95.

BOOKS EDITED BY AND WITH CONTRIBUTIONS BY SACHEVERELL SITWELL (sB1–sB67)

---

sB1   NEW PATHS 1917–1918   1918

[*For description, see* EB3]

CONTENTS

Pp. 70–71, "Fragment from 'Sirens'" by Sacheverell Sitwell [as in *The People's Palace*]

sB2   THE ETON CANDLE   1922

[*For description, see* OB2*A*]

CONTENTS

P. 52, "Portrait of a Harlequin" by Sacheverell Sitwell

sB2*A*   A MISCELLANY OF   1922
             POETRY 1920–1922

[*For description, see* EB8*A*]

CONTENTS

Pp. 165–166, "The Venus of Bolsover Castle" by Sacheverell Sitwell

sB3   MAGNASCO SOCIETY   1924
             CATALOGUE

First edition

THE MAGNASCO | SOCIETY | [*ornament*] | CATALOGUE | *of a* | LOAN EXHIBITION | *of* | ITALIAN PICTURES | *of the* | XVII. & XVIII. | CENTURIES | [*ornament*] | Messrs. THOS. AGNEW & SONS' | *Galleries* | 43, OLD BOND STREET | LONDON | *October and* | *November,* 1924

16 pages. 160 × 129 mm.

Grey paper wrappers, stapled. Untrimmed edges. Lettered in black on upper cover.

Published in October 1924 at the Exhibition.

CONTENTS

Pp. [5]–6, "The Magnasco Society" [by Sacheverell Sitwell, according to Osbert Sitwell. Sacheverell Sitwell is not now certain which introductions to the Society's exhibition catalogues he wrote. See also oC477]

sB4   ANTOINE WATTEAU   1925

First edition

MASTERS OF PAINTING | ANTOINE WATTEAU | FORE-WORD BY | SACHEVERELL SITWELL | [*device*] | 1925 | "THE STUDIO," 44 LEICESTER SQUARE, LONDON

12 pages, and 12 plates. 302 × 244 mm.

Pink paper boards. Trimmed edges. Lettered in black on green paper labels on upper cover and spine.

Published in January 1926 at 5s. (Publishers' records destroyed in the war 1939–45.)

CONTENTS

Pp. 1–7, "Foreword" by Sacheverell Sitwell

sB5   MAGNASCO SOCIETY   1926
CATALOGUE

First edition

THE MAGNASCO | SOCIETY | [*ornament*] | CATALOGUE | *of a* | LOAN EXHIBITION | *of* | PICTURES | *of the* | XVII. & XVIII. | CENTURIES | [*ornament*] | Messrs.

THOS. AGNEW & SONS' | *Galleries* | 43, OLD BOND
STREET | LONDON | *October,* 1926.

12 pages. 160 × 130 mm.

Blue-grey paper wrappers, stapled. Untrimmed edges. Lettered in
black on upper cover.

Published in October 1926 at the Exhibition.

CONTENTS

Pp. [5]–6, "The Magnasco Society" [by Sacheverell Sitwell; this is a
different preface to that in sB3, above]

sB6   THE HISTORY OF HARLEQUIN   1926

First edition

[*Within a border*]

THE HISTORY OF | HARLEQUIN | By | CYRIL W.
BEAUMONT | With a Preface by | SACHEVERELL
SITWELL | A Cover Design and Decorations by |
CLAUDIA GUERCIO | And Illustrations from Contemporary
Sources | [decoration] | London | C. W. BEAUMONT | 75
CHARING CROSS ROAD, W.C. 2 | 1926

156 pages, and 44 plates. 259 × 193 mm.

Vellum spine, parchment boards. Untrimmed edges. Lettered in gilt
on spine, with decorations in black on covers.

325 numbered copies printed. Published in January 1927 at 42s.

CONTENTS

Pp. ix–xviii, "Preface: Concerning Harlequin in Art" by Sacheverell
Sitwell

sB7   THE TRIUMPH OF NEPTUNE   1927

First edition

THE | TRIUMPH OF NEPTUNE | ENGLISH PANTOMIME
IN TWELVE TABLEAUX | *Music by* | LORD BERNERS |

Book by | S. SITWELL | [*decoration*] | J. & W. CHESTER, LTD., | 11, GREAT MARLBOROUGH STREET, | LONDON, W.I.

96 pages, and 4 engravings. 313 × 242 mm.

Stiff paper wrappers, sewn. Trimmed edges. Printed on the upper cover on coloured panels.

Published in October 1927 at 12s.

CONTENTS

P. vii lists the scenes and variations; the "book" as such is unpublished. (The ballet was first performed by Diaghilev's *Ballets russes* in London at the Lyceum Theatre on 3 December 1926, and in Paris at the Théâtre Sarah-Bernhardt on 27 May 1927.)

sB8　　　　SERGE LIFAR　　　　1928

First edition

SERGE LIFAR | SIXTEEN DRAWINGS IN BLACK AND WHITE BY | EILEEN MAYO | WITH A FOREWORD BY | BORIS KOCHNO | TRANSLATED FROM THE FRENCH BY | SACHEVERELL SITWELL | AND AN APPRECIATION BY | CYRIL W. BEAUMONT | [*decoration*] | LONDON | C. W. BEAUMONT | 75 CHARING CROSS ROAD | 1928

46 pages. 331 × 280 mm.

Linen spine, yellow paper boards. Sewing cord sewn over linen spine, with a tassel end. Trimmed edges. Printed in black on upper cover.

500 numbered copies printed (490 for sale). Published in December 1928 at 21s.

CONTENTS

Pp. 5–7, "Serge Lifar" by Boris Kochno, translated by Sacheverell Sitwell

sB9　　　LIFAR EXHIBITION　　　1930
　　　　　　CATALOGUE

[*For description, see* EB15]

Pp. [5–7], "Preface (3)" by Sacheverell Sitwell

sB10   THE MEN BEHIND THE MUSIC   1931

First edition

THE MEN | BEHIND THE MUSIC | *Edited by* | C. HENRY
WARREN | LONDON | GEORGE ROUTLEDGE & SONS,
LTD. | BROADWAY HOUSE: 68–74 CARTER LANE, E.C. |
1931

160 pages. 188 × 120 mm.

Smooth red cloth boards. Trimmed edges. Lettered in black on spine.

3000 copies printed. Published on 18 June 1931 at 2*s.* 6*d.*

Pp. 90–98, "Mendelssohn" by Sacheverell Sitwell [as "A most eminent
Victorian: Mendelssohn" in *Radio Times*, 6 June 1930]

sB11   FLASH=BACK   1931

a. *First edition, ordinary copies*

FLASH=BACK | *Stories of my Youth* | *by* | *CYRIL W. BEAU-
MONT* | *[short rule with asterisk]* | *With a Preface by* |
SACHEVERELL SITWELL | *[short rule with asterisk]* |
LONDON | *C. W. BEAUMONT* | *75 Charing Cross Road* |
1931

132 pages. 187 × 122 mm.

Smooth red cloth boards. Top edge red, others trimmed. Gilt
lettered on spine.

"About 1000" copies (according to the publisher) printed. Published
in September 1931 at 5*s.*

Pp. vii–xxi, "Preface" by Sacheverell Sitwell

b. *First edition, special copies*

[*Title and size as in ordinary copies*]

132 pages, with p. [iv]: "The Certificate. This Special Edition is limited to 60 copies (5 not for sale), signed by the Author. This is No." [in ink, with author's autograph signature].

Red buckram boards. Else as ordinary copies.

60 copies printed (5 not for sale). Published in September 1931 at 12*s*. 6*d*.

CONTENTS

As in ordinary copies

sB12   GRAND TOUR   1935

a. *First edition*

GRAND TOUR | A Journey in the Tracks of the | Age of Aristocracy | *conducted by* | Mona Wilson | Douglas Woodruff | Edmund Blunden | Janet Adam Smith | Richard Pyke | Sacheverell Sitwell | Malcolm Letts | *and edited by* | R. S. Lambert | *London* | Faber and Faber Limited | *24 Russell Square*

168 pages, and 29 plates and a map. 220 × 138 mm.

Black cloth spine, marbled cloth boards. Trimmed edges. Gilt lettered on spine.

2352 copies printed. Published 7 November 1935 at 10*s*. 6*d*.

CONTENTS

Pp. 103–117, "Venice, Florence, Rome and Naples" by Sacheverell Sitwell [revised and expanded from *The Listener*, 14–21 August 1935]

b. *First edition, American issue*

Note: This issue, printed in America, was published by E. P. Dutton & Co., Inc., on 22 January 1937 at $2.50. 1500 copies were printed. Bound in black cloth spine, rough pink and blue patterned paper boards. The contents are as in sB12a.

First edition

[*Within an ornamental border*]

DEAR MISS HEBER | An Eighteenth Century | Corres-
spondence | [*short ornamental rule*] | *Edited by* | FRANCIS
BAMFORD | *With introduction by* | GEORGIA & SACHEVE-
RELL | SITWELL | [*short ornamental rule*] | MCMXXXVI |
CONSTABLE · ORANGE STREET | LONDON

336 pages. 203 × 131 mm.

Smooth blue and black mottled cloth boards. Trimmed edges. Gilt
lettered on spine.

2000 copies printed. Published 26 November 1936 at 8*s.* 6*d.*

CONTENTS

Pp. xiii–xxxi, "Preface" by Georgia Sitwell—pp. xxxiii–xl, "Introduction" by Sacheverell Sitwell

sB14 CLASSICAL CRUISE TO GREECE 1938

First edition

[*No title; being the Messageries Maritimes' prospectus for the
cruise, printed in black on orange paper.*]

6 pages. 275 × 110 mm, folded.

Unbound folder.

Distributed free by the Company and their agents early in 1938, as
prospectus for cruise by S/S *Champollion* 11 April–1 May 1938.

CONTENTS

P. 2, "A Classical Cruise" by Sacheverell Sitwell

sB15 INTERNATIONAL CYCLOPEDIA [1938]
OF MUSIC AND MUSICIANS

First edition

[*Within a rectangular ruled frame*]

THE INTERNATIONAL | CYCLOPEDIA | OF MUSIC | AND |
MUSICIANS | [*decoration*] | EDITED BY | OSCAR THOMP-

SON | Music critic, *New York Sun*; editor, *Musical* | *America*; author, *Debussy, Man and Artist; The* | *American Singer; How to Understand Music*; etc. | DODD, MEAD & COMPANY · NEW YORK | 1939

2304 pages. 276 × 197 mm.

Dark blue buckram boards. Blue sprinkled top, other edges trimmed. Blue end-papers. Blue and white head and tail bands. Blind- and gilt-stamped on upper cover, gilt stamped on spine with light blue panels.

6000 copies printed. Published 12 December 1938 [*sic*] at $12.50.

CONTENTS

Pp. 1020–1025, "Franz Liszt" by Sacheverell Sitwell

sB16   THE CALL OF THE SIREN   1939

First edition

The Call of the | Siren. By Alex- | ander Polovtsoff | Selwyn & Blount, *Publishers*, Paternoster | House, Paternoster Row, London, E.C. 4

284 pages (including 28 pp. advertisements), and 12 plates from drawings by F. Galante. 214 × 138 mm.

Pink cloth boards. Trimmed edges. Lettered in black on spine.

Published 2 March 1939 at 10*s.* 6*d.* 1000 copies printed, of which 50 bound copies and 500 copies in sheets were destroyed by enemy action in 1941.

CONTENTS

Pp. 11–17, "Introduction" by Sacheverell Sitwell

sB17   MASSINE   1939

First edition

MASSINE | *Camera Studies by Gordon Anthony* | *With an Appreciation by Sacheverell Sitwell* | *London* | *George Routledge & Sons Ltd.* | *Broadway House: 68–74 Carter Lane, E.C.*

104 pages. 314 × 251 mm.

Green cloth boards. Trimmed edges. Gilt lettered on spine and upper cover.

1500 copies printed. Published 16 June 1939 at 25*s*.

Pp. 13–34, "An Appreciation of Leonide Massine" by Sacheverell Sitwell

sB18   THE FUCHSIA ANNUAL   1939

First edition

THE | FUCHSIA ANNUAL | 1939 | THE OFFICIAL PUB-
LICATION OF | THE FUCHSIA SOCIETY. | Copies may be
obtained from the Honorary Secretary, | W. W. White-
man, | Abbots Lodge, | Sandhurst, | Gloucester, | England. |
Price 5/–. | SECOND YEAR OF ISSUE. | Copyright. All
rights reserved. | [*rule*] | T. W. COLE & SONS, LTD.,
PRINTERS, GLOUCESTER.

64 pages (including advertisements), and 10 plates. 225 × 148 mm.

Red paper wrappers, stapled. Trimmed edges. Lettered on upper cover.

Published in Autumn 1939 at 5*s*.

Pp. 17–22, "An Argument for Victorian Fuchsias" by Sacheverell Sitwell

sB18*A*   A SELECTION OF RARE   1940
              BOOKS AND MANUSCRIPTS

First edition

Catalogue Thirteen January, 1940 | A Selection of | RARE
BOOKS | and MANUSCRIPTS from | FAMOUS LIBRARIES |
With a foreword by SACHEVERELL SITWELL | OFFERED
FOR SALE ON THE FOLLOWING TERMS | [*twelve lines*] |

[short rule] | *[nine lines]* | *[short rule]* | REGent 3209 | 26
OLD BOND STREET, LONDON, W.I | IFAN KYRLE
FLETCHER

44 pages. 213 × 138 mm.

White paper wrappers. Stapled. Printed in black, with black-and-white reproductions, on each side of both covers.

Distributed as bookseller's catalogue

CONTENTS

Pp. 3–4 "Foreword" by Sacheverell Sitwell. [Concerning books from the Hafod library.]

sB19   BALLET—TO POLAND   1940

a. *First edition, ordinary copies*

BALLET—TO POLAND | EDITED BY | ARNOLD L.
HASKELL | DECORATED BY | KAY AMBROSE | IN AID OF |
THE POLISH RELIEF FUND | ADAM AND CHARLES
BLACK | 4, 5 AND 6 SOHO SQUARE LONDON W.I 1940

156 pages, and 13 unnumbered plates. 245 × 184 mm.

Fawn cloth boards. Trimmed edges. End-papers decorated by Kay Ambrose. Stamped in red on spine and upper cover.

5000 copies printed. Published 21 May 1940 at 12s. 6d.

CONTENTS

Pp. 17–19, "The Sleeping Beauty at the London Alhambra, 1921" by Sacheverell Sitwell

b. *First edition, special copies*
[Title as in ordinary copies]

158 pages, and 13 unnumbered plates, with certificate following title leaf: "This Edition is limited to One Hundred copies all of which are for sale. This is No." [in ink, with editor's and decorator's autograph signatures]. 245 × 183 mm.

Buff buckram boards. Top edge red, others trimmed. End-papers decorated by Kay Ambrose. Gilt stamped on spine and upper cover.

100 copies printed. Published 21 May 1940 at 2 guineas. (Some extra copies—"not more than 25"—were in fact printed.)

CONTENTS

As in ordinary copies

sB20 COUNTRY HOUSE BAROQUE 1940

First edition

COUNTRY HOUSE | BAROQUE | *Photographs of* | *Eighteenth Century Ornament, mostly Stucco-Work* | *in English and Irish Country Houses* | *and in some Dublin Houses* | BY | ANTHONY AYSCOUGH | *With a Foreword by* | SACHE-VERELL SITWELL | *and a descriptive text by* | M. JOUR-DAIN | [*cross*] | HEYWOOD HILL LTD | 17 CURZON STREET · LONDON · W.1 | 1940

108 pages. 237 × 163 mm.
Yellow cloth boards. Trimmed edges. Lettered in red on spine.
Published in July 1940 at 12*s*. 6*d*.

CONTENTS

Pp. 7–10, "Foreword" by Sacheverell Sitwell—pp. 11–17, "English and Irish Stucco-Work" by M. Jourdain

sB21 PALMYRA OF THE NORTH 1942

First edition

CHRISTOPHER MARSDEN | [*decoration*] | PALMYRA | OF THE NORTH | *The First Days of* | St. Petersburg | [*decoration*] | *with a preface by* | SACHEVERELL SITWELL | FABER AND FABER LIMITED | 24 Russell Square | London

280 pages, and 15 plates. 217 × 140 mm.
Lilac cloth boards. Top edge pink, others trimmed. Lettered in silver on spine. (See below.)
2000 copies printed. Published 29 October 1942 at 12*s*. 6*d*. (Later bindings are found with coloured, not silver, lettering on spine.)

Pp. 5–13, "Preface" by Sacheverell Sitwell

sB22   SIR HENRY WOOD   [1944]

First edition

SIR HENRY WOOD | FIFTY YEARS OF | THE PROMS | *To Sir Henry Wood* | How many thousand times have you upheld | A batonette between two multitudes, | Each hushed to ready and receptive moods, | Waiting your mind's impulsion, that will bring | Oneness to beat, to breath and stroken string, | And beauty's presence, holding the house spelled? | Ah, many times to me, as to the race, | You have compelled this ecstasy of law | Lifting the human pattern from its flaw, | In the dry desert giving living dew. | Lord of sweet Music and of Langham Place, | Today, this Nation thanks and praises you. | *JOHN MASEFIELD* | THE BRITISH BROADCASTING CORPORATION | BROADCASTING HOUSE | LONDON, W.1

64 pages, and 2 plates. 210 × 156 mm.

White paper wrappers, stapled. Trimmed edges. Printed in blue on upper cover.

57,000 copies printed. Published 12 June 1944 at 2s. 6d., as B.B.C. Publication no. 1762.

CONTENTS

Pp. 60–64, "When such works were new" by Sacheverell Sitwell

sB22*A*   EXHIBITION OF MODERN   1944
            BRAZILIAN PAINTINGS

First edition

EXHIBITION OF | MODERN BRAZILIAN | PAINTINGS | Arranged by His Majesty's Government | in the United

Kingdom of Great Britain | and Northern Ireland | Being a collection of 168 paintings and | drawings presented by 70 Artists of Brazil | to be sold for the benefit of the Royal | Air Force Benevolent Fund | ROYAL ACADEMY OF ARTS | PICCADILLY, W.1 | November 23rd–December 13th | 10 a.m.–5 p.m.

36 pages, and 6 plates. 184 × 124 mm.

Pale green wrappers, stapled. Trimmed edges. Printed in green on covers.

Published as catalogue of the exhibition in the Royal Academy, organised by the British Council, in November 1944.

CONTENTS

Pp. 3–7, "Preface" by Sacheverell Sitwell

sB23 EXHIBITION OF HISTORICAL 1945 AND BRITISH WALLPAPERS

First edition

Exhibition of | Historical and British | Wallpapers | *organised by* | *the* | *Central Institute of Art & Design* | *National Gallery London* | *for* | *the British Wallpaper Industry* | MAY 1945

48 pages. 285 × 212 mm.

Pink and gold decorated printed wrappers. Stapled. Trimmed edges. Printed in black, with black and yellow and pink display titling, on upper cover, with blue-framed white panels.

Published at the exhibition at the Suffolk Galleries in May 1945 at 1s. 6d.

CONTENTS

Pp. 5–7, "Introduction" by Sacheverell Sitwell

First edition

DIVERSION | EDITED BY | HESTER W. CHAPMAN | *and* | PRINCESS ROMANOVSKY-PAVLOVSKY | *Published for the benefit of* | *the Yugoslav Relief Society* | [*device*] | COLLINS | 14 ST. JAMES'S PLACE LONDON | 1946

160 pages, and 2 plates. 194 × 125 mm.

Black cloth boards. Trimmed edges. Gilt lettered on spine.

Published 23 September 1946 at 7s. 6d.

CONTENTS

Pp. 31–33, "The Truth of Ghosts" by Sacheverell Sitwell

sB25   IRISES   1946

First edition

IRISES | THEIR CULTURE AND SELECTION | BY | GWENDOLYN ANLEY | FOREWORD | BY | SACHEVERELL SITWELL | LONDON: W. H. & L. COLLINGRIDGE LTD. | 2–10 Tavistock Street, Covent Garden, W.C.2

136 pages, and 10 plates. 215 × 132 mm.

Blue cloth boards. Trimmed edges. Lettered in maroon on upper cover, and in maroon and silver on spine, with maroon panel.

3000 copies printed. Published 12 November 1946 at 8s. 6d.

CONTENTS

Pp. v–xvi, "Foreword" by Sacheverell Sitwell

sB26 ENGLISH CHURCH MONUMENTS 1946

a. *First edition*

[*Within a border*]

ENGLISH CHURCH | MONUMENTS | 1510 to 1840 | *By* | KATHARINE A. ESDAILE | *With an Introduction by* |

SACHEVERELL SITWELL | LONDON | B. T. BATSFORD
LTD | 15 NORTH AUDLEY STREET, W.I | *and at Malvern*
Wells, Worcestershire

152 pages, and 41 plates. 223 × 146 mm.

Blue cloth boards. Top edge blue, others trimmed. Lettered in red on
spine.

9125 copies printed. Published in December 1946 at 21*s.*

CONTENTS

Pp. 1–43, "Introduction" by Sacheverell Sitwell

b. *First edition, American copies*

Note: 500/525 copies imported by Oxford University Press, New
York, with their imprint. Similar binding and the same contents as in
sB26a. Published 24 July 1947 at $4.00.

sB27   THE ROMANTIC BALLET   1948
        FROM CONTEMPORARY PRINTS

First edition

The | ROMANTIC BALLET | from Contemporary Prints |
With an Introduction | *and Notes on the Prints* | *by* | SACHE-
VERELL SITWELL | B. T. BATSFORD LTD | LONDON:
NEW YORK : TORONTO : SYDNEY

48 pages. 233 × 184 mm.

Grey paper boards. Trimmed edges. Lettered in blue on upper cover
and spine.

50,000 copies printed. Published in October 1948 at 6*s.* 6*d.*, in the
"Batsford Colour Books."

CONTENTS

Pp. 1–12, "Introduction" and "Notes to Ballet Prints" by Sacheverell
Sitwell

First edition

TROPICAL BIRDS | from Plates by John Gould | *With an Introduction* | *and Notes on the Plates* | *by* | SACHEVERELL SITWELL | B. T. BATSFORD LTD | LONDON : NEW YORK : TORONTO : SYDNEY

48 pages. 233 × 184 mm.

Yellow paper boards. Trimmed edges. Green lettered on spine and upper cover.

51,000 copies printed. Published in October 1948 at 6*s*. 6*d*., in the "Batsford Colour Books."

CONTENTS

Pp. 1–12, "Introduction" and "Notes to Plates" by Sacheverell Sitwell

sB29　　　INKY BLOSSOMS　　　1949

First edition

INKY BLOSSOMS | A Collection of Round-About Papers | by | C. B. MORTLOCK | (URBANUS) | With an Introduction by | SACHEVERELL SITWELL | 1949 | LONDON | MAC-DONALD & EVANS

206 pages. 184 × 123 mm.

Smooth buff cloth boards. Top edge lilac, others trimmed. Lettered in red on spine.

2000 copies printed. Published 6 April 1949 at 8*s*. 6*d*.

CONTENTS

Pp. xiii–xviii, "Introduction" by Sacheverell Sitwell

sB30　　　YESTERDAY WAS MINE　　　1949

a. *First edition*

Yesterday Was Mine | *By* *PRINCESS ANNE-MARIE*

CALLIMACHI | *Whittlesey House* | MᴄGRAW-HILL
BOOK COMPANY, INC. *New York London Toronto*

284 pages. 229 × 151 mm.

Smooth black cloth boards. Trimmed edges. Gilt lettered on spine.

3495 copies printed. Published 28 April 1949 at $3.50.

CONTENTS

P. xiii, "Foreword" by Sacheverell Sitwell

b. *First edition, English issue*

Yesterday Was Mine | *By* PRINCESS ANNE-MARIE
CALLIMACHI | [*with flourishes:*] *The Falcon Press* | 6 & 7
CROWN PASSAGE PALL MALL LONDON

284 pages (including back end-papers). 214 × 136 mm.

Red cloth boards. Trimmed edges. Gilt stamped on spine. (Copies
were later remaindered in royal blue plastic boards.)

Published 11 December 1952 at 17s. 6d.

CONTENTS

As in the first edition

sB31   THE SLEEPING BEAUTY   1949

First edition

EDITED BY ARNOLD L. HASKELL | SADLER'S WELLS
BALLET BOOKS, NO. 1 | [*swelled rule*] | The | Sleeping
Beauty | *by* | SACHEVERELL SITWELL | JOY NEWTON |
TAMARA KARSAVINA | DYNELEY HUSSEY | *published for* |
THE GOVERNORS OF SADLER'S WELLS FOUNDATIONS |
[*swelled rule*] | BY THE BODLEY HEAD LONDON

56 pages, and 7 plates. 184 × 122 mm.

Pictorial coloured paper wrappers, sewn. Trimmed edges. Printed
in colours on spine and covers.

7000 copies printed. Published 15 July 1949 at 2s. 6d.

Pp. 7–19, "The Sleeping Beauty" by Sacheverell Sitwell

sB32 AUDUBON'S AMERICAN BIRDS 1949

First edition

AUDUBON'S | AMERICAN BIRDS | from Plates by J. J. Audubon | *With an Introduction* | *and Notes on the Plates* | *by* | SACHEVERELL SITWELL | B. T. BATSFORD LTD | LONDON : NEW YORK : TORONTO : SYDNEY

48 pages. 233 × 184 mm.

Pale blue paper boards. Trimmed edges. Lettered in dark blue on upper cover and spine.

25,000 copies printed. Published in July 1949 at 6s. 6d., in the "Batsford Colour Books."

CONTENTS

Pp. 1–12, "Introduction" and "Notes on the Plates" by Sacheverell Sitwell

sB33 GALLERY OF FASHION 1949
1790–1822

First edition

GALLERY OF FASHION | 1790–1822 | from Plates by Heideloff and Ackermann | *With an Introduction* | *by* | SACHEVERELL SITWELL | *Notes on the Plates* | *by* | Doris Langley Moore | B. T. BATSFORD LTD | LONDON : NEW YORK : TORONTO : SYDNEY

48 pages. 233 × 184 mm.

Green paper boards. Trimmed edges. Lettered in red on upper cover and spine.

25,000 copies printed. Published in October 1949 at 6s. 6d., in the "Batsford Colour Books."

CONTENTS

Pp. 1–10, "Introduction" by Sacheverell Sitwell; pp. 11–12, "Notes on the Plates" by Doris Langley Moore

a. *First edition, ordinary copies*

[*Red*] PETER CARL | FABERGE | [*black*] Goldsmith and Jeweller to the Imperial Russian Court | and the principal Crowned Heads of Europe | *An Illustrated Record and Review of* | *his Life and Work, A.D. 1846–1920* | *by* | [*red*] HENRY CHARLES BAINBRIDGE | [*black*] With a Foreword by Sacheverell Sitwell | [*decoration*] | B. T. BATSFORD LTD. | *Publishers by Appointment to H.M. Queen Mary* | 15 NORTH AUDLEY STREET · LONDON W.1 | NEW YORK · TORONTO · SYDNEY

194 pages. 290 × 224 mm.

Red cloth boards. Top edge red, others trimmed. Gilt stamped on spine and upper cover.

1000 copies printed. Published 7 November 1949 at 7 guineas. (Certificate on p. [iv]: "This work is presented in two editions as follows: (1) An Edition de Luxe, the text printed on hand-made paper and the work specially bound in half-Niger morocco. (2) A Library Edition, printed on superior machine-made paper and bound in cloth. The Edition de Luxe consists of 250 copies for sale in Great Britain and 100 copies for the U.S.A. The Library Edition comprises 1,000 copies for sale in Great Britain and 750 copies for the U.S.A. . . .")

CONTENTS

Pp. vii–xi, "Foreword" by Sacheverell Sitwell

b. *First edition, special copies*
[*Title, pagination and size as in ordinary copies*]

Half blue Niger morocco, natural buckram boards. Top edge gilt, others trimmed. Gilt lettered, with raised bands, on spine. Yellow and blue headband.

250 copies printed (see Certificate in ordinary copies, above). Published 7 November 1949 at 14 guineas.

CONTENTS

As in ordinary copies

c–d. First edition, American ordinary and special copies

Note: These, printed in England, were published in New York by Messrs. Batsford some time in 1949, at $35.00 and $50.00 respectively. 750 and 100 copies, respectively, were printed. Except for variations in the imprint on the title and in the wording of the certificate of limitation, they are as sB34a–b.

sB35   LOAN EXHIBITION OF THE   1949
WORKS OF CARL FABERGÉ

First edition

[*Coat of arms & By Appointment* . . .] WARTSKI [*coat of arms & By Appointment* . . .] | LTD. | 138 REGENT STREET, LONDON, W. 1 | AND AT LLANDUDNO | A LOAN EXHIBI-TION | OF THE WORKS OF | CARL FABERGÉ | JEWELLER AND GOLDSMITH TO | THE IMPERIAL COURT OF RUSSIA | 1846–1920 | NOVEMBER 8th–25th, 1949

36 pages. 229 × 138 mm.

Grey stiff paper wrappers, stapled. Trimmed edges. Printed in red, black and yellow on covers.

According to Messrs. Wartski, "about 5000" copies printed. Published at the exhibition on 8 November 1949 at 5s.

CONTENTS

Pp. 1–8, "Foreword" by Sacheverell Sitwell

sB36   THE BEDSIDE LILLIPUT   1950

First edition

[*Within a border*]

THE BEDSIDE | LILLIPUT | HULTON PRESS LTD | 1950

480 pages. 197 × 135 mm.

Green cloth boards. Trimmed edges. Gilt lettered on a red panel on the spine.

25,000 copies printed. Published 26 October 1950 at 10s. 6d.

Pp. 59–63, "L'Inconnue de la Seine" by Sacheverell Sitwell [from *Lilliput*, April 1945]

sB37   BARON AT THE BALLET   1950

a. *First edition, ordinary copies*

BARON | AT | THE BALLET | [*swelled rule*] | *Introduction and Commentary* | *by* | ARNOLD L. HASKELL | *Foreword by* | SACHEVERELL SITWELL | COLLINS | ST JAMES'S PLACE, LONDON | 1950

224 pages, and 8 plates. 278 × 215 mm.

Red cloth boards. Trimmed edges. Gilt stamped on spine and upper cover.

17,500 copies printed. Published 30 November 1950 at 30*s*.

Pp. 7–8, "Foreword" by Sacheverell Sitwell

b. *First edition, special copies*
[*Title and size as in ordinary copies*]

224 pages, and 8 plates, with certificate on p. [2]: "This volume is number [in ink] of an edition limited to 150 copies, signed by the authors" [autograph signatures of Baron and Haskell].

Full green morocco. Top edge gilt, others trimmed. Gilt lettered on spine, gilt frames on covers. Ivory headband.

150 copies printed. Published 30 November 1950 at 4 guineas.

As in ordinary copies

sB38   DIVERSION   1950

First edition

[*Ornamental capitals*] DIVERSION | Twenty-two Authors on | the Lively Arts | [*row of O's*] | edited by | JOHN SUTRO | 24 PHOTOGRAVURE PLATES | AND | 40 DRAWINGS IN LINE | [*row of O's*] | MAX PARRISH · LONDON

224 pages, and 12 plates. 222 × 161 mm.

Brown cloth boards. Trimmed edges. Decorated end-papers. Gilt lettered on spine.

5000 copies printed. Published 4 December 1950 at 18s. 6d.

CONTENTS

Pp. 35–46, "The Sacred Rites of Pride" by Sacheverell Sitwell

sB39   THE PAVEMENT AND THE SKY   1951

First edition

THE PAVEMENT AND | THE SKY | [*swelled rule*] | TOM CLARKSON | *with a foreword by* | SACHEVERELL SITWELL | [*device*] | WINGATE | LONDON AND NEW YORK

216 pages. 183 × 123 mm.

Blue cloth boards. Trimmed edges. Gilt lettered on spine.

4000 copies printed. Published 20 June 1951 at 10s. 6d.

CONTENTS

Pp. 7–8, "Foreword" by Sacheverell Sitwell

sB40   SPECIAL CORONATION   1953
EXHIBITION OF CARL FABERGÉ

First edition

Special Coronation Exhibition of | the work of CARL | FABERGÉ | including selected items | from the Royal Collection | at Sandringham | WARTSKI LIMITED | 138 Regent Street London W 1 | *and at Llandudno*

32 pages, and 5 plates. 248 × 172 mm.

Grey paper wrappers. Unsewn. Trimmed edges. Printed on upper cover in red, blue and black.

5024 copies printed. Published 20 May 1953 at 5s.

CONTENTS

Pp. [3–5], "Foreword" by Sacheverell Sitwell

First edition

RUDDING PARK | [*heraldic decoration*] | *A Brief Description
and Guide*

24 pages. 139 × 225 mm.

Yellow stiff paper wrappers, stapled. Trimmed edges. Lettered in
black on front.

3000 copies printed. Published at Rudding Park, Harrogate, in early
March 1954 at 2s. (There have been five reprints, with "certain
changes both in illustration and in text.")

CONTENTS

Page [5], "Foreword" by Sacheverell Sitwell

sB41*A*   PAINTING IS A PLEASURE   1953

First edition

Coronation Exhibition of Paintings | "Painting is a Plea-
sure" | at The Trafford Gallery | 119 Mount Street W.1. |
Gros 2021 | Wednesday May 6 to Friday June 12 1953

20 pages. 232 × 140 mm.

Green paper wrappers, decorated by Cecil Beaton. Stapled. Trimmed
edges. Lettered in black on the decoration on upper cover. Published
by Toc H at the exhibition at the Trafford Gallery, May–June 1953.

CONTENTS

Page 2, Foreword by Sacheverell Sitwell

sB42   ALBUM DE REDOUTÉ   1954

a. *First edition, ordinary copies*

[*Within a ruled and ornamental border*]

[*Three words in decorative type:*] | ALBUM | DE | REDOUTÉ |
WITH TWENTY-FIVE FACSIMILE COLOUR PLATES |

FROM THE EDITION OF 1824 | AND A NEW REDOUTÉ |
BIBLIOGRAPHY | SACHEVERELL SITWELL | AND
ROGER MADOL | COLLINS | 1954

561 × 359 mm.

20 pp. (excluding plates): [1] half-title; [2] illustration; [3] title; [4]
"This book has been made and designed for William Collins, 14 St.
James's Place, London by George Rainbird and Ruari McLean at
8 Wyndham Place, London W.1. The plates have been reproduced
from a complete copy of the *Album de Redouté* . . . [and] have been
printed in six- and eight-colour photo-litho offset and collotype
monochrome by Van Leer of Amsterdam. The Text has been set and
printed in Monotype Bodoni by Joh. Enschedé en Zonen in Haarlem.
Original XIXth-century Didot types have been used for the title page
and headings. 250 numbered copies have been printed on mouldmade
paper made by Schut of Heelsum, and 2000 unnumbered copies on
specially made white cartridge. Bound by Mansell of London".
[5] Contents, the Colour Plates; 6–20 text.

Frontispiece sewn in, and 24 plates bound in.

Black buckram spine, yellow-green paper boards. Trimmed edges.
Decorated end-papers. Gilt lettered down spine.

2000 copies printed. Published 18 October 1954 at 10 guineas.

CONTENTS

Pp. 6–10, "The Pictures of Redouté" by Sacheverell Sitwell

b. *First edition, special copies*
[*Title, size and illustrations as in ordinary copies*]

20 pp. (excluding plates): As in ordinary copies, except p. [4]:
". . . Mansell of London. This is copy number" [in ink, with the
authors' autograph signatures].

Dark green leather spine and corners, marbled paper boards. Top
edge gilt, others trimmed. Marbled end-papers. Gilt lettered on
spine. Slip case of dark green cloth and light green printed paper
boards.

250 copies printed. Published 18 October 1954 at 20 guineas.

CONTENTS

As in ordinary copies

c. *First edition, subscription copies*

Note: I have not seen any of these copies. The following is derived from the publishers (who do not have a copy), the prospectus, and catalogue 17 (1967) of C. K. Broadhurst, Southport, item 1519.

The "subscription edition" consisted of 25 copies, quarter-bound vellum by Hiscox of London, with vellum tips on heavy boards of hand printed French paper of XVIII century design, with a slip case. Each copy contained an original Redouté plate from *Les Liliacées*, and was signed by the authors. Published on 18 October 1954 at 50 guineas.

sB43 THE BOOK OF WALLPAPER 1954

First edition

THE BOOK OF | WALLPAPER | A HISTORY AND AN APPRECIATION | BY | E. A. ENTWISLE | WITH AN INTRODUCTION BY SACHEVERELL SITWELL | [*decoration*] | [*device*] | LONDON | [*brief rule*] | ARTHUR BARKER

152 pages, and 34 plates. 246 × 185 mm.

Grey cloth boards. Top edge red, others trimmed. Lettered in red on spine.

Published 22 October 1954 at 30*s*.

CONTENTS

Pp. 11–18, "Introduction" by Sacheverell Sitwell

sB44 IMPERIAL RUSSIAN 1955
PORCELAIN FIGURES

First edition

[*Cover, printed black on lilac*]

[*Decoration*] | IMPERIAL RUSSIAN | PORCELAIN FIGURES

16 pages (including covers), and 12 plates. 153 × 203 mm.

Stiff paper wrappers, sewn. Trimmed edges. Printed in black on lilac on upper cover; lower cover white and blank.

1000 copies printed. Published by Wartski Ltd. in late May 1955 at 5s.

CONTENTS

Pp. [3–6], "Russian Porcelain Figures" by Sacheverell Sitwell

sB45 A BIBLIOGRAPHY OF P. H. GOSSE 1955

a. *First edition, ordinary copies*

A BIBLIOGRAPHY OF | THE FIRST EDITIONS OF |
PHILIP HENRY GOSSE, F.R.S. | BY | PETER STAGEMAN |
WITH INTRODUCTORY ESSAYS BY | SACHEVERELL
SITWELL | AND | GEOFFREY LAPAGE | [*device*] | 1955 |
THE GOLDEN HEAD PRESS, LTD. | CAMBRIDGE

100 pages, and 4 plates, with certificate on p. [iv]: "This edition . . .
consists of 480 copies for sale . . . Number 1 to 50 are specially bound
in quarter leather. Number 51 to 480 are bound in cloth . . . This copy
is number . . ." [in ink]. 215 × 136 mm.

Crimson cloth boards. Trimmed edges. White paper label, lettered in
black, pasted to upper cover.

430 copies printed. Published 9 August 1955 at 2 guineas.

CONTENTS

Pp. 7–16, "The Illustrations of Philip Henry Gosse" by Sacheverell
Sitwell

b. *First edition, special copies*
[*Title, pagination and size as in ordinary copies*]

Crimson leather spine, red cloth boards. Trimmed edges. Gilt lettered
on spine, with two raised bands.

50 copies printed (see certificate in ordinary copies, above). Published
9 August 1955 at 4½ guineas.

CONTENTS

As in ordinary copies

360

sB46 OLD CARNATIONS AND PINKS 1955

a. *First edition, ordinary copies*

[*Red*] Old Carnations | and Pinks | [*black*] [*ornamental half-
rule*] | by | C. Oscar Moreton | WITH AN INTRODUCTION
BY SACHEVERELL SITWELL | AND EIGHT COLOUR
PLATES BY RORY McEWEN | [*red device*] | [*black*] GEORGE
RAINBIRD | *in association with* | COLLINS | 1955

64 pages, and 8 plates. 342 × 228 mm.

Dark green buckram spine. Pictorial paper boards. Top edge terracotta, others trimmed. Gilt lettered on spine. (Remainder copies—
see below—have turquoise cloth spine, top edge plain.)

3000 copies printed (certificate on p. [ii] reads: "100 numbered copies,
signed by the author and artist, have been printed on tub-sized rag
wove paper ... and 3,000 copies have been printed on cartridge
paper ..."). Published 19 September 1955 at 3 guineas. (About 300
or 400 copies were remaindered in a variant binding—see above—
about three years later, at 18s.)

CONTENTS

Pp. vii–ix, "Introduction" by Sacheverell Sitwell

b. *First edition, special copies*
[*Title, pagination and size as in ordinary copies*]

Half morocco boards, remainder pictorial paper boards. Top edge
gilt, others trimmed. Gilt lettered on spine.

100 copies printed (see certificate in ordinary copies, which is here
followed by: "This is number" [number, with artist's and author's
autograph signatures]). Published 19 September 1955 at 7 guineas.

CONTENTS

As in ordinary copies

sB47   THE SPOKEN WORD   1955

First edition
THE SPOKEN | WORD | [*swelled rule*] | *A Selection from*
Twenty-Five Years | *of 'The Listener,' chosen and* | *introduced*

by | RICHARD CHURCH | COLLINS | ST JAMES'S PLACE, LONDON | 1955

320 pages. 209 × 139 mm.

Blue cloth boards. Trimmed edges. Gilt lettered on spine.

4035 copies printed. Published 17 October 1955 at 16s.

CONTENTS

Pp. 119–123, "Epstein on Himself" [from *The Listener*, 19 December 1940] by Sacheverell Sitwell

sB48   GALA PERFORMANCE   1955

a. *First edition, ordinary copies*

Gala | *Performance* | *[swelled rule]* | EDITED BY | *Arnold Haskell* | *Mark Bonham Carter* | *Michael Wood* | *With a Foreword by* | *H.R.H. The Princess Margaret* | COLLINS | ST JAMES'S PLACE, LONDON | 1955

248 pages, and 8 plates. 278 × 212 mm.

Black cloth boards. Top edge black, others trimmed. Gilt lettered on spine.

14,500 copies printed. Published 17 November 1955 at 2 guineas.

CONTENTS

Pp. 13–35, "Prologue" by Sacheverell Sitwell

b. *First edition, special copies*

[100 special copies were published on the same day. Bound in lambskin, top edge gilt, in slip case. The price was 105s. Contents as in the ordinary copies.]

sB49   GLYNDEBOURNE   1956
MOZART BICENTENARY FESTIVAL
PROGRAMME BOOK

First edition

[In black on a yellow panel]

[*Coat of Arms*] | Glyndebourne Festival Opera | Mozart Bicentenary Festival | 14 JUNE–14 AUGUST | 1956 | Programme Book

100 pages. 303 × 238 mm.

Yellow paper wrappers, decorated by Oliver Messel. Trimmed edges. Gilt lettered on upper cover.

Published at Glyndebourne in Spring 1956 at 5s., with "a circulation approaching 20,000" (according to Glyndebourne Festival Opera).

CONTENTS

Pp. 19–23, "Wolfgang Amadeus Mozart (1756–1956)" by Sacheverell Sitwell

sB50   THE SELECTIVE EYE   1956

a. *First edition*

The Selective Eye | [*brown*] 1956/1957 | [*black*] AN ANTHOLOGY OF THE BEST FROM L'ŒIL, | THE EUROPEAN ART MAGAZINE | [*brown*] EDITED BY GEORGES AND ROSAMOND BERNIER | [*black*] WITH 51 PAGES IN COLOR | [*brown*] G. & R. BERNIER PARIS LAUSANNE | REYNAL & CO. NEW YORK

192 pages. 311 × 239 mm.

Glazed pictorial boards, plastic spine. Unsewn. Trimmed edges. Gilt lettered on spine, printed in white on upper cover and in black on lower cover.

10,000 copies printed. Published in October 1956 by Reynal & Co. at $8.75.

CONTENTS

Pp. 65–68, "The Friday Mosque" by Sacheverell Sitwell. (Despite the note on p. [4], this was specially written for this volume and did not originally appear in L'ŒIL.)

b. *First edition, English copies*

Note: These copies, identical with the above except for a change of imprint on title and spine, were published by A. Zwemmer Ltd., in London on 9 November 1956 at 45s. 2000 copies were printed.

sB51   AMERICAN NOTES AND   1957
        PICTURES FROM ITALY

First edition (of introduction)

AMERICAN NOTES | AND | PICTURES FROM ITALY | *By* |
CHARLES DICKENS | *With Twelve Illustrations by Marcus
Stone | Samuel Palmer and Clarkson Stanfield | and an
Introduction by* | SACHEVERELL SITWELL | [*sepia decoration*] | LONDON | OXFORD UNIVERSITY PRESS | NEW
YORK TORONTO | 1957

452 pages, and 13 plates. 184 × 121 mm.

Brown cloth boards. Top edge brown, others trimmed. Lettered in
silver on spine.

5250 copies printed. Published 17 October 1957 at 12*s.* 6*d.* in "The
New Oxford Illustrated Dickens."

CONTENTS

Pp. [v]–x, "Introduction" by Sacheverell Sitwell

sB52   GLYNDEBOURNE   1958
        PARIS PROGRAMME BOOK

First edition

[*Within a lilac border*]

[*Coat of arms*] | GLYNDEBOURNE | *Festival Opera* | [*lilac*]
1958 | [*black*] *Paris* | *8 May–16 May*

56 pages. 304 × 239 mm.

Paper wrappers decorated in green and gold by Oliver Messel,
lettered in gold on upper cover. Trimmed edges.

4000 copies printed. Published in May 1958 on the occasion of the
Company's visit to Paris. (This edition is quite different from that
published for the English 1958 Festival at Glyndebourne.)

CONTENTS

P. 16, "Avant-propos" de Sacheverell Sitwell

[This item has now been placed in correct chronological order at sB41*A*]

sB54   AUSTRIA   1959

a. *First edition*

AUSTRIA | [*swelled rule*] | SACHEVERELL SITWELL | TONI SCHNEIDERS | [*short swelled rule*] | 194 PHOTO-GRAVURE PLATES | 7 PLATES IN COLOUR | [*device*] | THAMES AND HUDSON · LONDON

212 pages. 306 × 217 mm.

Green cloth boards. Trimmed edges. Gilt stamped on spine and upper cover.

2000 copies printed. Published 28 May 1959 at 50*s*.

CONTENTS

"Austria" by Sacheverell Sitwell, pp. 5–22; photographs by Toni Schneiders, pp. 23–184; "Historical Notes" by Hans Bernhard, pp. 185–196

b. *First edition, American copies*

AUSTRIA | [*swelled rule*] | SACHEVERELL SITWELL | TONI SCHNEIDERS | [*short swelled rule*] | 194 PHOTO-GRAVURE PLATES | 7 PLATES IN COLOUR | A STUDIO BOOK | THE VIKING PRESS · NEW YORK

Note: 2000 copies were imported and published in 1959. The contents are as in sB54a.

sB55   POEMS OF OUR TIME   1959

[*For description see* EB47]

CONTENTS

Pp. 322–325, "Ballad: White Rose"—"Rosario d'Arabeschi: Poems and Rose Portraits, I–II" by Sacheverell Sitwell

sB56   A CENTURY OF SANDERSON   1960

First edition

A CENTURY OF | *SANDERSON* | 1860–1960 | LONDON |
[*two rules*] | ARTHUR SANDERSON & SONS LTD | BERNERS
STREET W1

44 pages. 246 × 182 mm.
Grey paper wrappers. Trimmed edges. Lettered in white on covers.
60,000 copies printed. Privately distributed by Messrs. Sanderson on
19 February 1960.

CONTENTS

"Wallpapers and Chintzes: a little survey" by Sacheverell Sitwell,
pp. 9–26

sB57   TRAVELLER IN THE ORIENT   1960

a. *First edition*

TRAVELLER | IN THE ORIENT | MARTIN HÜRLIMANN |
Introduction by Sacheverell Sitwell | *223 photogravure plates* |
41 in colour | [*device*] | THAMES AND HUDSON

340 pages. 241 × 206 mm.
Blue cloth boards. Trimmed edges. Device gilt-stamped on upper
cover, gilt lettering on spine.
4000 copies printed. Published 26 October 1960 at 63*s*.

CONTENTS

Pp. 7–10, "Introduction" by Sacheverell Sitwell. (The German
edition of Hürlimann's book was published in 1959, without the
introduction)

b. *First edition, American copies*

JOURNEY THROUGH | THE ORIENT | *Text and photographs*
by | MARTIN HÜRLIMANN | *Introduction by Sacheverell*
Sitwell | A STUDIO BOOK | THE VIKING PRESS · NEW
YORK

Note: 3500 copies were imported and published in 1960 at $15. The
contents are as in sB57a.

a. *First edition*

[*Red:*] Great | Houses | of | Europe | Edited by [*black:*]
SACHEVERELL SITWELL | [*red:*] Photographs by [*black:*]
EDWIN SMITH | WEIDENFELD AND NICOLSON | 20 New
Bond Street London W1 | [*caption to frontispiece*]

320 pages. 312 × 241 mm.

Red buckram boards. Trimmed edges. Decorated end-papers. Gilt
stamped on blue panels on spine.

4000 copies printed. Published 27 October 1961 at 90*s*.

CONTENTS

Edited by Sacheverell Sitwell. "Introduction" by Sacheverell Sitwell,
pp. 8–17

b. *First edition, American copies*

[7000 copies were imported by G. P. Putnam's Sons, New York. The
date of publication was 24 October 1961 and the price was $22.50.
The contents are as in the English copies. The English publishers are
the holders of the copyright and were the designers of the book.]

sB59   DAME EDITH SITWELL: 1962
        IN CELEBRATION OF HER 75TH
                BIRTHDAY

First edition

[*Cover, drawn by I[rene] H[awkins]:*]

DAME EDITH | SITWELL | *IN CELEBRATION* | *OF HER*
75TH BIRTHDAY | ROYAL FESTIVAL HALL | TUESDAY
9*th* OCTOBER 1962

32 pages, including covers. 245 × 184 mm.

Glossy white paper wrappers. Stapled. Trimmed edges. Upper cover
printed as above.

1968 copies printed and sold as programmes at the concert on 9
October 1962.

P. [9], "Edith Sitwell: a tribute from her younger brother" by
Sacheverell Sitwell

sB59*A*   WITLEY PARISH CHURCH   1963

First edition (of introduction)

WITLEY PARISH CHURCH | A short history and guide | to
the Parish Church of | St. Michael's and All Angels, | Great
Witley. | *Compiled by* | BERNARD G. GOODWIN, J.P.,
F.R.C.S. | *Churchwarden.* | *3rd Edition*, 1963.

20 pages. 203 × 126 mm.

Buff paper wrappers, stapled. Trimmed edges. Printed in black on
covers.

8000 copies printed. Published in late 1963 at 1*s*.

P.3, "Introduction" by Sacheverell Sitwell, dated October 1963

sB60   GREAT PALACES   1964

a. *First edition*

[*Red:*] Great Palaces | [*black:*] Introduction by Sacheverell
Sitwell | Weidenfeld and Nicolson · 20 New Bond Street
London W 1

288 pages. 313 × 240 mm.

Brown cloth boards. Trimmed edges. Pictorial end-papers. Gilt
lettered on spine.

5000 copies printed. Published 9 October 1964 at 105*s*.

Pp. 8–11, "Introduction" by Sacheverell Sitwell

b. *First edition, American copies*

[2500 copies were imported by G. P. Putnam's Sons, New York, and
were published by them in 1964 at $22.95. The contents are as in
sA60a.]

a. *First edition*

[*Black:*] *Eighteenth Century* | [*red:*] GOLD BOXES | [*black:*]
of Europe | by | A. KENNETH SNOWMAN | With a Foreword
by | SACHEVERELL SITWELL | and an Appendix by |
F. J. B. WATSON, CVO, FSA | FABER AND FABER | 24
Russell Square | London

192 pages, and 150 plates. 309 × 248 mm.

Green buckram boards. Top edge gilt, others trimmed. Gilt stamped
on spine, with black panel.

2420 copies printed. Published 15 September 1966 at 15 guineas.

CONTENTS

Pp. 29–34, "Foreword" by Sacheverell Sitwell; pp. 118–144, "Some
Remarks upon a Number of the Gold Boxes Illustrated in Colour" by
Sacheverell Sitwell

b. *First edition, American copies*

[2080 copies were imported by the Boston Book and Art Shop and
published at $60.]

a. *First edition, ordinary copies*

[*Blue:*] SOME BIRDS | AND MAMMALS | of South America |
[*black:*] by | AXEL AMUCHÁSTEGUI | with an introduction
by | SACHEVERELL SITWELL | and descriptive text by |
CARLOS SELVA ANDRADE | [*artist's monogram in blue*
| [*black:*] THE TRYON GALLERY | LONDON | in association
with George Rainbird

78 pages, and frontispiece and conjugate stub. 529 × 351 mm.

Quarter dark blue morocco, blue marbled paper boards. Top edge gilt, others trimmed. Gilt stamped on spine and front cover. Dark blue cloth board slip-case.

250 numbered copies printed for sale, and four un-numbered copies for legal deposit. Published in July 1966 at £78 15s.

CONTENTS

Pp. [11–12], "Introduction" by Sacheverell Sitwell

b. *First edition, special copies*
[*Title and size as in ordinary copies.*]

78 pages, frontispiece and conjugate stub, and original drawing and tissue guard bound in before frontispiece.

Full natural vellum. Top edge gilt, others trimmed. Facsimile of artist's signature (on paintings) stamped on front cover, gilt lettered on spine. Slip-case as with ordinary copies.

Copies A to E reserved for the artist and his friends; copies 1 to 50 published in July 1966 at £157 10s.

CONTENTS

The Introduction as in the ordinary copies. (Most of the original drawings in the special copies were later reproduced in the artist's book *Studies of Birds and Mammals of South America*, 1967.)

sB63   TIBETAN VENTURE   1967

a. *First edition*

C. G. LEWIS | TIBETAN | VENTURE | *Foreword by* | SACHE-VERELL SITWELL | ILLUSTRATED | [*device*] | ROBERT HALE · LONDON

192 pages, and 4 plates. 215 × 135 mm.
Blue cloth boards. Trimmed edges. Gilt lettered on spine.
2000 copies printed. Published 26 May 1967 at 21s.

CONTENTS

Pp. 9–10, "Foreword" by Sacheverell Sitwell

b. *First edition, American issue*

C. G. LEWIS | TIBETAN | VENTURE | *Foreword by* | SACHE-
VERELL SITWELL | [*device*] | South Brunswick | New
York: A. S. Barnes and Co.

192 pages. 208 × 138 mm.
Black cloth boards. Trimmed edges. Lettered in silver on spine.
3000 copies printed. Published 28 March 1968 at $5.

CONTENTS

As in the first edition, but without illustrations

sB64   FLORENTINE JOURNAL   1967

First edition

Arnold Bennett | FLORENTINE | JOURNAL | *1st April–25th
May* | *1910* | Illustrated by the Author | WITH AN IN-
TRODUCTION BY SACHEVERELL SITWELL | 1967 |
CHATTO & WINDUS | LONDON

96 pages. 197 × 128 mm.
Brown cloth boards. Trimmed edges. Gilt lettered on spine.
1503 copies printed. Published 30 November 1967 at 25*s*.

CONTENTS

Pp. 9–15, "Introduction" by Sacheverell Sitwell

sB65   FOURTH INTERNATIONAL   1967
         CONGRESS OF BIBLIOPHILES

First edition

FOURTH | INTERNATIONAL CONGRESS | OF BIBLIO-
PHILES | LONDON 27 SEPTEMBER–2 OCTOBER 1965 |
Transactions | Edited by A. R. A. Hobson | QUATRIÈME
CONGRÈS INTERNATIONAL | DE BIBLIOPHILES |
LONDRES 27 SEPTEMBRE–2 OCTOBRE 1965 | LONDON |
1967

104 pages, and 6 plates. 253 × 175 mm.

Stiff blue paper wrappers. Trimmed edges. Lettered in black on upper cover.

400 numbered copies printed. Published in autumn 1967 in London by the Congress, for the Association Internationale de Bibliophiles, Paris.

CONTENTS

Pp. 63–80, "On Aquatints" by Sacheverell Sitwell

sB66   HOUSE AND GARDEN   1969
WEEKEND BOOK

First edition

[*Printed in white on a black panel:*] HOUSE | & GARDEN |
[*in black, parallel to, and in type twice the size of, the two preceding lines:*] WEEKEND BOOK

272 pages. 214 × 175 mm.

Yellow cloth boards. Trimmed edges. Green pictorial end-papers. Gilt stamped on spine and upper cover.

7500 copies printed. Published 24 April 1969 at 42s., by Condé Nast Publications Ltd. in London.

CONTENTS

Pp. 21–24, "The Art of Letter Writing" [from *House and Garden*, April 1947]

sB67   VICTORIAN MUSIC COVERS   1969

First edition

[*One line in ornamented type, curved over the second line:*]
VICTORIAN | *Music Covers* | *by Doreen and Sidney Spellman* |
with a Foreword by Sacheverell Sitwell | EVELYN, ADAMS
& MACKAY

72 pages. 198 × 155 mm.

White paper boards. Trimmed edges. Gilt lettered on spine.
Published 25 September 1969 at 25s.

CONTENTS

Pp. 6–7, "Foreword" by Sacheverell Sitwell

sC1 "Li-Tai-Pé Drinks and Drowns," *Wheels*, [*First Cycle*], p. 72, [December] 1916.

sC2 "Tahiti," "Barrel-Organs," "Song: The Feathered Hat," "The Nightingale," "Soliloquy and Speech from 'The Mayor of Murcia,'" "Trumpets," *Wheels, Second Cycle*, pp. 33–50, [December] 1917.

sC2A "Psittacus Eois Imitatrix Ales ab Indis," *The Egoist*, v. 5, no. 5, p. 70, May 1918.

sC3 "People of the Universe," *The Egoist*, v. 5, no. 6, pp. 85–86, June–July 1918. [Review of *Serbo-Croatian Plays* by J. Kosor.]

sC4 "Extract from 'Bird-Actors,'" *Art and Letters*, v. 2, no., p. 7, 1 Winter 1918–1919 [i.e., February 1919]. [There are two states of this issue, the earlier bearing "Winter 1918–19" on the front cover.]

sC5 "Fables," "Fountains," "Psittachus eois Imitatrix Ales ab Indis," "Whitsun," "Pindar," "Outskirts," *Wheels, Third Cycle*, pp. 43–56, 1918 [i.e., February 1919].

sC6 "Church and Stage," *The Monthly Chapbook*, v. 1, no. 1, pp. 15–16, July 1919.

sC7 "Serenade, from 'Bird Actors,'" "The Italian Air," "Mrs. H . . . or a Lady from Babel," "Valse Estudiantina," *Wheels, Fourth Cycle*, pp. 27–33, [November] 1919.

sC8 "Week-ends," *Coterie*, no. 3, pp. 12–14, December 1919.

sC9 "Laughing Lions will Come," "Et in Arcadia, Omnes," "A Swiss Rhapsody," *Wheels, Fifth Cycle*, pp. 66–82, 1920.

sC10 "A March Past at the Pyramids," *Art and Letters*, v. 3, no. 1, pp. 1–10, Winter 1920.

sC11 "Half Hours with the Best Authors," by 'Augustine Rivers', *Art and Letters*, v. 3, no. 1, pp. 49–51, Winter 1920. [Review of *Georgian Poetry, 1918–1919*.]

sC12 "Parade Virtues of a Dying Gladiator," "An Imitation," "Another Imitation," *Wheels, Sixth Cycle*, pp. 27–41, 1921.

sC13 "Serenade," *The Sackbut*, v. 2, no. 6, p. 33, December 1921.

sC14 "The Italian Air," *The Chapbook*, no. 26, pp. 12–16, May 1922. [Much enlarged from poem of same title in sC7.]

sC15 "Bolsover Castle," *The Chapbook*, no. 35, pp. 10–17, March 1923.

sC16 "Three Variations: Variation on a theme by John Lely; Daphne, an adaptation from John Milton; Variations on a theme by Alexander Pope," *The Criterion*, v. 2, no. 7, pp. 296–299, April 1924.

sC17 "Gardener's Song," *Spectator*, v. 132, p. 755, 10 May 1924.

sC18 "The Fiery Torch," *Vogue* [London], v. 63, no. 10, p. 44, late May 1924.

sC19 "Orange-Tree by Night," *Spectator*, v. 133, p. 58, 12 July 1924.

sC20 "On a Name Scratched upon a Window," *Spectator*, v. 133, p. 226, 16 August 1924.

sC21 "Two Odes in praise of Popular Music," *The Chapbook*, no. 39, pp. 14–15, 1924.

sC22 "Settecentesimo," *New Statesman*, v. 24, pp. 47–48, 18 October 1924.

sC23 "English Furniture, and a Note on William Kent," *New Statesman*, v. 24, literary supplement, p. v, 8 November 1924. [Review of *Dictionary of English Furniture, v. 1*, by Percy MacQuoid.]

sC24 "Every Picture tells a Story," *New Statesman*, v. 24, pp. 388–390, 10 January 1925.

sC24A "Song: A Creole Winter Have I Found," *The Decachord*, v. 2, no. 7, p. 13, January–February 1925.

sC25 "Spain," *Vogue* [London], v. 65, no. 3, pp. 48–51 and 78, early February 1925.

sC26 "The Monasteries of St. Bruno," *New Statesman*, v. 24, pp. 597–598, 28 February 1925.

sC27 "Reflections on the Royal Academy," by Osbert and Sacheverell Sitwell, *New Statesman*, v. 25, pp. 133–134, 16 May 1925.

sC28 "The Flemings in Spain," *New Statesman*, v. 25, pp. 196–198, 30 May 1925.

sC28*A* "Late Italian Art—at the Burlington Fine Arts Club," *Apollo*, v. 1, no. 6, pp. 334–335, June 1925. [See oB3.]

sC29 "The Gramophone Congress," *The Nation and Athenaeum*, v. 37, no. 16, pp. 485–486, 18 July 1925.

sC30 "Convent Thoughts in Cadiz," *The Chapbook*, no. 40, pp. 93–97, 1925.

sC31 "An Equinox," *Vogue* [London], v. 66, no. 8, p. 47, late October 1925.

sC32 "A Journey to Portugal," *Vogue* [London], v. 67, nos. 11–12, pp. 64–65 and 110, early and late June 1926.

sC33 "Dancer," *Poetry*, v. 28, pp. 276–277, August 1926.

sC34 "Igor Stravinsky," *Radio Times*, v. 16, no. 197, p. 65, 8 July 1927.

sC35 "Three Nights in Fez," *The London Aphrodite*, no. 2, pp. 84–85, October 1928.

sC36 "A Most Eminent Victorian: Mendelssohn," *Radio Times*, v. 27, no. 349, pp. 542–543, 6 June 1930.

sC37 "Glitter of Music Remembered from Youth," *Radio Times*, v. 29, no. 376, pp. 727 and 746, 12 December 1930.

sC38 "All Naples in a Christmas Day," *Radio Times*, v. 29, no. 377, pp. 813 and 818, 19 December 1930.

sC39 "Stravinsky's 'Sacré du Printemps,'" *Radio Times*, v. 30, no. 382, pp. 173 and 207, 23 January 1931.

sC40 "The World we Listen In," *Radio Times*, v. 30, no. 384, p. 288, 6 February 1931.

sC41 "The World we Listen In," *Radio Times*, v. 30, no. 385, p. 348, 13 February 1931.

sC42 "The World we Listen In," *Radio Times*, v. 30, no. 386, p. 414, 20 February 1931.

sC43 "The World we Listen In," *Radio Times*, v. 30, no. 387, p. 478, 27 February 1931.

sC44 "An Episode in the Life of an Artist," *Radio Times*, v. 30, no. 388, pp. 547 and 586, 6 March 1931.

sC45 "The World we Listen In," *Radio Times*, v. 30, no. 388, p. 542, 6 March 1931.

sC46 "The World we Listen In," *Radio Times*, v. 30, no. 389, p. 612, 13 March 1931.

sC47 "Lord Berners," *Radio Times*, v. 32, no. 415, p. 556, 11 September 1931.

sC48 "The Early Renaissance in Stone and Marble," *Architectural Review*, v. 72, no. 428, p. 22, July 1932. [Review of *The Quattro Centro*, *v.* 1, by Adrian Stokes.]

sC49 "Folk-Tale and Story," *The Observer*, no. 7387, p. 4, 25 December 1932. [Review of the *Pentamerone* of Basile.]

sC50 "We Are Hopeless Gramophonists" by Osbert and Sacheverell Sitwell, *Harper's Bazaar* [London], v. 7, no. 4, pp. 18–19 and 73, January 1933.

sC51 "Lady Cynthia Moseley," *The Times*, no. 46446, p. 18, 17 May 1933. [Anonymous obituary.]

sC52 "The Pictures of Richard Wyndham," *Architectural Review*, v. 75, no. 447, p. 61, February 1934.

sC53 "A Curious World," *Architectural Review*, v. 75, no. 448, p. 94, March 1934. [Review of *Stones of Rimini* by Adrian Stokes.]

sC54 "Italy—Venice and Florence," *The Listener*, v. 14, no. 344, pp. 258–261, 14 August 1935.

sC55 "Italy—Rome and Naples," *The Listener*, v. 14, no. 345, pp. 297–300, 21 August 1935.

sC56 "Record Achievement," *Harper's Bazaar* [London], v. 14, no. 1, pp. 86 and 120, April 1936.

sC57 "Mr. Bernard Van Dieren," *The Times*, p. 14, 25 April 1936. [Anonymous obituary.]

sC58 "The Russian Ballet," *The Fortnightly*, v. 140 (new series), pp. 239–241, August 1936. [Review of three books.]

sC59 "Tuscan," *The Fortnightly*, v. 140 (new series), p. 445, October 1936.

sC60 "Coronation Day," *Vogue* [London], v. 89, no. 9, pp. 103–109, 28 April 1937.

sC61 "A Persian Pilgrimage," *Architectural Review*, v. 82, pp. 33–34, July 1937. [Review of *The Road to Oxiana* by Robert Byron.]

sC62 "Lady Ida Sitwell," *The Times*, no. 47735, p. 16, 13 July 1937. [Anonymous obituary.]

sC63 "The Age of Competence: paintings in the exhibition of seventeenth century art at Burlington House," *Country Life*, v. 183, no. 2138, pp. 38–42, 8 January 1938.

sC64 "The Taste of the Seventeenth Century," *Journal of the Royal Society of Arts*, v. 86, no. 4444, pp. 225–240, 21 January 1938.

sC65 "Roumanian Wedding," *Geographical Magazine*, v. 6, no. 6, pp. 427–440, April 1938.

sC66 "English Pictures at Renishaw," *Country Life*, v. 84, no. 2180, pp. 419–421, 29 October 1938.

sC67 "Dancers on Dancing," *The Listener*, v. 20, no. 517, supplement p. xi, 8 December 1938. [Reviews of books by Anton Dolin and Serge Lifar.]

sC68 "High Up in Morocco," *Geographical Magazine*, v. 11, no. 5, pp. 295–303, September 1940.

sC69 "An Argument for Victorian Fuchsias," *My Garden*, v. 21, no. 82, pp. 139–145, October 1940. [From the Fuchsia Annual, 1939.]

sC70 "Mr. Frederick Dawson," *The Times*, no. 48763, p. 7, 2 November 1940.

sC71 "Kilvert Completed," *The Listener*, v. 24, no. 621, supplement p. vi, 5 December 1940. [Review of *Kilvert's Diary*, v. 3.]

sC72 "Epstein on Himself," *The Listener*, v. 24, no. 623, pp. 873–874, 19 December 1940. [Review of Epstein's *Let There Be Sculpture*.]

sC73 "Roumania," *The Fighting Forces*, v. 17, no. 5, pp. 409–416, December 1940.

sC74 "Genius Loci," *Spectator*, v. 166, pp. 65–66, 17 January 1941. [Review of *Cambridge* by John Steegman.]

sC75 "Van Dyck: an appreciation," *The Burlington Magazine*, v. 79, no. 465, pp. 174 and 177, December 1941.

sC76 "Welsh Costumes," *Geographical Magazine*, v. 14, no. 2, pp. 82–85, December 1941.

sC77 "Mr. Arthur Doble," *The Times*, no. 49132, p. 7, 13 January 1942. [Anonymous.]

sC78 "My Fancy Breeds" [of poultry], *The Countryman*, v. 28, no. 2, pp. 247–251, Winter 1943.

sC79 "English Book Illustration since 1800," *The Listener*, v. 30, no. 780, p. 726, 23 December 1943.

sC80 "Red Fog over London, 1843," *Lilliput*, v. 14, no. 1, pp. 45–47, January 1944.

sC81 "The Brazilian Style," *Architectural Review*, v. 95, no. 567, pp. 65–68 and 77, March 1944.

sC82 "L'Inconnue de la Seine," *Lilliput*, v. 16, no. 4, pp. 315–317, April 1945.

sC83 "The Children's Crusade," *Lilliput*, v. 16, no. 6, pp. 453–456, June 1945.

sC84 "The Arts in England," *Vogue* [London], v. 101, no. 8, pp. 33, 76 and 82, August 1945.

sC85 "Left Hand, Right Hand!," *Life and Letters To-Day*, v. 47, no. 98, pp. 52–60, October 1945. [Review of Osbert Sitwell's book.]

sC86 "A Note on Two Japanese Landscape Gardens by the monk Soami," *Life and Letters To-Day*, v. 47, no. 100, pp. 144–156, December 1945.

sC87 "Portrait of a Queen's Room," *Strand Magazine*, v. 112, no. 674, pp. 34 and 39–40, February 1947.

sC88 "The Art of Letter Writing," *House and Garden* [New York], v. 91, no. 4, pp. 95–96, 161, 165–166, 170, April 1947.

sC89 "Immortal Pierrot: a note on some engravings of Jean-Gaspard Debureau," *Ballet*, v. 4, no. 6, pp. 17–22, December 1947.

sC90 "Clockwork and Wax Figures," *Lilliput* v. 22, no. 1, pp. 6–8, January 1948.

sC91 "Mrs. Gordon Woodhouse," *The Times*, no. 50969, p. 6, 15 January 1948.

sC92 "The King's Pictures," *The Horseman's Year*, 1947–48, pp. 111–115. [Published 9 February 1948.]

sC93 "Lady Cunard: old world and new," *The Times*, no. 51126, p. 7, 17 July 1948.

sC94 "The Gipsy Caves at Guadix," *Journal of the Gipsy Lore Society*, v. 29 (third series), nos. 1–2, pp. 2–11, January–April 1950.

sC95 "A Retrospect of Flowers," *Books*, no. 248, pp. 104–107, May 1950.

sC96 "The Beauty of Flowers," *Spectator*, pp. 894 and 896, 30 June 1950. [Review of *The Art of Botanical Illustration* by Wilfrid Blunt.]

sC97 "The Feria in Seville," *Harper's Bazaar* [New York], no. 2864, p. 34, July 1950.

sC98 "Theatrical Paintings at the Garrick Club," *Country Life Annual*, 1950, pp. 81–87. [Published 2 November 1950.]

sC99 "Men, Women and Memories," *Sunday Times*, no. 6656, p. 6, 12 November 1950.

sC100 "Men, Women and Memories," *Sunday Times*, no. 6657, p. 4, 19 November 1950.

sC101 "Domestic Detail," *Spectator*, pp. 569–570, 24 November 1950. [Review of *English Furniture Illustrated* by Oliver Brackett.]

sC102 "Men, Women and Memories," *Sunday Times*, no. 6658, p. 4, 26 November 1950.

sC103 "Men, Women and Memories," *Sunday Times*, no. 6659, p. 6, 3 December 1950.

sC104 "Men, Women and Memories," *Sunday Times*, no. 6660, p. 4, 10 December 1950.

sC105 "Men, Women and Memories," *Sunday Times*, no. 6661, p. 4, 17 December 1950.

sC106 "Men, Women and Memories," *Sunday Times*, no. 6662, p. 4, 24 December 1950.

sC107 "More Books of the Year," *Sunday Times*, no. 6663, p. 3, 31 December 1950.

sC108 "Men, Women and Memories," *Sunday Times*, no. 6663, p. 4, 31 December 1950.

sC109 "Men, Women and Memories," *Sunday Times*, no. 6664, p. 6, 7 January 1951.

sC110 "Men, Women and Memories," *Sunday Times*, no. 6665, p. 4, 14 January 1951.

sC111 "Men, Women and Memories," *Sunday Times*, no. 6666, p. 4, 21 January 1951.

sC112 "Men, Women and Memories," *Sunday Times*, no. 6667, p. 4, 28 January 1951.

sC113 "The Conversation Piece," *Spectator*, no. 6397, p. 154, 2 February 1951. [Review of *The Devis Family of Painters* by S. H. Pavière.]

sC114 "Men, Women and Memories," *Sunday Times*, no. 6668, p. 6, 4 February 1951.

sC115 "Men, Women and Memories," *Sunday Times*, no. 6669, p. 4, 11 February 1951.

sC116 "Men, Women and Memories," *Sunday Times*, no. 6670, p. 4, 18 February 1951.

sC117 "Men, Women and Memories," *Sunday Times*, no. 6671, p. 4, 25 February 1951.

sC118 "The Grand' Place of Brussels," *Geographical Magazine*, v. 23, no. 11, pp. 521–523, March 1951.

sC119 "Men, Women and Memories," *Sunday Times*, no. 6672, p. 4, 4 March 1951.

sC120 "Men, Women and Memories," *Sunday Times*, no. 6673, p. 4, 11 March 1951.

sC121 "Men, Women and Memories," *Sunday Times*, no. 6674, p. 4, 18 March 1951.

sC122 "Dazzling Plumes," *Sunday Times*, no. 6675, p. 3, 25 March 1951. [Review of *The Birds of Paradise and Bower Birds* by Tom Iredale.]

sC123 "Men, Women and Memories," *Sunday Times*, no. 6675, p. 4, 25 March 1951.

sC124 "Ballad: Nymphs were Mentioned," "Nimrod," "Passe Virgo," *The Catacomb*, new series, v. 2, no. 1, pp. 58–59, Spring 1951.

sC125 "Men, Women and Memories," *Sunday Times*, no. 6676, p. 4, 1 April 1951.

sC126 "Men, Women and Memories," *Sunday Times*, no. 6677, p. 4, 8 April 1951.

sC127 "Men, Women and Memories," *Sunday Times*, no. 6678, p. 4, 15 April 1951.

sC128 "Men, Women and Memories," *Sunday Times*, no. 6679, p. 4, 22 April 1951.

sC129 "Men, Women and Memories," *Sunday Times*, no. 6680, p. 4, 29 April 1951.

sC130 "Men, Women and Memories," *Sunday Times*, no. 6681, p. 4, 6 May 1951.

sC131 "People and Memories, *Sunday Times*, no. 6686, p. 4, 10 June 1951.

sC132 "People and Memories," *Sunday Times*, no. 6687, p. 4, 17 June 1951.

sC133 "People and Memories," *Sunday Times*, no. 6688, p. 4, 24 June 1951.

sC134 "Brother and Sister: a ballad of the Parallelo," *The Catacomb*, new series, v. 2, no. 2, pp. 113–116, Summer 1951.

sC135 "People and Memories," *Sunday Times*, no. 6689, p. 4, 1 July, 1951.

sC136 "People and Memories," *Sunday Times*, no. 6690, p. 4, 8 July 1951.

sC137 "People and Memories," *Sunday Times*, no. 6691, p. 4, 15 July 1951.

sC138 "People and Memories," *Sunday Times*, no. 6692, p. 4, 22 July 1951.

sC139 "People and Memories," *Sunday Times*, no. 6693, p. 4, 29 July 1951.

sC140 "People and Memories," *Sunday Times*, no. 6694, p. 4, 5 August 1951.

sC141 "People and Memories," *Sunday Times*, no. 6695, p. 4, 12 August 1951.

sC142 "People and Memories," *Sunday Times*, no. 6696, p. 4, 19 August 1951.

sC143 "Away to the Sun," *Sunday Times*, no. 6697, p. 4, 26 August 1951.

sC144 "A Town in the Clouds," *Sunday Times*, no. 6698, p. 4, 2 September 1951.

sC145 "Giants in Tarragona," *Sunday Times*, no. 6699, p. 4, 9 September 1951.

sC146 "Foreword," "Thomas Goff's Clavichords," *Foyer*, no. 1, pp. 5–7, 29–32, Autumn 1951. [And, anonymously: "The Bibienas," p. 17, "Musée Dantan," p. 21, "The Greatest of the Castrati: Carlo Broschi Farinelli," pp. 22–23, "Juvara," p. 28, "Lithograph of Luigi Lablache by Chalon," p. 32, "Carnaval de Vénise," p. 51, and "Little Tich," p. 57.]

sC147 "Tombs of the Plantagenets," *Sunday Times*, no. 6701, p. 8, 23 September 1951.

sC147*A* "An Original Amateur," *Architectural Review*, v. 110, no. 660, p. 401, December 1951. [Review of *Thomas Archer* by Marcus Whiffen.]

sC148 "First Impact of Russian Music," *Foyer*, no. 2, pp. 9–12, Winter 1951–1952. [And, anonymously: "A Ballet Scene by Jacques Callot," p. 20, "A Note on Pantomime," pp. 26–27, "Lithograph by A. E. Chalon," p. 32, "Black Woodcut Silhouettes from the Musée Dantan," pp. 34–36, "Act Drop by Richard Dadd," p. 37, "A Typical Stage-set by Giuseppe Galli da Bibiena," p. 42.]

sC149 "A Tic-Toc World," *Spectator*, no. 6451, pp. 209–210, 15 February 1952. [Review of *Thomas Tompion* by R. W. Symonds.]

sC150 "The Life and Background of George VI: I. Younger Brother," *Picture Post*, v. 54, no. 9, pp. 33–39, 1 March 1952.

sC151 "Memories of A Great Artist," *Spectator*, no. 6454, p. 302, 7 March 1952. [Review of *Chiaroscuro* by Augustus John.]

sC152 "The Life and Background of George VI: II. From the Shade to the Sunlight," *Picture Post*, v. 54, no. 10, pp. 39–43 and 53, 8 March 1952.

sC153 "The Life and Background of George VI: III. War brings the Supreme Test," *Picture Post*, v. 54, no. 11, pp. 36–39 and 55, 15 March 1952.

sC154 "Distant Delights," *Sunday Times*, no. 6726, p. 5, 16 March 1952. [Review of *Breeding Birds of Kashmir* by R. S. P. Bates and E. H. N. Lowther.]

sC155 "The Life and Background of George VI: IV. The Price of Duty," *Picture Post*, v. 54, no. 12, pp. 46–48, 22 March 1952.

sC156 "Giants at Tarragona," *Geographical Magazine*, v. 24, no. 12, pp. 586–588, April 1952. [Different from sC145.]

sC157 "The World of Robert Ross," *Spectator*, no. 6458, p. 444, 4 April 1952. [Review of *Robert Ross, Friend of Friends*.]

sC158 "Watching People in Spain," *Spectator*, no. 6460, pp. 519–520, 18 April 1952. [Review of *Round and About Spain* by A. F. Tschiffely.]

sC159 "Gardens of Spain," *Réalités* [Paris], no. 19, pp. 50–55 and 76, June 1952.

sC160 "Two Songs: 'Sylphide and Magical Being'; Song of the Cherry Trees," *Nine*, v. 3, no. 4, pp. 303–305, Summer–Autumn 1952.

sC161 "The World of Arthur Devis," *Saturday Book*, no. 12, pp. 88–98, [Autumn] 1952.

sC162 "Mrs. H., or, a Lady from Babel," *New World Writing*, no. 3, p. 174, May 1953.

sC163 "A Photograph Album," *Spectator*, no. 6516, p. 630, 15 May 1953. [Review of *Italy* by Martin Hürlimann.]

sC164 "The Coronation," *Harper's Bazaar* [New York], no. 2899, p. 58, June 1953.

sC165 "Four Queens in their Element," *House and Garden* [London], v. 8, no. 6, pp. 61–64, June 1953.

sC166 "Portugal," *House and Garden* [New York], v. 103, no. 6, pp. 96–99, 131 and 133, June 1953.

sC167 "A Day of History," *The Queen*, v. 201, no. 5235, pp. 105–106, 3 June 1953.

sC168 "The Burden of Queenship," *Picture Post*, v. 59, no. 10, pp. 23–25, 6 June 1953.

sC169 "Mexico, Land of Bright Colours and Large Hats," *Housewife*, v. 15, no. 7, pp. 31 and 69, July 1953.

sC170 "The Duke of Westminster: a tribute to a friend," *Sunday Times*, no. 6797, 26 July 1953.

sC171 "The Ballerina: an appraisal of Fonteyn," *The New York Times Magazine*, pt. 6, pp. 18–19 and 35, 6 September 1953.

sC172 "The Duke of Alba: a memoir," *The Tablet*, v. 202, no. 5915, p. 322, 3 October 1953.

sC173 "The Palace of the Sun-King," *Books*, no. 281, pp. 72–73, November 1953.

sC174 "A House of Glass," *Daily Mail Ideal Home Book*, 1953–54, pp. 18–20 and 23. [Published November 1953.]

sC175 "This Year of Grace," *The Queen*, v. 201, no. 5247, pp. 44 and 113, 18 November 1953.

sC176 "Margot Fonteyn adds to her Triumphs," *Housewife*, v. 15, no. 12, pp. 69 and 121, December 1953.

sC177 "Winter Sunshine," *The Queen*, v. 202, no. 5251, p. 22, 13 January 1954.

sC178 "The Artistic Genius of Holland," *Atlantic Monthly*, v. 193, no. 4, pp. 117–120, April 1954. [This was published in a supplement entitled *Perspective of Holland and Belgium*, which was published both with the *Atlantic Monthly* and separately, 15,000 copies being separately published in May 1954 by Intercultural Publications Inc.]

sC179 "A Note for Bibliophiles," *Cameo*, [no. 1], pp. 76–85, [Spring 1954]. [Illustrated account of book jackets designed for his books.]

sC180 "Plastic Baronial: Scottish castles of the sixteenth & seventeenth centuries," *Architectural Review*, v. 115, no. 689, pp. 296–301, May 1954.

sC181 "Fantasy on German Toy Pigeons: leaves from a notebook," *Ark*, no. 13, pp. 44–49, [1954].

sC182 "The Miracle of Bourges Cathedral," *Réalités*, no. 45, pp. 46–53, August 1954.

sC183 "Slum Song," *Saturday Book*, no. 14, p. 88, [September] 1954.

sC184 "Ballad: Lines to a Succubus," *Encounter*, v. 3, no. 4, p. 60, October 1954.

sC185 "Italian Grotesques: the sculptures at Bomarzo," *Geographical Magazine*, v. 27, no. 6, p. 306, October 1954.

sC186 "When the United Nations occupied Paris," *Réalités*, no. 51, pp. 38–41, February 1955.

sC187 "French Romantic Jewellery," *Réalités*, no. 55, pp. 26–31, June 1955.

sC188 "Golden Age and Age of Gold," *The Listener*, v. 54, no. 1393, pp. 784–786, 10 November 1955.

sC189 "Rose is a Rose," *Spectator*, no. 6684, pp. 184–186, 3 August 1956. [Review of *Collins' Guide to Roses* by Bertram Park.]

sC190 "The Blue Mosque," *Sunday Times*, no. 6951, p. 6, 5 August 1956.

sC191 "In the Steps of Alexander," *Sunday Times*, no. 6954, p. 6, 26 August 1956.

sC192 "A Look at Teheran and Isfahan," *The Listener*, v. 56, no. 1436, pp. 502–503, 4 October 1956.

sC193 "Ulanova's Great Artistry," *Sunday Times*, no. 6960, p. 14, 7 October 1956.

sC194 "Nuptials of the East and West," *The Listener*, v. 56, no. 1438, pp. 609–610, 18 October 1956.

sC195 "Random Ebullience," *Spectator*, no. 6699, p. 685, 16 November 1956. [Review of *Butterflies and Moths* by Alfred Werner.]

sC196 "Gift Books," *Spectator*, no. 6703, p. 880, 14 December 1956. [Review of eight books.]

sC197 "Montgolfians," *Spectator*, no. 6705, p. 938, 28 December 1956. [Review of *Balloons* by C. H. Gibbs-Smith.]

sC198 "Visions and Nightmares," *Spectator*, no. 6709, p. 118, 25 January 1957. [Review of two books on Goya.]

sC199 "A Triptych," *Spectator*, no. 6711, p. 185, 8 February 1957. [Review of three books.]

sC200 "A Dual Personality," *Spectator*, no. 6712, p. 214, 15 February 1957. [Review of *James Wyatt* by Antony Dale.]

sC201 "Painter in Limbo," *Sunday Times*, no. 6989, p. 6, 28 April 1957. [Review of *John Singer Sargent* by C. M. Mount.]

sC202 "Spanish Churches," *Spectator*, no. 6723, p. 590, 3 May 1957. [Review of *The Cathedrals of Spain* by John Harvey.]

sC203 "Sailing to Byzantium," *Spectator*, no. 6726, p. 683, 24 May 1957. [Review of three books on Byzantium.]

sC204 "Caricature Sculptures," *Spectator*, no. 6730, p. 819, 21 June 1957. [Review of *Figures of Fun* by Janet Seligman.]

sC205 "The Aerial Beauty of the Châteaux de la Loire," *Réalités*, no. 88, pp. 50–55, March 1958.

sC205*A* "Denmark," *Vogue* [New York], v. 131, no. 7, pp. 44 & 50b, 1 April 1958.

sC206 "A Resounding Tinkle from 800 Artists," *Sunday Times*, no. 7042, p. 21, 4 May 1958.

sC207 "Chelsea's Cannonade of Flowers," *Sunday Times*, no. 7045, p. 22, 25 May 1958.

sC207*A* "Les Châteaux de la Loire," *Esquire*, v. 50, no. 3, pp. 48–51, September 1958.

sC207*B* "Some Memories of Scarborough," *The Municipal Review*, v. 29, pp. 517 & 546, October 1958.

sC207*C* "Impact of Spain," *Sunday Times*, no. 7112, p. 16, 6 September 1959. [Review of *Spanish Mercy* by Arland Ussher.]

sC207*D* "Buildings that Dance," *Daily Telegraph*, no. 32491, p. 14, 2 October 1959. [Review of *From Baroque to Rococo* by Nicolas Powell.]

sC207*E* "The High Road and the Low," *Time & Tide*, v. 40, no. 51, pp. 1409–1410, 19 December 1959. [Review of two books on architecture.]

sC208 "Encore Architecture," *Daily Telegraph*, no. 32836, p. 19, 11 November 1960. [Review of two books.]

sC209 "Cuzco, City of the Sun," *Geographical Magazine*, v. 34, no. 1, pp. 29–41, May 1961.

sC210 "Augustus John, O.M., Hon. President of the Gypsy Lore Society, 1937–1961," *Journal of the Gypsy Lore Society*, 3rd series, v. 41, nos. 1–2, pp. 1–3, January–April 1962.

sC211 "Now the English Spirit Flowers," *New York Times Magazine* pp. 42 and 60 and 62, 19 August 1962.

sC212 "The Essential Paris," *Geographical Magazine*, v. 35, no. 8, pp. 479–486, December 1962.

sC212*A* "Castles in Spain," *Opera News* [Metropolitan Opera Guild, New York], v. 27, no. 4, pp. 8–13, 1 December 1962.

sC213 "Flowers and Fronds," *Sunday Times*, no. 7302, p. 31, 28 April 1963. [Review of three books.]

sC214 "The Tides of Taste," *Portfolio* [New York], no. 8, pp. 48–59, Spring 1964.

sC215 "The Auricula," *National Auricula and Primrose Society (Southern Section), Year Book*, pp. 19–23, 1964. [Review of book by C. Oscar Moreton.]

sC216 "Nostell Priory: the golden age of English country houses," *Réalités*, no. 174, pp. 74–81, May 1965.

sC217 "Haunted Land of Green and Gold" [Sweden], *Daily Telegraph (Weekend Telegraph)*, no. 34, pp. 18–22, 14 May 1965.

sC218 "Promises of Summer," *Sunday Times*, no. 7409, p. 48, 16 May 1965. [Review of *The Concise British Flora in Colour* by W. Keble Martin.]

sC219 "Antonio Gaudí," *Saturday Book*, no. 25, pp. 30–39, [September] 1965.

sC220 "Portugal," *Daily Telegraph (Weekend Telegraph)*, no. 74, pp. 12–18, 25 February 1966.

sC221 "The Sun," *Daily Telegraph (Weekend Telegraph)*, no. 90, p. 25, 17 June 1966.

sC222 "Desiderata Lisztiana," *The Liszt Society, Newsletter* [Twyford, Berkshire], no. 5, pp. 2–4, September 1966.

sC223 "Passing through Pienza," *Réalités*, no. 199, pp. 44–49 and 98, June 1967.

sC224 "Forty-Eight Poems: On singing over to myself a hymn by J. S. Bach; To the self-portrait of A. Watteau; On the *Serenade* from *Il Seraglio*; Sousedská; Poetic exercise in the form of a fight with a giant bird; Singerie; Ballad: '*Sous un ciel chagrin*'; Eclogue obstiné; Devil's Cherries; Herb Paris; Madonna Lily; 'Limelight'; White Arum Lily; Blue Waterlily; Epiphyte Lily; Forty-four degrees in Córdoba; Serra da Arrábida; A Bronze

Head of a Girl from Benin; The Sacred Park; The Yellow-flowering tree; Perahera; Sandalwood Song; La Sampaguita; Ti Fai Fai; Parrot Pie; To a green parrakeet from São Tomé; Tai-Haku; Weeping Rosebud Cherry; 'Rose of Two Hearts'; Botanic Garden, Honolulu; On a Matching Set of Twelve Strawberry Dishes (with four more) by Paul de Lamerie [sixteen poems]; His Blood Colours my Cheek; No More," *The Poetry Review*, v. 58, pp. 75–120, Summer 1967.

sC225 "The Pleasures of the Senses," *Apollo*, v. 87, no. 2, pp. 129–139, February 1968. [French eighteenth-century exhibition at the Royal Academy.]

sC225*A* "Do One Thing Well," *Drum Beat* [Church Lads' Brigade, London], v. 1, no. 1, p. 2, April/May 1968.

sC226 "Death of a Flie," *Studies in the 20th Century* [Troy, New York], no. 2, pp. 27–38, Fall 1968.

sC227 "An unknown world of architectural beauty," *Journal of the Royal Institute of British Architects*, v. 75, pp. 540–541, December 1968. [Review of *Sicilian Baroque* by Anthony Blunt.]

sC228 "Invitation to Baroque delights," *Spectator*, v. 222, no. 7332, pp. 13–14, 3 January 1969. [Review of books by Anthony Blunt and Henry Russell Hitchcock.]

sC229 "High Coloratura," *Spectator*, v. 222, no. 7337, pp. 175–176, 7 February 1969. [Review of *Rossini* by Herbert Weinstock.]

SACHEVERELL SITWELL: BOOKS
ANNOUNCED BUT NOT PUBLISHED
(sD1–sD9)

sD1 "Sitwells' Omnibus." (See ED1.)

sD2 "The Santander Quartet, in a programme of Spanish music."
Announced as "to be published shortly" in *Façade*, 1922.

sD3 "Baroque Art of the Kingdom of Naples." Announced as "in
preparation" in *Spanish Baroque Art*, 1931.

sD4 "Forty or Fifty Siciliennes." Announced as "forthcoming" in
Canons of Giant Art, 1933.

sD5 "Ballads and Poems." Announced as "in preparation" in *Cupid
and the Jacaranda*, 1952; *Liszt*, 1955; and *Arabesque and Honeycomb*, 1957.

sD6 "Habaneras and Siciliennes." Announced as "in preparation" in
Arabesque and Honeycomb, 1955.

sD7 "Variations on Old Names of Hyacinths." Announced in
Arabesque and Honeycomb, 1957; a series of fourteen poems read
on the B.B.C. but unpublished in printed form.

sD8 "Rosario d'Arabeschi (Poems and Rose Portraits)." Announced
as "unpublished" in *Journey to the Ends of Time*, 1959.

sD9 "Ruralia: or Poems on Wild Flowers." Announced as "unpublished" in *Journey to the Ends of Time*, 1959.

(A few isolated poems from sD5–sD9 were published in *The Poetry
Review*, Summer 1967; see sC224.)

SACHEVERELL SITWELL:
TRANSLATIONS (sE1–sE11)

---

sE1 *The Rio Grande* by Constant Lambert. (1929–see next section.) This includes a German translation by Beryl de Zoete.

sE1A *Le Baroque Mexicain.* In: *Documents* [Paris], [v. 2], pp. 291–297, 1930.

sE2 *Por el Norte Africano.* [*Mauretania.*] Translated by Cayetano Romano. Buenos Aires: Espasa-Calpe, 1942.

sE2A *Le Dieu du Blé.* Translated by Ludmila Savitzky. In: *Aspects de la Littérature anglaise (1918–1945)*, edited by Kathleen Raine and Max-Pol Fouchet; Paris; Fontaine, 1947, pp. 329–330.

sE3 *La Tumba de Agamenon: fragmento.* [Part of "Agamemnon's Tomb."] Translated by J. R. Wilcock. In: *Sur*, año XV, pp. 431–435, Julio–Octubre 1947.

sE4 *Franz Liszt.* [*Liszt.*] Translated by Willi Reich. Zürich: Atlantis Verlag, 1958.

sE5 *Liszt.* Translated by Françoise Vernan. Paris: Buchet-Chastel, 1961.

sE6 *Die Grossen Schlösser Europas.* [*Great Houses of Europe.*] Translated by Peter Stadelmayer. Berlin, Frankfurt/M., Vienna: Ullstein, 1961.

sE7 *L'Olanda.* [*The Netherlands.*] Translated by Enzo Siciliano. Milan: Garzanti, 1961.

sE8 *Le Grandi Dimore d'Europa.* [*Great Houses of Europe.*] Translated by Paolo Gajani. Milan: Mondadori, 1962.

sE9 *Portugal.* Translated by Ulrike Simon. In: *Atlantis* [Zürich], v. 35, pp. 491–501, September 1963. [See sC220.]

sE10 *Grandi Palazzi.* [*Great Palaces.*] Translated by Rosalina De Ferrari. Milan: Garzanti, 1964.

sE11 *Berühmte Schlösser und Paläste.* [*Great Palaces.*] Frankfurt/M.: Ariel Verlag, 1964.

SACHEVERELL SITWELL: MUSICAL SETTING

---

sF1 *The Rio Grande* by Constant Lambert, for chorus, orchestra and solo pianoforte. (1929; but actually published 11 December 1930 in ordinary, chorus and solo piano editions, and a signed edition limited to 75 copies; Oxford University Press.)

SACHEVERELL SITWELL: RECORDING

---

sG1 Excerpts from *Spain, Mauretania* and *Roumanian Journey,* read by the author. ("Columbia Literary Series," set DSL-190, DSL-190E; released 5 October 1953 by Columbia Records [New York].)

INDEX

INDEX

Titles of original works are in small capitals with the entry number of the description in heavy type.

Titles of poems are in italic.

Titles of prose items are in single quotation marks.

Titles of periodicals are in roman.

Titles of books to which the Sitwells have contributed are in double quotation marks with the entry number of the description in heavy type.

Book reviews are indexed under the names of the books' authors and the titles of the reviews.

428

'When the Palace Band played the Wrong Tune,' oA40; oC398
When the Sailor, EA9, 20, 29, 45, 49
'When the United Nations occupied Paris,' sC186
Where is All the Bright Company Gone?, EA49; EC239; EG7
Which is the Triton true?, oA9, 18, 33; oG4
Whiffen, Marcus, sC147*A*
Whistler, Laurence, oC424
Whistler, Rex, EA19b, 24; oB56; oC374, 424; sA19b
White, Ethelbert, oB2*B*, 5*A*, 10
White Arum Lily, sC224
White Hyacinth[s], sA12, 29
'White Man's Burden, The,' oA25, 57; oC156
White Owl, The, EA49b
White Rose, sA49; sB55
Whiteman, W. W., sB18
'Whitman and Blake,' EC226
Whitsun, sA1, 29; sC5
'Who are the Sitwells?,' EC98
WHO KILLED COCK-ROBIN?, oA5
Who shall have my Fair Lady?, EG7
'Who wants Poets now?,' EC119
Who's Who in Heaven, oC52
Why, EA7, 20, 29, 49
'Why do you live in a Flat?,' oC194
'Why I don't like Games,' oA25; oC105
'Why I look the way I do,' EC249
'Why not Like Poetry?,' EC178
Why Should a Sailor Ride the Sea?, oA3
'Why Worry about your Age?,' EC123
Whyte, Lancelot Law, EB55
Widow Styles, EA10, 15
Wilcock, J. R., sE3
'Wild Parties,' oC230
Wilde, Oscar, oA48; oC444
'Wilfred Owen,' oA48; oC390, 442
'William Blake,' EC202
WILLIAM BLAKE: A SELECTION, eD3
Williams, Arthur, oA34a, 38a, 42a
Williams, H., and Son Ltd., oA37
Williamson, Malcolm, EE11, 12
Willis, George, EC17
Wilson, Angus, EB56
Wilson, Colin, EC269*A*
Wilson, John G., EB8*A*
Wilson, Mona, sB12
Wimborne, Viscountess, oA20
Wind as Husbandman, sA7, 29, 49
Wind of Early Spring, The, EA48, 49
Windmill Press, The, oA19

Wind's Bastinado, The, EA6ab, 7, 20, 32, 42, 43, 45, 47, 49; EG7
Wine & Food, oC261, 330
Wingate, Allan, Ltd., oB37; sB39
'Wink from the Great Beyond, A,' oA56
WINSTONBURG LINE, THE, oA2
Winston's Jamboree, oC41
Winter [1], EA7, 12, 20, 29, 49; EC60, 61
Winter [2], see *Four Songs of the Italian Earth*
'Winter in Italy,' oA22; oC138
'Winter Sunshine,' sC177
WINTER THE HUNTSMAN, oA11
Winter the Huntsman, oA9, 11, 18, 33; oF2, 3; oG4
Winter Walk, The, sA7, 29
WINTERS OF CONTENT [1932], oA22, 49
WINTERS OF CONTENT AND OTHER DISCURSIONS [1950], oA49
"Winter's Tales, I," oB52
"Wiser Woman, A?," oB56
"Witley Parish Church," sB59*A*
Wizardry, oC29
Wolfe, Edward, oB19
Wolfe, Humbert, sA16
Wolff, H., Book Manufacturing Co., EA42, 43b, 48b, 49a, 51b
'Wolfgang Amadeus Mozart,' sB49
Woman who could not Die, The, oA50, 58; oC451
Woman who Could Not Go Home, The, oA53
'Woman who Hated Flowers, The,' oA30, 45, 51; oC303
Woman's Journal, EC178
Women in War-Time, EB2
Wood, Sir Henry, sB22
Wood, Michael, sB48
WOODEN PEGASUS, THE, EA4
Woodhouse, Mrs. Gordon, sC91
Woodruff, Douglas, sB12
Woolf, Leonard, EB43
Woolf, Leonard and Virginia, EA11a
Woolley College, EB34
'Word to the Poetry Contractors, A,' EC125*A*
Wordsworth, Dorothy, EC165
'Work of Gertrude Stein, The,' EC92
"Works of Ronald Firbank, The," oB9
World-Hymn to Moloch, oA3, 18
'World of Arthur Devis, The,' sC161
'World of Robert Ross, The,' sC157
World Publishing Co., sA65b, 66b
World Review, oC450, 452